Inside the Roman Legions

Inside the Roman Legions

The Soldier's Experience 264–107 BCE

Kathryn H. Milne

Pen & Sword
MILITARY

First published in Great Britain in 2024 by
Pen & Sword Military
An imprint of Pen & Sword Books Limited
Yorkshire – Philadelphia

ISBN 978 1 39907 066 9

The right of Kathryn H. Milne to be identified as
Author of this Work has been asserted by her in accordance
with the Copyright, Designs and Patents Act 1988.

A CIP catalogue record for this book is
available from the British Library

Typeset by Mac Style
Printed in the UK by CPI Group (UK) Ltd, Croydon, CR0 4YY.

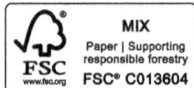

MIX
Paper | Supporting
responsible forestry
FSC
www.fsc.org
FSC® C013604

Pen & Sword Books Limited incorporates the imprints of After
the Battle, Atlas, Archaeology, Aviation, Discovery, Family History,
Fiction, History, Maritime, Military, Military Classics, Politics,
Select, Transport, True Crime, Air World, Frontline Publishing, Leo
Cooper, Remember When, Seaforth Publishing, The Praetorian Press,
Wharncliffe Local History, Wharncliffe Transport, Wharncliffe True
Crime and White Owl.

For a complete list of Pen & Sword titles please contact

PEN & SWORD BOOKS LIMITED
47 Church Street, Barnsley, South Yorkshire, S70 2AS, England
E-mail: enquiries@pen-and-sword.co.uk
Website: www.pen-and-sword.co.uk
or
PEN AND SWORD BOOKS
1950 Lawrence Rd, Havertown, PA 19083, USA
E-mail: uspen-and-sword@casematepublishers.com
Website: www.penandswordbooks.com

Contents

Spurius Ligustinus' Known Service   vi
Introduction   ix

Chapter 1   Mid-Republican Military Culture   1

Chapter 2   A Legion of Strangers   18

Chapter 3   Finding Your Place in the Ranks   37

Chapter 4   The Complete Army   53

Chapter 5   Moving an Army on Campaign   73

Chapter 6   Training   91

Chapter 7   On Campaign with a Mid-Republican Army   106

Chapter 8   The Disciplinary System   123

Chapter 9   Preparing for Battle   138

Chapter 10   Fighting a Battle   154

Chapter 11   The Aftermath of Battle   173

Chapter 12   Getting Out Alive   192

Conclusion: Looking Forward to The Late Republic   208
Glossary   215
Notes   219
Bibliography   236
Index   247

Spurius Ligustinus' Known Service (Livy 42.34)

PROVINCE	YEAR		COMMANDER	POSITION	Select Events and Sources
Macedonia	200	1	P. Sulpicius Galba, consul	Common soldier miles gregarius	Skirmishing against the cavalry of Philip: Livy 31.35, battle won by the cavalry near Athacus: Livy 31.36-7 Fighting through the pass to Eordea: Livy 31.39 Taking of Celetrum (surrendered), Pelium (garrisoned) Livy 31.40.
Macedonia	199	2	P. Villius Tappulus, consul	miles gregarius	Wintered in Corcyra and transported to mainland in Spring, but enemy hold the road into Macedonia, Flamininus already approaching: Livy 32.6 Maneuvering, skirmishing (Plut. Flam. 3.1)
Macedonia	198	3	T. Quinctius Flamininus, consul	(Centurion?) 10th maniple of hastati decimus ordo hastatus	Battle of the Aous pass: Livy 32.11-2; Plut. Flam. 4.1-5.1
Macedonia/ Greece	197	4	T. Quinctius Flamininus, proconsul		Battle of Cynoscephalae: Polyb. 18.20-7; Livy 33.7-10; Plut. Flam. 7-8.
Macedonia/ Greece	196	5	T. Quinctius Flamininus, proconsul		
Spain (Hispania Citerior)	195- 194	6	M. Porcius Cato, consul	First centurion of the hastati primus hastatus prioris centuriae	Mustered at Portus Lunae in Liguria: Livy 34.8.4 The Battle of Emporiae: Livy 34.13-16; App. Hisp. 40. Cato's year in command: Plut. Cat. Mai. 20.1-4; App. Hisp. 40-41. Triumph with donative of 54 denarii: Livy 34. 46. 2.
	193				
	192				

Region	Year	No.	Commander	Rank/position	Notes
Greece/Asia 'War against Antiochus'	191	7	M. Acilius Glabrio, consul	First centurion of the principes *primus princeps prioris centuriae*	Mustered at Brundisium: Livy 36.3.12 Cato 'tribune': Plut. *Cat. Mai.* 12.1; 'legate': Livy 36.17.1. Battle of Thermopylae: Livy 36.15–19; App. *Syr.* 17–20; Plut. *Cat. Mai.* 13.1–14.4.
Greece/Asia	190	8	L. Cornelius Scipio, consul*		*Ligustinus does not mention this commander, however, Livy and Polybius both say the army remained in place from 191 to 190: Polyb.21.5; Livy 37.7.7.
	189–183	9 & 10			Two one-year services: 'campaigns where the legions served for a year'
	182		Q. Fulvius Flaccus, praetor		Ligustinus could have joined the army in this year when it departed or been part of the *supplementa* sent in 181: Livy 40.16.8; 40.17.6.
Spain (Hispania Citerior)	181	11	Q. Fulvius Flaccus, propraetor		Battle with the Celtiberi: Livy 40.39–40; App. *Hisp.* 42. Army handed over: Livy 40.40.14
	180				Triumph at Rome: Livy 40.43.5–7; Bonus 100 *denarii*, double pay
Spain	179	12	Ti. Sempronius Gracchus, propraetor	First spear centurion *primus pilus*	Cato ambassador for consul: Plut. *Cat. Mai.* 12.1 Year in Spain: App. *Hisp.* 43 Triumph: Livy 41.7.2–3; Bonus 50 *denarii*
Macedonia	171	22	P. Licinius Crassus, consul	First spear centurion of first legion *primus pilus*	

Introduction

The main aim of this book is to explore the experience of military service in the Roman legions of the Middle Republic through the perspective of the ordinary soldier. In order to do this, we will follow the soldier in his journey through military service from his life and cultural environment as a Roman boy, through his recruitment and first military campaign, to his eventual discharge from the legions. The period of the Middle Republic offered a variety of different experiences depending on the times and campaigns in which a soldier fought, making it difficult to distinguish an average or typical soldier. The book therefore centres on one particular soldier, from whom we can extract a narrative of the progression of a real campaign with details like how he travelled there, the objectives of the operations in which he fought, and what the different military units were called to do on that campaign. This core example of a soldier's experience is supplemented throughout by reference to soldiers who took different paths or served in significantly different circumstances at other times or in other places.

The soldier who forms the core of the narrative is a man named Spurius Ligustinus, whose military experience is detailed by the historian Livy. He may or may not have been a real person, a question which we will consider in detail when he is introduced in Chapter 1. His story has been chosen because we have good evidence for the period of time in which he served, and in particular for the first two campaigns in which he took part. This began in 200 BCE with five years in Macedon and Greece, followed by a year in Spain, in the province of Hispania Citerior. These first years provide the most common experience of a Roman soldier of the era because the beginning of a soldier's career and the first campaign was the part that was shared by all soldiers. It would have been a more common experience to be in the divisions of the *velites* and *hastati*, where young men served first than to rise to become a first centurion or to stay with the army long enough to serve in the division of oldest men, the *triarii*. In addition, the sources for these two campaigns are particularly good, since we have extant works of the historians Livy and Polybius covering all or some of this period and Plutarch's biographies of the two generals who commanded the campaigns, among other sources. The general M. Porcius Cato, who commanded in Spain, was also an author. Parts of his works survive and his speeches and treatises were used as a source by other ancient writers.

The principal reason that there is not one typical soldier's experience during this era is because there were three phases within it that represent different characters of warfare. The Middle Republic as a period is usually dated from 264 BCE, the date of the beginning of the First Punic War. It is generally considered to extend to either 146 BCE, the date of the sack of Carthage that closed the Third Punic War, or 133 BCE, which is a date that marks a turning point in Roman political life. The first phase of warfare is the Punic Wars, which began with the Romans still fighting close to home and in a limited number of places further afield like Sicily, Spain and Africa. The Second Punic War involved the defence of Italy and saw Rome's most dramatic losses. It is from this phase that we have the most evidence about what happened to soldiers in the case of defeats. The next phase is the period 200–168 BCE, which is the period in which Ligustinus fought. This period was essentially expansionist and was one of the most rewarding periods to be a Roman soldier, especially in the lucrative campaigns in the East. The campaigns of this period were not defensive and soldiers spent much of their time engaged in the siege and takeover of cities in foreign provinces like Macedon and Spain. Lastly, there was the period of the wars mostly in Spain from the 160s to the 130s BCE, which were notoriously harsh and unpopular wars spent overcoming fierce and determined warrior tribes engaged in desperate defence of their land. It is clear that there were different motivations involved for those who repelled the invasion of Italy by the Carthaginians, and those who were sent as invaders themselves to strip land from others. Soldiers found the Spanish wars prolonged and unrewarding and, as a result, military service became an undesirable option. All three of these phases are part of the landscape of Mid-Republican warfare and an astute reader might notice that the greatest amount of literary evidence that is extant belongs to the first two, while the greatest part of the archaeological evidence belongs to the third.

The Sources

The author widely considered to be our best source for the Mid-Republican army is the Greek historian Polybius. Polybius was from Megalopolis in Greece, which in the second century BCE was part of an alliance known as the Achaean League. Polybius was very interested in military matters and had served as a cavalry commander for the League by the time that the Romans fought and won the Third Macedonian War in 168 BCE. At that point he and a thousand other prominent statesmen of the League were sent to Rome as hostages, for assurance of the league's good behaviour in that region. Polybius became friends with some of Rome's most prominent aristocratic families of the time, many of whom were magistrates and commanded armies. In particular he describes in the *Histories* how he came to be friends with the statesman Scipio Aemilianus when the latter was around eighteen, after the two had a conversation while leaving the house of Scipio's brother. This happened probably in the city of Rome in 166 BCE.[1] Two decades later, Scipio took Polybius along with him when he was a general during the Third Punic War. Polybius saw Roman armies in action and mentions that he personally witnessed the forces of Scipio sack the city of Carthage in 146 BCE.[2] Polybius has therefore always enjoyed a very good reputation for the reliability of his account, especially on military matters.

Polybius wrote his *Histories* not for the Romans themselves but an audience of educated Greeks, aiming to explain how Rome had come to dominate the Mediterranean region in a period of just fifty years. The start of this period is the Republic's least promising moment, in 216 BCE after defeat at the Battle of Cannae during the Second Punic War, when it seemed that destruction at the hands of the Carthaginians was all but ensured. Polybius wished to document the remarkable ascent of Rome from this terrifying low, through the slow climb back to eventual victory in the war, and finally to Rome's domination of the Mediterranean, which was widely thought to have been accomplished by victory in the Third Macedonian war in 168 BCE. As a key part of this story, in book six of the *Histories* Polybius wrote at length on the Roman military system as instrumental to Rome's ability to endure. There is, however, one problem that is central to this account, which is that his description of the Roman army in book six does not accord well to his own time period. Most suspect in this regard is his account of the levy, which Polybius may not have witnessed himself. The levy as he describes it would work well if all Rome's eligible soldiers were local, but implies long, superfluous travel for many soldiers in an era where citizens were spread all over Roman Italy. This has led some scholars to suspect that his account is not his own contemporary observation but derived from an earlier source, such as a handbook for tribunes or an earlier historian.[3]

One other note of caution about using Polybius as a source for the Roman armies of this time period is that he seems to have viewed a large swathe of Roman religious practices as mere superstition.[4] At the beginning of book six he warns, 'I am quite aware that to those who have been born and bred under the Roman Republic my account of it will seem somewhat imperfect owing to the omission of certain details' (6.11.3). Many of these details were religious rituals that we will come across as we follow the soldier on campaign. The Romans used divination extensively to check for opposition to their actions from the gods. Later we will see that the period during which the army fought a battle was marked by religious ceremony both before and after. Polybius usually fails to mention acts of divination or sacrifice that would have been important to soldiers, although he states that he knows that such matters were both pervasive and important to the state as a whole (6.56.6–8).

The second main source for Mid-Republican warfare is the historian Livy. He wrote a history of Rome *ab urbe condita*, 'from the foundation of the city' at the end of the first century BCE at the time of the first Emperor Augustus. This was originally in over 140 books, but only 1–10 and 21–45 are extant. For the lost books, we have summaries of their contents known as the *Periochae*. Books 1–10 deal with early Rome up to 293 BCE, and books 21–45 from the Second Punic War to 167 BCE. The surviving books are not all of the same quality. While about a hundred manuscripts have survived for books 31–40, only a single one bears books 41–45, and where it is damaged or there are copying mistakes, it is very difficult to reconstruct.[5]

For about two thirds of the narrative in books 31–45, Livy has based his writing on the *Histories* of Polybius, especially for events in the East.[6] It is harder to tell if he has done so for the period of the Punic Wars because the extant parts of Polybius' narrative break off after the battle of Cannae in 216 BCE. There were excellent sources available to Livy, however, including two writers who had served in the Second Punic War, Fabius Pictor and Cincius Alimentus, and two Greek authors who had accompanied the Carthaginian general Hannibal, Silenus and Sosylus. In all parts of the work he sometimes used the earlier historians Coelius Antipater, Valerius Antias and Claudius Quadrigarius. All of these works are now lost to us, but from the parts of the narrative where both Livy and Polybius' work is extant, it is apparent that sometimes Livy embellished or exaggerated what he found there. This has made some scholars deeply suspicious of the historical reliability of some of his work, and it serves as a warning that we must always use his evidence with caution.[7]

One source used by Livy is of particular interest to us, and that is the dispatches or *litterae*, 'letters' sent by commanders from the field back to the Senate. Livy narrates an occasion in which these dispatches were received and read out in the Senate in 177 BCE. Letters came in from two commanders, with one reporting that he had won a victory against two named tribes, citing the number of enemy killed, the location of the battle, the capture of the enemy camp, that he had burned the enemy arms as an offering to the god Vulcan, and that the soldiers had retired into winter quarters in the allied cities (41.12.4–6). In places in the narrative where the *litterae* are not specifically cited, their use as a source is suggested by Livy's formulaic language.[8] The very mundanity of these details is a good argument for their authenticity, for they are not literary tropes, and usually serve no purpose in the narrative except as historical record. Livy will thus often provide details of routine army activity that have been omitted by other ancient writers. In Chapter 7 these kinds of details are instrumental in examining when ordinary soldiers were in action and when they were left behind. Livy frequently specifies the location of sub-units of the legions, such as where garrisons were stationed in provincial towns or where the wounded were left when armies moved on. Behind these details are the stories of thousands of ordinary men whose wars looked a little different from the picture we would see if we only followed the largest body of the legion.

All of the sources for the campaign in Spain in the year 195–4 BCE, Ligustinus' second campaign, seem to have been influenced by the work of the commander himself, M. Porcius Cato, known also as the Elder Cato to distinguish him from a famous great-grandson. He was an author himself and wrote a work entitled *De Agricultura* ('on Agriculture') which has survived, but much of his other writing has been lost, including a handbook on military affairs that was the first such work in Latin. A number of his speeches were available in antiquity. Polybius may have used these works as a source, especially his military treatise, and Livy certainly used his account of his military campaign for the years 195 and 194.[9] Some fragments of speeches and other works are used in this book directly.

A number of more minor sources are also referenced throughout the narrative. The Greek biographer Plutarch, who lived in the Roman Empire in the second century CE, wrote a biography of the commanders of the first two of Ligustinus' campaigns, T. Quinctius Flamininus and the Elder Cato. Some references are from the works of the playwright Plautus, who was active in Rome in the early second century BCE. The fourth century CE writer Vegetius wrote a treatise on the military that is valuable because it refers often to the practices of the Romans of the Republic. Valerius Maximus was a compiler of *exempla*, or historical anecdotes, and noted in particular a number of stories about Roman discipline from this era. Appian is a Greek historian of the second century CE who wrote a history of Rome and is particularly useful for the campaigns in Spain. The last major source of information for the Mid-Republican army is not literary but archaeological, or what is now commonly called 'material culture'. This is of interest particularly for the soldiers' arms and armour and the Roman military camp. Real examples of equipment not only fill in details about dimensions and appearance, but allow for recreations that can answer difficult questions about its capabilities. The archaeological remains of army camps, most importantly the numerous camps around Numantia in Spain, give concrete examples of the model Roman camp described by Polybius.

Themes

The main theme of this book is to simply discover what happens when we turn our attention from leaders to followers, from large-scale politics to individual experiences, from the famous and the elite to the ordinary. This approach will highlight a number of themes that are worth introducing here.

Firstly, the real world of soldiers on the ground is a messy one. There are very few areas in which practice accords to any specific set of rules, let alone every time. Partly this is to do with gradual change, so for example, when discussing the techniques of wielding a sword, the evidence suggests that soldiers sometimes stabbed and sometimes slashed, and had different swords depending on the decade and circumstance. Soldiers in this era were conscripted, but at the same time it becomes clear that it was in the best interests of both soldiers and officers that there was a degree of self-selection to allow choice to those who wished to rush forward and those who wished to hang back. The basic unit of the army was the maniple, but sometimes the troops operated in cohorts. Polybius lays out the rules of the Roman camp with precise measurements, while the excavations of the camps at Numantia show that the Romans in real life simply did the best they could in order to accord with the terrain. When we come to questions where there is less evidence, such as how individual soldiers moved up and around divisions, or how promotion worked, the lesson from the lack of neatness elsewhere may well be that these things depended heavily on time and place and circumstance.

The importance of visual and oral culture

The ordinary soldier in the Roman Republic relied on both spoken words and visual signals for communication, with very little depending on something written down. This is what we would expect in a world where few outside of the elite could read and write, and it also means that these ways of communicating were more significant for Romans than for us. This began at home even before service, when exemplary tales of Roman military heroes and the stories of relatives started to prime the Roman boy for what would be expected of him. At recruitment, he would be required to take an oath of obedience to become a soldier, with the recitation of the oaths important both for announcing the terms or rules that were to apply as well as the verbal confirmation that the soldier accepted them. Equally important to oaths were witnesses, as men were needed who could independently verify that the oath had been taken by a particular individual. Through this action, the soldier's comrades were implicated as future witnesses and even deterrents for moments when the soldier might contemplate breaking his oath. Words that were spoken aloud were also important for rituals, where the declaration of the result of divination, for example, was spoken out loud, and the commander was relied upon to announce that these things had been done.

At other times, visual signals were the primary means of conveying meaning. These were things like the movement of military standards that showed men the location of the front line on the battlefield, or the colour-coded system of flags that provided reference points for the soldiers to build their camp while on campaign. There were also less obvious sets of visual codes, like the correspondence between awards given for bravery in battle and the particular acts that they represented, which allowed soldiers to see a man's decorations and know what he had done to earn them. Other types of symbols allowed the soldier to recognize the identity of individuals or groups, like the commander who wore a red military cloak, or division of *velites* marked by a piece of fur and the tall feathers on the helmet of a member of the *hastati*. In the wider context, the importance of visual and oral means of communication made the in-person attendance at ceremonies and events important too, as the communal nature of religious rituals and oaths helped to cement a sense of group identity.

Religion

Religion is another facet of Roman campaigns that was important to the soldier's experience. Many modern works on the Roman army make the same editorial choice that Polybius made thousands of years ago and omit religious ceremonies completely or mention them only in passing. It should become evident, however, that elements of religious obligation contribute profoundly to areas that have been of greater interest to scholars, like the level of cohesion that a Republican army might be able to achieve. Religion was tied to community, in the sense that most religious rites were communal events. There were a number of religious obligations that formed part of conducting an army in this period.

Many facets of group identity were fostered in processes that were essentially religiously based. Oaths, for example, depended upon the individuals who took them respecting the same deities, who as supernatural beings were able to guarantee oaths by observing behaviour when no human was around to do so. Similarly, there was the *lustratio*, in which the commander asked the gods for protection and success before the army departed on campaign. As part of the *lustratio* the whole army was physically and ritually encircled, emphasizing the unity of the group inside the circle.

Class and Elitism

One inescapable problem of the literary sources for this period is that a huge gulf of class and wealth separated the ordinary Roman soldier from the wealthy and aristocratic elites. Those who engaged in literary and intellectual pursuits, like writing historical accounts, belonged to the latter class and their audiences did too. Many of these authors had little concern or liking for soldiers. Their views are from the top down, as they empathized with the commanders of the age in matters like how to manage a legion of soldiers or compel the unruly to obedience. The discrepancy in perspective between ordinary and elite is nowhere more vividly shown than in the rules, punishments and demands of the Roman military disciplinary system. The idea of a harsh and unforgiving discipline appealed greatly to many later authors, for whom the high standards served as a mark of exclusivity and distinction. As a result, many of the authors of our sources have greatly romanticized incidents of harsh discipline that would have seemed to those suffering them as arbitrary and unjust. The instances of the horrifying punishments cited, such as the *fustuarium*, in which the soldier's comrades bludgeoned him to death, and decimation, in which one out of ten men in a unit was executed, are few and far between. Nevertheless, it seems that ordinary soldiers had little power over their circumstances once out on campaign, something which is especially evident in the disciplinary system.

Chapter 1

Mid-Republican Military Culture

Creating a Military Culture

The Roman boy who would become a soldier grew up in a culture in which military values were extremely important. Before he ever picked up a sword, the way that Roman armies, soldiers and wars were perceived and valued by those around him had already shaped his viewpoint and attitude towards his future endeavours. In order to understand what the soldier's experience was really like, this chapter looks at his life and influences prior to army service and examines what a Roman youth of the Mid-Republican period was likely to know, and how he might have approached his service. Messages from all directions about how to conduct himself while in the legions would have allowed him to develop an understanding of what was required to succeed as a soldier of Rome. We will examine what kinds of actions, attitude and person were regarded positively, rewarded, and glorified, what behaviours were discouraged, and how messages about military values reached the future soldier.

Boys living in the Roman and allied communities around Italy in the Middle Republic become eligible to serve in an army at the age of seventeen. Serving in the army was an entirely normal and expected life stage, not a one-time response to a particular conflict as it has been for citizen soldiers in modern times. A citizen militia was levied annually whether there was a current war or not. The potential soldier's father and grandfather had served before him and he would expect any sons he had to serve after him, as well as older friends and local men in the community with whom his family traded, socialized, and celebrated religious festivals.

Although not all new recruits would have joined at exactly seventeen, the vast majority of *tirones,* 'recruits' or 'novices', would have become a soldier for the first time when they were young and unmarried. The Roman male would then go on to pass his remaining teenage years and his twenties serving in Rome's campaigns abroad. This fitted into the patterns of Roman society, since unmarried men were the group whose absence could be borne best by both small landholdings and the agricultural economy as a whole.[1] Most of Rome's soldiers came from families around Italy and the average recruit would have spent his early life on the land, growing up on a family farm. There was a property requirement for army service, but it was never very large, and so many of these farms would have operated on a subsistence level.[2] The childhood and youth of boys, therefore, would have been mainly engaged in helping with a farm's labour, from the ploughing, hoeing, weeding and reaping of cereal production to the cultivation of beans and olives and the management of animals like oxen, sheep and goats.[3] It was thought then, as it is often thought now, that the hard labour and sheer physical effort involved in farming produced hardy and enduring men and so forged the best soldiers.[4]

The amount of time that a soldier would spend on campaigns is difficult to pin down. Polybius recorded the number of years that a man was required to serve as a soldier in the second century, but the number has become corrupted in the surviving manuscripts of the *Histories* and may have been six, ten or sixteen.[5] There are examples of legions dismissed after six years of service, perhaps in special circumstances, but also some left to languish in provinces for much longer. During the Punic Wars some soldiers certainly served for more than sixteen years. Despite Polybius' statement that there was a rule, it was likely not a hard and fast one, perhaps adjusted according to circumstance. A lot may have depended upon when the soldier was first called to service and to which campaign he was originally attached, whether this was one where the legions were detained for an extended period abroad or a short period closer to home. Soldiers could be conscripted between the ages of 17 and 46, and we would expect them to spend an average of twelve to fourteen years in a succession of different legions.[6]

Usually our sources tell us that after their service, they would return to their villages and regions to become husbands and fathers. This was certainly not true for every soldier, but one of the most persistent themes in the ancient sources is the idea that military values were created and sustained in a cyclical way by veterans who brought home with them the memories, spoils and tokens of their military experiences. These became integrated into both the historical and contemporary culture of communities. The intention was that the veteran would return as a living, aspirational example of a soldier, who could promote the value of courage and successful service by means of any decorations he had earned for valour and the narratives that accompanied them. The positive values attached to military prowess had the clear and practical aim of encouraging the young to anticipate their own military careers and, from early in their lives, form ambitious ideas about how they would perform. The first military virtue, no less key to the Roman conception of the soldierly ideal than bravery, was a deep attachment to ancestral lands.

Spurius Ligustinus

The fundamental Roman connection between land and the military brings us to the example of one particular Mid-Republican soldier, whose experiences will help us to structure our examination of the typical experiences of soldiers of this era. His name is Spurius Ligustinus, and he is attested only once, by the historian Livy. He appears during the recruitment of two legions for a campaign in Macedonia in 171 BCE to fight what would come to be named the Third Macedonian War. The consul of that year, Publius Licinius Crassus, was put in command of two legions that he would raise himself and take to Macedonia, and he received a special dispensation from the Senate to recruit veteran soldiers for his campaign.

The officers of this new army had the task of appointing volunteers to serve in various positions as they formed up the legions. A volunteer's rank in a new legion would not necessarily be the same as he had held in his last army, and so a group of twenty-three men who had previously served in the highest rank of centurion, as *primi pili* or 'first spear' centurions, protested that they had been placed in too low a rank. The consul was asked what he wished to do. Licinius replied that he did not want to hamper the ability of his military tribunes to enrol any soldier in any manner that benefited the Republic. One of the centurions, hearing this, asked and was granted permission to speak.[7]

This is when we meet Spurius Ligustinus, who tells us that he is a veteran of twenty-two years. Despite his wealth of military experience, instead of beginning by declaring his martial talents, he begins his speech by describing his circumstances prior to joining the army in 200 BCE. Ligustinus voices the idea that his previous home life and his relationship to his own land underpins his motivation for undertaking and persisting in military service:

> I am Spurius Ligustinus, a Sabine by birth, a member of the Clustuminian tribe. My father left me a *iugerum* of land and a small cottage in which I was born and bred, and I am living there today. As soon as I came of age my father gave me to wife his brother's daughter. She brought nothing with her but her personal freedom and her modesty, and together with these a fruitfulness which would have been enough even in a wealthy house. We have six sons and two daughters. Four of our sons wear the *toga virilis*, two the *praetexta*, and both the daughters are married.[8]

Ligustinus, we learn, has a strong patriotic commitment to his lands, which he has demonstrated in a lifelong attachment to his family home. Ligustinus' wife is a reflection of his own character, poor in terms of money but rich in moral value. Her virtues, ones valued by Roman men, were her chastity at marriage and her fertility, providing many children, the majority of whom were boys, which is a reflection of typical Roman patriarchal values.[9]

The tribe and area from which Ligustinus comes are evocative of both typical Roman soldiers and ideal ones. He was not an urban Roman from the city of Rome, who, by the time that Livy wrote during the time of the Emperor Augustus, had gained a reputation for quarrelsomeness and were not recruited very often.[10] Ligustinus was a Sabine. The Sabines had been, by legend, integrated into the Roman state at the time of Romulus, although historically Ligustinus' tribe, the Clustumina, originated sometime between 426 and 396 BCE.[11] The most common Sabine tribe was the Quirina, and in order to belong to the Clustumina, Ligustinus' home town must have been Forum Novum.[12] This was a Roman settlement in Sabine territory, modern Vescovio, about 38 miles to Rome's northeast. Ligustinus' father's *iugerum* of land was probably in this region rather than at Forum Novum itself, which, like many settlements named 'forum' had probably been created or taken over as a Roman centre of administration for the surrounding area.[13]

At the very end of the second century BCE when Ligustinus would have grown up, the region around Forum Novum was sparsely populated. Many of its inhabitants were in fact quite wealthy families, who had bought the land after the Roman conquest in the third century BCE, both 'Romanized Sabines' and Roman nobility seeking to take advantage of the rich agricultural land.[14] The large villas that took over the area in the course of the second century, however, were probably not what Livy's audience envisioned when they thought of a Sabine soldier. Sabine territory was famous for being rural and harsh, providing the backdrop for the kind of hard-working rural life that was thought to toughen men. The Sabines themselves were famous for living austere lives. The poet Horace writes that the soldiers who fought and won Rome's third-century wars were of this tough stock, whom he calls 'the masculine offspring of rural soldiers, taught to turn the clods with Sabine hoes.'[15]

Ligustinus' glowing war record, which he goes on to detail, is exemplary as might be expected of such a background, but it takes more than this to create the perfect soldier. His idealness also rests in his willingness to perpetuate Rome's military culture, to return to his farmland and to create the next generation of soldiers in his own tough image, and so his exemplarity begins with his attitude about the end of his service. Only by having the desire to return to his origins, and making it through service successfully enough to return, could he fulfil the whole cycle and make his experiences mould the world in which other males grew up.

It is unfortunate that we cannot say for certain whether or not Ligustinus really existed. It is possible that Livy, writing in the time of Augustus in the very late first century BCE, perhaps 150 years after this scene, might have consulted an earlier source which had preserved a genuine record of the speech.[16] On the other hand, the story could be a rhetorical device, with Ligustinus invented out of whole cloth to serve as representation of the ideal Mid-Republican soldier.[17] Or he may be a bit of both, a real soldier that Livy has embellished with some extra heroism. The advantage of following his story, despite this lack of certainty, is that it gives us an example to turn to for every stage of a soldier's potential career. Every campaign in which Ligustinus says he fought was a real campaign, and every one of those campaigns involved a real soldier at the rank he claims to have held. Even if Ligustinus' career as detailed in Livy might not truly reflect the experience of one man, it most certainly does contain within it the experiences of many real Roman soldiers.

We will continually return to Ligustinus' career as we move through the Roman military experiences in sequence, from recruitment, through deployment, training, combat, and finally return. For now, we can observe that his introductory words illustrate the idea that the beginning of a soldier's experience in the army was rooted in the end of the experiences of others. The individual gained societal esteem by sharing his story and so received a secondary benefit from it. He had been honoured in the army, and in being honoured again at home he became a perpetuator of military culture and a key part of a system of ennobling certain military actions.

Instilling Military Culture in the Young

In the modern world, most nation states maintain a permanent standing army which builds organizational continuity over time. Armies are entities, with tangible characteristics like physical buildings and permanent personnel distinguished by their uniform. While military culture can spread beyond the organization, it is largely centred on and stems from it, and so the study of military culture today distinguishes 'organizational culture' from 'national culture.'[18] The armies of the Roman Republic had no organizational continuity and maintained not even one permanent military building, and in fact, only had a real tangible existence at all as long as there were legions in the field. Roman armies were temporary citizen militia and there was widespread eligibility for service through the citizen and allied population. Roman military culture was not centred on a well-defined organization, as there was simply not one. It existed in a much more diffuse form across many aspects of the Roman daily experience. In other words, Roman military 'organizational culture' was inseparable from the wider context of Roman 'national culture.'[19]

We are told that particular care was taken to educate young men about what behaviour would be appropriate and desirable while in military service. Examples of individuals and armies performing deeds that were judged positively were publicly rewarded and commemorated, in order to show young men the kinds of behaviours to which they ought to aspire. A major proponent and documenter of this theory of military exemplarity was the Greek historian Polybius. Just as we see in Livy's account of Ligustinus, for Polybius, being attached to particular lands was an integral part of the motivation of Roman soldiers. He writes that unlike Carthage's army, which was largely built of mercenaries, the Roman citizen soldiers fought for their own homes and lands. In Polybius' estimation this gave them an edge, as with their homeland and children at stake, they could never give up.[20] The attachment to land, however, was more than this, because the soldier had to return to his homeland in order to reap the full rewards of success in the military for himself and to be an exemplar for others. Polybius outlined certain practices and traditions that he believed 'encourage[d] the young soldier to face danger.' He envisioned these practices as a kind of cycle, in which the awards given for certain deeds would make a man 'famous in the army and at his own home', and so the young would be inspired to face dangers in emulation of these deeds so that they, too, could enjoy fame and esteem.[21] For Polybius, the Roman army's tradition of awarding prizes and decorations to the brave was a kind of deliberate social engineering.[22] We will come back to this as a set of actions that reflected individual desirable acts on the part of ordinary soldiers. First, though, we will look at his second example, the practice of exemplary storytelling.

Exemplary Narratives

As a means of cultivating and spreading military values, Polybius cites the dissemination of tales of famous figures, often referred to as exemplary narratives. These stories purported to be true accounts of men and women who had performed extraordinary deeds at some point in the past. Typically, they relate the story of an individual who performs some kind of heroic or extraordinary deed. The deed is witnessed by an audience internal to the narrative, who judge the deed and assign it a positive value. The deed is afterwards commemorated with some sort of visual representation like a statue or painting, which then acts as a cue for the story to be re-told, hence presenting the deed and its positive and aspirational nature before a second audience of youths who were motivated to emulate it.[23] Although some exemplary stories modelled behaviour for women or maidens, Polybius notes that the youth who would become a soldier was the primary target of this system of instilling values. We can sketch out some of the most common themes and the behaviours promoted by them using a couple of the most widespread exemplary stories of the Roman Republic.

The stories that involved proper conduct in the legions generally emphasize bravery, discipline, and devotion to the state over private or family concerns. Polybius highlights one story particularly as an example, the tale of a soldier named Horatius Cocles. This man was present during the invasion of Rome by the Etruscans, and was stationed guarding the *pons Sulpicius*, a bridge over the river Tiber, against an enemy force. When Cocles saw reinforcements of the enemy coming, he urged his fellows to retreat while he held the bridge, to allow them time to destroy it:

> The bridge once cut, the enemy were prevented from attacking; and Cocles, plunging into the river in full armour as he was, deliberately sacrificed his life, regarding the safety of his country and the glory which in future would attach to his name as of more importance than his present existence and the years of life which remained to him. Such, if I am not wrong, is the eager emulation of achieving noble deeds engendered in the Roman youth by their institutions.[24]

Although Cocles does not die in all of the many versions of this story, the value that is encouraged is very clearly self-sacrifice, especially considered and deliberate self-sacrifice. Polybius emphasizes that Cocles put himself forward wilfully and voluntarily. Here the encouragement is towards cultivating a particular mentality that augments the moral good of the deed. It is a detail that is clearly aimed at the audience to whom the story was told, rather than an important historical detail about Cocles himself. Polybius can hardly have known what Cocles was thinking at his moment of sacrifice, especially since he apparently knew the version in which Cocles did not survive to tell his own story. Polybius does know, however, that key values to convey to youths were that they should approach their service with a willingness or even an aspiration to sacrifice the self, to take on danger oneself on behalf of others, and to relieve the burden of the many through the volunteerism of the few.

Polybius also references another widely known exemplary story that showcases strict adherence to military discipline. The value of discipline is key to his estimation of what Romans were inspired to do by such tales:

> Some even when in office have put their own sons to death contrary to every law or custom, setting a higher value on the interest of their country than on the ties of nature that bound them to their nearest and dearest.[25]

The most famous of such stories was that of Titus Manlius Torquatus, the consul of 340 BCE, who punished his son with execution for engaging in single combat without his father's permission. The young man had responded to a challenge from Geminus Maecius, the leader of the Tusculans, slain him in combat, and returned with the spoils, but he had neglected to ask his father the commander's permission to leave the camp and so was executed. This story gave rise to the phrase 'Manlian orders' meaning severe or extreme discipline, and was a well-known and established tale by the first century BCE.[26]

Grim and unforgiving tales like this may seem off-putting and, like some of the rules we will explore later in Chapter 8 on the disciplinary system, they may have been more popular with the upper classes of a later era, who could admire them without being subjected to them, rather than contemporary soldiers. Strict standards, on the other hand, can actually give groups an air of exclusivity and hence desirability. Extreme discipline can seem poignant and appealing, especially to outsiders and to those who anticipate entry into the group. Consider, for example, the study of entrants to the US Marine Corps in the 1990s, who confessed themselves charmed by stories of perfection, iron discipline, and codes of honour. Those troops were at their most motivated and committed at the very start, but they soon discovered that their jobs did not live up to the glamour that was promised, nor their fellows to the honest image that had been advertised.[27] In the case of our young Romans, the threat of iron discipline was a dire warning about even the slightest wrongdoing, but it need not have dimmed the army's appeal. The draconian discipline could also be an enticing lure to become a part of something distinctive and special.

Individual Spoils and Veterans' Stories

If sacrificing his life was what was expected from every soldier, joining Rome's armies would have been an unappealing prospect for most. For those less desirous of trading their lives for fame, there were models for smaller acts of continued good service that would bring a fainter, but perhaps more palatable glory. One famous soldier from the stories was credited with many continued and consistent acts of exemplary behaviour. L. Siccius Dentatus was said to have been a common soldier from the fifth century BCE who 'never shirked from danger' and who single-handedly turned several battles, recovering the standards that had fallen into enemy hands, saved numerous fellow soldiers, and won every kind of award available, most of them more than once.[28] Rome's armies had a standardized system of military awards and decorations, each of which corresponded to a particular achievement. In the small communities of rural Italy, any military decorations that had been won by a soldier were hung on the door frame of his private house, and it was forbidden to remove these decorations even if the house changed hands.[29] Since the correspondence between award and deed was consistent over time, young and potential soldiers could pass by, and upon seeing decorations on display they would know what achievements they represented.

Looking at the specific acts that were singled out for reward will show us what the Romans valued in their soldiers.[30] Polybius gives us a list of awards and their corresponding deeds. A man 'who, faced with no compulsion, in skirmishing or any other opportunities voluntarily and deliberately endangered himself' won the *hasta pura*, a type of spear, for wounding an enemy. For killing and stripping an enemy, a member of the cavalry earned *phalera* (horse-trappings) and an infantryman a *patella* (a shallow dish).[31] There was the *corona muralis*, an award for the first soldier to scale the walls of an enemy fortification, and the *corona vallaris*, for the first over the wall of an enemy camp. There were also some rewards that related to defending or preserving life. The *corona civica* was awarded to a soldier who saved the life of a fellow citizen in battle, provided that he held the ground where the deed had happened for the rest of the day. This award implies that the soldier had been part of the halt of a reversal or a retreat.

The specific behaviours that were directly encouraged by these awards involve aggressive, proactive violence. They could be won only by eager soldiers rushing to the front, risk-takers, and even in the case of a reversal, those who stayed in their place rather than retreating. Although all the awards imply violence, some were specifically for wounding or killing enemies. This was reinforced by the fact that any spoils that the soldier displayed on his house like helmets, breastplates and swords, had been stripped directly from a slain enemy, and explicitly conveyed that the owner had killed someone in battle. Displaying awards and spoils was common, and it encouraged and normalized the act of killing and, in turn, elevated it to a desirable act that had a positive value to Roman society.

As we will see later, the widespread glorification of war and specific violent acts by individuals need not imply that violence and killing came easily to the Romans or that they were in any way uniquely warlike.[32] It might in fact indicate that Roman culture had adapted or developed to reward and therefore incentivize acts that men naturally found unpleasant and were reluctant to do. It is generally recognized today that killing is difficult behaviour for human beings, and few possess the temperament to do it happily. Two famous psychiatrists who worked with soldiers of the Second World War, Swank and Marchand, called two per cent of American soldiers 'aggressive psychopaths.'[33] These men felt no remorse about the men they had killed. Sometimes they are referred to as 'natural killers', and since they have certain traits of birth and behaviour in common, they can be identified and used. Not only do they kill, but they motivate others to kill, and are competitive and aggressive.[34] The decorations point to an overall culture that elevated and ennobled the kind of soldier who displayed aggressive and proactive violence.

For each individual decoration that was displayed on a house, there was a narrative that accompanied it, that of the soldier who had won it. There were many markets, festivals and social events in ancient Italy where people from one town or village came together with neighbouring communities. These would have been opportunities for charismatic ex-soldiers to relate their tales of war to eager audiences, tales which were likely grimmer and more triumphal in tone than any veteran would tell now. These stories would then be associated with their owners and passed again by word of mouth as a form of entertainment. Each story offered a concrete example of desirable behaviours that brought admiration and esteem, even those which did not correspond exactly to a deed as laid out by Polybius. The implication of his account that the young could elevate their social standing within the community is that these stories were welcome to the people living back at home and that they engaged audiences. Social distinction was known to be a particularly powerful lure even in ancient times. 'No-one' wrote Valerius Maximus, 'is so humble that he is not touched by the sweetness of glory.'[35]

Public Displays of Collective Military Success

While visual cues like military awards referred to the achievements of certain individuals and hence gave an idea of what was desirable for a single soldier to do, there were also many modes of commemorating collective Roman military success. The landscape of the city of Rome was engaged in a process of using successes and victories to build a lasting impression of Rome's power and influence, both within the population and to visitors and foreign states.[36] Many temples in particular had a direct relationship with successful warfare. This was the result of two different religious conventions. The first is that commanders called upon a god at some point during battle, either to promise them honours if they should help the Romans achieve victory, or as thanks for success. The temple of Castor, for example, was either dedicated by the dictator Postumius at the moment his troops broke the enemy line at Lake Regillus in 496 BCE, or more enticingly in a different version of the story, because Castor and his brother Pollux had materialized at the head of the cavalry to inspire the Romans to victory.[37] There was also *evocatio*, in which a commander called out the god from an enemy city, offering them honour in Rome if they should deign to switch sides. The *evocatio* of Juno Regina in 396 BCE from the city of Veii, for example, was the origin of the temple of Juno Regina on the Aventine hill in Rome, standing as a testament to Rome's domination of that city.[38]

In the latter half of the fourth century and during the third there was a boom in religious building that largely corresponded to military successes.[39] Any of our potential soldiers visiting or living in Rome would have been able to view temples dedicated to divinities of war, victory, and other associated value systems, like the temple of Victory on the Palatine, the temple of Bellona and the temple of Fors Fortuna (good fortune or luck).[40] These temples signalled power and were intended to be impressive to those who visited the city, and by the latter half of the second century, large temple projects had sprung up in surrounding smaller cities like Praenestae and Tusculum as well.[41] For those about to fight for Rome, the important part of the message would have been the reassurance of being on the side of a powerful state that was, moreover, divinely favoured. A state such as this was likely to field a winning army, and in turn, offered a good chance of both safety and profit in its forces.

Temples and other public buildings were often used as a setting for displaying the spoils of war and fortified the impression of a militarily powerful state. Plutarch writes that by the late third century BCE the city of Rome was full of the arms and armour of its defeated enemies.[42] In 216 BCE after the disaster at Cannae, there was enough equipment displayed or dedicated in temples to arm at least some of the troops raised to meet the emergency.[43] It was possible to see spoils in the city temples in Rome, placed there by successful commanders, and these spoils were also sent out for display to other towns in Italy.[44] Sometimes these trophies were very large. When in 338 BCE the Romans defeated Antium, a Latin city notorious for its piracy, they demanded the Antiates give up their ships. They removed the rams from the fronts and affixed them to the wall attached to the *comitium* building from which speakers addressed the public in the forum below. This new decoration gave the speakers platform its name, the *rostra*.[45] The fixation of the ships' prows was probably connected to the monumental complex of the *comitium* and the *curia*, a project likely also funded from the profits of the campaign against Antium and other Latin states.[46]

By the third century BCE, the focus had shifted to using spoils and profits from wars to also aggrandize the individual generals under whose commands victory had been achieved. Prominent men sought to turn a success during their military commands into longer term political power by advertising their own personal achievements, and hence to court votes for future positions.[47] It would have been common to see statues of particular individuals in public spaces, like that of C. Maenius atop a column that commemorated his naval victory in the Battle of Antium dating to 338 BCE, as well as the imitation it probably inspired, the statue and column of C. Duilius commemorating the Battle of

Mylae in 260 BCE.[48] Increasingly into the second century BCE, the private houses of the elite classes were decorated with spoils, not just weapons and armour but artwork and statuary taken from conquered territories in the Greek world.[49]

It was not just ambassadorial visitors who would be affected by such displays. For those with an eye to their future service, such commemorations would have had a bearing on their perception of the competence of individuals and the elite classes whose members served as officers. Although Rome's generals did not frequently repeat commands unless they served during a prolonged war, previous commanders did often accompany armies in other capacities. Someone with a reputation for excellent command did not have to be in charge of the army to inspire confidence. In 190 BCE, for example, when Scipio Africanus accompanied an army to Asia Minor because his brother was commanding it, there were many volunteers who signed up because they trusted his military judgment and were reassured by his presence.[50]

In addition to spoils and statuary, any young boy who had occasion to visit the city of Rome or another thriving urban centre in Italy might have come across triumphal paintings, which were large painted scenes of battle displayed on temples or other public places.[51] Four examples are known from the period of the Middle Republic. One was displayed in the temple of Mater Matuta from 174 BCE, and since it commemorated the conquest of Sardinia was made in the shape of that island. We are specifically told that this painting had a caption underneath which identified the occasion and the name of the commander who had presided, Tiberius Sempronius Gracchus.[52] Another successful commander, L. Hostilius Mancinus, who had commanded the fleet in the Third Punic War, had a triumphal painting made of his troops breaking into the city of Carthage. According to the Elder Pliny he was fond of lingering by this painting where it was displayed in Rome and recounting the story of the battle to passers-by. Just as in the case of the soldier's personal decorations, a visual cue suggested an accompanying narrative. Vividness in war accounts was both desirable and popular; an artist's visual depiction was good, a first-hand oral description to go along with it was better. Hostilius became so popular that he won the consulship the following year.[53]

There is evidence that there were similar commemorations of military victory in smaller cities and towns in Italy where many soldiers would have lived. In Fregellae, a Latin colony of Rome, for example, three houses dating to the Middle Republic displayed terracotta friezes at about eye level on the outside, depicting scenes of victory, battle and trophies.[54] Images of war and symbols of victory have been found in middle-class houses in the allied town of Pompeii, dating to the second century BCE, which likely allude to the victorious campaigns of the Romans and their allies in this period.[55] For our soldiers this means that, although Rome would doubtless have provided the most splendid and large-scale examples of the ennoblement of martial exploits, they could easily absorb the same types of messages elsewhere in Italy.

Sometimes military values were conveyed not by fixed and permanent commemorations, but by one-time events. The aristocratic funeral mentioned by Polybius is one such example, where stories were told about the famous ancestors of aristocratic families. Another example, even more useful for learning about future military service, was the triumph, which was instructional about many different aspects of campaigns. A young Roman might have opportunity to witness a triumph if he were living in the city or nearby. Sometimes the road back to Rome through Italy was also treated as a quasi-triumphal procession, with rural crowds that may never have witnessed a triumph in the city given the chance to see the army's march home. Such was the case in 201 BCE, when Scipio Africanus returned from Africa by traversing the length of Italy from Sicily through rural crowds, and a few years later in 194 BCE when T. Quinctius Flamininus made the march from Brundisium to Rome with his soldiers and their captured booty on display in a procession that was evocative of a triumph.[56] On one occasion in 167 BCE, the conqueror of Macedon, Aemilius Paullus, sailed the spoils from his campaign up the River Tiber while crowds lined the banks on either side.[57]

The triumph proper was a military parade, in which a conquering army and its general entered Rome and processed through the city, while spectators cheered from the roadside. During triumphs, the audience of civilians paid attention to the soldiers as they paraded and especially to those who wore decorations they had earned. We are told that onlookers particularly enjoyed it if there were a high number of soldiers distinguished for their service.[58] Triumphs were highly descriptive tools that provided visual details for understanding what a particular campaign had been like. They included 3D models of the towns the soldiers had captured, made out of wood, ivory, and other materials. Often the real siege engines and missile weapons that had been used to capture them were included in the procession.[59] The swords, shields, and other weapons and armour taken from the enemy rolled along on carts. Enemy prisoners followed along behind, providing real, living, breathing examples of the people that the soldiers had fought.[60] As a portrayal of what the army did, and was likely to do in the future, triumphs provided a highly accurate and vivid impression of the people, places and materials involved. In this way, distinctly military sights and sounds were brought in front of the gaze of the civilian world, and some of their most important witnesses were young men who knew that their future included the kind of military service that was reflected therein.

The frequency with which details of campaigns and especially violent acts were showcased specifically to civilians, in a way that framed them as valuable to society and ennobled and elevated the individuals and groups who accomplished them, points to one major way in which the ancient perspective differs from the modern. War creates a discrepancy between the soldier's experience and the civilian's, especially if that experience involved extreme violence. Modern soldiers have reported feeling this gap profoundly. For them, the instinct has been to hide, not to celebrate, any violent actions in which they had participated. Veterans returning from Vietnam to the US feared what others would think of them if they knew what they had done abroad.[61] Similarly, Italian combatants of the Great War felt that there was a gulf between themselves and civilians that was impossible to bridge, because their experiences could not be adequately described to those who had not lived them. The presence of death in particular – the possibility of their own, and the deaths of others around them – bound them to their immediate group of companions and made them feel profoundly separated from those who had stayed at home.[62]

Such reported experiences might prompt us to look for evidence of the same gap between civilian and military in Roman society. What is striking is that, on the contrary, many facets of Roman culture around warfare seem geared towards minimizing any potential gap and making the separation between the two minimal. The visual cues and accompanying narratives described here involve bringing the details of military experiences into civilian life as vividly as possible. Although, as we will see later, there were religiously based ceremonies that marked moments of transition between the two, at a fundamental level the military and civilian spheres in Roman life were very closely connected; soldiers were citizens and citizens were soldiers. We should expect the boundaries between a military and a civilian state of being to be blurred, because it was advantageous to the state and more comfortable for individuals if the path between these two domains was easy to traverse. And so all over Italy, the details of what to expect in army service and how to conduct oneself to be a successful soldier were readily available.

The Dark Legacy of Military Failure

All of the elements that we have considered so far have reflected what a young Roman might have experienced when Rome's campaigns were largely successful. When the military world was deliberately brought before the gaze of the civilian, it was in celebration, to glorify individual and collective success and to promote, perpetuate and commemorate the achievements of community members as widely as possible. The emphasis was on victory. Of course, the

Romans lived through difficult times, too, and sometimes the experience of the young potential soldier would be the remnants of a defeat rather than a victory. All members of a community could be put in immediate personal danger by the failure of Rome's armies.

In the case of Ligustinus, who was born around 220 BCE, in his young lifetime from birth until he joined the army in 200 BCE, Rome had faced the very real possibility of her own total destruction. The expedition of Hannibal into the Italian peninsula during the Second Punic War had threatened the city of Rome itself. By the time Ligustinus was a teenager, Rome had clawed her way back into the fight, and by 202 BCE they had won it. Ligustinus' most enduring impressions would have been of Rome's improbable resurgence; he joined the army just after they had soundly defeated the only power in the Mediterranean that was their equal. The next thirty years in which he served were those in which Rome completed her domination of the Mediterranean region, culminating in the defeat of the Macedonians at Pydna in 168 BCE, a battle in which Ligustinus could well have fought.[63]

Other Romans and allies who were a little older, including presumably Ligustinus' parents, had lived through the darkest days of the Second Punic War, and their memories would be quite different. Hannibal's armies came down from their famous trek over the Alps in the autumn of 218 BCE, and they proceeded to soundly defeat Roman armies in battles near the Ticinus River, the Trebia River and Lake Trasimene. For many Roman families, relatives who had departed for the war simply never came home. For others, the terror was on their doorstep, as the Carthaginian army plundered the countryside, attacking the villages and towns of northern Italy and murdering the people they found within.

After the defeat at Lake Trasimene the Roman Senate consulted the prophetic scrolls known as the Sibylline Books, texts of mysterious origin which were consulted during crises and prescribed various means of propitiating the gods.[64] The books advised several tasks for the Romans to complete in order to make peace with the gods and turn their fortunes around. Among the vows, plans for new temples, and sacrifices, the books prescribed a *supplicatio*, in which both men and women flocked to the temples to entreat the gods.[65] This would have been what Ligustinus' parents did. Clustumina and its environs was too close to Rome for them to have fallen victim to Hannibal's men, but they, like those in the city of Rome themselves, would have expected the rampaging army to appear on the horizon at any minute. The message from Rome to all its allies was that the gods must be supplicated in prayer. Within the city of Rome itself, after the *supplicatio*, a *lectisternium* was held, an appeal to the gods in which their statues were displayed on couches outside of their temples. This would have been an obvious visual representation of the state's distress, and it formed the backdrop as citizens both male and female engaged in the prayers for divine help for their salvation.

Even if Rome's citizens and allies did not live at a time when they were attacked by an invading force, or called upon to appeal to the gods for their safety as Ligustinus' were at that frightening time, the activity of Rome's armies could still cast a dark shadow. One might, for example, have lived through a display of Rome's vengeance upon those who scorned her authority. Not only did exemplary stories like that of T. Manlius, mentioned above, encourage the idea of a merciless, draconian discipline, but this same idea was sometimes shown to the general public. A Roman who lived early in our era might remember the contingent of Campanians who went rogue and seized the city of Rhegium in 280 BCE, who ten years later were dragged to Rome and publicly scourged and beheaded in the forum as punishment.[66] In 214 BCE, while recovering cities that had revolted from them during Hannibal's invasion of Italy, the Romans discovered 370 deserters from their armies, whom they also sent to Rome to be beaten in public before being hurled from the Tarpeian Rock, the precipice on the Capitoline Hill that was used to execute criminals.[67] One imagines that such a grim lesson was not easily forgotten, both augmenting and reinforcing the morals of the exemplary stories.

A conspicuous reminder of the unpleasant consequences of failing in war was the constant presence of slavery. For soldiers and potential soldiers, the captives who were marched in triumphs were not just examples of Rome's defeated enemies, they were very real reminders of what could happen to them should they find themselves part of a losing army.[68] Romans could, and did, become enslaved through war. Ligustinus would go to Macedon in 200 BCE with an army that would fight and win the battle of Cynoscephalae. This battle signified the liberation of Greece from Macedon, and it also allowed the release of 1,200 slaves living in Greece who had been Roman soldiers during the Second Punic War but had been captured and sold by Hannibal. These men were taken back to Rome to march in commander T. Quinctius Flamininus' triumph, wearing the caps of freedmen. Their return was a celebration and a victory, but their twenty years of slavery were also a dire warning about the cost of failure even for those who survived it.[69]

The Roman Youth

The Roman boy would have known from early in his life that military service was part of his future, and tales of war would have been pertinent to him in anticipation of his own participation in a Roman legion. The behaviours required to be successful in that setting were known in advance through both legendary stories and those of individual veterans, and the tokens of success that accompanied them: be brave, be eager, be obedient, cultivate a mindset of self-sacrifice, develop a talent for effective battlefield violence. In the city of Rome, and increasingly in other cities in Italy, the tokens and commemorations of victory provided constant reassurance that the Roman state was powerful and divinely favoured. The history of past success, brought before the gaze of future soldiers, encouraged them to estimate favourably their own chances of serving in a victorious and profitable campaign.

The prospective soldier also knew once he started down the road of military service, any path that was not successful was likely to lead him to some dark and dangerous places. Sometimes he would have remembered witnessing a stark display of what could go wrong for an individual Roman soldier, especially if he had the memory of seeing violent executions of deserters. Sometimes he would be prompted to think of the consequences of his whole army coming to defeat, a possibility reflected in the presence of slaves traded up and down the Italian peninsula. Each enslaved face was a reminder of how quickly one's fortunes could reverse and how easily freedom could be lost in the ancient world. Consequently, men would also look to Rome's evidence of past successes, hoping they too would serve with competent colleagues, generals and officers, to have the good fortune to join a well-run legion that would not fall afoul of an ambush or be entered into a battle against hopeless odds.

It would have been clear that the life and prospects of an eager soldier were better than those of a reluctant one. The ideal path was to excel as a soldier and to retire from Rome's armies alive, able-bodied, rich, and with a considerable amount of societal esteem from what he had achieved. Of course, there would have been men among their number who harboured doubt about their ability to be good soldiers, who thought such a life would suit them not at all, and for whom the prospect of facing an enemy in combat was terrifying. Perhaps these men wished only to be acceptable soldiers, to perform averagely, fulfil their duties as required, and escape uninjured to a more pleasant life. We will see throughout this book that many facets of Roman military life conspired to make the two paths of excellence and acceptability the easiest, if not the only, options. Other paths that might seem at certain points to be better, like deserting or running away from a battle, carried consequences that were difficult, painful or impossible, such that continuing to serve as well as he could was the easiest and most realistic option.

Chapter 2

A Legion of Strangers

The soldiers who fought for Rome during the Middle Republic were largely willing to do so. They had to be, as the Republic lacked any effective way to compel compliance from its citizens. There was no large-scale police force or other means of widespread law enforcement. The agents of the Republic therefore could not even make eligible men come forward, let alone recruit them, have them turn up when required, and stay in service for the months and years that campaigns commonly lasted.

There are many reasons why men were willing to enrol in the legions. So far, we have seen that Roman society had a strong martial culture that assigned a positive value to success in war. The result was men who had grown up in a climate in which military prowess was both well regarded and a path to social and financial success. We are explicitly told that it was aspirational for soldiers to return from campaign with evidence of great achievement in warfare, and thus get to enjoy the resultant esteem and social capital this distinction would bring. This aspiration was probably sharpened by the circumstances of many young Roman citizens, who would have found their normal rural lives both dull and uncomfortable, with little stretching ahead of them except the prospect of continued poverty and never-ending farm work. Faced with this alternative, it is little wonder that they found adventure in war preferable to what one historian has called 'the grinding miseries of civilian existence.'[1]

In this chapter we will walk through the process of a young soldier entering the legions through the *dilectus*, the levy. A signature feature of the legions of this period is that they sought to avoid a concentration of men from any one town or area in the same legion, preferring instead to separate neighbours from one another by distributing them evenly across the new legions. This model flies in the face of many decades of military theory about how to best form armies in order to create maximum cohesion, the greatest morale and thus military effectiveness. It has, however, recently been largely redeemed by modern studies into combat effectiveness. In the end there are a number of specific reasons why breaking up pre-existing friendships would have not caused a detrimental effect to the legions that the Republic ultimately fielded in battle.

Underlying the recruitment process was a kind of moving push-and-pull between the interests of the individual and the state. There were a number of reasons that a Roman man might wish to serve or not wish to serve, and a set of rules about the kind of man the state wished to recruit and the kind of man it did not. These distinctions rested largely on widespread beliefs about what constituted the proper motivations for a soldier of Rome. Military service was normal and routine at this time, and broadly speaking, the soldier hoped for excitement, social distinction, and financial advantage from it. The collective societal expectations represented by the state privileged land as a requirement for motivating a soldier, casting this as the one tangible asset that bound the soldier in loyalty to the state through the literal ownership of part of it. There were additional practices that mediated in what capacity or role someone could serve, depending on interplays of previous service, level of wealth, and someone's social or familial links. Here, we will explore what all this looked like and how it worked.

Eligibility

The men who were liable to service in the legions under normal, non-emergency circumstances were citizens from the age of 17 to 46. Army service in this period fit into the stage of a man's life between childhood and marriage, and for this reason the vast majority of serving men would have been under 30.[2] There were a few categories of men who were not eligible. Men who had a civic role as priests or magistrates were excused for the duration of the terms of those duties. Debtors and criminals were excluded, as were those in professions considered by the Romans to be disreputable. The profession of acting on a stage, for example, pretending to be someone the person was not, was deemed to be too lowly for the military. This indicates that there was some kind of a moral component involved in selecting recruits, who needed to have some claim to good character in order to serve.

Anyone who was not considered able-bodied would be rejected by the recruiting officer, either because they were suffering from an illness that made them unfit for service at that time or because they had a permanent disability. The standards of fitness were probably much the same as for modern conscript armies, based on the range of duties that needed to be performed. The soldier needed to be able to stand, to march for many miles in a day, to dig, to lift a certain amount of weight, and to wield a weapon. They should hear and see clearly, as they needed to be able to respond to orders conveyed by the sound of a horn or the movement of their unit's standards. All of this would have added up to a general impression of fitness to serve, with the authority to reject on health grounds possessed by the recruiting tribune at his discretion, rather than the application of any formal tests or rules. Due to the sheer amount of recruits and the time it would take to check each, it would have been the responsibility of those individuals who did not wish to serve to present themselves and point out the evidence for the condition that made them unfit.

An inability to serve in the legions was, naturally, undesirable, as it went against societal ideals of the Roman man as a brave and successful soldier. It seems that exceptions were made if the injury that ought to have been disqualifying was acquired in combat during previous service, as some heroic narratives indicate. The Elder Pliny tells the tale of a soldier by the name of Marcus Sergius, who lost his right hand in his second campaign and was subsequently wounded so badly that he could barely use hands or feet, serving as a 'disabled soldier' (Plin. *HN* 7.104–105). What kinds of duties he performed is not specified. The figure of early legend Mucius Scaevola, caught in an assassination attempt of the enemy king, allegedly thrust his right hand into the fire and held it there to show the king the determination of the Romans. He was given afterwards the cognomen Scaevola, 'the left-handed' (Livy 2.12.1–13.1). The fact that he had disabled his sword hand seems to render him no less heroic. These kinds of stories, although most likely subject to the exaggeration of legend, suggest that a physical deformity or handicap acquired in the course of a war was considered a different category to a civilian disability, in both wider Roman culture and during the levy. Fighting in a war and becoming wounded, injured or disabled thereby was a distinct moral category from something that had prevented service in the first place.

Roman citizens who were considered to have already made a satisfactory contribution to the Roman state were not liable to be called again. Usually these were men who had already completed their required years of military service, but it was also possible for men to be granted exemptions from serving if they had rendered some extraordinary assistance to the state. This could be under arms previously, or for some good deed done while a civilian.[3] Later we will see that discharge from the legions was sometimes used by commanders in the field to reward soldiers for performing particularly brave deeds. Release from service as a reward suggests that the main attractions of army service were the opportunities it provided to enrich and advance soldiers' subsequent civilian lives, and that for most, the actual experience of being in the legion was not particularly desirable or enjoyable. Although some, like Ligustinus, were willing to re-enrol voluntarily time after time, apparently many others welcomed a quicker end to their service in the legions if they could manage it.

The last and most important criterion for army eligibility was the ownership of land. Eligibility for the legions was determined by a man's census class, and thus the levy had a relationship to the census, which was taken every five years by a magistrate called the censor, and took into account any property the citizen owned, both land and other possessions.[4] The legions were made up of men from five property classes whose wealth made them *assidui*, the name given to the classes between the wealthy *equites*, who qualified as cavalry, and the extremely poor *proletarii*. This last and most impoverished class were sent to serve in the navy instead. The recruit who was young and unmarried would not have had an independent census class of his own, but rather his class would depend on the holdings of the oldest living male in the family, the *paterfamilias*.

Surprisingly, we find Ligustinus so far at the bottom of this scale of wealth that we would not expect him to be recruited into the legions at all. Technically, Ligustinus' meagre holding of 1 *iugerum* of land (about 1 acre) should have made him ineligible for service, as the minimum land qualification for the fifth and poorest class of *assidui* seems to have been 2 *iugera*.[5] At a holding of 1 *iugerum* he ought to have been counted among the *proletarii*, and no explanation is forthcoming from Livy's text to explain his recruitment into the infantry in 200 BCE. Perhaps Ligustinus' family had other assets not mentioned in his speech, or maybe Ligustinus had presented himself with the appropriate equipment and persuaded the recruiter to allow him to join. It will become evident as we follow the soldier's experiences in service that matters of administration were often discretionary and could be bent and changed in response to circumstances. It is also possible that the discrepancy is simply a narrative adjustment by Livy, deciding that placing Ligustinus in poverty with the minimal amount of land would create a pleasing contrast between his humble origins and his exemplary service to the Republic.

The Levy

When Rome's international landscape was quiet, it enlisted four legions per year. Two of these legions were sent to serve with one consul and two with the other, making up what is referred to as a 'consular army' or 'consular legions.' These legions were originally formed at the beginning of each summer and disbanded at its end. Perhaps the most important difference between the Roman Republican army and most others in history is that the legions raised by Rome lacked even the most basic sources of continuity. There were no individuals who served on a permanent basis and there were no physical building or facilities which belonged to the military. The bodies raised by Rome in this era cannot even properly be called an 'army', singular, which implies a standing institution, and so are better referred to as the Romans did themselves, in the plural as 'armies' or more specifically 'legions.'[6] Every legion, every year, was an entirely unique combination of soldiers and officers.

The Mid-Republican armies had naturally grown out of the military organization of previous eras. In Rome's early period it had been one town among many on the Italian peninsula and had not really been any more powerful or distinctive than any other. These early communities were frequently at war with one another. Rome's armies at that time were not, as they were later, levied and commanded by agents of the centralized state. Rather, the wealthiest and most powerful families in the city and surrounds led private armies, made up of members of their own clans and other followers who owed them loyalty. The soldiers in such armies are referred to as *sodales*, 'swordmates'. This word was in use from the early Republic, where it refers to the followers of aristocratic warlords, to the Middle Republic, where the playwright Plautus used it to describe close male friends, to the beginning of the Empire, where Livy used it to refer back to the early war bands.[7]

The term *sodalis* also had a religious dimension, as it referred to members of archaic priesthoods. Although these priesthoods were restricted to members of the elite, while the *sodales* were followers of the elites rather than aristocrats in their own right, the dual usage of the word might well be significant. Later we will see how the soldiers of this period, soldiers who were not otherwise related by tribe or clan, were bound together as a group by means of an oath that could only derive its power from their shared religion. Instead of a common affiliation to a particular family, the identification with the group came to rest firstly on the fact that they all shared a respect for the same divinities that were thought to secure their word. Before they departed to war, they would be physically marked off as a group by means of the *lustratio*, a religious ceremony that emphasized that the group possessed a certain unique identity.

The first armies of Rome that had been technically under the control of the state were still semi-private in nature. There were specific magistrates who exercised military authority in the field and these magistracies were entirely separate positions from those who exercised civilian authority in the city. Only later did individual Roman magistracies come to involve responsibility for both civilian affairs and military authority. By the time of the Middle Republic, although local leaders no longer commanded armies of Roman citizens who happened to be directly loyal to them, they were still highly influential figures in their communities. Roman society still operated through systems of patronage, where the most powerful men in a community were attended upon by less powerful men who were their clients. A client supported his patron's campaigns for magistracies and contributed to him financially, for example with a daughter's dowry or expenses of public office. The client enjoyed a kind of sponsorship in return, where the patron's influence in the community could help them increase their business or social standing. A patron might explain the law to his client or bring a suit on his behalf.[8]

A Roman citizen living in a small Italian town would have been involved somewhere in the patronage system as a patron, a client, or both. Most likely he belonged to an extensive network that extended up to the town's most powerful men and down to its very least influential. He would be beholden to those higher up in his network and in turn there would be others beholden to him. Even during military service, while ostensibly loyal to the Roman state, he could potentially leverage these loyalties, and others could claim his. The state levy, which had been designed with these connections in mind, was intended to prevent a concentration of men with these pre-existing bonds in any one unit. This was a means of preventing sedition before it started and encouraging soldiers to view their common bond to one another as resting on Roman citizenship rather than local allegiance.

Prior to 241 BCE the levy was conducted using the political divisions of the *comitia centuriata*. This assembly was a voting body that organized all Roman male citizens into six different property classes according to their wealth. At the top was the senatorial class, consisting of the men and families who made up the greater part of the ruling elite. A large number of these were patrician families, whose members claimed histories dating back to the original Senate of Romulus in the days of the city's earliest foundation. They had names that were easily recognizable, like the Claudii, the Aemilii and the Cornelii families. The patricians had initially had a monopoly on priesthoods and magistracies at Rome. During the third century BCE and following a plebian rebellion known as the Conflict of the Orders, plebians had been guaranteed a share of political power, and this had given rise to wealthy and influential families of plebian origins as well. The men from the resulting senatorial classes of the third and second centuries BCE, both patrician and wealthy plebian, were Rome's officers.

For the ordinary soldier, officers were an elite class set apart from the everyday Roman by a number of factors, such as their wealth, their family history, and their deep and longstanding connections to the city of Rome itself. This was a centralized leadership that was embedded in the heart of Rome's oldest history, which claimed not only an almost exclusive right to rule but the right to communicate with the gods on behalf of the whole state. This right of conducting religious ceremony in particular was tied up with military leadership, as it was necessary in this era to consult the gods before both moving large bodies of men and committing them to combat.

The second class in the *comitia centuriata* were the *equites*, or knights. In the Republic of this era the equites were largely businessmen. As the Republic expanded the *equites* became heavily involved with ventures abroad, such as imports, exports and the transportation of goods to and from the provinces. Also ranked as *equites* were the elite families of smaller towns in Italy that enjoyed Roman citizenship. It was very difficult for these men to break into politics in Rome because of the monopoly enjoyed by both the patrician families and the wealthy plebian families with long histories of holding magistracies, so they usually remained as local leaders with equestrian status. The *equites*, by tradition, made up the citizen cavalry of the Roman armies because they had originally been the class wealthy enough to provide a horse or horses. Underneath the *equites* were five divisions of citizens arranged by wealth class, with the first and wealthiest providing an additional two units of engineers and the fifth and poorest providing also two units of horn-blowers for military signalling. In the pre-241 division of the army by class, members of the first class were asked to provide helmet, corselet, greaves, shield, spear, and sword, the second the same minus the corselet, and the third the same minus the corselet and greaves. The fourth had only a spear and a javelin and the fifth only slings and stones, making them both light-armed infantry.[9]

It is difficult to make out from the available evidence how the levy by century actually took place. The *comitia centuriata* was both a political body, as it was the basis of the voting system, and a military body, as it was used to organize the legions. The divisions it created were called centuries and they contained members from all of Rome's thirty-five tribes. The levy based on this organization would result in legions which represented both a cross-section of property classes and a large number of different tribes. Since the tribes represented geographically distinct, contiguous areas, this would separate men from others who originated in the same region. This would minimize the local influences and maximize the control of officers and, in turn, the central power of the state. So the system of levy which persisted until 241 BCE deliberately split up friends, relatives and neighbours to avoid putting pre-existing civilian groups into one legion. Like its later iteration, the levy would have removed previously existing and potentially conflicting loyalties which might have detracted, disturbed or usurped the primary purpose of the legion.

A greater amount of evidence exists for the levy after 241 BCE, as it is described in some detail by Polybius in Book 6 of the *Histories*, where he tells us that it was conducted on the basis of the tribes. Although Polybius was a contemporary of the Roman armies he described and had even witnessed them in action, his account of the *dilectus* poses certain challenges. He writes that all the eligible men, from all thirty-five Roman tribes, travelled to the city of Rome to participate in the levy. There is more than one problem with this picture. The first is that not all men who were eligible in a given year were needed to serve, and so if there was only one centralized levy, we must accept a situation in which some men would have had to travel for days or weeks to reach Rome, only to be forced to turn around and go back without being enrolled. This was clearly not practical, for either the travelling men or the tribunes who would be faced with sorting through many more prospective soldiers than were actually required for their armies.[10]

The problem of unnecessary movement can be solved by conjecturing some sort of preliminary local recruitment, and indeed there is evidence that one existed. There are references to men acting as recruiters, who were either local magistrates or an official sent from Rome for that purpose. L. Cincius, an antiquarian writer, tells us that if a man were prevented for some reason from going to meet the army at its mustering point, then he should report on the following day to the person 'in the district, village or town' responsible for dispatching the men.[11] This indicates the presence of an official in charge of the men who departed from a particular region, but it does not entirely clarify exactly how the preliminary levy was organized.

There are two ways in which towns and villages in Italy with Roman citizenship could have done their recruitment. The first is that local communities assembled their eligible men and chose those who would make up their contingent to send to the *dilectus*. We know that Roman magistrates sent messages to the towns and cities that possessed Roman citizenship, informing them of the number of soldiers required for each campaign. Under this model, soldiers who knew they would definitely be serving would still have to present themselves at Rome and be assigned to a legion and a division within that legion, the *velites*, *hastati*, *principes*, or *triarii*. They needed to know to which legion they had been assigned in order to know which army to join at which mustering point, and they needed to know the division in which they had been placed in order to bring the correct equipment.

The alternative possibility to a preliminary levy followed by enrolment at Rome is for the men to be enrolled through a levy held locally and then sent straight to the mustering point. This is how the Roman allies organized themselves, in their case sending whole units from their towns that were also commanded by locals. For this model to work, the request from Rome would have to specify the numbers they required and for which legion, and also how many of each division the district was to send. The assignment to divisions was technically the responsibility of the military tribunes, but this need not be too much of a difficulty, as the Romans could simply ask for an approximate number and reserve the right to change a man's assignment at the mustering point if they disagreed with his designation. This leaves us with a central levy that involved either just Roman citizens close to Rome, who would meet their countryside comrades for the first time at the mustering point, or enough men to make up four legions converging on the Roman capitol to be sorted. Although the first seems more logical, in fact our sources all insist upon the second model and name the city of Rome as the place where troops were raised and sorted, and so this is where we ought to imagine the levy taking place.[12]

The Soldier's Experience at the Levy

If the preliminary levy did indeed dispatch men from the Italian countryside to be sorted at Rome, as the sources insist, then the *dilectus* of four completely new legions represented the registering and marshalling of 18,000 men. This would have been a huge and time-consuming task that was effective but not very efficient. At minimum it would have taken several days for the tribunes to sort by merely glancing at the men, much longer if they were actually examining them, and longer still if they were adjudicating for those who had turned up to plead injury or ineligibility on health grounds. At one point Livy writes that a *dilectus* of four legions and some reinforcements was completed in eleven days and he implies that this was fast.[13] The whole process seems both massively impressive and despairingly tedious. It is plausible, however, that it was rarely necessary in the second century to raise an entire legion anew, as legions were increasingly kept in provinces and sent reinforcements from Rome instead. Even in Ligustinus' first campaign in 200 BCE, when the war against Macedon was newly declared, the legions contained 2,000 already-serving soldiers transferred from Sicily.

Polybius describes the *dilectus* in detail (Polyb. 6.19–20). He writes that the officers were separated into four groups first, one group of officers for each of the four new legions. The military tribunes of each legion would then go on to select the recruits. The order in which the tribes were brought forward was determined by lot. The eligible citizens were then brought forward tribe by tribe. As they came up to be sorted, they were brought before the selecting tribunes in groups of four men of roughly the same age and build. The tribunes of the first legion would pick one of the four men. The second choice, from the remaining three men, went to the tribunes of the second legion, then the tribunes of the third legion would choose between the remaining two men, with the last man going to the fourth legion. For the second batch of four, the tribunes of the second legion would have first choice, and so on until the division of the whole tribe had been completed. The next tribe would then be brought forward and the process repeated. The division as described by Polybius means that a man's chance of serving in the same legion as his best friend or his neighbour was one in four. The odds were worse if they were of the same size and build, and better if they were of a different height, weight and age.

The enormous scale of the *dilectus* might incline us to be dubious about Polybius' account, or to conclude that the model of the citizens coming straight from the countryside to the mustering point must be the only practical way it could have been conducted. There are, however, considerations specific to the ancient world that make it more likely that this mass organization did in fact take place. The levy and other large-scale political institutions, like the census and the voting assemblies, had the character of a mass ritual.[14] Since large preindustrial societies could not easily enforce obedience, the ritualistic element served to enhance their legitimacy and foster a collective sense of identity. The individual's brief participation in this ritual of categorizing and stratifying both assigned him a place and would have served to impress upon him that he belonged within this grouping despite its massive scale. The levy was a spectacle, doubtless visually impressive, and one in which others were witness to his sorting and he was witness to theirs. Hierarchy, too, was enforced by this system, as the tribunes and their aides ordered the individuals about, sometimes physically directing and moving them.

For the individual, it must have been excruciatingly dull. At the same time, there was something important dawning among the soldiers involved in all the ritualistic sorting and prolonged, unpleasant boredom. The drawn-out process of the levy marks the very first experience the soldiers shared. The levy was the first thing that they undertook as a group, of which no-one outside of that grouping was a part. As the men waited to be chosen and sorted, the two obvious and available sources of entertainment for them were watching the choices of the tribunes as they were made and holding conversations with one another.

As they each came to their own turn and were ushered into one of the legions, they would immediately have something in common with their new grouping, that they were about to serve together, to travel to the same place on the same campaign. The fresh legion had its starting point here in more ways than one, for it is here, surely, that the men started to build a community and a sense of common identity. For many hours there was no other activity for them to do but chat, mingle, play games, and share food as they watched the sorting, which was long and repetitive. According to Polybius the tribunes made 4,200 selections. There is no evidence of how the new soldiers passed these hours and days. Their own selection lasted perhaps less than a minute or two, as they were brought forward from their tribe with three others, chosen, and then directed towards the appropriate legion where an administrator recorded their name, town, and possibly census class.[15]

Perhaps they amused themselves by calling out advice to the military tribunes to pick this or that man, and cheered the new additions. Perhaps they turned away from the sorting altogether to talk among themselves, where the topic of conversation was likely the most pertinent, namely their experiences of war, the commander and the officers of their new legion, and the campaign to which they were being sent. Perhaps they wandered off or slipped away to see the sights of Rome, to buy food from street vendors and marvel at the temples built with booty from campaigns, the shields and swords stripped from enemies displayed on the walls. Here they might have been able to absorb the sights mentioned in Chapter 1, the memorials and commemorations that were concentrated in the city that more provincial citizens would not otherwise have had opportunity to see. We simply do not know, because no source tells us, whether strict military discipline was exercised at the levy, or whether the tribunes were happy enough to see the men out of the way once they had been assigned to a legion, as long as they returned to take their oath at the end.

The *Sacramentum*

At the end of the levy, after the soldiers had been sorted into their legions, they were required to take the *sacramentum*, the military oath. The taking of the oath was organized in a ceremonial fashion, as the culmination of the experience of the levy, and all the members of the new army participated in and witnessed the spectacle. We are not told if the soldiers were all required to stay at or close to the levy in order to take the oath at the end, or allowed to disperse at some point after they had been sorted. This seems sensible, as that way the crowd of men would have gradually diminished, creating more space and less noise, and, as we have seen, the levy must have happened over the course of days rather than hours.

That the oath was not merely a quiet formality, but intended as a spectacle, is implied by the fact that one man was carefully chosen to be the first to step up and recite the whole oath. This action was witnessed by the whole of the new army, and the fact that the first man was deliberately selected indicates that the ceremony was supposed to convey something particular. The first soldier who stood up, observed by all, was intended to create a picture that was both aspirational and meaningful to the soldier so that he would determine to do his best during his own service. As they all watched him speak, each soldier knew that he would be expected to step up in his turn and join him in his promise.

We are told that the tribunes selected the first man by choosing whomever they deemed 'the most suitable' (Polyb. 6.21.1). This rather vague phrase of Polybius' does not help us to specify what his qualities were. Good soldiers for the Romans were made by actions, not looks, and so the ideal soldiers in our sources are generally described in terms of their behaviour and temperament. Polybius remarks when considering ordinary legionaries as candidates for centurion positions that the Romans favoured soldiers whom they judged stalwart and steady.[16] We need to look for other sources of evidence from the Roman world to come up with a picture of what the tribunes were looking for when they scanned the assembled troops to select a man who looked like an appropriate soldier to recite the oath.

Firstly, they would have been searching for someone strong and healthy.[17] The good soldier maintained excellent physical fitness, and it was thought that the professions least suited to soldiering were craftsmen and artisans because those men were sedentary (Livy 8.20.4). This does not mean that the tribunes were looking for a heavily muscled or very tall man. Physically, fitness was more typical of the Roman soldier than being of above average size or possessed of extraordinary muscularity. These qualities do not seem to have been aspirational to the Romans or how they perceived the average Roman or Italian man to look. Large men were remarked upon as unusual, reminiscent of Gauls and Germans rather than Romans. The early Roman hero T. Manlius Torquatus was described as a man of average height matched in single combat against a Gaul of enormous size; the first spear centurion M. Centenius Penula was distinguished from the others for his huge size (*magnitudine corporis*); and the Late Republican general Mark Antony was ridiculed by Cicero for the 'gladiatorial strength of [his] whole body'.[18] In short, strength was good but conspicuous muscular bulk was not.

A suitably impressive man for the oath would also have to accord to broader criteria that applied not just to soldiers, but were typical standards for men across Roman society, like good hygiene. Poets addressing advice to young men desirous of girlfriends warned that they should smell pleasant but not perfumed. Having a pleasant smell was an attribute of the gods and, perhaps more importantly, the famed Macedonian king and commander Alexander the Great.[19] The poet Ovid specified that ideally men should not have 'tartar on their teeth', and Martial advises that one should not be so hairy as to appear scruffy, nor so plucked as to be effeminate.[20] It might have been desirable to choose someone who had a scar on some visible part of his body like his face or arms, as this was considered proof of having stood and faced an enemy in combat.

Physical attributes would not have been the only criteria for suitability. According to Cicero the first enrolled soldier was always someone whose name was propitious.[21] Similarly, the man called to take the full oath would probably also need to have a lucky name, or at least not an unlucky one. Propitious names were those related to words of positive meaning, like Valerius from the verb *valeo*, meaning to be strong or powerful, Salvius from *salveo*, meaning to be well, to be in good health, and Statorius from *stator*, meaning one who stands fast, is abiding.[22] Since the nature of oaths is to make a promise with a divine power as witness, here too it would have been desirable that the words be spoken clearly and articulately, as they needed to be in Roman religious ceremonies. In that context spoken words needed to be said precisely and exactingly: a stutter, for example, prohibited a girl from becoming a Vestal Virgin, and the Republican magistrate L. Caecilius Metellus, who had some kind of speech impairment, is said to have practised for months to correctly articulate the dedication of a temple.[23] Livy writes of P. Licinius Crassus, a commander during the second Punic war, as an ideal soldier because 'at that time no citizen was better put together than he, of surpassing handsomeness and physical strength, he was most eloquent.'[24]

These various pieces of evidence allow us to make a very educated guess about the type of man the tribunes were searching for. He should be someone handsome, who also appeared neat and clean. He might bear a previous wound, but it should be on the front of the body and not be disfiguring or embarrassing. He should be visibly strong and fit but not overly muscular or unusually tall. He must be called something propitious, and be well spoken in such a way as to be able to pronounce his oath clearly without stuttering. The oath was, in essence, a promise of mutual reliability. The more capable that first man looked, the more heartened the new soldiers would feel to be joining a group where he had been chosen as representative. When this first man pledged confidently that he would stay under arms, the intended effect was to encourage the new soldiers and instil optimism.

The specifications of the oath itself come from three different sources. From Polybius, we learn that the oath was that 'he will obey his officers and execute their orders as far as is in his power.'[25] From Dionysius of Halicarnassus we get a slightly different version of the oath, as spoken by the consul Cincinnatus, reminding his troops they had sworn that 'they would follow the consuls in any wars to which they should be called and would neither desert the standards nor do anything else contrary to law.'[26] There is one other source of evidence for the *sacramentum* but it must belong to an imperial context. Servius' commentary on the Aeneid has three examples (Serv. *Ad. Aen.* 8.1; 2.157; 7.614) which state that the soldier must do 'nothing against the state' and that the soldier must not leave the ranks until he had completed the *stipendia*. This word, meaning essentially 'pay' or 'salary' refers to an entire length of service in the Empire but is also used, for example by Ligustinus, to refer to each campaign that he undertook.

Livy's evidence for the *sacramentum* complicates the picture, as he writes that the oath changed in 216 BCE:

Then a new departure was made; the soldiers were sworn in by the military tribunes. Up to that day there had only been the military oath binding the men to assemble at the bidding of the consuls and not to disband until they received orders to do so. It had also been the custom among the soldiers, when the infantry were formed into companies of 100, and the cavalry into troops of 10, for all the men in each company or troop to take a voluntary oath to each other that they would not leave their comrades for fear or for flight, and that they would not quit the ranks save to fetch or pick up a weapon, to strike an enemy, or to save a comrade. This voluntary covenant was now changed into a formal oath taken before the tribunes. (Livy 22.38.2–5)

From these four accounts, some common threads allow us to say a few things for certain about the oath, at least as it was before 216 BCE. Firstly, it involved the soldier verbally consenting to becoming a soldier by promising to submit himself to the authority of his appointed officers. Secondly, he consented to remain a soldier by promising to stay with the standards until he was formally released by the appropriate authority. Thus, the immediate effect of the first oath was to bring the soldier under the command of the consul. It also secured the very first order of the general, one that was difficult to enforce by any other means, that the members of each consular army would assemble at a particular place on a particular day, 'to be in Ariminum on a certain day before bedtime' to give an example from Polybius.[27]

Livy's account makes the picture more difficult, since he writes that there were originally two oaths, which in 216 BCE were merged into one and the same. Frontinus, repeating this information, clarifies that the first and original oath was the *sacramentum* that obliged the soldier to come under arms and not leave until he was dismissed, and the second, sworn voluntarily among the soldiers of the unit that they would not flee the battle line, was called the *iusiurandum*.[28] If we are to believe Livy, then by the time of Ligustinus the oath taken would be both to become and remain a soldier until dismissed, with the important addition that he would not abandon his colleagues in the battle line.

Part of the problem of Livy's text is that one oath including these two parts does not really fit anywhere in the enrolment process. Polybius has the army organized through no less than three different meetings, once to gather together and enrol those who were eligible, once to sort these men into an appropriate division, maniple and century, and once at the mustering point, where the legionaries assembled with the allies and were taught how to build a camp. Livy, however, writes that, previous to 216 BCE, the oath to remain in the battle line was taken by each *centuria* of the infantry and each *decuria* of the cavalry at the time when they were sorted into those units. If we follow Polybius, this would be at the second meeting, although he says very little about this meeting except that it was arranged at the end of the first: the 'tribunes in Rome, after administering the oath, fix for each legion a day and place at which the men are to present themselves without arms and then dismiss them.' (6.21.6)

If we attribute the whole oath to the first meeting of enrolment, then this would have significantly diminished the impact of the second part. In Polybius' model, at enrolment only the soldier's legion had been decided, not his division or maniple. The nature of the second oath was that it was made personally to the people it affected, one's comrades in the same unit. If it were done at enrolment, it would cease to be an oath made to particular men that he would not abandon them, and become the rather more theoretical oath that he would not abandon the battle line. If we place the oath at the second meeting, then the soldiers would not, technically, have been sworn in until then and would not have been under oath to turn up at this meeting. We would also have to reject Polybius' explicit statement that the oath was taken at the first enrolment session.

Livy presents the oath to remain in the battle line as an organic practice that had grown up among the soldiers that was subsequently institutionalized by the state. Since the oath is reported by no other source, it remains too problematic to accept Livy's account as true, or at least to accept that this part of the oath was adopted by the state. There is reason to think it may have existed as an informal oath among Roman soldiers at some time. The idea that fleeing the battleline was the most dangerous thing one could do was well-established in antiquity. The late Republican author Horace wrote that 'death chases the soldier who runs' (Horace, Odes 3.2) and it is true that it was usually more dangerous to flee than stand one's ground, as the fleeing soldier was especially vulnerable to being cut down from behind. Right up to a pivotal point of the line's collapse when it was clear he would be cut down otherwise, the soldier's safest option was to stay firm and face forward.[29]

After the first soldier had spoken the whole oath, the rest would come forth one by one and say *idem in me*, 'the same for me.'[30] The verbalizing of the oath affirmed that the soldier was a member of this particular group and that he had something in common with the men present that he did not have in common with anyone who was not. In addition, the word *sacramentum* indicates that it was not just a secular promise but a religious guarantee, which relied on the notion of a widely recognized supernatural power. The idea was that when the oath was sworn to a divinity, the responsibility for sanctioning the oath breaker was given over to that deity, whose knowledge and power reached far further than that of a mortal. The other soldiers were both audience and participants in this swearing, as it was important for the oaths to be vocalized out loud so that they could be witnessed by both gods and men. While the soldiers came from different places in Italy, had different levels of military experience and for the most part did not know one another, they recognized the same general pantheon of gods. In the absence of any truly effective body that could compel their obedience to the state, the oath served to create a moral obligation and, at the same time, created a consequence of disobedience by invoking the threat of divine wrath. In this way the binding quality of the oath was not primarily based on the reliability or honour of the participants, but was rooted in understandings about the nature of the supernatural that they held in common.

The immediate practical effect of the oath was that each man promised to obey his officers until he was released from the oath he had just taken, and the first thing that he guaranteed was that he would turn up at the next meeting to be further sorted into his division and maniple. The more abstract effect relates to another function of oaths, that the swearing of an oath can effectively be the act of creating a group.[31] In the case of the *sacramentum*, the oath cannot qualify as an initiation, because there was no pre-existing institution of the army into which to be initiated.[32] Rather, the oath created the army group and defined its membership. This is important in the Middle Republic in particular, when there was no standing army and sometimes no army of Rome in existence at all.

The uttering of those three words *idem in me* had given the soldier membership into a new group. At this stage this would have seemed quite abstract; the barest psychological connection among members who had promised to embark upon a campaign together and to remain a part of the army until legitimately dismissed. The new soldier had the bare bones of a vision of his immediate future, now knowing with which of the four legions he would serve, under whose command, where he was expected to assemble and to where he was going. Perhaps he had made some new friends during the sorting, or he had spent time with those men with whom he had come to Rome from his own region. The men who would come to be vital to him, the members of his new maniple, the others who would share his tent in camp, he was yet to meet.

Division and Cohesion

The purposeful division of recruits to the legions across lines of friendship, kinship and regional origin raises a number of questions about the character of the new army that was created and the soldier's experience within it. It has been plausibly argued that the intent of the mixing that took place during the *dilectus* was to encourage a sense of Roman identity among soldiers who might otherwise have viewed themselves with primarily local or regional identities.[33] The potential problem is whether these men, who served in units with men who were strangers on the day of enrolment, would develop a sufficient cohesion to be militarily effective.

The Roman practice is the diametrical opposite of a long-held theory that soldiers would fight more fiercely and more effectively with friends and relatives, on the basis that these men were people whose welfare and safety was more important to them. It was thought that relationships that existed before military service would serve as a built-in motivator and could be leveraged to create better functioning units. The principle seems intuitive and attractive, that camaraderie based on origin and common life experiences would generate cohesion, and military effectiveness would thrive when based on a solid foundation of lifelong friendship. This theory was tried on a massive scale during the First World War in the form of the 'Pals Battalions' raised by the British Secretary of State for War, Field Marshal Horatio Herbert Kitchener, from August 1914 to June 1916.

The original principle of the battalions was to encourage recruitment by promising men that they could serve with their friends and colleagues. The battalions were raised from workplaces and social clubs, and friends were encouraged to sign up together. While local battalions were common for purposes of home defence, sending such units to engage in large-scale actions abroad was a new idea.[34] For the men of Edwardian Britain, the Pals units allowed them to avoid certain problems of units that had drawn men from a mix of places, for example, there was a profound difference between the highest and lowest social classes at the time. Problems had also arisen due to differences in local and regional dialects and languages, and even from units that had a mix of urban and rural troops.

Advocates of the Pals units thought that the men who served in them would have a 'better spirit', and indeed they were often observed to have a high *esprit de corps* and social cohesion.[35] The authorities had expected this to translate directly into a higher combat effectiveness, but this turned out not to be the case. The Pals units showed no discernible superiority in combat compared to mixed units.[36] There was also one solidly negative effect that Kitchener and his staff had not foreseen. The high rate of casualties suffered by Britain in the Great War meant that a Pals battalion devastated in battle led to a village empty of men back home, a pattern that replicated itself across the country.[37]

The experience of the Pals Battalions suggests that the Romans were not necessarily sacrificing a great potential advantage when they mixed their soldiers' regional affiliations. In order to understand why, we need to look into the reason why the cohesion observed in the Pals battalions did not translate into a superior combat performance. Principally it is because, despite enjoying a long tradition of study in the field of military psychology, cohesion cannot be understood to be one concept that is applicable to all aspects of a soldier's interaction with his comrades. Specifically, there is a marked difference between cohesion as it describes soldiers liking one another and getting along together in a social sense, and the type of cohesion that allows a given group of people to complete specific actions. The first type is called social cohesion, and the second is task cohesion.

> The definitions of the two are as follows: task cohesion is the shared commitment among members to achieving a goal that requires the collective efforts of a group. A group with high task cohesion is composed of members with a common goal and who are motivated to coordinate their efforts as a team to achieve that goal. Social cohesion is the extent to which group members like each other, prefer to spend their social time together, enjoy each other's company, and feel emotionally close to one another.[38]

Before this distinction was made, it was assumed that task cohesion, applicable in the military context as fighting together or combat performance, had a strong relationship to social cohesion. This was the assumption behind the Pals Battalions. The reason that this turned out not to be true, and the reason why it might not matter very much how the Romans grouped their soldiers, is that the two types of cohesion have a very weak relationship to one another.[39] How well a soldier gets along with someone else in a social context has very little to do with how the two will work together under pressure. Numerous modern examples have illustrated that even people with pre-existing hostilities, who actively dislike one another, are capable of performing tasks effectively. This has been observed in modern military units that were divided up and mixed with others and then swiftly after had to respond to combat situations without any time to get to know their new comrades.[40]

What these studies have shown is that task cohesion in particular does not need to be rooted in long-standing, pre-existing ties, because human beings are remarkably good at working on tasks even with those they actively dislike. A second reason that military units, or groups of any kind, do not need to draw from already existing bonds is that human beings have a capacity to quickly develop ties with new people who are placed in a group with them. Simply defining people as a group is enough for individuals to start identifying with one another and developing positive attitudes to each other, even if that grouping is completely arbitrary or random. This is called 'ingroup favouritism', and while it happens naturally as people drift towards groupings with others of similar traits, it also happens simply through being placed in a group for any reason or none at all.[41]

These findings by modern researchers are, of course, of limited use in a population whose behaviour we cannot study first hand. The main value is as a warning that we ought not to fall into making old assumptions about the cohesive potential of strangers thrown together in the military. It was not necessarily a disadvantage to mix a Roman citizen into a unit with strangers, either to the kind of social interactions the soldier might enjoy or the level of combat effectiveness his unit could achieve. It also ought to alert us to the importance of groups and prompt us to pay attention to how group identity was emphasized. As we follow Ligustinus through his first campaign it will become apparent that for the citizen soldiers of the Middle Republic there were all sorts of different experiences that impressed upon them that they were a group and that this group was important. We saw this first in the taking of the *sacramentum*, in which each member individually vocalized his assent to become a soldier and the repeated phrase *idem in me*, 'and the same for me', emphasized that each had taken an action in common, witnessed by the other members of the group. The soldiers were also subject to a number of rituals surrounding travelling and departure that represented them as a group. In such rituals, the consul exercised his right to consult the gods on behalf of the army as a whole, and to receive divine warning relating to the fate of the army grouping.

In addition, the history of the Pals Battalions, particularly that their common origin was not an advantage to them, should warn us to keep an eye on the length and quality of shared experiences that the Roman soldiers built before they even reached enemy territory. Ligustinus started building common points of reference with others beginning from his experience watching the *dilectus* with others and being sorted into divisions, and arguably earlier, as he walked to Rome with others from his town. There was a long road to come, from assembling at the mustering point, to his deployment via the navy and long routine of marching, camping and training. These events, which are most often skipped or severely abbreviated in our sources, made up a huge percentage of the time spent on campaign, and represent weeks and months of living and working with the same comrades.

Chapter 3

Finding Your Place in the Ranks

The Second Meeting: Divisions and Maniples

Polybius writes that before the recruits were sent back to their homes, they were dismissed temporarily, with each legion being given a day and a place to reassemble for a second meeting. The vagueness of this statement is unhelpful, as we have no real idea whether this meant days later, weeks later or the day after, and whether a 'place' means simply somewhere in Rome and its environs or another town entirely. It is very unlikely by the Middle Republic that the soldiers were expected to return home between the two meetings, and so it is best thought of as happening shortly after the first.[1] The existence of a second meeting suggests that the first sorting into four groups was a quick and rough way of dividing the men into groups of a more manageable size, and that it was done in order that a more detailed sorting could be done of four or five thousand men at a time instead of sixteen or twenty thousand.

We are told that three things were taken into consideration when sorting the available men into their appropriate divisions: age, experience, and wealth. It is not clear what the rules or norms surrounding these factors were, nor what the interaction between them might look like. There is also some suspicion that the exact positions into which the soldiers were divided would have been chosen by the tribunes based on a number of factors beyond the ones that Polybius lists, including the current needs of the army, the influence of patronage systems, and negotiation between the tribunes and the soldiers.

Polybius says that the soldiers presented themselves to the tribunes at the second meeting without arms to be placed in their divisions, after which they were instructed what equipment to bring to the mustering point depending on the needs of their new division (6.21.6–23.14). Military tribunes allocated all the soldiers into one of the four divisions of the army, the *velites*, *hastati*, *principes* or *triarii*, and then to a maniple and a century. This would be a fairly neat system during most of the third century BCE, when it seems that the soldiers had to supply their arms and armour themselves. It would reflect a division based on wealth, not pertaining to the man's census class exactly, but rather in the form of the equipment that the soldier could afford to supply.

The system was not so straightforward by the time of Ligustinus. At some point after Ligustinus' time, by the very end of the second century, the Roman system had changed so that weapons and arms were supplied by the state. We do not know when this happened, as there is no record of a decree or policy that points us to a specific date for the change. It may always have been quite a loose requirement.[2] Polybius tells us that Roman citizens had deductions made from their pay for corn, clothes and 'any additional arm they might require' (6.39.14). This may mean that there were spare arms for any the soldier had broken or lost, but it also implies that arms were available for those who did not have them. Certainly, during the Punic Wars legions were supplied with arms by the state on several occasions, or the allies were asked to supply them. This certainly seems to be a much more practical policy for all involved, as the availability of weapons would have allowed the tribunes more flexibility in assigning soldiers to the various divisions, and the ability for a soldier to essentially lease a sword would have given men opportunities that they otherwise would not have had. The other advantage is that it would streamline the process of recruitment and mustering, as the soldiers would not have had to make an extra journey to their homes to retrieve their equipment, which is the largest and most obvious inefficiency in Polybius' description of the *dilectus*.

When the soldier could supply his own equipment as a proxy for wealth, it is possible that he could find or borrow some in order to advance a case for placement in a different division. If a soldier could influence his appointment in the ranks through any means, it was certainly in his best interests to do so. There was a pressing and tangible incentive for soldiers to qualify for the further divisions as soon as possible because the most dangerous roles in a battle were in the *velites* and front lines of the *hastati*. The *velites* faced the most danger because they were skirmishers who wore the least amount of protective armour in order to remain light and mobile. The *hastati* were the front line of heavy infantry, who were the first to fight and faced the freshest opposition. The level of risk gradually diminished as one moved through the divisions to the *principes*, who were rotated to the front when the Romans were pressed, and the *triarii*, who were held in reserve and usually only used when a battle was going badly.[3]

Polybius does not simply say that the young started in the *velites*, but that the youngest *and* poorest were placed in this division. The idea that there were two different criteria for placement in the *velites*, an age basis and a wealth basis, suggests that neither could represent a hard and fast rule. It might mean that serving in the *velites* was required only of citizens who were both young and poor. If this were the case then a soldier of higher wealth could bypass the *velites* entirely and begin his service in the *hastati*, as could someone who came to his first army service a good few years after his first eligibility, as apparently Ligustinus did, and as might have happened regularly through some of the Republic's least tumultuous years. Or Polybius might mean that every soldier had to start in the *velites* regardless of wealth and only the poor were made to remain there. In this case the 'youngest' would refer to the members of the *velites* who were in their first years of service, while the 'poorest' would refer to those soldiers who had more years of experience but were placed in the *velites* only because of their poverty.

It is not clear that progress through the divisions represented any distinction or promotion. In other words, it does not seem that the *principes* was a higher rank than the *hastati* or that one could be advanced there quickly on account of bravery or distinguished service. Instead, progression seems to have been a function of age, years of experience, and perhaps wealth. We do not know if there was a normalized schedule for this progression, meaning a specific time of service that automatically granted assignment to a more senior division. If soldiers in the second century were serving for six to fourteen years, we might be tempted to think the rule of thumb was two or three years in each of the *velites*, *hastati* and *principes*. Since the *triarii* contained half the number of men that populated the other three divisions, it would almost always be made up of those who had elected to stay with the army voluntarily. During Rome's quieter years, the *triarii* must have represented a self-selected body of men who had found a talent and a liking for military service. At some moments, such as during the Punic Wars, the *triarii* would have been men who were pressed to remain in the legions because they were sorely needed.

There was a way to progress upwards in rank through distinguishing oneself, and that route led not to more senior divisions but to positions in the centurionate. The smallest unit of the legion's combat organization was the century, and each century had one centurion and a rearguard officer called an *optio*.[4] Two centuries made up a maniple and there were ten maniples per division, giving us two centurions and two *optiones* per maniple, and twenty centurions and twenty *optiones* per division, per legion. The most senior of these was the centurion of the right-hand or 'prior' century of the first maniple. It is unclear how the hierarchy of centurions worked in this period. We know that the most senior centurion in the whole legion was the prior centurion of the first maniple of the *triarii*, suggesting in turn that generally, the seniority was with the smaller maniple number, the prior rather than the posterior century, and the oldest division. It is not known, however, how much weight was attached to each of the factors, for example, whether the fifth centurion of the prior century of the *hastati* was senior, junior or equal to the third centurion of the posterior century of the *principes*.

The implication of the fact that one could move around the legion either by means of age and experience or by means of distinction is that even in the Mid-Republican citizen militia there was an ambitious, proto-professional route, and a quieter, less dramatic and safer way to serve. Ligustinus chose the former, making his performance distinguished enough to catch the attention of his officers and gain recommendations for promotion to leadership positions, on up through its progression until he eventually arrived at the pinnacle of what was achievable for someone who came up from the ordinary soldiery, the *primus pilus prioris centuriae*. This was the 'first *triarius* of the prior century' where the word *pilus* or 'spear' has come to replace *triarius* when the Romans meant the centurions of that division. The *primus pilus* is sometimes translated 'first spear centurion'.

Many more soldiers of Rome would have taken the second route, in which they performed entirely adequately to complete their required number of years without deliberately seeking out danger. As we will see later, numerous rules and traditions mapped out a path that must have been extremely common. The path of least resistance and trouble required neither extraordinary acts of courage nor the problems and difficulties of trying to leave the army and make a life after mutiny or desertion. This path was relatively safe. It did not lead to positions that were the most famously dangerous, like that of the centurions, nor did it lead to extraordinary individual awards and distinctions. Rather, it would have been a quiet route through the middle of maniples that were increasingly further back from the front lines, a long routine of showing up where ordered, remaining steady in group combat, and hoping that no enemy bow or spearman managed to get in a lucky shot.

Approaching the levy, many young Roman men would have seen their chance to take their future into their own hands. Success offered material reward and economic gains to every soldier, and none would have desired this more than those who began in near-poverty. For most of the Mid-Republican period, families that sent a son to military service received an immediate boon in the form of a tax benefit. From the early Republic until 167 BCE, Rome's wars were financed by its citizens through a monetary contribution called *tributum*. It was framed as a loan to the state for the purpose of waging particular wars, after which the money was supposed to be returned from the resulting campaign booty, but in reality we know of few occasions upon which the money was refunded. In effect the *tributum* was a tax, from which serving soldiers and their families were exempt.[5] The soldier meanwhile drew pay for military service called the *stipendium*. For most of the second century BCE this was probably no more than an allowance for expenses incurred, since the cost of a soldier's food was deducted from it. An ordinary legionary received three *asses* a day, a centurion received double that, although his individual food requirement would be the same, and a cavalryman received nine *asses*.[6]

The appointment of centurions was done at the same time as the division into units. This was what was happening during the levy of 171 BCE when we first met Ligustinus. In his case, the experienced soldiers who were volunteering to go to Macedon were asking to be reappointed at a rank they had achieved in a previous army. There was not necessarily continuity between a soldier's rank in one legion and his place in the next. Ligustinus made his speech as part of a request to be appointed at the highest rank he had achieved in his years as a soldier, that of *primus pilus*, the highest-ranking centurion. The fact that Ligustinus was making the request to return to his former rank, and his remark that 'four times in a few years' he served as *primus pilus*, illustrate that these rankings were not attached to the individual like a modern military rank, but were slots that were available to appropriately qualified individuals in particular armies. One characteristic of a permanent army institution is that when a soldier achieves a particular rank he can be expected to retain it, barring any disciplinary infraction he might commit. This was of course not at all possible when all armies were unique and temporary formations. Ligustinus, when he travelled from legion to legion, was not a *primus pilus*, but a soldier who had the necessary experience to be appointed to serve in that position.

In the case of the levy of 171, there is a sense of negotiation between the soldiers and the tribunes who were administering the sorting of recruits. Experienced men were desirable in any campaign, and since the men were under no compulsion to serve, the fact that the discussion was being held at the levy and not at the mustering point implies that they were able to give or withhold their services depending on the position in which they were appointed. There was likely a convention or idea that a soldier ought to be reappointed at a comparable rank to his last position, but constraints on the number of officer positions alone would have meant it was not compulsory. There were, for example, only two positions of *primus pilus* in a consular army, one in each of the two legions.

So in addition to the criteria of age, wealth and experience, we can reasonably expect a very human process of negotiation about how these elements should be weighted to find each soldier an appropriate position. There is good reason to believe that other factors were at play. As we saw, the original division of the tribes into four legions was intended to break up the influence of patronage networks, with the biggest threat to army unity coming from influential local leaders. Of course, the consul who commanded and the tribunes who performed the bulk of the administrative work in recruitment had their own networks of patronage, which had been the foundation of Rome's early private armies. The word *dilectus* originally meant a selection rather than an enrolment, and is probably a remnant of the older army system in which commanders had been independent of the state and had chosen their soldiers from their own clans, families and patronage networks. Even in the fourth and third centuries when the commanders were technically magistrates of Rome and acting as representatives of the state, there seems to have been an effort made to privilege parts of the population most friendly to the commander.[7]

By the time of the Middle Republic, it was not possible to select particular tribes or men from certain areas because of personal choice, but it is not overly cynical to suspect that it was not an entirely fair and egalitarian exercise, either.[8] The consul and tribunes could still allocate divisions and ranks as they saw fit. In a society that functioned very much through the use of personal and patronage connections, the appointment of centurions and other positions was an area where the general and officers could use their powers to benefit their own networks. This was occasionally done blatantly, as when in 134 BCE the commander Scipio Aemilianus took 500 clients and friends with him to war in Numantia (App. *Hisp.* 85). Most often, it is reasonable to suspect that recruits with a connection to the army's officers would be shuffled into positions that were more distinguished, or safer, or both.

Rome, 200 BCE

Although the role of the *velites* often seems overlooked or treated briefly in ancient battle narratives, it ought to be remembered that this division was in fact very large, comprising almost a third of citizen infantry.[9] The *velites* is where we would expect the newly recruited Ligustinus to have been placed in 200 BCE. Livy, for whom the days of divisions and maniples were long gone, does not have him use this term, saying instead that for the first two years of his service he was a *miles gregarius* a 'common soldier' or what we might now term a private. It may be that Ligustinus started in the *hastati*, for after two years he says that on account of his bravery he was appointed as *decimus ordo hastatus*, literally 'tenth-rank *hastatus*'. There is something strange here, for usually 'tenth *hastatus*' would refer to a centurion, and be followed by either *prioris centuriae* 'of the prior century' as they are in the rest of his list of centurion positions, or *posterioris centuriae* 'of the posterior century'. The word *ordo* means a group of soldiers in formation or rank and does not usually occur in the title of a centurion, although there remains much confusion about how the centurions were named during the Republican period.[10] The wording here may simply mean that Ligustinus was literally 'a tenth-maniple *hastatus*' or, in other words, made an ordinary member of the *hastati*.[11]

If we agree with most of the commentators on this passage of Livy that Ligustinus became a centurion in 198 BCE, then his first two years as a 'miles gregarius' were probably served in the *hastati*, for it makes little sense to promote a *veles* to command of a division in which he had never served. This, too, seems wrong, for it should not have been possible for someone very poor like Ligustinus, who should not technically have met the land requirement for infantry service, to skip service in the *velites*. Perhaps the tribune responsible for the divisions found Ligustinus too old to be a *veles*. Certainly by the time he was called at the age of twenty, three years after he was technically eligible, he hardly seems like an ideal *veles*, whose role as swift runners and second riders on cavalry horses, as we will see, makes them sound more the age of boys than men. In such a case perhaps he was found some heavier equipment and enrolled straight into the *hastati*, whom Livy called 'the flower of adolescent youth', making them also sound quite young.[12] Perhaps Ligustinus had inherited equipment from a relative or friend and was able to negotiate a start in the *hastati*, meeting the direct equipment requirement rather than the census requirement. It might also be that in his speech Ligustinus has omitted a move from the *velites* to the *hastati* during his second year, and that *decimus ordo hastatus* does indeed mean that he distinguished himself and was promoted to centurion for the following year. Since we are unable to say for certain that Ligustinus was a real person with the career he describes, there is little use in picking apart this problem. Due to his extreme poverty and inexperience, and for the sake of following the more typical experience of a young man who began in the *veles*, we will place him there in the beginning and advance him swiftly to the *hastati*. This does not seem a stretch, as Ligustinus was a few years older than the qualifying age for enrolment.

As Ligustinus set off back to Forum Novum from Rome, thinking of the role he had been given in the new army, he would have considered what he now needed to collect in order to show up correctly equipped at the mustering point, which had been set as the town of Brundisium. The *velites* are often referred to as light infantry, because their role was to be quick and mobile. They primarily used a javelin called the *hasta velitaris*, with each *veles* carrying perhaps three to five of them into battle. These were small and numerous, and cannot have been expensive, nevertheless, they would not have been provided by the recruits themselves. They needed to be available in bulk and so would have been provided by the army or its allies, as, for example, we hear the city of Arretium offering arms and armour in large numbers during the Second Punic War.[13] That means Ligustinus would only have had to acquire a plain helmet, a small round shield called a *parma* and a sword. Most likely in this period he obtained these himself, if he could, or had them deducted from his army pay if he could not.

The quality of any Roman soldier's equipment, when he provided it himself, would have depended on how it was obtained. An item handed down from a family member, for instance, could either be higher quality than the young man would otherwise be able to obtain, or rather worn out, depending on where it had originally come from and for how long it had been used. By the time that Ligustinus fought in the first half of the second century, basic military equipment had become overwhelmingly of a standard, mass-produced type. The archaeological record indicates that this had already happened by the middle of the third century and so, although there was a variety of equipment circulating in Italy, most soldiers would have had a very similar set of basics.

The best illustration of this homogenization of equipment is the Montefortino helmet, which is overwhelmingly the most common design found in Italy from the fourth to the first century BCE. These show a marked deterioration in quality in the second and first centuries BCE, both in manufacture and finishing. This points to mass production, as does the fact that they begin to be marked with Latin maker's stamps, indicating that the workshops were making enough pieces for it to be worthwhile for them to create a special die to mark them.[14] These new, mass-produced, cheaper and lower-quality items corroborate the written sources in giving us a date sometime in the second century when equipment was being provided to soldiers. On the one hand, these low-quality pieces would have made warfare slightly more hazardous and certainly more uncomfortable. On the other hand, the availability of first cheap and then free equipment would have lowered the financial barriers to participation in the Roman legions.

In addition to these items, Ligustinus would have packed at least one spare tunic. These were fairly simple garments, either sleeveless or with short sleeves, extending down to the thigh and pulled in at the waist with a leather tie.[15] If he had one, he would have taken his *sagum*, a wide woollen cloak that could be pinned to the right or centre of the chest with a pin called a *fibula*.[16] This could be used at night as a blanket or folded up to serve as a pillow.[17] These items would not last through years of service and they were not expected to, as along with grain, our sources often mention clothing as being sent out to the armies in the field from Rome or one of her allies.[18] In 198 BCE, for example, two years into his service in Macedon, Ligustinus could have requested a new tunic from a batch of clothing that was sent out from Sicily and Sardinia (Livy 32.27.2–3).

Ligustinus would also have been in search of some fur. The *velites* were marked out from the rest of the army, Polybius writes, with wolfskins 'or similar' that covered their helmets (6.22.3). These markers were probably not as dramatic as they are often portrayed in movies and recreationist groups, where the whole skinned head of a wolf is poised on the top of the helmet.[19] For the vast majority of the *velites* it was more likely a covering of pelt that had once belonged to something more common and easy to come by, perhaps a rabbit. Polybius says that this pelt was intended to allow their officers to distinguish the *velites* and so judge if they fought bravely or not. The more obvious use of a visual marker for *velites* was for centurions to be able to distinguish which individuals were their own troops, as they skirmished with enemy light infantry in front of the static front lines and were required to move both around and behind Roman maniples.

One additional and very important item that Ligustinus needed was a pair of soldier's sandals, called *caligae*. The military sandal would become a staple of Roman armies for the rest of its history. The term *caligati* 'those in caligae' came to mean 'common soldiers' because this type of shoe was worn only by soldiers and not officers. Although there is no extant use of the word *caligae* as the name of these specific sandals dating to this era, the general design of a vegetable-tanned shoe, held together by dozens of hobnails, certainly existed. The hobnails are distinctive and have been found at military sites dating from the Second Punic War. The nails fell or were knocked off the bottom of sandals frequently enough that when they are discovered through archaeological field work, they can be used to track the movements of Roman armies. The trails of these scattered hobnails can be attested as early as the site of the Battle of Baecula in 208 BCE, where they lead from camp to battle site.[20]

So Ligustinus would have obtained a sword, shield, and helmet, either now before setting out from home if he had them, or from the army at the mustering place. He would have donned his hobnail sandals and packed a spare tunic and a woollen cloak into a bag or satchel called a *sarcina*.[21] When he entered his service, he and the small group of soldiers with whom he shared a tent would transport, or have their mule transport, the tent and tent pegs, cooking equipment, tools for entrenching, and rations. For now, Ligustinus would only have had personal basics, like a cup, a spit, a pot, a waterskin, some food, and perhaps a few coins.[22]

Ligustinus would not travel straight from home to a campaign again until five years later, by which time he was a centurion in the *hastati*. As soldiers were moved from the *velites* to the *hastati* they went from light to heavy infantry, and thus were required to be more heavily armed and armoured. This represented the biggest change in equipment between army divisions, as the *principes* and *triarii* were equipped in much the same way as the *hastati* except that the *triarii* carried long spears called *hastae* instead of the *pilum*. In order to qualify for the *hastati* a soldier would have to acquire a longer shield called the *scutum*, a pectoral, which was a round bronze disk placed over the heart to protect it from injury, and a greave for the left leg, which was the one planted in front during combat. Since Ligustinus became one of the *hastati* in service in Macedonia, he would have acquired these items from the army or by using his pay or monetary rewards from service to buy them from traders. If he chose the latter option, he might have chosen to invest in some arms and armour beyond the basics.

As an example of how Ligustinus could have upgraded his equipment, we can again look at helmets. Polybius indicates that the helmet of the *velites* was 'plain' (6.22.3) while the helmet of the more senior divisions was made of bronze. The plain helmet is probably the Montefortino type. Most soldiers would have worn this common and easily available helmet during their time in the legions and never sought nor needed anything else. For those eyeing a longer relationship with military service like Ligustinus, it might have made sense to make an investment in a more elaborate or customized type. Other helmet types were available that boasted various advantages, from which the soldier could choose according to his needs. Attic and Etrusco-Corinthian types were most popular after the Montefortino, which itself could be obtained with just a plain bowl or have additional cheek pieces. Some helmets provided additional protection like a neck-guard, while others provided good ventilation and were better for vision and hearing. All types benefitted from being well-fitting, as they were less liable to be struck out of place by a blow and impair the soldier's sight, as well as less tiring to wear for long periods of time.[23]

There were similar improvements available in other pieces of arms and armour, but the finest would probably always be out of reach for Ligustinus. Polybius tells us that the soldiers who rated over 10,000 drachmas in the census wore a coat of mail, of the fine-ringed variety given the modern name *lorica hamata*. This amount of money translates to the first Roman census class, which was the wealthiest class of citizens after the equestrians who made up the citizen cavalry. At the time of the Punic Wars and down into the second century, mail would have been very rare indeed. There are very few archaeological remains of this type of armour that can be securely attested to the Romans in this time period, and even sculptural depictions only appear in the second century BCE.[24] These may not be true reflections of reality, as in monumental contexts like the altar of Domitius Ahenobarbus and the victory monument of Aemilius Paullus, we might suspect that the soldiers depicted are uniformly and finely dressed only because the elites who commissioned the sculpture wished them to appear that way. Even as a *primus pilus*, Ligustinus may not have worn a coat of mail, which our evidence suggests may only have been sported by the very elite.

Travelling to the Mustering Point

When the legions were dismissed and told to reconvene at a mustering point (Polyb. 6.21.6), this was not necessarily at or near Rome, but was more often a town somewhere in Italy. Livy specifies a number of these towns which can be cited as examples. There is Arretium (130 miles North of Rome), Brundisium (335 miles South East of Rome), and Cales (115 miles South of Rome).[25] Only during the Second Punic War, while defending Italy, were armies mustered at Rome and towns close by like Tibur and Praenestae.[26] Polybius gives us an idea of what kind of instruction the soldiers were given when he mentions legions ordered to make their own way from one point to another, with the tribunes exacting an oath from each soldier that they 'would be in Ariminum before bedtime.'[27] For men travelling for days or weeks in the ancient world, arriving during a particular day was about as precise a timeline as could possibly be achieved. Latecomers, however, were unlikely to miss the army entirely, as its organization and departure could take weeks.

Ligustinus' first army in 200 BCE was ordered to assemble at Brundisium, about 335 miles from Rome. Brundisium was Rome's port in the southeastern part of the Italian peninsula. It was a common place for armies to muster when the army's destination was in the East, so that the soldiers might immediately be transported with the fleet. Since Ligustinus' home town of Forum Novum was nestled at the foot of the Sabine mountains, he would have had no option to travel directly toward the east coast, where Brundisium sat, much further to the south. The first days of his journey would have been southwest, down from the area of his family's rural landholding towards the Tiber River, which he could follow towards Rome.

It is very unlikely that Ligustinus made this trip alone. Even the busiest thoroughfares of the ancient world were dangerous. Travelling in numbers reduced the risk of being robbed by the highwaymen and bandits that targeted the rich and the vulnerable. Men from the same areas would have travelled to the mustering point together, either making their own informal organization at the levy about when they would get together, or grouped together by a local magistrate. The soldier's journey to his mustering army was apparently too mundane a detail to be addressed in any source, so we are left to extrapolate from how people in the ancient world normally moved around. The poor generally travelled by riding a mule.[28] The soldiers in their groups probably walked using mules to carry their belongings, as the contemporary writer Plautus wrote in his play *Epidicus*, where the titular character describes soldiers returning to their city leading *iumenta* (Plaut. Epidicus 208–9). This term means 'beasts of burden,' commonly mules and donkeys. It makes sense in logistical terms to think that mules or donkeys were organized locally for soldiers to travel to their muster point and to use after discharge to return to their homes.[29] This would have kept the numbers of mules proportional to the number of soldiers in the army and avoided the impractical exercise of collecting thousands of mules at the mustering point and distributing them among the soldiers.

The obvious advantage to groups of soldiers travelling with their mules was that the animals would transport their belongings. There is also another, less apparent advantage, which is that it was the perfect time for brand new recruits to learn or to practice being on the back of a horse. As we will see in the later chapters, the *velites*, as light-armed infantry, often operated with the cavalry, and unlike the aristocratic young men who served in the legions as citizen cavalrymen, they had probably not had the means or opportunity on their small farms to become experienced riders. Although they would not have had to control a horse themselves while in the *velites*, it is not possible to be a passive passenger on one, but rather one needs to move with the motion of the animal in order to avoid becoming bumped and bruised and interfering with the horse's gait. With a mule on which to practise, the young recruits could start to learn these military skills here, to quickly mount, dismount, and travel comfortably on a swiftly moving equine.

When Ligustinus and his companions reached Rome, or perhaps, skirted its environs, the route was either along the via Appia or the via Latina, which converged at the town of Beneventum. The via Appia seems the more sensible choice here as it was the wider and more even road, being already paved by this date, and it was also some 22 miles shorter.[30] From Beneventum the via Appia continued all the way to Brundisium. There was another route, which the geographer Strabo tells us was *hemionikos*, 'a mule road' or 'road fit only for mules'. This road saved a day of travel time in comparison to the via Appia, and was probably the choice of those who favoured efficiency over comfort.[31] Future soldiers could choose to walk the mule road in order to avoid the carriages and large carts of merchants transporting goods, or decide that they preferred the paving and width of the via Appia.

The whole journey from Forum Novum to Brundisium was some 370 miles, and would have taken around 20 days to complete. For the *veles* or the *miles gregarius* as Ligustinus calls himself, it was a good opportunity to soak up some advice, listen to war stories, and perhaps learn the rudiments of swordplay or riding. Although the *dilectus* had distributed the local men among the legions, and the division into their centuries at the mustering point would separate them more, these men had a common origin, and a common point to which they would hopefully return. Probably they hoped to see each other again at home when their service was over. For some, they would continue to be able to visit friends made on this journey during spare moments by taking a short walk through the camp. Although the recruitment and allocation policies that were practised sought to ensure there was no great concentration of locals in one unit, there was no reason that a soldier could not seek out a familiar face in another maniple or even legion if he so chose.

Since there were only two roads that led from the north to Brundisium and all the soldiers were headed to the same place on the same day, the closer the party got to the city, the more men there would have been on the road. The groups would have become larger and so would have the variety of men of all divisions and from different areas of Italy. It is not hard to see how a youth travelling this road for the first time would suddenly find the world opening up for him even before his true military service had really started. Ligustinus' family was very poor and the long journey through the southern Italian peninsula was likely the furthest from home he had ever been. For the young man in search of excitement, as the crowd of men grew and brought with them an expanding range of personalities and stories, perhaps it felt like the adventure had already begun.

200 BCE, Brundisium

On the day appointed for the mustering at Brundisium, we should imagine the town bustling with activity as thousands of legionary infantry, allies and cavalrymen arrived. The gathering of the army would have been a good opportunity for traders, entertainers, food sellers and diviners to mingle among the arriving soldiers to sell them goods and services. Brundisium was a busy port city, full of not just Romans and Italians but foreign merchants and travellers too.

Soldiers would be arriving continually throughout the day. As each soldier reached the environs of Brundisium he knew in which of the three divisions of the army he was to serve and in which century, maniple, and legion. As there were tens of thousands of Roman citizen soldiers, allies, and slaves, and each was required to find their legion and maniple, there must have been some way to guide the soldier from his arrival on the road, to the gathering army, to the appropriate spot. The allies were organized first. Polybius explains that the Roman officers appointed to be in charge of the allies, the *praefecti sociorum* 'prefects of the allies' picked out the best men from the allies to make into a unit called the *extraordinarii*. This unit had about a fifth of the total allied infantry and about a third of its cavalry. The remaining allies were divided in two and assigned to an *ala*, a 'wing', either the *ala sinistra*, the left wing, or the *ala dextra*, the right wing, where they would be stationed in a pitched battle. Polybius then explains that the tribunes took the allies and Romans and taught them how to pitch camp (Polyb. 6.26.1–12).

The sequence of events described here strongly suggests that the camp system was also the basis of organization at the mustering place. Since the allies had come directly from their own towns without attending the *dilectus*, they were the only troops who did not already have a unit designation, which was needed to know where they would be camped. Rather than there being some sort of preliminary stage in which the soldiers gathered in their maniples, and afterwards were taught castramentation, the system of castramentation itself could be used to facilitate each arriving soldier in locating his maniple. In other words, the camp would be being slowly built throughout the day, with the arrivals gathering on the spot that was designated to their maniple in an army camp. The organization of the camp, which was always laid out in the exact same way, reflected both the order of the march and the order of the battleline. In such a large grouping, learning the layout of the camp and one's place within it was vital knowledge that allowed soldiers to organize with the minimum of supervision. Older soldiers would be able to find their way to their maniple without direction and to point their younger comrades in the direction of theirs.

For new soldiers like Ligustinus, coming to a camp for the first time would be an exercise in learning how to navigate its layout. Primarily this skill was built on learning patterns and responding to visual cues, the very same skills that were used to keep the army together and manoeuvre it on the field. When the Roman armies were on the move, it was the job of specialist troops to go ahead of the army and lay out the camp with coloured flags, which acted as reference points for the soldiers to know where to build. The camp was then built from the officers' tents outwards, with every maniple of citizens and allies orientating themselves to their spot.

At this point Ligustinus did, for the very first time, something that he would do thousands of times during the course of his military career. He looked around for his immediate comrades to orientate himself and find his assigned place. As a member of the *velites* he and twenty-three others would be attached to a century of sixty-four men, which could have belonged to the *hastati*, *principes* or *triarii*. This century, in turn, would be encamped with another century from the same division to make up a maniple with a number from one to ten.

In 200 BCE Ligustinus' division might have been men barely older than himself, who had been too young to fight at the end of the Second Punic War and were now beginning their military service in a new arena. On the other hand, two thousand of the troops at Brundisium, about half a legion's worth, were veterans from the armies that had successfully conducted the invasion of Africa under Scipio. These men had served three years in North Africa and brought the war to a successful conclusion at Zama in 202 BCE where, according to Polybius, the battlefield had been so slick with blood it was treacherous to walk (Poly. 15.14.2). They were probably the oldest and most experienced set of soldiers to be found in all Rome's armies in 200 BCE.

When Ligustinus arrived the centurions of the maniple were probably already there, allocating men to *contubernia* and putting soldiers to work counting out space and pitching tents. The *velites* had no centurions from their own ranks, the only division that did not have them. Nor do we hear of any other kind of unit or group leader for the *velites* specifically. Instead, they were commanded by the centurions of the unit to which they were attached. The character of this centurion would have varied depending on the division to which the young *veles* had been attached. It could have been a young centurion of the *hastati*, but equally it could have been any centurion up to a *primus pilus*, the most senior centurion of the *triarii*.

As the tribunes and centurions formed and organized each maniple and the *velites* that would be attached to it, Ligustinus would have been introduced to the rest of the *velites* in his century and his maniple with whom he would be assigned the same duties. They were probably placed in a tent together, *velites* with *velites*, while the division to which they were attached was assigned to tents with men of their own division. The reason for this is that the tents housed eight men but only realistically had room for six.[32] The men traded places as the two men on watch returned and two more went out, so the tents sheltered eight men through the night but only six at a time. As the night-time guard duties varied by division, it would be easiest and neatest to keep the tents of one division only.

The seven other *velites* who shared his tent would be the men closest to Ligustinus both socially and militarily for the campaign of that summer, and perhaps for longer. Their faces were immediately tremendously important, as were the faces of the other *velites* and those of the men in the rest of the maniple. They were the faces that would help to place him on the battlefield and orientate him in the camp, the faces with which he would become intimately acquainted over many months as he walked with them in the march, the faces that he would scan for reaction in a crisis, faces that would register suddenly familiar and draw him back to his own place if he ran too far in a battle.[33]

At the mustering point, presumably any necessary changes were made due to soldiers who had not turned up, or not turned up on time, slight adjustments were made to ranks and positions or shuffling around of personnel. Since the order to assemble involved arriving on a specific day, at least the majority of the sorting and counting of men and castramentation ought to be completed by nightfall. The camp was in friendly territory with no danger to threaten it, and for now it served purposes other than defence. It helped to organize the arriving troops into their maniples, to teach the new recruits how to find their legion and maniple within a camp, to familiarize all of the troops with the art of camp building. Perhaps most importantly, it provided the whole army somewhere to pass the nights from the day of the soldiers' arrival until it was ready to deploy in the following weeks.

195 BCE, Portus Lunae

In his third year in Macedon, Ligustinus was appointed to the *hastati*. He would go on to stay in this division for at least five years, serving in centurion positions for various maniples. Ligustinus left Macedon before this campaign had come to a formal end, and evidently opted to go straight out on a second campaign, this time to Spain. This campaign, for which he would have mustered as a member of the *hastati*, was under the commander M. Porcius Cato and began in 195 BCE.

This army mustered at *Portus Lunae* (Livy 34.8.4), the harbour near the ancient town of Luna, this time on the West coast of the Italian peninsula and the modern day Gulf of Spezia. This was about 220 miles north of Rome and it would have taken about twelve days to walk to from Rome via the roads. The commander Cato travelled to the mustering place by boat, as Livy reports him as departing with a warship, a route which cut the time taken from twelve days to four. It is likely that many of the soldiers did the same, as although there are frequent mentions of even the very rich returning to Rome from Brundisium via land, for some other destinations it was often swifter and cheaper in the ancient world to travel by boat.

As a member of the *hastati*, with five years of military service under his belt, Ligustinus would have been far more knowledgeable, probably navigating to his assigned maniple with ease. His equipment would have improved somewhat since the last time he had mustered with an army, including now a pectoral to protect his chest. Instead of fur on his helmet, the *hastati* wore tall, upright feathers, which Polybius specifies were purple and black, and were intended to make each man look twice his height (Polyb. 6.23.13). These were distinctive of the *hastati* and would have been helpful in allowing both soldiers and officers to distinguish a maniple of *hastati* by sight.

When he mustered at Portus Lunae, Ligustinus had been appointed as *primus hastatus prioris centuriae*, centurion of the prior century of the first maniple of *hastati*, one of only two men holding this position in a standard army of two consular legions. As a centurion he might have arrived early to help orientate his men, and he would have been taking orders directly from the military tribunes. Despite the fact that he had already served for five years, this was his second experience at a mustering point and his first as a centurion with others under his orders. Forty-eight young *velites* would now be under his charge and 128 *hastati*. His closest and most important colleague would now be the *primus hastatus posterior centuriae*, who was essentially his co-centurion. There should be two, Polybius writes, in case something happens to one of them, so that the maniple will always have a leader (Polyb. 6.24.7–8).

Chapter 4

The Complete Army

Whenever a soldier came to the mustering point for his campaign, the most important people for him were his new immediate colleagues. There were plenty of other sights to see, however, as now it was not just the citizen legions in attendance, but the whole army assembling for the first time. A wide variety of other groups were also arriving and settling in, from Latins, Italian allies, and foreign auxiliaries to priests, servants and scribes. There was a large animal contingent of thousands of cavalry horses, mules in every corner of the camp, chickens at the *praetorium* to be carried for the purposes of divination, and sometimes, as in 200 BCE, elephants.

The Citizen Cavalry

The citizen cavalry was made up of men who had sufficient wealth to meet the requirement for the equestrian census class, the second highest of all the wealth classes. Some of these men were from very aristocratic and politically active families at Rome, who were serving the ten years required to qualify to stand for their first political offices.[1] Others were men from equally wealthy families who had no political aspirations and whose ancestors had never held political office at Rome, but rather represented a more local kind of nobility: the wealthiest and most influential families within other cities in Italy that held Roman citizenship. These men, called the *domi nobiles*, quite literally 'the nobles at home' were the kind of men whom it was feared could rally large groups of their own local clients and countrymen, should too large a number of them be allowed to congregate in one particular legion of the army. The separation of friends and neighbours described in Chapter 2 was intended to mitigate any threat posed by these local leaders, who often enjoyed a great deal of respect in their own cities, and prevent them from having too wide a base of personal support within the army.

The cavalry, like the officer class, were a distinctly different category from the ordinary infantry soldiers. The cavalryman brought two servants with him and three horses. He received a higher rate of pay and a greater wheat allowance in order to feed the servants and horses and to compensate him for the greater expense they created. Situated near the centre of the camp opposite the *praetorium* and *quaestorium* and the bodyguard cohorts of the senior officers, the area of the cavalry would have been busy with snorting, neighing horses and their grooms. The cavalrymen themselves would have been upper class, wealthy, and Latin-speaking, and despite their disparity in class from men like Ligustinus, they would soon become important for the *velites*, as the units often operated together in combat and scouting duties.

The Italian Allies

When the ancient sources mention the *socii*, 'the allies', they are usually not referring to any and all forces allied to the Romans, but rather the towns, municipalities and tribes in the Italian peninsula that had an agreement with Rome to provide them military forces. The Italian allies played a massive part in Rome's war efforts during the years that Ligustinus was in service in the early second century. Their contingents were larger than the citizen legions and during this period they often seem to have borne the brunt of Rome's military efforts. Polybius says that there were the same number of allied infantry as citizen infantry but three times as many allied cavalrymen as citizen (6.26.7). This seems to be an overly schematic or theoretical number as, even in other places in Polybius' own account, there are different numbers and proportions depending on the campaigns, and these numbers usually reveal more allied infantry than citizen.[2]

The allies were organized into a unit of elite *extraordinarii* and two units or *alae*, 'wings', in each consular army of two legions. The *extraordinarii* were about a fifth of the total allied force, and both their infantry and cavalry camped on the opposite side of the *via principalis* to the citizen legion. A further body of '*delecti extraordinarii*' acted as a bodyguard to the consul and quaestor. Since *extraordinarii* means 'men out of the *ordines* (ranks, lines)' the *delecti extraordinarii* are something like 'men selected from the men out of the ranks' or the most distinguished of the distinguished. This small detachment of men was camped near the *praetorium* and *quaestorium* across from the citizen cavalry.

Of all the allies, the *extraordinarii* would have been the closest in culture and language to the Roman citizen soldiers. Their role was vital to security while the army was on the march since they led the column and would be the first to encounter any danger, unless the enemy was suspected to be behind, in which case they would take up the rear. For this reason, and because the *extraordinarii* were hand-picked as the best soldiers of the allies and enjoyed distinction, members of the Latin colonies were probably dominant among them.[3] The Latin towns were those geographically closest to Rome and her oldest allies, and when in the fourth and third centuries Rome sent out colonies to other parts of Italy they were populated with Roman and Latin citizens and given 'Latin' status in respect to Rome. This gave their citizens a particular set of rights that included the right to marry and form business contracts with Roman citizens.

Unlike the citizen legionaries, the Italian allies were grouped together in maniples and cohorts by their town and area of origin. Sometimes these groupings are highlighted in the sources, such as when Livy describes the actions of the *cohors Paeligna*, which distinguished itself in leading the assault on a Carthaginian camp during the Second Punic War in 212 BCE (Livy 25.14.2–13). The Paeligni were a tribe centred in the ancient towns of Corfinium, Superaequuum and Sulmo, in central Italy east of Rome, in the modern-day region of Abruzzo. They spoke a dialect between the Italic languages of Umbrian and Oscan.[4] These kinds of local dialects were probably one of the reasons that the Italian allies were levied at home and sent their contingents straight to the mustering point.

Despite having a different language and origin from the citizen soldiers, the Italian allies also had a lot in common with them. Like the Romans, the majority of them would have been unmarried men from their late teens to their early thirties.[5] They would have been dressed and armoured similarly, with perhaps their own distinguishing marks in place of the fur of the *velites* and the black and purple feathers of the *hastati*. The homogenization of equipment is noticeable in the archaeological record from all over Italy, so their helmets, pectorals and weapons would have been the same as their Roman counterparts. Lastly their ambitions would have been essentially the same, to use their time in service to achieve whatever advancement in wealth and social status they could.

How much interaction could and would have taken place between the Italian allies and the Roman citizen legions is still an open question. Socially, the allies would have remained closest to their own native contingent, with whom they camped, fought, and shared a language. Their closest interactions after that would be the contingents with whom they could most easily communicate, for example in the case of the Paeligni, their Oscan and Umbrian-speaking neighbours. We have no real idea of how many of the Italian allies spoke Latin or how many of the Romans spoke other Italian languages. The leaders of the allied cohorts, the *praefecti cohortes*, will have been able to speak Latin as a requirement to translate orders and messages from the Latin speaking officers.

The biggest regular point of contact between the Romans and their Italian allies was the street where the allied cavalry camped directly across from the maniples of the *hastati*. The allied cavalry were, like their Roman counterparts, from families wealthy enough to take one or more horses to war. As such, the men of the cavalry would have been the most likely to possess skills in the Latin language. Boys who had grown up working on their family farms had little time to spend in education, but the sons of local elites had more opportunities to learn language and literacy, and some of their families may have had business ties in Rome.

It seems inevitable that over the months and years of army service, Italian allies, Roman citizens and even foreign troops would have come to socialize and share activities in camp.[6] We know there were at least some speakers of Latin among the allies, the leaders of cohorts as well as others who, even if they were a minority, could help to facilitate conversations in groups and translate for their comrades. Even living in different parts of the camp need not have been much of a hinderance, as Polybius says that the soldiers liked to drift out to spend their spare time on the *via principalis*, the biggest road in the camp. What the frequency and quality of their interactions were truly like, unfortunately, is lost to history.

Foreign Allies

Contingents who were allied to the Romans but non-Italian are referred to as *auxilia externa*, 'foreign allies'. In a single consular camp they were placed across the *via principalis* opposite the legions and the Italian allies. Sometimes these men had been sent from Roman allies in various places to help their campaigns; for example, during Ligustinus' first campaign, the army was joined in Macedon by 1,000 Numidian cavalry from North Africa, sent, along with wheat and barley, by the Numidian king Massinisa (Livy 31.19.3–4). Sometimes the foreign allies were contingents sent from areas local to where the Romans were campaigning, as when that same campaign was joined in 197 BCE by Aetolians from Greece with both infantry and cavalry, Cretan and Illyrians, and troops from Athamania south of Epirus. These types of foreign troops were likely a great curiosity to the young Roman *velites*. They had specialities that the Romans did not have, like the Cretan archers and the Numidian light cavalry. These latter rode without bridle or saddle, bore only a shield and javelins, and favoured a wide, loose formation. More disconcertingly, it had not been that many years since this cavalry had fought on the side of the Carthaginians, cutting down the Roman *velites* at the Ticinus River in 218 BCE.[7] Unfortunately, we can only imagine what the Roman soldiers thought of this addition to their forces.

Non-combatants

Besides the Romans and their allies, there were a number of individuals travelling with the army who were non-combatants, both slaves and free men, whose job was to attend the animals or serve the soldiers. In some cases, these men would have been private slaves brought by the wealthier soldiers to help them and their units. As well as being distinguished by their clothing, the officers would have had a whole retinue of private slaves around them, whom they had taken from home to help with all kinds of daily activities and duties. The Elder Cato is said to have had five servants in total with him in Spain, with the general implication that this was the height of restraint, so the normal number for a commander was probably dozens.[8] Plutarch tells us that on the march Cato had only one servant with him for carrying his effects, while he carried his own armour (Plut. *Cat. Mai.* 1.7). This anecdote too was intended to show Cato's austerity, and we can infer that it was more usual for generals to have several slaves with him while on the march, to carry camp equipment and, normally, the general's weapons and armour. Each member of the citizen cavalry had two servants to take care of their horses, and either two or three horses depending on the time period.[9]

In addition to the private slaves and servants that surrounded the senior officers, the broader army had military slaves, called in the singular a *calo* and in the plural *calones*. This term might have applied to private slaves as well, but it seems to have referred primarily to state-owned slaves who had been brought with the army to handle the soldiers' baggage and equipment and act as support personnel for mules, other pack animals and wagons of supplies.[10] The sources pay these men little attention, which is why it is difficult to know much about them. They are mentioned only in passing, or when pressed into unusual service, like fighting with the soldiers, or when they were killed.[11] Vegetius mentions that they had leaders, called the *galearii* 'men with helmets (*galea*)' who were chosen for their experience and ability and 'put in charge of up to 200 pack animals and grooms (*pueri*).'[12] The *galearii* appear nowhere else in our sources, but it makes sense that the *calones* were organized under some kind of structure, which would be especially necessary if they came under attack.

We do not know how many *calones* might have accompanied the army. Nor do we know where they slept and ate. What we do know is that these men would have been unarmed, and mainly working in a logistical capacity, organizing and transporting goods for the soldiers, or a kind of domestic capacity, helping soldiers make food and keep their spaces clean and sanitary. Perhaps it was their duty to clean away the dung generated by the mules and horses. Since the *calones* were enslaved, they would have been from a variety of foreign nations, captured in wars either as combatants or inhabitants of enemy towns and villages. This had not necessarily been done by the Romans themselves, as there was a large Mediterranean slave trade, but it could have been. Just as the Roman soldiers ran the risk of being captured and sold as slaves during a campaign, so did the combatants of other states and the inhabitants of territories defeated by any hostile force.

A group of people called *lixae* are also frequently mentioned in the sources as accompanying the army, but the role of these men is never explicitly told to us, and some of the references are contradictory.[13] Unlike the *calones*, the *lixae* were free men, although they seem to have been held in some contempt and considered the very lowliest part of the army.[14] Their role is linked to the handling or acquisition of booty, including human beings taken as slaves, and the word *lixae* is often rendered by translators and commentators as 'sutlers', i.e. those who followed the army buying and selling goods. As the group were ill-defined and seem to have had a number of roles, they are perhaps best thought of as hopefuls or opportunists, who followed the army offering services in handling human captives, selling items and joining the plunder of enemy countryside with the soldiers.

For Ligustinus, men who were non-combatant and had the status of servants or slaves would have been a familiar sight around the camp. Some made up an officer's retinue as he moved around, some could be found packing and moving mules and wagons. The *calones* were also associated with firewood by the antiquarian Festus, who suggests that the name derived from the Greek for firewood, *kala*.[15] Among their other duties, they would have helped the soldiers forage for food and collect firewood and fodder. A story told by Plutarch involves slaves who came out to meet the soldiers returning from the Battle of Pydna in 168 BCE to light their way back to the camp with torches (Plut. *Aem.* 22.1). This suggests that perhaps providing light for the soldiers at night was one of their duties, in an age where a soldier with a shield and spear would not have had a free hand for a torch.

Several times in the sources we hear mention of a commander attempting to toughen up his troops and improve discipline by the reduction or elimination of servants and pack animals. In 108 BCE, Metellus took over the army in Numidia and declared that it could not be attended upon by *lixae*, and that no soldier could have a pack animal or slave (Sall. *Iug.* 45.2–3). Similarly, all except the 'most necessary' *calones* and baggage were sent away from the camp of P. Cornelius Scipio at Numantia in 133 BCE. What we can infer from this is that the military servants made the soldiers' lives easier, helping them with foraging, carrying equipment, lighting their way at night, and cooking and cleaning. During the march they drove the baggage train and guarded it. Like many of the marginalized peoples of antiquity, they are often invisible to us, but their presence is important to the soldiers' experience in particular. The camp was busier than we might imagine, and less heterogeneous, with Roman citizens, their allies and slaves of various ethnicities and nationalities.

Animals

A Roman camp was no place for someone who disliked animals, as they were everywhere and quite inescapable. Not only did officers and cavalrymen have a number of horses each, there were mules tied not far outside the soldiers' tents. In the army of 200 BCE there were elephants. Livy says that these had been captured from the Carthaginians in the war that had ended just a few years ago, and were used for the first time in a battle near Athacus, one of the first encounters of the campaign (31.36.4). These enormous beasts were probably the largest animals the soldiers had ever seen. They would have known of them before their service only from descriptions by the men who had fought them in the Punic Wars and the invasion into Italy of Pyrrhus of Epirus, where they were no doubt described as enormous, destructive, trampling beasts.

Besides the mules for transport and the horses and elephants who went to war, there were other animals in camp that were there because they were needed for religious purposes. Oxen were present as draught animals, but also some were taken along to use as sacrifices, and were probably kept along the *intervallum*, the space between the tents and the camp walls. The *haruspices*, specialized Etruscan priests, would read any warnings from the gods in their entrails. Up at the *praetorium*, a special attendant called a *pullarius* looked after the sacred chickens, which, like the oxen, were to be used in divination. These birds were not killed but used in augury, in a specific ritual where their behaviour determined whether a particular action was ill-advised or not. We shall come back to the role of these animals a little later.

The Roman Officer Class

Almost all commanders of armies and senior officers in the Roman Middle Republic came from a small class of aristocrats who enjoyed hereditary wealth and status. There was a massive discrepancy in wealth, privilege, and societal standing between these men and the soldiers they commanded. By the time of the Middle Republic, the elite class was made up of members of both of Rome's two orders, the patricians and the plebians. We met the patricians in Chapter 2, as Rome's oldest families who claimed to be able to trace their family lineage back to the city's earliest days.

The patrician order had enjoyed power and privilege for much longer than the plebians. For many hundreds of years Rome's patricians had styled themselves as an exceptional class, whose distinction of birth made them uniquely suitable for the more important affairs of state. They enjoyed a monopoly on both public offices and priesthoods, this latter because communication with the gods was thought to be reserved for only the most worthy in society. Even spontaneous signs that were believed to be sent from the gods were only regularly accepted if someone of a certain class reported them.[16] By the time of the Middle Republic the patrician families had been joined in public office and military command by wealthy and established plebian families. Although they did not have the highest prestige associated with the ancient names of the patricians, they still stood at the other end of the societal scale from a man like Ligustinus.

The Roman aristocracy was very competitive, and military service was one way for men to distinguish themselves while young and gain advantage and fame for their future careers. They were advantaged by their upbringing in this aspiration, for their wealth allowed them much more free time than was available to poorer boys. Thus we hear of the sons of aristocrats being trained in physical fitness and also with weapons. During his second campaign, Ligustinus would serve under a very famous figure of his time, Marcus Porcius Cato, often called 'the Elder Cato' to distinguish him from another famous descendant of the same name. Cato personally trained his son in military arts, teaching the boy to hurl a javelin, ride a horse, and fight in armour, as well as in swimming and enduring heat and cold (Plut. *Cat. Mai.* 20.4). Although it is possible a father of the poorer classes could have also taught his son these things, when both were required to work on a subsistence farm there would have been much less time to do so. Men like Ligustinus' father could have snatched time to train his sons in the skills he had gained in his own service, but he would not have been able to dedicate days and weeks to physical and technical military performance as the aristocrats could. For the poorest, like Ligustinus, any military skills gained in advance of service would have to be acquired during spare moments, from fathers and older brothers, from local veterans at festivals, and on the road by local soldiers on their way to the mustering point.

Poorer citizens might come into contact with the elite class during political speeches if they lived in Rome, or were close enough to attend the capital when they voted. For many others, their major point of contact with this class would be in the army. The army's officers would have been distinguishable immediately. They were made visually distinct from the common soldier because they wore tunics with a purple stripe. They also wore boots instead of the soldier's military *caligae*. As they moved around the camp, they would have a small crowd of servants and bodyguards around them at all times. When they spoke, their aristocracy would have been obvious. The kind of Latin that was spoken in oratory, for example, in the political speeches that the soldiers might have attended, was distinct from the ordinary parlance of poorer Romans. This occurred not just in word choice but in distinctive pronunciation, where certain letters and sounds had come from rural contexts and were associated with both rural and poor urban communities.[17] While an aristocratic officer would have been very distinctive, the soldiers themselves may not have found this particularly off-putting. They would have been used to the idea of the nobility monopolizing state and religious authority, and especially the idea that the right to lead men, as well as the right to consult with the divine on behalf of the state, were the particular domain of these elite families.

Despite the large difference in wealth and social class, in Republican Rome even the highest ranking officers were frequently seen on the ground in person, and their faces were recognizable to the ordinary soldier. The tribunes, especially, who had the biggest role in organization and discipline, and who oversaw the building and guarding of army camps, would have been recognizable to the legionary soldiers, but the commanders were too. The general made announcements and gave exhortations to the soldiers from the tribunal in the *praetorium*, distributed awards to the soldiers in person during the award ceremony, or *contio*, held after battles, and could be witnessed presiding over religious rituals like the taking of auspices. Upon his arrival in Spain in 210 BCE to take over the army of his father and uncle, Livy has P. Scipio say, 'You recognize a likeness to my father and my uncle in figure, face, and expression, I will soon show you that I am like them also in character and fidelity and courage', showing that Livy, at least, believed that soldiers were familiar with the faces of their commanders (Livy 26.41.24).

It was in the best interests of the senior officers to treat their soldiers fairly and cultivate a good reputation. They were part of a small class of politically active elites that competed for election to public office, and the military was a fruitful area to target to help advance their careers. The position of military tribune, in particular, was a favourite one to hold just before a man launched a political career in Rome, because it offered an opportunity to cultivate popular support.[18] Soldiers could hope to impress a tribune, seeking to gain awards and reap the benefits of having come to the attention of a powerful person, and at the same time tribunes and other officers wished to gain a good reputation among the soldiers, who could advantage them in a future political career.[19] This would not have been limited to the soldiers themselves and their individual votes. The soldiers could also sway their friends, family, patrons and clients with their accounts of their personal experience and what they had heard while in the army. Reputation was built through the soldiers and would have eventually added up to a general popular opinion about how a particular officer had performed during his military service.

The performance of officers was clearly a favourite topic of discussion among the soldiery, with conversations turning into prevailing viewpoints and developing reputations. Here was where the soldiers weighed their officers against all the values they had learned as boys, looking for the kinds of heroism and martial prowess that they had heard in the stories of famous Romans. They would also have learned the value of less flashy and dramatic deeds, of respect for level-headed men who were competent and fair in the camp and made sensible decisions under pressure. Ordinary soldiers do not seem to have been overly cowed by the obvious class gulf, or at least they were comfortable passing judgment on their officers' abilities and intolerant of abuses of power. Socially, politically, and militarily, the elite class who made up Rome's officers wielded a huge amount of power over the common men in their armies, and not all of them were careful with their men's lives. Thus we hear of generals slammed for recklessness, while others were lauded in triumphal song without us ever hearing of any deed extraordinary enough to make it into the history books. At the triumph of M. Livius Salinator, for example, we are told that the cavalry songs praised two legates, and 'urged the plebs to make them consuls for the coming year.'[20]

Commanders

The generals of Roman armies were usually the consuls. The consul was the highest magistrate in the state and there were two elected every year, hence the creation of two consular armies. These were the core component of Rome's forces and were always generated in a year, whether there was an ongoing war or not. The consuls usually served part of their magistracy with authority over political affairs in the city, and the summer campaigning season in command of two legions or more. If there was a pressing war, the consuls could go out immediately. Most of Ligustinus' commanders were consuls, including the first three with whom he served in Macedon, P. Sulpicius Galba, P. Villius Tappulus and T. Quinctius Flamininus.

The other regular position in the state that granted its magistrate the right to command an army was the praetor. The origins of the praetorship are a little confused, with some ancient authors dating its creation to 367 BCE, when one of the offices of the consul was reserved for a plebian for the first time, with the idea that the patricians conceded to this only if another office was created that would be reserved for patricians. This, however, cannot be true, as other ancient sources tell us that the consuls were originally called praetors, and it is in fact far more likely that the consulship grew out of the original praetorship. The two roles are almost identical in their range of powers.[21] There were two praetors until 218 BCE, when two more were added with a specific remit, one for Sicily and one for Sardinia. In 197 BCE two more were added for Spain, which in itself was divided into two provinces called Hispania Citerior and Hispania

Ulterior. The ongoing campaigns in these regions were to be commanded by praetors. When Ligustinus first joined a campaign in Spain, it was that of M. Porcius Cato, who was a consul, in Hispania Citerior. This is because unrest in Hispania Citerior was thought to be serious and so the Roman Senate declared the province consular instead of praetorian.[22] Later, when he returned to Spain in 181 BCE, Ligustinus' commanders, Q. Fulvius Flaccus and then Ti. Sempronius Gracchus, were both praetors.

The right to command an army did not rest on the magisterial office itself per se, but rather that the office holder was eligible to be granted the rights necessary to do so, called *imperium*, 'military authority' and *auspicium*, 'the right to take the auspices'. These were conferred by the centuriate assembly. *Imperium* could only be held outside the city boundaries and, unlike the magistracy itself, it did not automatically expire after one year. A decision was made at Rome depending on the state of the campaign, whether it had been brought to a conclusion, and, if not, whether the same commander was to continue or a replacement was to be sent. If the commander was to continue, then his command of the province was said to be prorogued, and he became a proconsul or propraetor. It was as a proconsul that Flamininus stayed on in Macedon, and as a propraetor that Ti. Sempronius Gracchus remained in Spain.

There was only one other public office that came with the state power to lead an army, and that was the dictator. The position of dictator was an emergency appointment, specifically of a military commander, who was not appointed to a particular province but whose remit was especially appointed to deal with a military crisis. The dictator appointed would be highly experienced in both military and political affairs and well respected, but the wars to which he was called were dark, urgent moments. Under normal circumstances, for the ordinary soldier it probably did not matter a great deal whether one served with a consul, a praetor, or a promagistrate. Partly this is because a large part of the commander's duties were religious, and partly it is because he had a great deal of advice to rely upon when making military decisions.

Advisors Travelling as Officers

Although a commander on campaign in the Middle Republic held the highest and most authoritative position in that army, he was usually not the most experienced or knowledgeable person travelling with it. It would not have been his first campaign by far, as candidates for office needed a minimum of ten years of military experience, but it might easily be their first campaign as a commander. To mitigate the lack of command experience, generals were routinely assigned former consuls and praetors who had previously commanded their own campaigns to act as advisors.

There are plenty of examples of this to be found in the armies in which Ligustinus served. During his first campaign, he spent five years in Macedon. He went out with P. Sulpicius Galba, who was succeeded by P. Villius Tappulus. When Ligustinus was in his third year and serving under his third commander T. Quinctius Flamininus, Sulpicius and Villius were both appointed to the consul's staff as legates, to act as advisors regarding the conduct of the war that they had previously commanded (Livy 32.28.12). L. Quinctius Flamininus, the consul's brother, was placed in charge of the fleet. Similarly, having served under M. Porcius Cato in a season that extended from 195 to 194 BCE, Ligustinus saw him again as a military tribune aiding M. Acilius Glabrio in Greece in 191 BCE (Plut. *Cat. Mai.* 12.1).

Perhaps a more startling example is the army that Ligustinus joined in 171 BCE, when he made his speech during enrolment. It was an army which would take him back to Macedon, the province where he had first served almost thirty years before. By this time Ligustinus had a wealth of experience, and had served four times as *primus pilus*, part of the commander's *consilium* (council of military advisors), and the highest rank achievable by someone who was not of noble origin coming up through the army system. His wealth of experience is all the more striking when we consider that the consul commanding the army, Licinius Crassus, had no command experience at all. As praetor in 176 BCE he had been excused command in Nearer Spain due to religious obligations.[23]

As a mitigation of the consul's distinct lack of command experience, Licinius had been provided an entire retinue of advisors of extensive experience as well as some older soldiers. Ligustinus was among a group of veterans whom the consul had been allowed to recruit as a special dispensation from the Senate and it seems that there were rather more soldiers who had been *primi pili* than positions available in the legions. Licinius' officer corps contained two former consuls, Q. Mucius Scaevola and C. Claudius Pulcher, and a further three men that we know of serving as legates or military tribunes who had seen command at least once as praetors.[24]

There were, therefore, in most army camps, not one but up to about a dozen accomplished members of Rome's most noble and elite families, either as informal advisors or holding ranks like legate or quaestor. They would each have been accompanied by a retinue of slaves and so would have been conspicuous as they moved around, just like the commander. In the Roman army system, just as the ordinary soldier did not keep or carry a rank from army to army, so the officer class could serve as commander one year and as a tribune the next. This was quite normal and not in any way considered to be a demotion, despite the fact that technically an officer of more experience was acting in a junior capacity to a man of less experience. The reason for this is because the general's authority, duties and responsibilities were not exclusively military, they were also heavily religious. The magistracy that the consul held enabled him to consult and communicate with the gods on behalf of the state, thus forming the foundation of his authority.

The *cohors amicorum*

When a commander left on campaign, he took along with him a retinue of friends, relatives, and others invited along at his discretion. Such men were termed the *cohors amicorum*, literally, 'the cohort of friends'. The historian Polybius gained his first-hand army experience travelling with Scipio Aemilianus as part of this group. The *cohors amicorum* also commonly included the commander's sons and the young sons of other elite families who needed to gain military experience. This meant that there were young aristocratic boys with the armies, who came on their first campaigns at around the same age as the youngest recruited *velites* of seventeen.[25]

Of the *cohors amicorum*, some, like Polybius, were purely advisors who were not expected to participate in combat. Others, like the young *nobiles*, would have been conscious of the stories of exemplary heroism and the weight of expectations they laid out for the behaviour of aristocratic Romans in particular. Thus we hear stories like that of the young Scipio Aemilianus, who went missing after the Battle of Pydna and was believed dead before he came in 'covered in the blood of the enemies he had slain' (Plut. *Aem.* 22.7). At the same battle, another young noble, M. Porcius Cato Licinianus, the son of Ligustinus' general M. Porcius Cato, was driven to great lengths to avoid dishonour. We are told that he had lost his sword in battle, something that was potentially a source of great shame and embarrassment to a soldier.[26] Running through the ranks he persuaded a group of men to help him retrieve it, and together 'with a great struggle, much slaughter, and many wounds, they drove them [the enemy] from the ground, and when they had won a free and empty place, they set themselves to looking for the sword' (Plut. *Aem.* 21.4). Having pushed the enemy line back, they sorted through the armour and bodies and eventually found the sword. All of the aristocratic officers wished to gain the favour and support of their troops, but the young especially were determined to impress them.

Senior Officers

There were two legates in each legion and these were important senior officers, although their role seems to vary a great deal. As we saw above, this was the role most often chosen for experienced advisors. Unlike the tribunes, who had numerous clearly defined roles organizing and administering the army, the legates do not seem to be as frequently in contact with the soldiers. Instead, we find them with diplomatic and advisory functions, as ambassadors and envoys to foreign states. The term is also used loosely, with men who were at one point mentioned as a military tribune called later a *legatus* in deference to their role at that moment.[27] The ordinary soldiers would perhaps have the least interaction with the legates, save that, like the other officers, they each had two groups of guards at their tents.

The officers with the most frequent contact with ordinary soldiers were the tribunes. Ligustinus would have seen some of them already, as they had a large part in military organization. They were responsible for the division of men into the four legions at the *dilectus* and for assigning the soldiers to their divisions at the second meeting. It was the tribunes who administered the *sacramentum* to the soldiers, and it was they who had the overall responsibility for directing the building of the army's camp. Polybius' account of the army in Book 6 of his histories may even be derived from a handbook for military tribunes, something which is suspected because it outlines their pivotal role in the camp.[28]

The military tribunes were elected by the *comitia tributa*, the tribal assembly, the units of which were divided by tribal designation rather than by wealth. There were twenty-four military tribunes after 207 BCE, distributed among the four legions, making twelve in a consular army and six per legion. This is a relatively small number, and the tribunes, more than any other rank of officer, were closest to the rank-and-file. This is fitting as part of their job was to defend the interests of the common soldiery, which in practice meant looking out for the interests of the sick and wounded, responding to complaints, ensuring the fairness of disciplinary action and taking care of the food supply. Sometimes the military tribunes were placed in direct command of detachments. The rank of military tribune illustrates the legions as a rare part of the Roman world in which the elites had extended interaction with ordinary men. No known tribune of the Middle Republic came from a background less wealthy than the equestrian class. Unlike most of the ordinary soldiers of the army, the military tribunes came from the city itself and its immediate surroundings, at least until the Second Punic War, and it was only by the end of the second century that their origins started to expand to the north and south of Rome.[29]

There was also one quaestor for each army, whose primary task was to handle the administration of money and supplies on behalf of the state. They were usually young men close to the beginning of their magisterial careers at Rome, and although younger, were every bit as aristocratic as the commanders and tribunes. Their tents were set up next to the commander's, where they also seem to have stored supplies. Polybius says that they were responsible for deducting from the soldier's pay any arms he might need, although he, like the other officers, would be attended by servants and slaves and probably did not discharge the duty himself.

The commander's official body of military advisors was called his *concilium*, and it was made up of the senior officers, the prefects of the allies, the prefects of the cavalry, and the advisors and friends of the commander. Polybius writes that the first man elected to the centurionate had a seat on this council, which must mean the *primus pilus*, of which there were usually two in a consular legion, one representing each legion. This might not have been the soldiers' only representation at the *concilium*, as the evidence for the *primus pilus* as the only centurions present is not strong, and by the first century BCE the first centurion of each of the heavy infantry divisions was represented at the council.[30] The council's mandate was deliberative, aimed at advising the commander about matters of military strategy. Unfortunately, we are not able to say much about the contribution of the centurions as we know very little. Perhaps their role was to advise on the condition and mood of the soldiers, or what their capabilities were at any given moment, if their ranks were heavily wounded or they were worn out by marching. Perhaps they had seen enough to comment on strategy and be taken seriously by the senior officers, but the evidence is simply not there.

Volunteering, *Tumulti* and Mercenaries

As discussed in the introduction, Roman practice often appears far less neat and tidy than the stated rules might suggest, and practical solutions to manpower needs provided many opportunities for alternative ways of joining the army. Being called up during a *dilectus* was not the only way that men made their way into the Roman legions. Some men volunteered there, as Ligustinus did in 171 BCE when he apparently simply attended the *dilectus* to offer his services. Others came by less usual means and from less-usual parts of society. The Middle Republic had a number of wars that sent them into crisis and long, drawn-out and unpopular campaigns that provided opportunities for volunteers to join, even those that Roman recruiters disdained when the state's military affairs were under control.

In the days of profound crisis during the second Punic War, when Hannibal had led a Carthaginian army across the Alps and down into Italy, decisively defeating the Roman legions at the Battle of Cannae, normal recruitment rules ceased to apply. The Roman senate refused to pay a ransom for the Roman prisoners taken in that war, deciding that their capture was evidence of their cowardice and unsuitability for further service. Instead, they formed legions from different sources. As both men and women packed the temples to pray for the gods' indulgence, refugees from the northern Italian allies were arriving at Rome, fleeing towns and cities ravaged by the invading army. Even as the occupants of the city were fearfully watching the horizon for the dust kicked up by the approach of Hannibal's army, some men's lives were about to suddenly change for the better. Emergency measures authorized the enrolment of criminals and slaves, who were offered their freedom in exchange for service. Young boys answered the call if they had grown strong enough to wield a weapon, and old men who were still capable of the same were organized in defence of the city.

Sometimes, volunteers simply showed up and asked to join the army. In a time of crisis, it could work simply to present yourself to the officers of an already formed legion, like those who joined the troops of C. Claudius Nero in 207 BCE. While that army was on the march, veterans and young men turned up to volunteer their services, and those judged strong enough were incorporated into the legions (Livy 27.46.3). Some soldiers re-volunteered with commanders that they trusted and with whom they believed they had a good chance of victory, such as in 190 BCE, when Scipio Africanus accompanied an army to Asia Minor because his brother was commanding it, followed by many volunteers reassured by his presence.[31] Some responded to calls for volunteers by commanders who, for one reason or another, had not been allowed to hold a normal levy.[32]

Volunteers were probably always welcome, and not always just in a crisis. During the second century Rome fought some difficult and markedly unprofitable wars against tribes in Spain. These campaigns against men who were both notoriously tough warriors and somewhat poor were unpopular, apparently offering too much danger for too little reward. Rome had trouble drafting enough soldiers for the legions and the recruiting consuls were reluctant to enrol anyone who did not wish to serve. The unwilling, of course, were likely to make bad fighters, and their lack of enthusiasm would not have been welcome in camp either. On any occasion, volunteers motivated to make some money, perhaps with some experience behind them, were infinitely preferable.[33]

Many of the men who volunteered for the army were, like Ligustinus in his later years, those who had served the required amount of time already. Until the age of 46 a citizen man was an *evocatus*, eligible for future service if the Republic needed him or he needed it. He might be called to serve in a crisis, or he might be attracted back to the legions when they were recruiting for lucrative campaigns in rich areas where it was possible for ordinary soldiers to make a tidy profit.[34] Some men were career soldiers who, probably in groups of long-time comrades, volunteered their services to recruiting tribunes. Tribunes picked centurions for their units, and these would certainly have been men of experience and proven ability. After the second century it may even have been more difficult to move into a centurion position from recruitment as an ordinary soldier because of the growing number of men who were essentially professionals.[35]

There was also a way to declare a state of emergency that would allow Roman magistrates to generate manpower immediately without having to hold a *dilectus*. Such a directive was called a *tumultus*. It suspended any legitimate exemptions that individuals might have had that excused them from military service, like holding a public service position, and at the same time it widened the scope of recruitment, for example to older men.[36] This characteristic of the *tumultus* is indicative of its origins in a period when Rome was a much smaller city, when in a crisis it might need to call every man even if he was not of the age or fitness that was usually required. There were two types of *tumultus* depending from where the danger originated, a *tumultus Italicus* or *tumultus Gallicus*. A *tumultus Italicus* was a danger that originated within the borders of Italy, and a *tumultus Gallicus* an invasion or threatened invasion from Italy's northern border with Gaul. The *tumultus* was thus intended to provide a response to a threat that was immediate, both in time and proximity.

When soldiers were recruited into service as the result of a *tumultus*, they did not swear the *sacramentum* but another kind of military oath, the *coniuratio*, the 'swearing together'. As the name suggests and as we might expect for a group assembled for rapid response, this was not the ceremony of soldiers swearing one by one as in the *sacramentum*. Instead, the man who was to command the new soldiers called out, 'he who wishes to save the republic, follow me' and the soldiers then 'swore together,' presumably that they would.[37] This form of oath bound the men as soldiers for only as long as the emergency lasted, as opposed to the *sacramentum* that applied for the campaigning season of a particular commander. They were required to be released as soon as the threat had been dealt with.

On rare occasions the Romans employed mercenaries. These were groups of professional soldiers who sold their services to the various states, kingdoms and empires of the ancient world. They are usually identified to us by national origin, which implies that mercenaries found one another in their home states and preferred groups of one language, although of course there must have been exceptions. Sometimes we are told that the mercenaries were of a particular speciality, such as the Cretan archers that accompanied at least two of Ligustinus' campaigns, in Greece in 197 BCE and again in Macedon in 171 BCE.[38] Livy claims that the first time mercenaries were in a Roman camp was in 213 BCE in Spain, where the Romans hired some Celtiberians, and Diodorus Siculus tells us it was not the Roman custom to hire them, implying that mercenaries were infrequent comrades.[39] From the Punic War onwards, however, there are examples and at other times, units listed as *auxilia* who were not allied nations and are suspected of being mercenaries. In addition to the Cretan archers mentioned, Ligustinus' campaigns included a mixed group of Thracians and Macedonians who accompanied his army into Greece when he was a centurion of the *principes* in 188 BCE, and Ligurians and Numidians who went to Macedon in 171 BCE.[40]

The Camp Oath

Polybius specifies that the camp oath was taken by everyone who was to be resident in the camp, whether those men were 'freemen or slaves' (Polyb. 6.33.1). This means that the soldiers and officers were required to take the oath, but also the officers' slaves, the *calones* and *lixae*, and the servants of the cavalry. This oath thus bound together the third and widest group, not the group of citizen combatants, as in the first oath, and not the organic and informal oath to stay in the battle line that might have been a practice of closer groups of soldiers, but a group defined primarily by physical space, namely, those enclosed by the boundary of the camp.

The antiquarian Aulus Gellius (16.4) has preserved what seems to be the wording of the oath from 190 BCE, dated by the names of the consuls that are given in the text of the oath.[41] It is very possible that Ligustinus was in service with L. Cornelius Scipio during that year, and so the words here are the very words he would have spoken at that time. The oath constitutes a promise not to steal anything from the camp. It names and exempts certain small items, which are here left in Latin so as to be better explained following the text:

> In the army of the consuls Gaius Laelius, son of Gaius, and Lucius Cornelius, son of Publius, and for 10 miles around it, you will not with malice aforethought commit a theft, either alone or with others, of more than the value of a silver sesterce in any one day. And except for *hasta, hastile, ligna, poma, pabulum, uter, follis* and *facula*, if you find or carry off anything there which is not your own and is worth more than one silver sesterce, you will bring it to the consul Gaius Laelius, son of Gaius, or to the consul Lucius Cornelius, son of Publius, or to whomsoever either of them shall appoint, or you will make known within the next three days whatever you have found or wrongfully carried off; or you will restore it

to him whom you suppose to be its rightful owner, as you wish to do what is right.[42]

The items that are named as exceptions to this rule are *hasta* and *hastile*, a spear and the shaft of a spear respectively. *Ligna* is wood, meaning specifically firewood that has been gathered. *Poma* is plural, 'fruits' and can refer to fruit like apples, but also things we might not immediately think of as fruit, like nuts, berries, figs and dates. *Pabulum* means food specifically for animals, or 'fodder'.[43] *Uter* is a bag or bottle made of animal hide for carrying water. *Follis* is a small bag for coins. *Facula* is a torch, or more precisely, the diminutive of the word for torch, *fax*, and so meaning a small torch or a splinter of wood used for a torch.

These seem to be either items that were foraged by the soldiers themselves (the fruit, firewood and fodder) or small items that were considered as communal use (spear and spear shaft, waterskin, bag, torch), perhaps because they were military issue. Some of these small items we do not know much about, but they are likely items produced by or for the legions. The *uter*, for example, could be made by soldiers, as we learn from Sallust when he writes that the general Marius had cattle delivered to each of his centuries with the order to make *utres* from the hides before taking the legions into the desert (Sall. *Iug.* 91.1). Animal skin cured by oiling and salting tends to be quite fragile when full, vulnerable to punctures and breakage, and can crack if left dry or while drying.[44] For this reason *utres* were probably common items supplied to the soldiers as, like tunics, even if the soldier brought one or even several with him, they needed frequent repair and replacement. Similarly a *facula* is a splint of wood with something flammable tied to it, like straw or cloth, that could be dipped in oil and set alight. Such things were apparently for the common use of soldiers and camp attendants who could take one if needed.

The oath specifies a 10-mile radius around the camp, which seems an exceptionally large area. This is certainly enough to have covered any soldiers or camp attendants working around the camp and possessions they had put down or misplaced in the course of creating defensive works or foraging. It must have also covered the battlefield, which was usually not more than ten miles away from a camp. It also covered any towns that were taken by storm and the plunder that was seized there, as Polybius explicitly tells us when he discusses how the Romans sacked cities. The soldiers stacked up everything they had found for the tribunes to distribute equally among the soldiers, including those who had been left on guard and the sick and wounded. Polybius gestures back to the camp oath, writing 'I have already stated at some length in my chapters on the Roman state how it is that no one appropriates any part of the loot, but that all keep the oath they make when first assembled in camp on setting out for a campaign' (Polyb. 10.16.6).

The oath itself had a number of purposes, intended or unintended. The most obvious of them was to announce the camp rules.[45] Not all soldiers would have been literate, and so distributing the rules of the camp in the form of an oath solved a number of problems. Every soldier was told the oath verbally and was required to assent to it, meaning that he could not later plead ignorance of its conditions. Further, introducing the rules in the form of an oath meant that the penalties for violating the rules were elevated from an act of petty theft to the violation of an oath.[46]

There are numerous advantages to an oath of this type which, we are told, had an extremely severe deterrent attached in the form of capital punishment for anyone caught violating its terms (Polyb.6.37.9). One of these is peace of mind for the soldier. The camp tents were small and arms and armour needed to be kept outside while the soldiers slept. Although there were guards posted by each maniple at night, they would surely not be protection against every petty theft. No-one needed to be kept awake by the worry that someone passing in the night would be tempted to steal the sword that had been his father's, or the helmet passed down from his brother. Even items that were not of sentimental value had immense practical value, like the cooking implements and utensils, and would cause the soldier great inconvenience and annoyance if they went missing. Disappearing utensils and equipment were likely to cause accusations, disputes, and distrust, and could lead to outright fighting. The prohibition against stealing, in guaranteeing each man's personal possessions, would have provided a basic sense of security against undue annoyance and inconvenience. This might not seem like a large concern but a repeated, grinding everyday annoyance like a missing tool could certainly grow in the imagination.

Chapter 5

Moving an Army on Campaign

Departure of the Commander from Rome

Since the soldiers made their own way to the mustering point, they would not have been present when the commander and his immediate retinue left Rome. There was a great deal of ceremony involved in this moment, and several tasks and rituals that were necessary for the commander to perform before leaving. The right to perform these depended on the commander's perceived ancestral and elite privileges to commune with the gods on behalf of the population. For the soldier, what was perhaps most important was that the commander arrived at the mustering point having performed all the appropriate rituals that were required of him in order to gain the gods' favour for the campaign. The soldier will have wanted to have confirmation that the commander had obtained the appropriate rights to lead the army.

At Rome, the consular commanders and the rest of the Senate were obliged to expiate any negative signs that had been reported to them before the armies left on campaign. These were *prodigium*, 'prodigies' or unusual events that had been observed anywhere in Rome's territory, which were thought to be communications from the gods indicating their displeasure at some transgression or slight. In the year that Sulpicius sailed for Macedonia, there were reports of the sky on fire in Lucania, the sun glowing red all day in Privernum, a 'terrible noise' in the night at the temple of Juno Sospita in Lanuvium, as well as a spate of deformities in humans and animals, including a lamb with a pig's head and a pig with a human head.[1] As was the usual procedure, these events were reported to the Senate, referred to the appropriate religious body, and expiated in accordance with that body's expert advice. It was the responsibility of another college of priests, the fetials, to make sure that the war was just and had been declared properly.

The commander himself was required to take auspices and to make a sacrifice, both of which were observed to make sure they contained no fault. These rites were consultative in nature, intended to query and confirm the gods' approval for a particular proposed undertaking, which was, in this case, the departure of the commander to assume control of a Roman army. We will look at the auspices in more detail later when they were taken in the presence of the soldiers, as performing augury and sacrifice would be repeated before any significant action. In 200 BCE, since the state was launching a new war soon after the end of the Second Punic War, it seems the Senate took pains to make sure all religious duties were scrupulously correct. Sulpicius was asked to make an offering to Jupiter and vow games in his honour (Livy 31.9.6). A departing general was always required to visit the temple of Jupiter Optimus Maximus to ask him for success and make a vow promising that further sacrifices would be made to the god, should that success come to pass.

When the commander had performed all the necessary rituals he came to the border of the city. The city of Rome was surrounded by a religious boundary called the *pomerium*. The *pomerium* formed the threshold between two spheres of Roman life, civil life in the city and military life outside the city's walls. When he crossed the *pomerium*, the consul's special assistants, called the lictors, robed him in the *paludamentum*, the distinctive red military cloak of a Roman commander, and accompanied him on his journey. Only then, having performed all the rituals properly and crossed the *pomerium*, did the commander possess the right of *imperium*, the right to command soldiers, and *auspicium*, the right to consult the gods on behalf of the army.

When the commander arrived to take command of the army, either at the mustering point or the camp of an army already in its province, it was important that all the correct procedures had been conducted without fault. Occasionally a commander attempted to take over an army without having done this preparation. C. Claudius did this in 177 BCE, but it seems that he was given away by arriving without lictors, whose presence would normally attest to the fact that he had done the correct ceremony at the *pomerium* and by extension, the correct rites up to that point as well.[2] Perhaps the commander appeared at an assembly of the soldiers to declare that these things had been done successfully, as it would have been important for the soldiers to know that the gods had been solicited for any opposition to their war, that any unsolicited signs that could pertain to the army's campaigns had been expiated, and that the war itself and the individual who commanded had both legality and divine approval. If these were not in place, it was likely that, just as they did in the case of C. Claudius, the current commander would refuse to hand over the army and the soldiers would refuse to obey him.

Naturally, none of the rituals or sacrifices performed by a commander ensured or guaranteed the fortunes of an individual soldier. It was perfectly possible for one man to become a casualty even in the case of a stunning victory. What it would have done, however, was check for any divine opposition to their war that would guarantee disaster for everyone. Failing to do such a thing would have been considered reckless neglect, and would have made a commander appear careless and incompetent in the eyes of his soldiers. All campaigns, therefore, ought to begin with the commander's declaration that the gods had been appropriately solicited and they had confirmed that all was well.

Transportation by the navy

At Brundisium, military tribunes and administrative staff would have been directing the loading of the transports for the short journey across the Adriatic to begin the campaign, and Ligustinus would have witnessed, probably for the first time, a fleet of the Roman navy. Besides its own military duties the navy provided military transport for the legions, not only carrying troops to their provinces, but also supplying grain and other provisions to feed, clothe, and equip the army. Few serving soldiers would have managed to avoid transportation by ship during the years that Ligustinus was active, as the patterns of warfare at that time favoured Spain and the East, theatres of war serviced by established sea ports on their Roman-controlled coasts.

A fleet carrying soldiers usually comprised of large transport ships accompanied and protected by warships. Roman warships of the Middle Republic were typically quinqueremes, although there were also quadriremes and triremes supplied by the allied nations. These names mean literally 'fives', 'fours' and 'threes' and refer to the numbers of banks of oars in the sides of the ship. For the ships named triremes, 'threes', the name refers to the fact that the oars were set at three different height levels, one on top of the other, which seems to be the maximum number of levels that could be used effectively. The names of the quadriremes, 'fours', and quinqueremes, 'fives', came from the number of oarsmen assigned to each oar and the number of levels. The typical Roman five would therefore have had either two levels, with three men pulling one oar and two men pulling the other, or three levels, with one man on the lowest level and two each at the two higher levels.[3]

Quinqueremes were very large ships with a broad beam. This created a spacious deck that was high above the waterline, where a warship destined for combat would place its marines and any artillery and grappling equipment. At the bow of the ship at the waterline there was a bronze ram called the *rostrum*. This widened at one end where it was fitted to the prow, and at the other, the bronze piece jutted out in a rectangle shape tapering to a vertical point. The *rostrum* also had three horizontal projections sticking out at the top, middle and bottom, designed to look like the three points of a trident as it rammed into the hull of an enemy ship.

Above the ram there was a smaller structure that projected out from the prow of the ship called a *proembolion*. This was a 'fore ram' or 'subsidiary ram', set at the point where the wales that strengthened the ship came together, about half-way up the stem post.[4] This was intended to protect this important point of the superstructure at the bow, as well as causing more damage to the upper hull of the ship under attack.[5] Examples of these survive, as well as depictions on various friezes and relief sculptures. Sometimes they were left rectangular, or were a smaller version of the lower *rostrum*. Frequently they were detailed in the form of animal heads, like a boar or a wolf.[6]

Behind the *proembolion*, in a panel on the port side, was painted a large eye. This was the *oculus*, a traditional symbol that is called apotropaic, meaning 'to turn away evil', in this case set there to turn danger and malevolent forces away from the ship. Underneath the eye would be painted a distinguishing figure, a merman called a triton, or a dolphin, which served as a way of naming the ship. The stempost curved out and back over the ship's deck, ending in a decoration, like the forward looking helmeted head in the representation of a quinquereme on the funerary monument of C. Cartilius Poplicola.[7] The warships were painted *venetus*, marine blue, or *caeruleus*, a dark blue or green.

There was nothing plain or unassuming about the ships docked at Brundisium. They were large and bright, the colour of the Mediterranean in the sunshine. They stared resolutely forward with their painted eye while the bronze wolf or boar snarled underneath. Just as they were intended to intimidate Rome's enemies, they likely inspired confidence in Rome's soldiers. The soldiers would see little of the navy while they were fighting inland, but they would receive news of their operations. These ships that were fighting another part of the campaign were more than an abstract idea, they were particular ships and particular sailors that they had seen and perhaps even spoken to during their departure. Perhaps it cheered the soldiers to know that these fierce blue boats were fighting on their side.

The sailors who manned the Roman warships came from a few different places. Some of them were the *socii navales*, the 'naval allies', whose alliance with Rome stipulated that they provide sailors for the warships and sometimes ships complete with crews. The *socii navales* were usually coastal towns in Sicily and the south of the Italian peninsula, which had a tradition of seafaring that dated back to their origins as colonies of the Greeks.[8] Rome also had maritime colonies that were liable for naval service like Ostia and Tarracina. The rest of the crews, primarily the oarsmen, came from the poorest of Rome's citizens, whose wealth was rated under 400 *asses*, and freedmen, men who had once been slaves but had either bought their freedom or had it granted by their former owner.[9]

We usually hear of the soldiers travelling on transports, called an *oneraria* in Latin and translated as transport or cargo vessels. Certainly this was what was done whenever a large number of troops like an invasion force needed transportation. The sources, however, are often unspecific about the exact travel arrangements and it was possible for soldiers to be moved by warship, especially in quinqueremes with their large decks.[10] In 214 BCE, Marcus Valerius moved his soldiers on warships and only when they ran out of room were troops put on transports. At Brundisium, Livy says that Sulpicius chose ships from the fleet that had been under the command of the consul of the previous year. There had been fifty in that fleet, and from Livy's remarks later about fleet numbers we know that there were about thirty-seven vessels in the naval force of Sulpicius' campaign.[11]

As the army prepared for its departure, there was a great deal to be done. Everyone and everything went by boat, the legionaries, the allies, the cavalry, the *calones*, as well as horses, mules, baggage, and initial supplies of grain. It would all have been very familiar to the 2,000 veterans who had joined Sulpicius' legions from the armies serving in Africa. Just a few years earlier, in 204 BCE, they had embarked on a voyage from Lilybaeum in Sicily to begin the invasion of Africa and, as they had hoped, bring the Second Punic War to a close. The organization of that large fleet had been particularly difficult and, unusually, it was overseen by the commander himself. The details given about that fleet are instructive. The admiral of the fleet had organized the boarding of the sailors followed by the soldiers to be transported. A praetor was responsible for gathering forty-five days' worth of food and sufficient water for men, horses and pack animals. The ships were ordered to have the correct number of lanterns to identify themselves to each other at night, and each ship's captain, pilot, and two other crew needed to attend a meeting to receive orders (Livy 29.25.4–11).

Something very similar, on a smaller scale, would have happened at Brundisium. Scipio commanding at Lilybaeum was said to have had 40 warships and 400 transports, but even Livy was unwilling to put a number on how many soldiers he transported (29.25.1–4). P. Scipio's landing in Spain in 217 BCE, along with 30 warships had carried 8,000 men, generating what Livy calls 'an enormous column of transports' visible from a distance to the Romans' allies (22.22.2). Generally it is thought that around 250 men per vessel would have been able to travel on a transport.[12]

As Ligustinus splashed through the water and climbed the ladder to the deck of the ship, perhaps he thought of those many banks of oars where his poverty really ought to have placed him. He had avoided being cramped under the decks of a warship, but he still had a great effort ahead of him if he wished success in the army to be profitable enough to prevent his future sons from owning so little that they qualified only as oarsmen.

In timeless military fashion, moving two legions, allies, equipment and baggage from camp to ships would have involved a lot of waiting, then a very small window of activity, and then a great deal of waiting again. As they were loaded onto the ships, the soldiers were probably given orders similar to those given to the soldiers under Scipio Africanus as they departed in 204 BCE, 'to remain quiet and decorous and to keep out of the way of the sailors performing their duties'(Livy 29.25.9). On any given occasion, they might have been tough-looking, competent men, executing their duties efficiently, or on the other hand, weak, disorganized, and prone to mistakes. We are never told such details and most of our sources would not have known them, but Ligustinus would have known. Later in the war, when the soldiers were told about the operations of the navy, their crews, their ships, and their weaponry were much more than an abstract, far-away concept.

The Lustratio Exercitus

Before an army departed on campaign, the Romans performed a ritual called the *lustratio exercitus*, 'the lustration of the army'. The best source for what happened at the *lustratio* is the Greek historian Appian, who records how the Emperor Augustus lustrated the fleet:

> Altars were erected on the margin of the sea, and the multitude were ranged around them in ships, observing the most profound silence. The priests who performed the ceremony offered the sacrifice while standing at the water's edge, and carried the expiatory offerings in skiffs three times around the fleet, the general sailing with them, beseeching the gods to turn the bad omens against the victims instead of the fleet. Then, dividing the entrails, they cast a part of them into the sea, and put the remainder on the altars and burned them, while the multitude chanted in unison. In this way the Romans perform lustrations of the fleet (App. *B Civ.* 5.19.96).

Although the sources often describe separate lustrations of the army and lustrations of the fleet, it seems that when an army was to depart by sea, the *lustratio* was done for the army and the navy at the same time, while the infantry and cavalry were already onboard naval transports ready for departure.[13] We know that the sacrifice mentioned was called a *suovetaurilia*, the sacrifice of a pig, a ram, and a bull, and that it was offered to the war god Mars. When an army marched out from Rome, this ceremony took place on the Campus Martius where an altar to Mars stood. As the Romans ventured further afield over the years, the *lustratio* was done at the point of mustering and departure. When done on land, the pig, the ram and the bull were led around the army three times before they were sacrificed, just as was done here, with the exception of the additional use of a skiff to sail with the victims around the fleet.

At a *lustratio*, the commander presided over the sacrifice and spoke the words of the prayer to Mars and other deities for the protection of the army. We know the words that Scipio spoke at Lilybaeum, words that no doubt were very similar to those that Sulpicius spoke at Brundisium:

> When the moment for departure came, Scipio ordered the herald to proclaim silence throughout the fleet and put up the following prayer: 'Ye gods and goddesses of sea and land, I pray and beseech you to vouchsafe a favourable issue to all that has been done or is being done now or will be done hereafter under my command. May all turn out happily for the burghers and plebs of Rome, for our allies of the Latin name, for all who have the cause of Rome at heart, and for all who are marching beneath my standard, under my auspices and command, by land or sea or stream. Grant us your gracious help in all our doings, crown our efforts with success. Bring these my soldiers and myself safe home again, victorious over our conquered foes, adorned with their spoils, loaded with booty and exulting in triumph. Enable us to avenge ourselves on our enemies and grant to the people of Rome and to me the power to inflict exemplary chastisement on the city of Carthage, and to retaliate upon her all the injury that her people have sought to do to us.' As he finished he threw the raw entrails of the victim into the sea with the accustomed ritual. Then he ordered the trumpeter to sound the signal for departure, and as the wind which was favourable to them freshened they were quickly carried out of sight. (Livy 29.27.1–5)

The words 'beneath my standard, under my auspices and command' evokes the same elements of ritual that had marked commanders' departure from Rome. The first points to the standards, solid and material symbols of the army that the commander had brought to the campaign from the city. The auspices underline the more abstract idea of the importance of ensuring safe movement, and gestures in particular to the general's role as responsible for the success of the army's journey by ensuring that it was always done with the approval of the appropriate divinities. The general alone had the right to consult the divine on behalf of those commanded just as he had the exclusive the right of *imperium*, to give orders to those men for the good of the state.

The *lustratio* is one of the rituals that would have made it seem natural to the soldiers of this era that they served in a sequence of temporarily constituted Roman armies. Its performance obliged the soldiers to sit silently for some time as they were encircled by the sacrifices, and then to chant together. Even if they did not consciously reflect upon it, the fact that every new army, new commander or reconstitution of an army went through this ritual would have served to emphasize the nature of a Roman army as one very specific body of men. The words of the prayer to Mars, like the words of the camp oath, were exclusive to that army and its particular commander.

It has been thought that the *lustratio* was a ritual of purification, but it does not fit easily into that reading. A *lustratio* was also performed for towns and fields, and a freshly constituted army would surely not need to be purified before it went to war, rather than afterward. A more likely explanation is that the ritual is a constitution or reconstitution of an entity. This is suggested by the concept of the encirclement, which by its very nature indicates that everything within it was henceforth to be considered a unity.[14] As the words of the prayer of Scipio Africanus show, it was further a request for the protection of the constituted entity, an entreaty to Mars to protect the soldiers and all others subject to the commander during the campaign.

Ligustinus, like all Romans of his day, was used to seeing and participating in ritual and sacrifices. He would go on to be a part of a minimum of twelve *lustrationes* during his long career, as one was necessary whenever a new commander came to take over an already existing army and whenever a new legion was formed.[15] When Ligustinus departed from Brundisium on his very first military campaign, sitting quietly during the *lustratio*, listening to the sound of the music that covered any ill-omened screech of a gull or bray of a horse, the whole experience might have seemed particularly poignant. As a ritual of encirclement, the *lustratio* implied the common identity and purpose of everyone within that circle, the Roman and allied soldiers, sailors and cavalry, the *calones*, the slaves and attendants of the officers, even the mules, horses and chickens, all of which had some contribution to make towards the furtherance of the war.

When the ritual had ended, the sound of trumpets signalled the departure, just as it would signal the off for Ligustinus many hundred more times during his military life; off to campaign, off on the march, off to battle. On this first occasion the journey was not a long one, as the fleet arrived in Macedonia two days after its departure (Livy 31.14.2). In his next campaign the transport by ship would be much longer. In 195 BCE, setting out from Portus Lunae on the Italian west coast, Ligustinus would journey to Emporiae in Spain via Portus Pyrenaei, the modern Port-Vendres on the French south coast near the Spanish border. Here the fleet stopped at a pre-arranged rendezvous for other ships to join them. From there, the fleet stopped at Rhode, modern Roses, where they expelled a Spanish garrison from the town, and from there across the bay to Emporiae. The whole journey would have taken more than thirty days by ship, excluding the time taken for the military operation at Roses.[16]

Building a Military Camp

When Ligustinus' first army embarked on ships from Brundisium it was transported to the territory of Rome's allies in Illyria, sometimes referred to as the 'Roman Protectorate'.[17] Here, the ancient port cities of Dyrrachium (Epidamnus) and Apollonia both lay within the areas allied to the Romans, which had been established by a settlement in 228 BCE between them and the local tribes, after the Romans had interfered to prevent piracy in the Adriatic off Italy's east coast. The Romans also controlled Corcyra, an island to the south that was a useful naval base for an invasion of Greece. The area was of strategic importance to the Romans, and by the time that Ligustinus arrived there in 200 BCE, it had been an important stronghold during the recent Second Punic War, when Hannibal's forces had controlled the southern part of Italy.[18]

When the Romans arrived in Illyria we are not told what their immediate action was, but it was most likely to build a camp. This was a common thing to do in the vicinity of the army's disembarkation point, as, for example, happened after Ligustinus' arrival at Emporiae in 195 BCE, when Cato is said to have stayed near the town 'for a few days' while he sent out scouts and exercised the army.[19] The camp would have been built at the disembarkation point for the same reasons it was built at the mustering point, because it was a way to reorganize the army, to account for all the soldiers, and to provide accommodation while this process was completed. Everyone had his place and everyone could be located by his place, and so it would be easy for each tent and maniple to recognize if everyone were present and accounted for or not. As in Cato's case, it was always sensible to pause and allow the scouts to survey the land and provide a picture of the immediate area, including the number and disposition of nearby towns and the location of any tribes.

There were two types of Roman camp during the Middle Republic. Camps made while on the march might be used for as little as one night, or could be used for several, while winter camps were semi-permanent quarters where the troops passed the cold months before starting up campaigns again in the summer.[20] When the Romans intended to build a camp while on campaign, specialist troops were sent out ahead of the army to choose a spot. When they had picked somewhere suitable they marked the ground out with coloured flags that showed the rest of the army where each part ought to be built (Polyb. 6.41.1). The units that Polybius uses for the dimensions of the camp are the Hellenistic foot and the *pletheron*, an area of 100 x 100 Hellenistic feet.[21] Happily there is an easy correspondence between the Greek and Roman measurements; 100 Hellenistic feet is 120 Roman feet, and so a *pletheron* is the equivalent of what the Romans called an *actus quadratus*, where *actus* is a unit of measurement 120 Roman feet

Diagram reproduced with kind permission of Mike Dobson.

long and *quadratus* means 'square' or 'squared', thus 120 x 120 Roman feet. The *actus* was the base unit of measurement in the Republican Roman camp, and it was one with which most of the soldiers would be familiar, because it was also the basic unit of measurement in agriculture. An *actus* was the distance that an oxen yoked to a plough was driven before it was turned around. It was also the basic unit of the civic grid system, used when a town or a colony was created by making a grid of straight streets that crossed one another at right angles.[22]

The camp was built outwards from the *praetorium*, the area that would house the tent of the consul and the area where he and his attendants would perform augury and sacrifice. Polybius tells us that a flag was placed that marked the centre of the *praetorium* and the four walls were each created 120 feet from this central spot to form a square. The front of the *praetorium* was angled to the east for the purposes of augury, and this orientation indicated what would be considered the front of the camp. The soldiers thus had a common vocabulary for the front, back, and left and right sides of the camp.

Having marked out the *praetorium*, one of its square sides was then chosen to be the area where the legions would be camped. Polybius says that this ought to be the direction 'which seems to give the greatest facilities for watering and foraging' (Polyb. 6.27.3). This may have been the consideration if all other things were equal. In the evidence provided by known Roman military sites of this period, the orientation is in no consistent direction, but appears to be chosen in accordance with the local topography.[23] The other consideration is that Polybius is describing a double consular camp, one with two consuls and four legions, built when the two consuls had joined forces. In a single consular camp, the ones that Ligustinus would have helped to build, the *praetorium* was effectively in the middle, and the legions would not be camped all to one side of it, but one on each side. In this type of camp, the forum was built to the east side of the *praetorium* and to the west, a strip 60 feet broad was left as a street running north to south, called the *via quintana*, 'fifth street', because it ran between the camping spot of the fifth maniple and the sixth maniple (Polyb. 6.30.6).

Parallel to the *via quintana*, on the other side of the forum, was built the *via principalis*. This was the largest and most important road in the camp, measuring one *actus* or 120 Roman feet in width. On the opposite side from the forum were built the tents of the legates, and then on each side of them, a little further down, opposite where the tents of the maniples would be, the tents of the tribunes were built. Six of these faced one legion, and on the other side another six faced the second legion. On the other side of those tents were the tents of the prefects of the allies, facing the allied infantry and cavalry. Behind this line of tents was another half *actus*, a 60 foot gap where the baggage, horses and mules of the legates, tribunes and prefects were placed.

Polybius then describes how the space for the soldiers' tents would be created. In the single consular camp, the rows of soldiers' tents were built along roads at a right angle to the *via principalis* and the *via quintana*. All of these streets were sixty feet wide, or half an *actus*. The rows of soldiers' tents were essentially built outwards by seniority, so that closest to the central *quaestorium* and *praetorium* were the citizen cavalry. Like all the troops, the cavalry was divided into ten units, where the first was the most senior. This first *turma* was directly across the *via principalis* from the tribunes' tents. Each subsequent *turma* was then built down the street in the direction of the outer walls. A gap was left between the fifth and sixth *turmae* to allow for the *via quintana*. The layout of the camp thus indicated the hierarchy. The divisions ran from the most senior, closest to the *praetorium*, to the most junior, nearest the walls, either north to south or south to north, depending on the legion, and the senior to junior maniple numbers ran from east to west from the first maniple or *turma* near the tribune's tents to the tenth nearest the walls.

Behind each *turma* of cavalry was a maniple of *triarii*, also running in order of importance with the first maniple directly across the *via principalis* from the tribunes' tents and continuing down in numerical order. Thus the first *turma* of cavalry had the first maniple of *triarii* directly behind it. This makes logical sense because these units both contained fewer soldiers than the other maniples, and so the *turma* with thirty men and their horses backed onto the maniple of sixty men. The maniple of *triarii* that effectively had its 'back' to the cavalry opened onto another street, across which was the first maniple of *principes*. The *principes* in turn backed onto the first maniple of *hastati*, who lived, in effect, across the street from the allied cavalry. The tents were pitched along three sides of the allotted space of each maniple or *turma*, with a space outside the tent left for arms and armour 5 feet deep, called the *arma*, a further 9-foot space for the mules called the *iumenta*, and the resulting space in the middle called the *conversantibus*. There seem to have been no borders or barriers between the maniples or *turmae* and the ones behind them. An individual from say, the third maniple of *principes* could cross into the area of the third maniple of *hastati* behind it, probably not by going between the tents where the guy ropes were pegged, but by walking along one of its sides and passing through the gap at the corner where the row of tents pitched along the back of the *conversantibus* did not quite meet the row of tents pitched at its sides.

The entrenching of the camp was done by the citizen legions and the Italian allies, with the allies taking the wall closest to their wing and the Romans responsible for the other two walls. This must mean that the allies each took the slightly shorter walls running east to west while the Romans created the longer walls running north to south. Polybius says a space of 240 feet called the *intervallum* was left between the last tent and the wall in order to prevent missiles reaching the tents from outside, to house cattle and booty, and to allow the soldiers to march out (6.31.11–14). This is not backed by the archaeological evidence from the camps at Numantia, where the *intervallum* was always much narrower than this.[24] Like the other aspects of the camp that were tweaked to circumstance, it seems that the *intervallum* was sized to accord with the terrain.

Each maniple carried entrenching equipment, and was assigned a section of the wall to build. This consisted of digging a ditch around the perimeter and erecting a rampart with the earth, on top of which they would build a defensive wall made of wooden stakes. The stakes themselves were essentially branches which had three or four lateral offshoots that allowed the soldiers to weave them together. Each soldier could carry several with him over his shoulder, and when they were planted together they were difficult to remove.[25] A line of branches like this was not intended to be a solid defence, but it prevented anyone coming unseen into the camp by night. If the camp did happen to be attacked, the wall would slow down or stop an enemy at a point where he would be vulnerable to attack by guards. The entrenching work was supervised by the centurions of each maniple, which was certainly a perk of this position. After his first campaign, upon his promotion to centurion, it seems Ligustinus left his digging duties behind him.

Navigating the Camp

The camp is perhaps most comprehensible when we imagine a soldier's movements within it. When any soldier started out from his tent, he would first have to go past the collection of arms and armour propped outside and then the animals and baggage. Beyond that, the soldier would emerge into a rectangle of space, where the rest of the tents of his maniple and the *velites* attached to it occupied three sides. The fourth side led out onto the street. One end of this street led towards the *intervallum* and the wall of the camp. The other led towards the centre. If he belonged to a maniple numbered six to ten, a soldier proceeding down that street towards the centre of the camp would first come to a crossroads, the *via quintana*, that separated the fifth maniple from the sixth maniple.

The soldier could follow the *via quintana* down to the *praetorium* and *quaestorium* in the very centre of the camp. Both areas had a cohort camped next to it as a bodyguard to the consul and quaestor, on one side the *delecti extraordinarii*, and on the other the *evocati*. These were essentially the elite troops of the citizens and the elite troops of the allies, and in the army in Macedon in 200 BCE, the *evocati* were probably made up of the Punic War veterans. On one side of the *via quintana* was the *quaestorium*, where one went for supplies, pay, and replacement arms, and on the other, the *praetorium* with the tent of the consul and the members of the *cohors amicorum*.

If the soldier crossed the *via quintana* and continued, he would come to the largest street, the *via principalis*. Directly across that street were the tents of the tribunes, each with four guards posted in front and, although he would not be able to see it, four behind. He would then need to turn right or left, depending on the legion of which he was a part, in the direction of the centre. At the centre he would reach the forum, the area where the soldiers gathered to be addressed and exhorted. This backed on to the *praetorium*, and since the commander and his attendants would have used this side of the *praetorium* to take auspices and make sacrifices, it would also have been an area where the soldiers could witness them.

The systematic layout of the camp meant not only was it easy to find one's way around, it would also be possible to find any given person within it as long as one knew his legion, division and maniple. When the soldiers travelled to the mustering spot from their regional homes, they already knew this information, and so it would be entirely possible to find local friends simply by following the camp numbering system to the area where his maniple was encamped. Even knowing just part of that information would allow someone to locate the approximate area of his friend's tent and ask around. Similarly, any soldier singled out for distinction or discipline could be summoned by messenger and any centurion could be found simply through the name of his position.

The tents of the soldiers were very small, with the implication that the soldiers would not wish to spend time in them unless they were sleeping and would naturally seek to spend time in the *conversantibus* instead, where meals and socializing took place, and in the wider camp. Polybius says that during the day the soldiers went to the *via principalis* to spend their time (6.33.3–4). Since this was adjacent to the forum in the centre, the area where the forum met the main road would provide the largest space for soldiers to congregate.

The most important aspect of the camp was its uniformity no matter where it was built. Polybius explained why this was done. While the Greeks made their camp differently depending on terrain, the Romans insisted otherwise: 'The Romans on the contrary prefer to submit to the fatigue of entrenching and other defensive work for the sake of the convenience of having a single type of camp which never varies and is familiar to all.'[26] The camp could always be built the same way along one unchanging plan that could easily be learned by all the soldiers with the minimum of supervision. The tents were all pitched in the same relationship to one another so that each *contubernium* of soldiers had the same neighbours and the camp would look the same, no matter where in the world it happened to be.

The effect of this, generally, was to create something analogous to a moving town or a city. The fact that the streets and the layout were unchanged each time the camp was rebuilt, creating the same neighbours every time, and the routine practice of building that camp, must have provided a kind of psychological solace for the Roman soldier.[27] It was also a huge part of the soldier's experience. Soldiers spent days, weeks, months, and even years in camp during their campaigns, in temporary camps with tents during the summer campaigning season, and in winter quarters living in one semi-permanent camp for the season. In winter the tents were replaced with timber or stone, or the tents had low walls built around them and were thatched to keep out the cold.[28] It would have come to feel much like a native city, with the same familiar faces, roads, tents and animals.

The religious boundary around the city of Rome, the *pomerium*, and the need to take auspices while travelling to extend the commander's authority across natural boundaries have already hinted at the importance of physical space in Roman life and thought. The same was true of domestic life. The Roman word for home, *domus*, was defined by the physical space occupied by the house, which had clearly delineated thresholds and boundaries, and implied a common connection between those who lived there. It would be natural for the young Roman, who had come into the legions straight from his family home, to start to feel connections to the people with whom he shared common physical space. In other words, to begin to see those around him, and especially those with whom he shared a tent, as a kind of military family.[29]

Auspices

In order for a Roman army to move around, to undertake military operations, or to engage in a pitched battle, the commander and an assistant first needed to take the auspices. In the Republican army the legions marched with a designated chicken-keeper, the *pullarius*, and a number of chickens kept in a cage. When the *pullarius* released the chickens from the pen they were fed grain. If they squawked, beat their wings, or tried to escape, the omens were bad. If they simply settled down to eat the grain hungrily, the signs were good, especially if they ate so fast that the grains spilled from their beaks. The best signs were called *tripudium sollistimum*, which refers to the fall of the food or its bounce on the ground, although the etymology is disputed.[30]

Favourable auspices were necessary for the army to undertake any significant endeavour. This is very different to the actions of modern armies, that may take decisions, form policy and initiate action based solely on military considerations. In the Middle Republic, sometimes what was best militarily had to be subordinated to the results of this consultation of the gods, who were thought to send signs to aid men by warning that a proposed action was destined to end badly. The obedience to religious directive was pervasive in the military sphere and was taken extremely seriously.

Taking the auspices was essentially consulting the gods regarding the advisability of one clearly defined, particular action. The answer was necessarily binary: the ritual could only solicit a yes or no, and so it always questioned a specific action that the Romans were proposing to begin immediately or shortly afterward. In a work on divination written in the Late Republic and referring back to this time period, Cicero refers to matters that needed the confirmation of auspices as essentially any military initiative:

> Our ancestors would not undertake any military enterprise without consulting the auspices; but now, for many years, our wars have been conducted by proconsuls and propraetors, who do not have the right to take auspices. Therefore they have no *tripudium* and they cross rivers without first taking the auspices.[31]

Cicero's example of such a military enterprise is crossing a river, which ought to give us an idea of what did and did not require divine approval. The need to stop and take auspices before launching military actions, however, was not as cumbersome as it may first appear. In fact it seems that by the time of the Middle Republic, the *auspicium ex tripudiis* had been streamlined so that it could be done quickly and efficiently. The chickens were captive, and managed and looked after by the *pullarius*, who also participated in the ceremony and was probably responsible for setting it up. It was also mostly formulaic and intended to produce a positive result: Cicero, in fact, says that the chickens were starved in order to make them peck hungrily at the grain every time.[32]

Despite these drives toward making the auspices routine, they could and did interfere with military operations. A negative auspice could prevent an army from taking an action even if it would otherwise be considered vital. For example, in 215 BCE one of the consuls of the year, Ti. Sempronius Gracchus, was in occupation of Cumae and threatened by the army of Hannibal nearby. His fellow consul, Fabius Maximus, was unable to come to his aid because, we are told, he was encamped across the river Volturnus, and was unable to cross the river or otherwise move his troops while he took fresh auspices and tried to expiate negative portents that had been reported to him (Livy 23.36.9–10).

Marching

The soldier of the third and second centuries BCE did not carry his own equipment. The army provided mules for this purpose and there were large numbers of them. Although it is sometimes suggested that there may have been as many as one per soldier, the archaeological evidence regarding Republican legionary camps makes this seem unlikely.[33] When the army camped, the mules were tied up to rest in the space outside of the legionaries' tent. Here they were close at hand so that they could be loaded by the soldiers when they prepared to move out (Polyb. 6.40.3). Each tent sheltered eight men, and if each were assigned a mule we would need to allow for a group of eight mules resting outside each tent, which seems an excessive number. It is likely that there were only one or two per *contubernium*. The mules seem to have kept the soldiers relatively unburdened. In Ligustinus' third year of service, with the commander Flamininus, we are told that while the army was in Thessaly the soldiers were ordered to carry stakes for a palisade. While Greek soldiers have trouble carrying their pikes due to the weight, Polybius says, Roman soldiers can sling their shields over their shoulders with leather straps and only need to hold their javelin in their hands, and can therefore carry stakes along with them easily (Polyb. 18.18.3–5).

Mules were favoured as pack animals because they boasted a variety of advantages over the horse. They had been used since the fourth millennium in Sumeria, and since the time of the Roman Republic have been used as pack animals in wars all over the world, proving themselves integral even to modern, highly technological armies when faced with action in mountainous terrain. The mule is less susceptible to colic (the name given to various potentially-fatal intestinal disorders of equines) and founder (laminitis, inflammation of the soft tissues of the hoof), and endures age and infirmity better than the horse.[34] The soldiers often walked thousands of miles with their mules, so this hardiness would have been welcome. If a mule died, it might be difficult to secure a replacement. Soldiers on the march seem to have had some discretion about the use of their mules; in 134 BCE, when Scipio issued a set of rules to his army to prevent them lagging and straggling, he specifically banned the men from riding the mules. This suggests that soldiers had been distributing one mule's burden among the rest in order to provide mounts for the weak and the sick. On the same occasion, we are told that there were many overloaded mules slowing down the march (App. *Hisp.* 86).

It is perhaps unsurprising when common soldiers were required to walk for such a long period of time that there is plenty of evidence that the march was often conducted with less than perfect precision or discipline. Straggling in particular seems to have been a common problem, as both individuals and parts of the train fell behind. We are told that in Spain in 134 BCE, straggling had become such a problem that the general Scipio Aemilianus attempted to solve it by making the soldiers march in a 'small square' in which each soldier was assigned a particular place that he was not allowed to change (App. *Hisp.* 86). The meaning of this seems to be that, just as in the battle line, the soldier was to take note of the men to the right and left of him and ensure they were walking at the same pace. At the same time he was forbidden to fall gradually backwards through swapping his place in the line with the men behind him, which would have allowed the square to continue to march at the same pace, but the individual to progressively fall behind. Scipio Aemilianus had come up with his solution to the straggling problem because on previous occasions men had become scattered, and we learn that the lagging was a particular problem with those who were ill, whom Scipio was apt to mount on horses instead of cavalrymen (App. *Hisp.* 86). We might suspect that these soldiers who fell behind were not weak from wounds but had contracted some kind of illness, just as in Burma during the Second World War, soldiers who were suffering from dysentery were forced to leave the lines to relieve themselves.[35]

Polybius tells us that there were two different formations of Roman armies on the move, one for movement through friendly territory and another for when danger was anticipated. The difference between the two was the manner in which the baggage, carried by the mules, was interspersed with the marching men. In friendly territory, a whole legion would march together, followed by the baggage of that legion. If the enemy was known to be close enough to attack, then the legions marched in three columns according to their divisions, the *hastati*, *principes*, and the *triarii*. These went in the order of their numbered maniples, with the baggage of the maniple going in front of the soldiers. Thus in the first column, the mules bearing the baggage of the first maniple of the *hastati* went first, followed by the first maniple of soldiers, followed by the baggage of the second maniple and then its soldiers, and so forth all the way down the line. Marching parallel to the first maniple of *hastati* was the second column headed up by the first maniple of the *principes*, and parallel to that a line of the maniples of *triarii*. This formation, according to Polybius, meant that each maniple could step in front of its respective baggage train, either to the left or to the right, depending from where the danger came. It would have been harder to fall behind in this formation, as any slow soldiers would be crowded from the rear by the pack animals of the next maniple and encouraged to hasten.

Chapter 6

Training

Basic Movements

During the time that Ligustinus fought with the Roman legions, new recruits would always have been trained, despite the fact that there was no formal period of training or boot camp. Only during the darkest days of emergency were untrained and inexperienced troops allowed into a battle situation. Although there would almost always have been some soldiers with previous experience, the higher the proportion of new troops, the more vulnerable was the resulting army. The absolute worst off were emergency legions made up almost entirely of new recruits. There are a few examples of such legions. A whole legion was made out of volunteer slaves during the Second Punic War in 216 BCE, after the Romans lost the Battle of Cannae. The people at Rome expected to see the dust of Hannibal's army appear on the horizon at any minute, and they engaged extreme emergency measures in their own defence. One of these included offering freedom to slaves and prisoners who would take up arms for Rome. Similarly, an entirely new legion was made for the Lusitanian war in 145 BCE (App. *Hisp.* 65). In these legions, new recruits would not even have benefitted from the kind of urgent, spontaneous training that could be given by experienced soldiers while on the march or during evenings spent in camp.

The most basic and essential piece of training was for the soldiers to learn how to assemble and move in their maniples. Without being trained in how to move or turn as a unit, the legions could not be deployed in their correct positions in the field, and so this type of organization was a basic essential for the legions to be able to operate at all. Thus Livy writes that before the inexperienced legions of 216 BCE were engaged, their commander Sempronius Gracchus exercised them so that they would 'become accustomed to follow the standards and in the battle line [*acies*] recognize their own ranks [*ordines*]' (Livy 23.35.6). He writes similarly of the centurion Statorius, loaned to a Roman allied king as a trainer for his troops, that his first task was to drill them in the Roman manner 'to follow the standards and stay in their ranks [*ordines*].'[1]

In moving from camp, to marching formation, to battlefield, the soldiers were guided by a sequence of signals. Many centuries after Ligustinus fought, Vegetius would write that the signals of the Roman army had come to be thought of in three types: voiced, semi-voiced, and mute (Veg. *Mil.* 3.5). Voiced were the orders conveyed by a human voice, while semi-voiced were sounds created by breath through an instrument, i.e. the sounds of three military instruments: the trumpet, the horn and the bugle. Mute signals were the movement of the standards. All of these types of signals would also have been pertinent in Ligustinus' day and earlier. Each soldier needed to become familiar with signals and their meanings whether they were given by voice by centurions and other officers, the sound of the horns and trumpets, or the mute visual signals conveyed by the standard bearer.

In the camp, the red standards of the commander called *vexilla* were raised to signal that the army was to move out to battle. The *vexillum* was made of a spear shaft with a crosspiece, from which was hung a cloth. This signal would have been accompanied by the sound of the trumpet. The trumpeter sounded the intention to move out of camp, and also, at the end of the day or the end of a battle, the intention to retire back to camp. The trumpet also sounded the charge.[2] A unit that was pursuing the enemy and was to be recalled to the lines would have heard the sound of the bugle (Polyb. 15.14.3). Vegetius tells us that the horn sounded an order, technically, to the standards and not the men (2.22), and so the sound of a horn signalled the standard bearer to move the standards to convey an order to those who were in visual range but perhaps not able to distinguish the sound of the horn among the other noise. *Signa*, the standards, were for directing centuries and maniples. In general, the trumpeter conveyed an order to the whole army, while the horns and bugles conveyed an order to a particular maniple, division or wing via the standard-bearer.

The movement of soldiers onto and around the battlefield was guided by the standards. According to several ancient sources, the standards had originally given their name to the maniples, *manipuli* being Latin for 'bundle' and referring to the bundles of hay that had been tied to spears in early times to create a primitive standard.[3] There were two standard-bearers per maniple, one per century, meaning that each standard-bearer was the principal guide for sixty-four men of one the three heavy infantry divisions and their twenty-four *velites*. The standard-bearer held the standards up at a height to aid their visibility. The standards attached to the units had three essential purposes: to allow the soldiers to align themselves, indicate by their movement what actions the soldiers needed to take, and to serve as a visual aid for the soldiers to identify where to regroup.[4] The soldier thus learned to be guided by a number of signs and cues, both oral and visual.

During the initial training on how to move in his maniple and line, each recruit would need to become familiar with the centurion closest to his position and look to him for cues. Each maniple had two centurions. The centurion who was the more senior commanded the century on the right and was called the *prior* centurion, and the centurion commanding the left was called the *posterior* centurion. Thus in the three centurionate positions that Ligustinus says that he held during his career, he commanded the right century in each: *primus hastatus prioris centuriae*, 'first *hastatus* of the prior century', *primus princeps prioris centuriae*, 'first princeps of the prior century' and *primus pilus prioris centuriae*, 'first *triarius* of the prior century.'

This very basic training in how to manoeuvre as a unit was vital to every member of the army. Even a soldier with a great deal of experience needed to practice moving with his new maniple. A soldier who had been moved into a new division needed to learn how to move in his line while bearing heavier arms and equipment. He also had to familiarize himself with his new colleagues, standards, and place in the legion's geography on the battlefield. A new soldier, particularly a young member of the *velites*, would benefit from seeing the gaps between the maniples and the depth of the ranks, with an eye to understanding how to move around them during a retreat, where to go when signalled to retire, and the route to take to restock his weaponry. At the beginning of each new campaign season, every soldier would need to be taught how to form up in the streets of the camp and file out in order.

Combat Training Through Skirmishing and Plunder

Training the soldiers how to move together onto the battlefield was, of course, not nearly enough to create an effective army. It was generally thought to be a bad idea to commit troops to combat without allowing them to practise and gain experience. By the time of Polybius it seems that the Romans were acutely aware that soldiers needed more than just practical skills in order to participate in combat successfully. They also needed the psychological element of confidence in their own abilities, the knowledge of what to expect in a fight, and familiarity with the appearance and techniques of the enemy. Thus, when new legions were created from solely or primarily new recruits, these legions were trained through skirmishing in smaller groups and kept out of large-scale battles until the commander thought they were ready. This type of combat meant that different units of soldiers were sent to smaller and more-controlled clashes with the enemy.

In 216 BCE just prior to the Battle of Cannae, Polybius writes that new recruits were hastily levied. The consul Aemilius Paullus sent instruction to the other commander:

that he should by no means hazard a general engagement, but contrive detailed skirmishes, as sharp and as frequent as he could, for the sake of practising the raw recruits, and giving them courage for a pitched battle: for they held the opinion that their former defeats were owing, as much as anything else, to the fact that they were employing troops newly levied and entirely untrained.[5]

The attribution of this piece of military theory to Aemilius Paullus in the weeks before Cannae might well be apocryphal, especially since the Romans did go on to give Battle at Cannae somewhat unadvisedly. The overall lesson, though, was indeed learned around this time and for the reason that Polybius writes, due to the string of defeats suffered by the Romans at the hands of Hannibal after his descent from the Alps and invasion into North Italy. By the time Polybius wrote, around the 150s BCE, it would have been established wisdom, and it would have been current military thought during the time that Ligustinus was in service from around 200 to 167 BCE.

The two reasons given for training of the recruits are significant. The first was to practise the recruits and give them time to develop the skills they would need. The second was to give them courage. Thus the training was intended to be practical, physical and psychological. A man trained to follow the standards needed to also have the confidence to remain in the battle line, while a man trained to wield the *gladius* needed the courage to thrust it into the flesh of his opponent. Skirmishing, or taking part in combats with fewer participants, or at a farther distance than pitched battle, would build both the recruits' skills and their confidence. This somewhat mirrors the current modern method of training armies by means of combat simulations, where the aim is to produce experiences as close to the real thing as can be achieved under controlled conditions.[6] For the Romans, the situations were real, and there were only so many ways that they could endeavour to control the conditions. One of these was to make sure that a soldier's first encounter was small scale. The other way was to introduce the soldier to combats from a distance using missile weapons, the primary offensive weapon of the *velites*.

Hispania Citerior 195 BCE

Polybius' account of the hastily mustered soldiers in 216 BCE details the practice of seeking out small engagements with the enemy for the explicit purpose of training the soldiers before they needed to be committed to a pitched battle. In less urgent situations, the soldiers could be trained through carrying out some of the army's early strategic objectives when they arrived in a new territory.

Some of these strategic objectives, like foraging or raiding, were well-suited to allowing the soldiers to gain gradual experience. Ligustinus would have been a part of an operation of this kind when he served as *primus hastatus prioris centuriae*, centurion of the prior century of the first maniple of *hastati*, for the commander M. Porcius Cato in Hispania Citerior in 195–4 BCE.[7]

We are told that in Spain Cato had two legions, 15,000 allies from the Latin confederacy, and 800 cavalry (Livy 33.43.3). It is not specified whether the citizen legions had been newly recruited or were transferred from another campaign, but it is certain that Cato thought them in need of training. This was started immediately upon arrival in Spain while the army was still near its debarkation point at the half-Spanish, half-Greek town of Emporiae. There were a number of tribes hostile to the Romans in Spain and they probably amounted to more soldiers than Cato possessed. At the time of the army's arrival it was harvest time in Spain, or, as Livy puts it in an account that most likely derives from a work of Cato himself, 'they had the grain on their threshing floor.'[8] Cato thus set his troops to plundering the countryside with the aim of obtaining these grain supplies, in order to monopolize the resources of the region at a time when they were especially vulnerable to attack.[9] These raiding parties could thus achieve a strategic objective while building the confidence of the new soldiers.

The fact that Roman soldiers were often trained in real military operations does not mean that no care was taken for what and how they learned. A fragment of one of Cato's own speeches attests to what his aims were for the soldiers during this the early part of his campaign in Spain:

> [Meanwhile] I was testing the capabilities of each squadron, maniple, and cohort in turn; in light engagements I was observing the quality of each man; if anyone had performed especially well I rewarded him fairly, so that others should wish to do the same, and before the assembled troops I praised him profusely.[10]

This fragment reveals some important aspects of the soldier's training. The mention of the squadron, *turma*, which was a group of cavalry, and then the maniple and cohort points to the fact that various sizes of units were used for different tasks during normal military operations. The cohort, according to Polybius, was the Roman name for three maniples operating together.[11] Cato was a contemporary of Polybius and his use of the word confirms that it was indeed in use at this period, although it was not the base unit of the legion as it would become by the end of the first century BCE, when it generally consisted of a maniple of *hastati*, a maniple of *principes*, and a maniple of *triarii* working together.[12] Although we do not know whether the cohort was mixed in this way at this time, the existence of a cohort as a unit shows that the soldiers would have had to learn, and so also practise, how to be a part of three maniples breaking from a line to form a cohort and act as an independent unit. Polybius explains this term as an aside during his description of action at the Battle of Ilipa, showing that maniples moving into cohorts was a manoeuvre that needed to be done during a pitched-battle situation. While Cato was testing the capabilities of his units, he would have been observing how well a cohort could move and fight together, as well as how the more standard units of the maniple performed.

The second observation to be made from this fragment of Cato is that the training that he implemented was designed to create a particular psychological effect. Just as Polybius wrote that building confidence was a concern of the generals in 216 BCE, a key component of a soldier's training in Spain was providing positive feedback for those who performed well in combat. Cato's description of praising the troops and offering them rewards for good performance is probably a reference to the *contio*, an assembly held after battles to reward soldiers for their individual courage. This practice was not unique to Cato, but the way he describes it implies that he was holding small and frequent assemblies after even minor engagements to reward soldiers who performed well. This would set a precedent for the rest of the campaign. Cato encouraged the soldiers to develop an expectation that anyone who engaged in these behaviours would be recognized and rewarded. Thus, the effect would have been to show that bravery could and did happen often among the soldiers, that it was encouraged, and that it was positively interpreted and appropriately rewarded. The intention was clearly to build confidence in the soldier's own abilities and highlight the positive qualities and reliability of his comrades.

When the *contio* was held after battles, the deeds of the soldiers that were being rewarded were described to the audience of soldiers. This made them instructional, as they showed examples of the kinds of behaviour that were particularly valued. As we saw in Chapter 1, there was a schematic component to these rewards, where particular items were awarded that corresponded to particular deeds. The most valued actions were aggressive and proactive ones, in which soldiers surged forward to seek out combat even when it was not strictly necessary. In the context of what Cato calls 'light engagements', a benefit for the young and inexperienced soldiers would have been that the achievements highlighted in these assemblies were manageable and realistic. They were deeds that had been done on that very campaign and by men that they could see. These were not the very dramatic deeds of legendary stories, in which a whole army was in crisis, but simpler acts of courage performed by living men. This would have given any new soldier a very clear idea of what was required of him and given promising soldiers an immediately positive and supportive response to performing actions that were valued.

Velites

While at the very beginning of new campaigns there was drilling and practice in movement, and on the job training in smaller and more-controlled combats, there were also skills unique to each of the divisions that had to be learned before the soldiers encountered any enemy soldiers at all. For the *velites*, there were three essential skills that a new *veles* might need to learn in order to be effective in his role. The *velites* were light-armed skirmishers, who frequently operated alongside the cavalry. They participated in small-scale clashes where speed was necessary. They also opened battles by attacking the enemy from a distance by throwing their spear, the *hasta velitaris*, literally the 'spear of the *velites*.' They were also supposed to be trained in combat with a sword so as to defend themselves if the enemy closed with them. Thus the three skills of the *velites* were:

- to quickly mount and dismount a horse behind its rider, while carrying a shield and javelins
- to throw the *hasta velitaris* using its attached leather loop
- to wield a sword and defend themselves in close combat.

It is not at all certain that each member of the *velites* would be required to be equally skilled in all three of these activities. It would make more sense for there to be some selectivity in the duties assigned to each *veles* according to where he showed the most talent or aptitude. Probably not all of the *velites* were suitable to fight with the cavalry, for example. Vegetius says that the Romans of the Middle Republic selected the 'swiftest runners' from the *velites* to accompany the cavalry, and Livy (quoted below) adds that they looked for agility. The necessity to have two adults on horseback, even temporarily, suggests that one would want to keep the weight low so as not to strain or injure the horse that carried them. Those chosen to work with the cavalry, as well as being the quickest, ought to also have been the lightest.[13]

Livy claims that the origin of the *velites* arose from an innovation of hard-pressed troops fighting near Capua in the Second Punic War in 211 BCE:

Young men of exceptional speed and agility were selected from all the legions and supplied with bucklers somewhat shorter than those used by the cavalry. Each was furnished with seven javelins, four feet long and tipped with iron heads similar to those on the darts of the *velites*. The troopers each took one of these upon his horse and trained them to ride behind and leap down briskly at a given signal. As soon as they came within range the signal was given and the *velites* sprang down to the ground. The line of infantry thus formed made a sudden attack on the Capuan horse; shower after shower of javelins was flung at the men and horses all along the line (Livy 26.4.4–7).

Despite what Livy states, this cannot be an accurate description of the origin of the *velites*, as he has mentioned this division in action many times earlier in the histories.[14] Rather, it might be the origin of the practice of using the *velites* in concert with the cavalry, which Livy also says was invented on this occasion by a centurion by the name of Quintus Navius. Livy's account does give us an idea about how this collaboration worked, and hence we can identify some skills that the *velites* working with the cavalry would have needed.

Firstly, they would have to learn how to quickly mount and dismount a horse behind its rider, and to balance while the horse was in motion. Horses have four different gaits, a walk, a trot, a canter and a gallop, in order of increasing speed. In a trot the rider typically 'posts' or 'rises' so as not to collide with the horse's up and down motion. In a canter or a gallop, the rider uses their legs to maintain a position above the horse's back to allow it to move uninhibited. A second rider would need to learn how to balance steadily during each of the horse's gaits, while not interfering with its motion or signalling an order to the horse by mistake. In turn, the horse would need to become accustomed to having two riders on its back.

As Livy writes, this skill was only mastered as the result of daily practice of *veles*, horse, and cavalryman. The *velites* picked for this duty would have spent time with cavalry riders and their horses, dressed in their tunics and carrying their equipment of several javelins and a small round shield. The aim would be to get used to how their arms and armour shifted in response to their necessary movements, how to mount and dismount with shield and weaponry in hand, and how to ride along with the horse. All of these would be basic competencies that needed to be learned before the pair could start engaging in skirmishing against real enemies.

This set of particular skills implies that certain members of the *velites* began their military journey with a significant amount of practice time with members of the cavalry. There was a distinct discrepancy of class between these two groups, since the *velites* were the youngest and poorest of Rome's citizens, and, as we have seen, those placed with the cavalry were perhaps even the youngest of those. The citizen cavalry, on the other hand, were largely the *domi nobiles*, the ruling families of towns and cities in Roman Italy that enjoyed Roman citizenship, and wealthy families in Rome itself. We have already observed that the tribunes were in daily contact with the ordinary men, and the relationship between the two units of the *velites* and the citizen cavalry suggests another area where two disparate classes were in regular contact and cooperation.

The second basic skill in which the *velites* needed training was how to throw the *hasta velitaris*, the light javelin. Famously, these had a metal tip which bent upon impact so that it could not be picked up and serve as a weapon for the enemy (Polyb. 6.22.4). This does not, however, seem to hold true, as the *hasta velitaris* was long and thin, and in experiments conducted with reconstructions, it was fairly easy to bend the tip back into shape.[15] There is evidence that this weapon was not readily available for use of the enemy for another reason, namely that it required practice to throw it properly. It could not simply be picked up, straightened out, and returned by anyone, or at the very least the distance it could be thrown from an inexperienced hand was nowhere near that of the trained *velites*. Livy specifically tells us that '[the *velites*'] weapon is unmanageable to return for the inexperienced.'[16] The reason for this is that it was not thrown by gripping the shaft and running forward to propel it using the strength of the arm, as is done in the sport of javelin throwing. Rather, it was thrown by use of an attached leather strap called the *amentum*. The exact mechanism of using these straps is rather mysterious, as no ancient source describes how to do it. Several enterprising archaeologists and historians, however, have conducted practical tests using replicas.[17] These have shown that there are a few ways to throw the *hasta velitaris* that result in a dramatically increased throwing distance. The leather strap is wrapped around the shaft, after which the javelin is thrown by being propelled by the strap using two fingers. All the experiments that tried the weapon with and without the *amentum* found that the distance and speed of the javelin was increased by its use.

The fact that the *hasta velitaris* required practice to be thrown properly is key to understanding its use as a weapon of the *velites* in particular and in the Roman system in general. The distance it could be thrown was more dependent on a skilled technique than the strength of the thrower.[18] The weapon was therefore well suited to the young, slight, and nimble *velites*, whose relative lack of strength could be overcome by technique. The damage rendered by a missile depends on the velocity with which it enters the body: the greater the speed, the greater the damage.[19] The skilled use of the *amentum* increased the velocity of the *hasta*, which in trials was shown to also increase the ability of the missile to puncture armour.[20] The *hasta velitaris* worked on the same principle as the heavier *pilum*, which was in fact designed to bend and resist being returned, and the *gladius*, used for a unique thrusting motion that was not the common use of most other swords. They were weapons which intended to be only truly effective in Roman hands and could not arm their enemies in a significant way if retrieved during a battle. Like learning to mount and dismount a horse with armour and weaponry, throwing the *hasta velitaris* was a skill that needed to be learned in safety before it could be practised with a real enemy.

The last of the three skills required of a *veles* was to learn how to wield a sword. The *veles* carried a smaller shield than a *hastatus* or *princeps* and so was not ideally suited for engaging in a hand-to-hand fighting with a sword, as was done by the heavy infantry, whose longer shields curled around their bodies and covered them from shoulder to ankle. Thus it would be prudent for the *velites* to avoid taking on any heavy infantry and a *veles* would not use his sword in a pitched battle unless other light infantry or the heavy infantry of the opposing line managed to close with him. This did happen: Livy says that in 189 BCE when fighting the Gauls, the *velites* bombarded their ranks with missile weapons, which caused some of them to rush at the ranks of the Romans. Livy writes specifically that it was the *velites* who slew these men with their swords and he adds the detail that they passed their javelins into their left hand in order to take the sword in their right (38.21.12–13). Thus sword training (described below) ought to have included the *velites* as well as the other ranks.

It is worth noting that there would have been spare time for the *velites* to receive informal training in swordplay, especially from the men in the heavy infantry part of their maniple. It would have been in everyone's best interests for the senior men to mentor, drill, and teach the *velites*. At the beginning of a new campaign, many of these youths would be brand new recruits to the legions. Helping them learn would have been especially pertinent for the maniples of *hastati*, who made up the first stationary line in a battle. Every maniple would have wished to boast the lightest, quickest and most vicious of the *velites*, who might be needed to cover their retreat or provide a break in the enemy line in front of them, and so it seems reasonable to speculate that the centurion and at least a few of the men who were inclined to teaching lent a hand to their development.

The *hastati* and *principes*

The shield

A recruit to the *hastati* needed to learn how to effectively fight with the shield, *pilum* and sword. The Roman technique of fighting hand-to-hand used the shield not just as a piece of defensive equipment, but also to push against the enemy and unbalance him, or as a weapon to hit him.[21] Livy describes such a usage during the Battle of Zama, when the Roman legionaries beat back the Carthaginians 'with their shoulders and the bosses of their shields' (Livy 30.34.3). Blows could be delivered either with the front face or the top edge. Polybius writes that shield of the Mid-Republican type, called the *scutum*, was rimmed in iron on the top and bottom edge, the top to protect against blows from a sword, and the bottom to preserve the shield from damage from being rested on the ground (Polyb. 6.23.4).

The first task of a trainer, then, was probably to accustom the recruit to the use of this shield. Polybius says that it was 4 by 2.5 Roman feet. A Roman shield of this type was found preserved in the Fayum region of Egypt.[22] It is oval and measures 128cm long and 63.5cm wide, dimensions broadly in line with those given by Polybius.[23] The recruit would grasp the shield in his left hand in an overhand grip using its handle, a horizontal bar in the middle of the back of the shield directly behind the boss. For the average 5′5″ Roman man, when his arm was hung straight with no bend in the elbow, the top of the oval would sit at his shoulder and the bottom at his ankle. This is both where the measurements would naturally cause it to fall, and how we see it depicted on two Mid-Republican monuments, the Altar of Domitius Ahenobarbus and the victory monument of Aemilius Paullus.

The recruit would be instructed to stand with his left foot forward and shown how to turn himself and his shield to meet the blows of an opponent. Practice would allow him to get used to the weight of the shield and, if the army had enough time, to develop the muscle in bicep, shoulder and back required to lift and lower the shield quickly using his overhand grip. This type of shield is thought to have weighed about 10kg.[24] Vegetius tells us that it was the habit of the ancients, by which he means the Romans long before his own time like our Mid-Republicans, to train the soldiers with equipment that was double the weight of their normal gear, so that they would find their own sword and shield light in comparison and become quicker and safer (Veg. *Mil.* 1.12).

The Pilum

The recruit had two more skills to learn along with his shield work, to throw a *pilum* and to fight with a sword. When Polybius describes Scipio's training of his troops at New Carthage in 210 BCE, he says that one day was allotted for weapons training, when the soldiers practised with swords and missile weapons (Polyb. 10.20.3). These were specifically practice weapons. Livy, in his version of these same events, calls the swords *rudes*, the Latin word for a wooden practice sword. He refers to the missile weapons as *praepilatus*, literally 'ball-topped.'[25] This means that they were blunted or fixed with a button like a modern fencing foil. Livy has taken this account from Polybius, who specifies that the swords were fixed with leather buttons, a technique wherein a piece of leather is placed over the point and tied on with string.[26]

While the *velites* were learning to throw the *hasta velitaris* in ways that increased its speed and distance, the *hastati* would have been practising how to throw their *pila* with force over short distances. The javelins of the *velites* were designed to whip down on an area of the enemy army in one big mass, but the *pila* were thrown directly at the front line of the opposing soldiers and would have required more accuracy. Polybius says that there were two types, light and heavy. They were the same length, but the heavy one, which could be either square or round, was thicker than the light (Polyb. 6.23.9–11). The iron parts of many *pila* dating to the Middle Republic survive and display variation in design, but the overall model is always the same, a javelin consisting of a wooden shaft attached to a long iron shank with a pointed head.[27]

As a missile weapon, the *pilum* was technically a weapon intended to be used at a distance, but it was not very much of a distance. Experiments with reconstructions of Mid-Republican type *pila* discovered that they could not be used at further than 25 metres. In addition, most of the types of head that the researchers tried could not penetrate the three-ply wood they had set up to mimic an enemy shield. Out of five tested, only one type, with a long, thin, pyramidal shaped head, would have gone through a shield and penetrated the man behind.[28] It seems that the ideal use of the *pilum* was not to thrust through a shield but rather to be targeted directly at flesh.

We can easily imagine our centurion trainer clarifying the objective of the *pilum* to the members of the *hastati*. For those who had recently been *velites*, he might explain that the purpose of their missile weapons was different now, not to generate many quick missiles raining down on a designated area, but a heavy weapon thrown at a chosen individual. He might have shown them how to aim the *pilum* at the body of a man charging towards him, teaching that, like someone with a modern gun, his best chance was to aim for centre mass, the torso, not the head. He might have shown how the *pilum* could be used to penetrate the chest of a cavalry horse or the side of an elephant, all things which could, and did, happen in combat. And he would have shown them how to throw from behind a shield, using its weight as a counterbalance to lean back and discharge it over the top without exposing his own body.[29]

The Sword

The Roman soldier's most famous weapon, of course, was the *gladius*, the type of sword which by the time of the Empire would become standard issue to all soldiers. The two most well-known types are the Mainz type and the Pompeii type from the first century CE, with the Mainz coming first chronologically and the Pompeii type its later evolution, a smaller sword in both breadth and length.[30] The gladius is characterized by its small size in comparison to most swords of the time, the fact that it was sharp on both edges of the blade, and in its use both as a cutting and thrusting weapon. The blades of the Mainz and Pompeii types vary from about 429mm to 644mm in length.[31] As a general rule of thumb, around 350 or 400mm to 550mm is a gladius, while around 600mm is a long sword or *spatha*.[32]

The swords used by the Mid-Republican soldiers and the wooden practice swords modelled after them were not the easily recognizable type of the Mainz and Pompeii *gladii*. The later Romans certainly believed that the standard sword of the Imperial army had come from Spain and termed it the *gladius Hispaniensis*, but the sources on the matter tell us only that it was adopted sometime during or after the Hannibalic war.[33] There are not many examples of the *gladius* securely attested as coming from a Republican context, but all of those known or suspected to be of Republican date are longer than the later models. The upshot of this is that in the Mid-Republican period, the soldier fighting before the Punic Wars would have had a *xiphos* type thrusting sword. Those fighting during or after the Punic Wars, in Ligustinus' time down to the end of the second century, would be more likely to have, not the imperial *gladius*, but its longer ancestor.[34] It was also possible to have something completely different. We should not, of course, forget that swords were passed down, taken from enemies on the battlefield, as well as ordered from local armouries on campaign, and thus were going to be very far from uniform in design and origin across the soldiers of the legions.

Since the swords that were in use were both cutting and thrusting weapons, the skills that the soldier needed to develop were both how to inflict cuts with the long edge of the blade and also how to thrust with the tip. In a battle, the *hastati* would throw a volley of *pila* and then close to fight with the sword. Although the thrusting ability of the *gladius* type sword is often emphasized, some of the iconography that belongs to the era clearly shows the soldier slashing with his sword from a drawn back arm. Such is the case in the victory monument of Aemilius Paullus from the mid second century, which depicts an infantry soldier with his right hand raised high above his head to deliver a blow.

When using a sword to slash, the target was often the face or neck, judging by the kinds of injuries that are indicated by both literary and archaeological sources. The eyes were frequent sites of injury, and we hear of many combatants from commanders to ordinary soldiers who had lost one eye. A little later than our era, during the Social War of 90–88 BCE, the commander Sertorius lost an eye from a blow sustained through being at the forefront of a battle (Plut. *Sert.* 4.2); according to Caesar, four of his centurions lost eyes during the siege of Dyrrachium in the Civil War against other Roman soldiers (Caes. *BCiv.* 3.45.4). It would have been difficult to land a killing blow directly, so the Romans would have been taught a two-part process. The first move was to deliver a sharp blow to the head in order to stun the opponent, and in the second, to take advantage of his momentary confusion in order to cause a fatal wound. This was why the face was such a common target. A cut or slash of an arm or leg would cause a man to flinch, and while he might pull back momentarily or fold his body towards the wound, it might not halt the momentum of his attack. A powerful blow to the head was better because it could momentarily stun, or, since head-wounds are painful and bleed profusely, was likely to make the man stop due to pain or interference with his vision.[35]

One tactic used by the Romans was to fight by pushing in close to their opponents, closer than most fighters of their times expected. Polybius tells us that in the battle against the Insubres, the Romans came in so close to their Gaulish opponents that the Gauls did not have the room to use their swords, which were used by means of a slashing motion. In this case the second type of sword use would have come into play, which is also shown on the monument of Aemilius Paullus, a stab or thrust from an arm held level rather than swung up high. The technique in this case is described by Dionysius of Halicarnassus:

> While their foes were still raising their swords aloft, they would duck under their arms, holding up their shields, and then, stooping and crouching low, they would render vain and useless the blows of the others, which were aimed too high, while for their own part, holding their swords straight out, they would strike their opponents in the groins, pierce their sides, and drive their blows through their breasts into their vitals. And if they saw any of them keeping these parts of their bodies protected, they would cut the tendons of their knees or ankles and topple them to the ground roaring and biting their shields and uttering cries resembling the howling of wild beasts. (Dion. Hal. *Ant. Rom.* 14.10.2)

The Greek historian Dionysius wrote this in the first century BCE in reference to the time of the dictator Camillus some three centuries before, and its description is likely to be more accurate to his own day than the fourth century, which, as we have seen, pre-dates the use of the *gladius*. It is, however, very similar to depictions of Roman soldiers on the Adamclisi monument, dating to 109 CE, several of whom are shown attacking with underhand stabbing motion. One, on metope 32, is shown with his shield held high against his enemy's face as he stabs underhanded. This is much like Livy's description of the Romans using their shields to strike at the enemy (30.34.3) and suggests that over time, the method of using the shield to create space for a sword thrust became standard Roman practice. Vegetius tells us that a thrust was deadlier than a slash and harder for the enemy to see it coming, considerations that would have added to its popularity (*Mil.* 1.12).

Despite its distance from the events it describes, Dionysius' rendering of the Romans' fighting technique rings true in a number of aspects. The first move is a defensive one, to catch the blow of the opponents' slashing sword with the shield. The alternative move suggested by Livy was to smash the shield suddenly and violently upwards, into an opponent's head or jaw if possible. We know this happened in Greek hoplite warfare and that a hard enough blow from the rim of a shield could inflict considerable blunt-force trauma.[36] When facing a soldier wearing a helmet, the upward force of a shield would be a more effective hit than a downward slash of a sword that met with the protection of metal. As the enemy staggered or reeled in shock, the soldier thrust with the *gladius*. The ideal finish was to drive the sword up under the ribs and cut into one of the vital organs in the chest cavity. Another common target, just as when using the sword to slash, was the face and eyes, as Polybius writes about the Romans battling Celts 'striking one blow after another on the breast or face' (Polyb. 2.33.6).

It is most likely that the centurions who trained and drilled the soldiers had no real preference for teaching their soldiers to thrust over teaching them an effective slash, even though the deadly thrusting ability of the *gladius* seems to have become a Roman signature in later centuries. Vegetius says that the recruits in ancient times were taught 'not to cut but to thrust with their swords' (*Mil.* 1.12) but in the Mid-Republican era, when the sword types were still longer than the classic *gladius* of the Empire, slashing must have been commonplace. It is doubtful that an infantryman delivering a slashing blow would be depicted on an idealized monument like that of Aemilius Paullus at Delphi if the Romans were at that time actively trying to train their soldiers out of that technique.

The trainers would have been concerned to impress upon their infantrymen the need to avoid any blow to the head that would make them vulnerable. Vegetius tells us that in the training of the 'ancients' the recruit was 'above all particularly cautioned not to lay himself open to his antagonist while aiming his stroke at him' (*Mil.* 1.11). They were taught also to act fast, as any attack with the sword endangered the right hand, arm and side. Working with the heavier practice equipment was designed to make them quicker in the striking movement and thus safer. The whole technique would have been to try to go in hard and fast, aiming straight for vitals or sensitive areas like the face, with the object of stunning or felling the individual quickly and delivering a killing blow. A blow from a shield and a thrust with the *gladius* into the abdominal cavity would become the professional ideal, but, as Dionysius' account indicates, in the citizen legions of the third and second centuries, a slash to the knees or legs would do just fine.

Chapter 7

On Campaign with a Mid-Republican Army

Macedonia, 200–199 BCE

D uring his first two years of service in Macedonia as a member of the *velites*, one of Ligustinus' primary duties would have been taking part in low-level skirmishing. As we have seen, this was done partly as training and partly to secure strategic objectives, especially in areas that were new campaigns, as Macedon was in 200 BCE. In the first two years there was plenty of this type of fighting to be done, according to Plutarch, who wrote a biography of the third commander to take over this army, Titus Flamininus. Of this command he writes,

> Titus learned that the generals who had preceded him in this field, first Sulpicius, and then Publius Villius, had invaded Macedonia late in the season, had prosecuted the war slowly, and had wasted time in manoeuvring for position or in long-range skirmishes with Philip to secure roads and provisions (Plut. *Flam.* 3.1–2).

This brief account of two years of campaigning hints at something that also occurs in the accounts of the historians of antiquity, who assigned importance to military events in a very different way to how actually living through these years must have seemed to soldiers like Ligustinus. The historians typically show a great deal of interest in set-piece battles, particularly those that were decisive of a war or campaign, while a mere sentence or two often suffices to record a great multitude of other operations. In describing events of the early years in Macedon, Livy describes some combats as being 'like a real battle' with the implication that these engagements were too insignificant to rise to that title. He uses it to describe the numbers of King Philip's army during an encounter near Acathus in 200 BCE, writing that there were so many infantry and cavalry that it was *prope iusta acies*, 'nearly a real battle-line' (31.37.3). Just after Flamininus had come to take over the army and was still deciding whether to try to take the pass at the River Apsus or go round a more circuitous route, the army forced Philip's forces to retreat up a hill. Many were wounded, writes Livy, *ut in proelio iusto*, 'just like in a proper battle' (32.10.12).

As a result of these historical accounts that give a great deal of prominence to decisive battles, it is very difficult to come away with an accurate impression of how soldiers spent their time. Ligustinus was in fact in his fourth year under his third commander before he entered a battle that turned out to be decisive, at Cynoscephalae in 197 BCE. Despite Plutarch, or Flamininus, branding these first years as 'wasted time' there was a need to complete specific objectives first, to create a safe road behind the army, to make sure there was adequate food and water for the soldiers and the animals, and to gain advantageous positioning. Nor did an enemy leader generally accept a pitched battle very readily, for to commit a whole force was extremely risky. This was the case in Macedon, for although we are told that on several occasions Sulpicius sent out the legions to offer battle to Philip's army, none of these offers were accepted.

For many soldiers, some battles or encounters that are passed over in the sources would have been longer, harder or more dramatic for them personally than the decisive pitched battles. When that day came, it could easily have been the one in which they were left to guard the camp or placed in a reserve unit. In the very early days of campaigns, soldiers were still trying to prove themselves. We saw Cato give rewards during the early days of his campaign in Hispania Citerior while he was still testing his units. When describing the Roman awards system, Polybius writes that certain awards were reserved for those who had voluntarily put themselves in danger 'during skirmishes or in similar circumstances' (Polyb. 6.39.4). This may hint that a higher proportion of combat was actually done in smaller units than in situations that involved the entire army. Many soldiers, perhaps the majority, will have won their renown, rewards and promotions in this form of fighting rather than in the battle line. As skirmishing and combat with smaller units allowed the soldier more choice about his level of involvement, the more proactive and violent of the soldiers could use these early engagements to distinguish themselves.

The army had gone into winter quarters at Apollonia shortly after its arrival in Illyria. When it emerged in the spring, Sulpicius marched it north along the coast and camped at the River Apsus. Here he turned a large part of the army over to his legate L. Apustius, for reasons we are not given by Livy, but the later historian Zonoras writes that it was because Sulpicius was ill at this time (9.15.3–4). We are not told exactly what proportion went on this expedition and what proportion were left to guard the camp. For those who accompanied Apustius, their introduction to the campaign proper was abrupt and violent. Livy, however, does not go into much detail about the expedition:

Apustius, having plundered the frontiers of Macedonia and having captured at the first assault the towns of Corrhagum, Gerronius and Orgessum, arrived at Antipatrea, a city situated in a narrow pass. There he first summoned the leading men to a conference and tried to induce them to put themselves under Roman protection; then, when they scorned his suggestions, relying on the size and walls and site of the city, he stormed and captured it by force of arms and killing all the men of military age and giving the booty to the soldiers he tore down the walls and burned the city (31.27.2–4).

The first part of this description, 'having plundered the frontiers' implies activity in the fields and farmland, especially since Livy shows that it was a separate action from attacking the towns. It essentially means moving through the countryside, taking grain, crops and animals. Buildings would have been searched for any valuables, although there was probably little to find in these rural spaces. Any inhabitants were most likely to have simply fled when they heard of the advancing army, as there was no hope of defending themselves. Even the inhabitants of larger towns sometimes simply chose to flee, as Livy writes about events a little later in the year, when the army marched through the lands of the Dassaretii. Livy writes that as they did so,

> Some of the towns and villages on his [Sulpicius'] route surrendered voluntarily, others through fear, some were taken by storm, others were found to be abandoned, the inhabitants having fled to the neighbouring mountains (31.33.5).

These descriptions show us that the towns responded with various degrees of defiance. The three towns that Livy mentions as being captured on Apustius' route are otherwise unknown to us and so we have no details of their size or population. That they were captured after being attacked suggests that the inhabitants put up some sort of defence, thus the towns were likely large enough settlements to have walls, without which an attempted defence would be hopeless. In order to attack a fortified town or city, the army had a choice of approach. They could either try to break in through engineering, by undermining or destroying the walls and building siege towers and earthen ramps, or they could launch a direct assault using ladders and manpower.[1] For these towns that fell on the first assault, probably little of the engineering work was necessary.

Before attempting to assault a town, the Romans usually built their camp close by. This was partly as intimidation, and partly because the assault on a town required men to be freshly rested and highly motivated.[2] The Romans' high level of organization and the swift and efficient way in which they built their camp could convey to the defenders that they were both determined and formidable.

The legions would then deploy outside the walls in order to show strength and frighten the inhabitants. Livy's list of the possible responses to the arrival of the Romans probably refers to the different stages of capitulation, first abandonment before the Romans approached, then surrendering voluntarily, surrendering through fear, and finally taken by storm. The first towns who surrendered 'voluntarily' probably opened their gates to the Romans and surrendered at their initial contact before any military action could be taken. Others who surrendered 'through fear' may have initially intended to stay behind their walls but surrendered when they saw the number of the Roman soldiers or witnessed the beginnings of siege preparations. The fate of these towns is unknown, but in general the Romans would take only goods from such cities, like supplies, animals, and valuables, and leave the rest of the town and its inhabitants untouched. They usually refrained from unleashing violence upon settlements that surrendered, on the general principle that future towns, cities and peoples should be encouraged by example to give in without resisting.[3]

The next step in the assault of towns was a testing stage, firstly with the exchange of missile weapons and then by a trial assault. The *velites* could have been employed here as the only Roman infantry with missile weapons capable of reaching up and over the walls. The tactic of discharging a volley of missiles that whipped down on one area in a mass could be used to try to thin the defenders at the walls. Apustius had probably also taken the Cretan archers that accompanied the army in Macedon for just such a purpose, to pick off the defenders or deter them from releasing their own missiles from the walls.

When the general had determined to make an assault on the town, he and any senior officers he had accompanying him would decide where to assign units, to walls, gates, and any vulnerable spots that the army might have found. Storming a city was particularly dangerous for soldiers because of the defence of the walls by inhabitants using missile weapons and other improvised projectiles like stones and roof tiles, which they could launch down at the invaders while remaining in relative safety themselves. The armies of this period typically had a particular style of approach to the assault of a town, because, unlike a pitched battle where all the soldiers were required to be in a particular formation, the storming of towns needed a group of men to lead the assault who were aggressive and fearless. For this reason, the vanguard of such assaults were always volunteers in one of two different senses, either overt volunteers who voiced their willingness to lead beforehand, or aggressive soldiers who naturally surged to the front while others hung back.[4]

Despite the fact that mounting a wall against defenders was very dangerous, there were always men who were willing to do so. Polybius writes that during the Roman siege of New Carthage in 209 BCE, 'the front ranks advanced confidently to mount the ladders' (10.13.6). Some of these ladders broke because of the weight of the men or were broken by defenders, while some of the attacking soldiers grew dizzy from the height and fell. Despite this, 'nothing could restrain the dash and fury of the Romans, but while the first scalers were still falling the vacant places were instantly taken by the next in order' (10.13.10). There were certainly incentives to do so. We saw earlier an especially privileged place in the system of rewards for acts that displayed proactive behaviour, for seeking out danger when it was not strictly necessary. There was a rich reward offered to 'the first man to mount the wall at the assault on a city', a crown of gold (Polyb. 6.39.5). Even for those who were less proactive, any valuables found inside the town would be distributed among the soldiers as booty, or sold and the money distributed, ensuring that there was a benefit to the army as a whole.

Even though the potential rewards were high, we are still told by our sources that not every soldier was motivated by them. There was a natural variance in behaviour by temperament that meant that while some soldiers were eager to climb the ladders to the walls, others hung back or seemed afraid. This was Sallust's interpretation of the soldiers at the siege of Zama in 109 BCE, who displayed a kind of stratification of military behaviour:

> The Romans fought according to their temperament, some standing off and slinging stones or bullets, others charging up to the wall and trying to dislodge it or climb it with ladders because they were eager for hand-to-hand combat ... Even those who were fearful and unwilling to go near the walls did not escape without injury, for they were hit by spears thrown by hand or launched from machines; thus the danger, although not the glory, was shared by the good men and fearful men alike (Sall. *Iug.* 57.4.6).[5]

Today, perhaps, we would not be happy to label the men who attacked eagerly as 'good' in opposition to those who were not so enamoured of climbing the walls to seek out combat. Sallust's evaluation of these men's characters is reflective of the prevailing Roman opinion about how men should behave in warfare. It was apparently not so easy to live up to these expectations when one was actually in that situation. One further consideration is that Sallust portrays it as just as dangerous to hang back as to try to climb the wall and fight the defenders, which is manifestly not the case, as we learn from other sources, and even at other points in Sallust's own work.[6] It was more dangerous to be proactive than to hang back, and in addition to a stratification by natural temperament, each soldier had to make his own judgment about how much he valued the potential rewards of wealth, glory, and social advancement against the risks he was willing to take.

In the case of the first three towns taken on Apustius' expedition, we are not told what was done with the town or its inhabitants. It may be that the fact that the towns were captured was all that was conveyed in the general's records from his campaign and thus all the information that was available to the historians. From the general habits of the Romans of this era in storming towns, we can surmise that the scene was not a happy one. At the very least, the men of the town who were actively defending it would have been killed as the Roman soldiers swarmed over the wall. The treatment of the town may then have depended on the strength of the opposition they had put up or how quickly they surrendered.

We have a little more detail, but not much, about the treatment of the town of Antipatrea. About it, Livy writes, 'he [Apustius] stormed and captured it by force of arms and killing all the men of military age and giving the booty to the soldiers, he tore down the walls and burned the city (31.27.4).' Antipatrea apparently had better defences and was better situated than the three previous towns, a fact which had caused its inhabitants to scorn surrender in the first place. The storming of it was thus probably more labour intensive and may have involved forcing the gates or building siege towers. After the soldiers had taken the town, the aftermath seems to have been correspondingly more violent. The particular elements of Antipatrea's fate were things that were ordered by the commander, in line with the same rule of thumb that we saw earlier, that the degree of defiance corresponded to the degree of violence unleashed upon the town upon its capture.

The order to kill all men of military age would have been carried out in several stages. First was the combat stage, where the men would have been killed defending their city as the Roman soldiers breached the walls. The second stage was after the breach had been accomplished and the soldiers were inside the city. This part of the storming was often particularly violent, and on many occasions the Romans are known to have killed not only armed defenders but anyone else who crossed their path. An example is Polybius' description of the seizure of New Carthage in 209 BCE:

When Scipio thought that a sufficient number of troops had entered he sent most of them, as is the Roman custom, against the inhabitants of the city with orders to kill all they encountered, sparing none, and not to start pillaging until the signal was given. They do this, I think, to inspire terror, so that when towns are taken by the Romans one may often see not only the corpses of human beings, but dogs cut in half, and the dismembered limbs of other animals, and on this occasion such scenes were very many owing to the numbers of those in the place (10.15.4–6).

The Romans had seized New Carthage from the Carthaginians, a particularly bitter foe who had invaded their own lands and cities, doubtless adding to the vehemence of the slaughter there. In cities like Antipatrea, the violence was strategic, aimed primarily at males of military age because they posed the greatest threat to the soldiers.[7] This does not mean that no one else was killed in this initial stage, as they certainly would have been, the violence of the sack, as Polybius says, being used as a deterrent to other places mounting their own opposition.

The sources emphasize two distinct stages of the capture of a town, this initial storming that was intended to eliminate any active opposition and force the townspeople to submit, and a stage after when the signal was given for pillaging.[8] The pillaging stage was when the soldiers were released into the city to take whatever valuables they could find. Soldiers broke into houses and temples to seize valuables including coins, weapons, and anything made of precious metals. If the whole population had surrendered, the people would be rounded up and taken as prisoners. If they had not, then what to do with the people they came across would have been up to the discretion of the soldiers who found them. Able-bodied adults and children could be captured as potential slaves, but they were also sometimes killed or raped. Older people were more likely to be killed because they were unsuitable to be sold as slaves and so were, in the eyes of their attackers, worthless.[9]

Those who were taken prisoner were usually sorted into various groups at the order of the commander. Some were turned over to the quaestor to be sold into the slave trade, possibly via the *lixae* accompanying the army, or taken directly to be public slaves of the Romans. Some were allowed to go free, perhaps depending on their status, as, for example, the citizens of New Carthage were allowed to return to their homes (Polyb. 10.17.6–8). Others were executed, especially if they were the ruling leaders of the town that had defied the Romans, or, as in this case, an order had been given to kill all the men of military age.

A skeleton from Cerro de la Cruz, in modern day Córdoba in Spain, gives us a vivid illustration of what might have happened to the people of stormed towns. This area was called Lusitania in the second century BCE when the Romans fought there, where the resistance was led by a native named Viriathus. During the course of this war the Romans sacked several towns that had been loyal to Viriathus, of which Cerro de la Cruz was probably one. In the archaeological remains of this town, in the street were found two skeletons dating from the period. One had had his foot nearly severed at the ankle and his thigh cut, the other had a sharp injury to the spine. All of these injuries had been inflicted by a *gladius*. Most tellingly, the second individual, a male in his twenties, had a large cut almost completely through his right shoulder blade. This was most likely from a *gladius* swung to behead him that had missed and sliced instead through the bone of his shoulder. It seems clear that these two men had died after being attacked on the street by Roman soldiers who had used their swords to first cripple, and then kill them.[10]

Some of the men in the town of Antipatrea, who were not cut down by the initial onslaught or during the pillaging phase, would have been rounded up and executed, most probably by beheading. This was the customary form of Roman execution, used for prisoners and criminals alike. It would always have involved some degree of organization to kill a group of people that was relatively large, like the military-aged male population of a town. Prisoners were usually bound by the soldiers before being taken to a particular place for execution by men designated for the purpose, where they were made to bend or kneel and beheaded using an axe or, as at Cerro de la Cruz, the *gladius*.[11]

Once the pillaging stage was over, and the human population of the town had been sorted according to their fates, there would normally be further orders pertaining to the physical structure of the town. Livy writes that at Antipatrea the commander 'tore down the walls and burned the city'. The general aim in sacking towns and cities was to leave them permanently or semi-permanently unable to regroup themselves. The population was vastly reduced, either through mass executions or through the enslavement of large groups. The walls were destroyed so that it would take a very long time for the town to mount an effective defence of itself again. Similarly, the burning was probably intended to make the town uninhabitable or very difficult to inhabit without significant rebuilding.

The destruction of a whole town or a city like Antipatrea would have been quite labour intensive. The Romans could use entrenching equipment to pull down walls, which were usually made of stone, or they could use siege equipment to ram them, or undermine them until they collapsed. The wall would need to be destroyed in a number of key places to discourage rebuilding. Similarly, the buildings that were destroyed within the city were burned, as Livy specifies. Sometimes the Romans put each house to the torch as they took out the plunder, but it is unlikely that they took care to burn every building. Instead, key targets would be picked out, like granaries, arsenals and temples. Some of these would burn well when set alight, while others would need to be stacked with kindling and their walls demolished if they did not burn sufficiently well.[12]

Polybius tells us that in the aftermath of the sack of New Carthage, as night fell and the guards began to be placed, that the *velites* were summoned from the camp to the city (10.15.10). These men had apparently been excluded from both the storming of the city and its sack. This was likely to have been a typical Roman practice, for a number of reasons. Firstly, the *velites* fought primarily via missile weapons, which as we saw were useful for the beginning exchange of volleys with the defenders, but not while storming the town. The assault on the walls was done by soldiers armed with swords and required close fighting, not distance weapons. Secondly the *velites* had a smaller shield than the other divisions and no pectoral, meaning that they had a more limited ability to defend themselves at close quarters than the other divisions. Finally, the *velites* were young and inexperienced. Assaults on towns were often done in the first stages of campaigns when many of the *velites* would have been brand new recruits with no experience of an enemy or warfare at all. Both the level of danger and the level of violence present on those occasions were likely judged unsuitable for beginners.

After Apustius' expedition had finished the destruction of Antipatrea, the soldiers were taken back to the camp of the consul and the whole army started to move through the countryside together. At this point there had been no specific activity in which we know the *velites* took part. Just as happened in Spain and at the beginning of Apustius' expedition, we can assume that they took part in the foraging and pillaging of farms and buildings in the countryside, most of which would have been unopposed. The men on the expedition had stormed several cities, but the *velites* were likely to have taken little part in these events. Apustius' train was attacked on the march on the way back to the consul's camp, fighting that might have involved some *velites*, but Livy passes over it in a sentence and it is very hard to say how many men Apustius had with him, let alone what proportion were *velites* or how many were involved in this fight. The army had not yet located the main defensive force that they expected to encounter, the army of King Philip of Macedon. There was a cavalry clash when these units from both armies were sent out as scouts, but no *velites* are mentioned as being present. Subsequently, the two armies learned the location of the other through deserters.

Livy tells us that when the armies learned of each other's location, King Philip moved his army about a mile away from the Roman camp, and then neither side moved for two days. This was to turn into what was a typical sequence for armies of this time period, consisting of waiting, offering battle, and manoeuvring for advantage. Committing to a pitched battle was a very serious undertaking. A battle could end indecisively if no side really gained an advantage and nightfall broke up the fighting. It could also potentially end in a rout and disaster for one side or the other, so it was not unusual in the ancient world for battle to be offered and declined repeatedly over days or weeks, as each side was only willing to commit when it saw advantageous conditions for itself.

Thus far there had been very little action for a *veles* with this particular army. The first action of the campaign that we know for certain involved the *velites* was a skirmish between a force of Roman *velites* and cavalry and King Philip's forces. The Romans had moved their entire army out of camp as a means of offering battle, but instead of sending out his whole army to meet them, Philip sent out a contingent of light infantry and some cavalry. These were specified to be Tralles from Illyria, about whom we know very little, and Cretan archers, contingents of which served on both sides of this war.[13] In response the Romans sent about an equal number of cavalry and their own light-armed infantry, the *velites*:

> The king's forces assumed that the type of fighting would be that to which they were accustomed, that the cavalry, alternately advancing and retreating, would now discharge their weapons and then retire, that the swift movements of the Illyrians would be useful for sallies and sudden charges, and that the Cretans would shower arrows upon the enemy advancing in disorder. The Roman attack, no more vigorous than stubborn, prevented the carrying out of this plan; for just as if they were in regular line of battle, both the skirmishers [*velites*], after hurling their spears, came to a hand-to-hand combat with their swords, and the cavalry, as soon as they had charged the enemy, stopping their horses either fought from horseback or leaped from their saddles and fought mingled with the footmen. So neither the king's cavalry, unused to a stationary battle, could stand against the Romans, nor his infantry, running to and fro and almost unprotected by armour, against the light-armed Romans, equipped with shield and sword and prepared alike for defence or offence. So they did not sustain the struggle, but relying on nothing else than their swiftness of foot they fled to the camp (Livy 31.35.5–7).

This incident is the first of a sequence of several in which Livy writes that the Romans engaged in a miniature version of a battle situation, with the *velites* discharging their spears and then closing to fight with swords. Although he specifically names the light-armed troops as *velites*, the actions that they took were the same sequence as taken by a line of *hastati* before they closed with an enemy front line in a pitched battle situation; they hurled their *pila* at the enemy first and then came to close quarters. The cavalry here seem to be following the same model, in fact they confuse the enemy by fighting like infantrymen rather than using the traditional advance and retreat of the cavalry. The Roman general had countered like with like, ordering out light-armed infantry and cavalry to meet the light-armed infantry and cavalry that had been advanced by Philip, and in about equal number. Upon reaching their opponents, neither Roman unit had used the usual tactics employed by their type in the ancient world, and instead had forced their way in close to their counterparts on foot like heavy infantry.

This type of skirmishing reminds us of the training quality of some of the earliest operations in a campaign. The difference between the light and the heavy infantry was their weight and hence their movement. As observed earlier, those distinguished for skirmishes were those who pressed forward when they did not have to, emphasizing that in light infantry engagements the soldiers had much more freedom to move. Although their technique sounds much like the technique of the front lines of *hastati*, unlike that division they had no standards or rules about keeping to a certain line and could break backwards or forwards more easily.[14] In other words, they fought at close quarters with a sword, but more independently than the *hastati*, so that they had the option to retreat or run if they felt the need.

Skirmishing as a form of training at the same time as for strategic objectives was still extremely dangerous, but it is easy to see how it could be used to build the soldier's psychological resilience. During his first encounters with the enemy he was not bound to the spot, as he would be later in a battle line, but rather had an escape. Matched against similarly lightly-armed infantry, he would not be at a significant disadvantage. The progression of the military experience of the *velites* can be seen in the first activities of the Romans in Macedon and in Spain, and their activities do seem to be quite subdued in these early phases. The storming of cities came first, in which they were not required to participate or only participated in the preliminary stages that involved the exchange of missiles.

On Apustius' expedition, which was only an early and quite small part of the whole campaign in Macedon, the soldiers took three towns at the first assault and successfully besieged a fourth that was apparently larger and better defended. The commander of Ligustinus' second army, M. Porcius Cato, boasted that he had captured more towns than he had spent days in Spain (Plut. *Cat. Mai.* 10.3). Plutarch adds that the captured towns were supposed to have numbered more than 400. Although this must be an exaggeration, similar to other seemingly-aggrandized details that stem from Cato's own account of his exploits in Spain, it does give us some idea of the large amount of time that the armies spent moving through the country taking settlements.

If, as we suspect, the *velites* did not have a large role in storming towns and cities, then their military activities at these times would have been as guards, as Scipio had used them at New Carthage, first to protect the camp and then further as guards stationed to protect the city after it had been taken. Guard duty was a large part of the *velites'* role as part of their routine when in camp. Their first actions outside of this were to engage in foraging or raiding in the countryside and in scouting activities with the cavalry. They might also, either as a result of scouting or while another army was in the vicinity, take part in a small-scale combat with similar contingents from the enemy army.

Their fairly subdued amount of activity and their lack of independence as a unit, operating either with the cavalry or the heavy infantry, suggests that their purpose was less tactical than intended to acclimatize new and young recruits to army life. A young *veles* would strike his first opponent from a distance, either in a small group or as part of a barrage of missile weapons when this happened in pitched battle. He could be required to fight at close quarters with a sword, but in a small-scale encounter where he was able to retreat or commit himself only when he felt confident. Otherwise, the youngest soldiers spent their time performing guard duties, learning how to deploy with the whole army, and in foraging and pillaging. That the *velites* did not have any crucial tactical function ought not to surprise us, for as we will see in the regard for religious practices, the army often conducted itself the way that it did for other considerations than tactical efficiency.

The notion that the *velites* were held back from the storming of cities but gradually acclimatized to combat through small-scale skirmishes can be related back to the stratification of behaviour that we saw in the descriptions of sieges. In those situations, there was real need for men willing to engage in hazardous behaviour, who wished to take on a higher level of risk in anticipation of a higher level of reward, and violent behaviour – men who were willing or eager to cut down citizens and execute people in groups. In the *velites*, those who pushed forward and assumed risk were also rewarded and distinguished. It is possible that serving in the *velites* operated as a kind of audition, where the best and boldest could prove themselves for admission to the *hastati*. Those happy to engage with an enemy, to be proactive and to be violent would always have a place in the legions.

Although we are told that the citizen army required service from every able-bodied citizen, and we know that it certainly did during times of crisis, by the second century there was an increased scope for men to self-select into longer service with the military. We have already seen the preference for volunteers over men brought in through the draft and the fact that there was a reluctance to press into service those who did not wish to go. This certainly matches up with the picture we get from Polybius that the army reward structure specifically incentivised fearlessness and eagerness for combat. The logical conclusion is that the tribunes who organized the legions did not wish to enrol just anyone, but rather eager soldiers who were more effective in the type of undertakings that made up the majority of the active combat time on campaigns, not fighting battles *per se* but skirmishing and storming towns. It is possible that the strongest argument for being included into the legions, even if a citizen was impoverished, was not in fact social connections or having the appropriate equipment, but having a reputation for being fearless and violent.

One further conclusion we can draw from looking at the early activities of a campaign is that there was variety among the experiences of the soldiers, because different groups were regularly sent to do different tasks. At the beginning of the Macedonian campaign a thousand infantry soldiers had been sent with the fleet to Athens, where they breached the city of Chalcis and, similarly to the events at Antipatrea, killed any men of military age (Livy 31.23.1–8). We did not follow the story of these particular soldiers but, like the men on Apustius' expedition, their first significant actions involved storming cities rather than combat against an enemy army. Meanwhile a division of the Romans stayed camped with the consul in Epirus, remaining in one camp for months with perhaps only guard and foraging duties. The division that went with the legate Apustius took three towns, then Antipatrea, received the surrender of Codrio, where a garrison was left, and took another town named Cnidus. They were then attacked on their way back to the consul's camp and engaged in combat with a contingent of the Macedonians. Although the majority returned to the consul, some men were left to garrison Codrio. We hear nothing else about this town or its garrison. The men left there might have been citizens or allies, or a mixture. It is worth noting, however, that the mention of garrisons shows us what some men's war looked like: a long journey to a foreign land, a short period with a moving expedition as it assaulted a handful of towns, and then a long period stationed in one town, with perhaps no further direct participation in the campaign.

Life in Camp

All of the soldiers, whether they went with the expedition to Athens, the one to Antipatrea or if they stayed with the consul in Epirus, would have spent a significant amount of time in the army's camp. There, duties were assigned according to the soldiers' divisions, and were especially onerous at night. The Roman camp seems to have operated on the principle that at any given time during the night, a quarter of the men were awake and on watch. There were four watches of the night, which were marked by the sound of a bugle, the *bucina*. The *primi pili*, the 'first spear' centurions were responsible for making sure the watches were sounded, although the actual sound was made by a bugle-player, the *buccinator*.[15] The number of men on watch seems a high proportion, but the evidence rests between the testimony of Polybius and the archaeological evidence of Roman winter camps, which points to there being barely enough room to fit six men in a tent, and never eight.[16] In effect the only way there was space in the small tents for soldiers to sleep was if a quarter of them were away at all times. As we will see, this causes us to have to account for a very high number of guard stations throughout the camp.

The *velites* were given guard duty around the perimeter of the camp, at the *vallum*. As we have seen from the making of the camp, this was neither high nor solid, but rather made of intertwined stakes that were hard to separate, at the top of an earthen mound with a ditch below it. The *veles* would have stood just behind this wooden wall, 240ft from the line of tents behind him, watching and listening for anything unusual in the darkness beyond the camp. Polybius does not specify how far apart the soldiers were posted or how many were assigned to each station. Elsewhere in the camp, guards who protected the tribunes' tents and the *quaestorium* were stationed in groups of four, but whether the *velites* were placed in groups along the wall or strung out in a row is not known. Ten *velites* stood on guard at each entrance.

The number of *velites* guarding the camp at any one time was quite high. If we use the numbers that correspond to the evidence of the archaeological remains of the camps at Numantia, as we have done so far, and consider a legion's strength of *velites* to be 1,280, that gives us a total of 2,560 *velites* for the 2 legions in a consular camp. A quarter of these on duty during each watch of the night is 640 men, from which we need to take away 60, counting 10 for each of 6 gates. That leaves 580 *velites* ringing the rest of the perimeter of the camp, which was, in the single-consular camp as reconstructed, a total of 10,920ft around. A very rough calculation gives us 1 *veles* per 18 feet, or perhaps a round number of about 1 every 20 feet.[17]

The reason that even a rough number like this is useful is that it helps to illustrate what the *velites* were looking for. They were not there to watch for a large-scale attack, although those did happen on occasion. They were rather watching out for individuals or small groups of men attempting to infiltrate the camp, either for the purpose of assassination or espionage. Livy writes that in 297 BCE a force of Samnites at war with the Romans snuck up to one of their camp gates at twilight in some heavy fog. After slaying the soldiers keeping a careless guard and entering the camp and *quaestorium*, they killed the quaestor before the alarm was raised (Livy 10.32.7–9). The fact that a watchword was given to the citizen soldiers every night was so that the guards could challenge anyone they saw and did not recognize, in case that person had come from the outside and had already entered the camp unseen.

At some point during the night the watches would be checked by a member of the citizen cavalry, who proceeded round the guards to check they were present and awake. Each cavalryman sent to check the watches took some friends with him to act as witnesses, presumably so that there could be no dispute. Polybius says that they were assigned to check each *phulakeion*, 'post' or 'station', where, if the soldiers were awake and present, they would pass to the cavalryman their *tessera*, a small, square, wooden token with marks upon it that identified the soldier's guard station. These were returned to the tribune at dawn, and if any were missing, the tribune identified which guard station it had been, and summoned the centurion of the appropriate unit to find the soldiers responsible (Polyb. 6.35.11–36.8).

The maniples of *hastati* and *principes* were liable for service to the tribune, which was needed during the day as well as at night. Three maniples were assigned by lot to each tribune, and so one maniple was on duty to the tribune every third day. Of the 128 men in the maniple, 8 were required to form 2 sets of guards which would alternate duty, providing at all times 4 soldiers to act as guards at the front and 4 at the rear of the tribune's tent 'near the horses' (Polyb. 6.33.7). Others put up his tent for him, levelled the ground around it, and protected the tribune's baggage.

At night, the model of a quarter of the men being on guard duty at any one time, necessitated by the small size of the tents, also suggests a very high number of guard stations manned by the *hastati* and *principes*. Unfortunately, Polybius' account is not detailed enough for us to work out if this is accurate or not. The main duty of these two divisions was to set guards around their own maniples. Each maniple's area consisted of a square in which there were 26 tents, 24 for the ordinary soldiers and one each for the centurions. Polybius does not specify how many guard stations each maniple needed to set up, but if each maniple had 128 men, a quarter of them is 32 men, and a guard of 4 each would allow them to supply 8 stations.

Polybius says that each unit provided its own guards, which would indicate that the allied and foreign units provided their own watch and did not need to be guarded by the citizen legionaries. If we follow the pattern of the *triarii* stations (below) that supplied two guards to the cavalry and two guards to their own maniple, remembering that both these units were half the size of the maniples of the *hastati* and *principes*, that would imply that the latter had four guard stations per maniple. This would leave a further four that could be stationed elsewhere in the camp.

Since the guard stations were all numbered or named for the cavalrymen to check, this must have been formulaic, a certain number of men at a certain spot. We know that the tents of the tribunes had two guard stations each, which makes twelve stations per legion. One maniple at a time was on duty for the consul, and since the consul was more important than the tribunes this probably means that all four of that maniple's 'spare' stations guarded the consul's tent, and more would have been required for the rest of the *praetorium*, including the tents of the *cohors amicorum*. The quaestor would have had at least two stations for his personal tent, like the tribunes, and the *quaestorium* that had supplies and military pay would have needed stations. The two legates of each legion would also have had two guards each, like the other officers.

This still leaves a number of stations, especially since the duties in the central part of the camp like the *praetorium* and *quaestorium* were shared between two legions. There remain the less visible members of the camp, the *calones* and *lixae*, and probably there were guard stations by the areas set aside for them. Partly this would have been to guard those men from danger and to guard the soldiers from them in the case of sedition or unrest. Partly it would have been to prevent the *calones* slipping away and deserting to the enemy with information about the size and location of the Roman forces. As slaves of the Roman state, they had every reason to wish to do so. We do not know for certain where the *calones* and *lixae* might have been encamped, although the obvious location is in the *intervallum*. This area would have needed guard stations whether or not there were people camped there, because it was also the location of various types of plunder like cattle.

It seems that it was the duty of the *optiones*, the rearguard leaders, to organize the night-watches. They were responsible for taking a soldier from the first watch to the tribune to receive the *tessera*, and the *optiones* of the cavalry were responsible for sending the patrols around the various watches at the right time. This hints at the function of the *optiones*, both in the cavalry and in the maniples. Their role was as aides to the decurions and centurions, apparently primarily administrative, or what we might call an adjutant. They were called *optiones* because the centurions were allowed to choose the man they wished from their maniple.[18] The Latin word *optio* is a feminine noun meaning 'choice', and when used as a masculine noun forms the name of this military position. The *optiones* appear to be rather undistinguished, as unlike the centurions they did not receive extra tent space, nor do they occur among the positions noted for having courageous individuals like the standard-bearers and the centurions.

The calculation of guard stations is a little easier regarding the *triarii*. The *triarii* provided a guard for the *turma* of citizen cavalry behind it, both during the day and during the night. This was to keep watch but also to make sure the horses did not get tangled in their tethers or break free (Polyb. 6.33.10–11). They also needed to provide a night guard to their own maniple. As their division was smaller than the others, they would only have sixteen men available per watch of the night, making four guard stations, and this must mean that they guarded their own area with two stations and the *turma* of cavalry behind them with two stations.

There are some conclusions that can be drawn from the study of the Roman camp. The first is that the Roman camp and military organization in general most frequently operated in base 4. There were 4 legions created in a year, and the soldiers within them were organized into 4 divisions. There were 4 soldiers to a guard detachment and 4 watches of the night. This multiplied up to 8 men in a *contubernium* and 152 in a maniple, 128 heavy infantry and 24 *velites*. Quite why this should be so is not easy to tell, although it is not at all exclusive to the legions. The use of base 4 occurs elsewhere in the Roman world as well. We saw that the Roman *actus* on which the camp system was based was 120 Roman feet, which was a measurement common to agriculture and urban planning. For our soldiers, it means that they would be used to working in groups of 4, as in a guard, and 8, as in their *contubernium*.

The sheer number of guard stations gives us an idea of what was the purpose of security and in turn, what it was that the guards were guarding against. Only the *velites* were truly a lookout for enemy activity. Many of the guard stations' primary duty must have been to prevent malicious actions of individuals, either those originating outside of the camp or within it. The officers and the high status individuals who accompanied the consul were provided protection against assassins, whether that might come in the form of an enemy infiltrator or someone who was already present in camp. It would not have been effective to try to bribe a citizen, allied or foreign soldier serving with the army to kill an officer in camp, for example. The same applied to all the soldiers, who posted their own guards around their maniple as surety that no-one could come into their tents and kill them as they slept. The guards would also be looking out for anyone intent on theft or sabotage. All this suggests that movement around the camp at night when it was dark was tightly controlled and possibly discouraged.

Chapter 8

The Disciplinary System

So far we have mostly looked at the influences upon the soldier that incentivized him to perform in ways that were desirable for the legion and its objectives. There were rewards for fearlessness and proactive violence, for successes in combat, for being the first over the wall in a siege. There was also the binding quality of the oaths that the soldier had taken to obey his officers and to steal nothing from the camp. These oaths and their surrounding ceremonies might have helped him to form a group identity, in which he thought favourably of his group members and in turn wished to be respected by them and preserve their esteem. The weeks and months of marching and living and camping closely with the members of his maniple would have strengthened these bonds and created relationships that he wished to maintain by saying and doing things that were commonly held to be correct and acceptable.

While we have considered the positive incentives to engage in desirable behaviours, we have also seen that there was the possibility to have an entirely unremarkable service in the legions. As with all armies, a high percentage of time was spent in non-combat activities, while assignments like garrisoning and guarding would only involve active combat situations in extraordinary circumstances. There were soldiers who hung back during skirmishing and in the storming of the walls, whose efforts were undistinguished but not so unacceptable as to invite punishment from the army's officers. Although these soldiers would not have been suitable for promotion and would not return home having been highly decorated, their performance was apparently quite normal for soldiers in an army in this era. At the very least, we hear of no dire consequences for any soldier failing to push forward or displaying hesitancy, only for running, dropping arms or fleeing.

There were, however, a number of disciplinary measures used in the army to punish soldiers who had done something wrong. In general, in order for behaviour to be punishable, it had to be more than simply average or reluctant performance. For something to invite actual punishment, it had to be an act that transgressed the boundaries of acceptable behaviour. These were things like deception, theft, negligence and cowardice, many of which related to violations of the oaths the soldiers had taken. The consequences for committing any of these faults were, quite famously, often very severe, although as we will see, not quite as severe as they are often reputed to have been. The intention, and very likely the result, of punishments in the legions was to make the least dramatic and dangerous path for the soldier to remain under arms and obey his orders. A soldier in a situation that was frightening and dangerous, like a wavering battle line, would know that the alternative to standing his ground was also extremely dangerous. In fact, dropping his arms and running away would invite disciplinary measures that would very likely result in a worse consequence for him than continuing to fight.

Polybius gives us a summary of punishments used in the Roman army. The mildest were fines and flogging, as he tells us, 'a tribune, and in the case of the allies a prefect, has the right of inflicting fines, of demanding sureties, and of punishing by flogging' (6.37.8). He does not specify what acts resulted in these punishments and there might not have been set rules linking particular transgressions to particular penalties. It may have been left up to the tribune or prefect's discretion. There are, however, examples that help to illustrate what kinds of things resulted in these punishments. We hear mention of a fine in a fragment of the Elder Cato, Ligustinus' second commander, who wrote 'our general, if anyone leaves his place in the rank in order to do battle, makes a fine for him.'[1] The context is unclear but it might relate to this description of Cato by Livy, 'if anyone too eagerly stepped ahead of the line, he himself rode between the ranks and struck him with his spear and ordered the tribunes and centurions to punish him.'[2] This context involves a legion moving across a battlefield, as it had been ordered to approach and attack the enemy camp from where it was waiting in reserve. It seems that moving forward eagerly was only desirable in skirmishes and storming of towns, but on the battlefield when a unit was in motion, a soldier was not permitted to go ahead of the standards.

There are a few more examples of fines being levied from soldiers in the army, which fall into the same general area of military negligence or incompetence. In 319 BCE a praetor was fined for bringing up his unit too slowly. In 176 BCE the general Q. Petillius Spurinus was killed in battle and the Senate punished the whole legion by having its military year effectively cancelled, in that they were deprived of their pay and the year was not allowed to count towards their time in service. On another occasion, soldiers who had been incorrectly dismissed by a tribune, rather than properly released by the commander, and who actually left the camp to head home were fined half a year's pay.[3] It seems clear in these situations that the soldiers involved had committed no deliberate act of disobedience or malice. The fines that were levied seem to reflect an opinion that in some unspecified way, they simply ought to have known or performed better.

The second punishment that Polybius mentions, 'demanding sureties' or the seizure of property, may not relate directly to a military context at all, but be a solution to private disputes between soldiers.[4] While fines would be deducted from the soldier's *stipendium*, thus reflecting the fact that they were levied for some fault in his service, a private argument would not be understood to be in the same category. Thus the soldier's private possessions could be seized to correct a private dispute, when a soldier was judged to have wronged or slighted another. It could not pertain to theft of another's property, as that would have amounted to violation of the camp oath and, as we observed at the time, this served to elevate the crime to oath breaking and had a more severe penalty.

The last of the three punishments that were within the powers of the tribunes or prefects of the allies was flogging. Livy writes of the commander Scipio Aemilianus at the siege of Numantia in 133 BCE, 'When he found any man out of rank [*extra ordinem*], he ordered him to be flogged with vine twigs, if a Roman; if a foreigner, with rods.'[5] This is part of Livy's account of Scipio's clamp down on discipline, and the implication is that the offence was rendered more severely here than in other armies, not punished by a fine but apparently the next step up, a flogging. Similarly, P. Aurelius Pecuniola was flogged in 225 BCE when he was left in charge of a siege and the besieged enemy defending the town burned the earthworks and almost captured the Roman camp (Val. Max. 2.7.4). Flogging was intended to be both painful and humiliating, as the soldier would be stripped and flogged in the camp where others would be able to see. Moreover, flogging was a punishment associated with slaves rather than free men and was intended to shame as part of the penalty.[6]

The implication of one officer being able to act unilaterally in imposing fines, property seizure and flogging is that these were penalties for supposedly minor crimes, as opposed to a longer list of infractions that warranted the death penalty. In those cases, a panel of all six tribunes from the legion was required to come to an agreement (Polyb. 6.37.1). The incidents punishable by fining and flogging all fall into a general category of unintentional military incompetence. The seizure of private property only comes into our evidence when the circumstances were extremely dramatic, such as in the incident above of the soldiers dismissed by a tribune. Those who did not return were sold as slaves and their property seized (Livy 40.41.11). There were probably many incidents of minor infractions by individual soldiers that would never have been recorded, let alone make it to a historical account of the era.

Polybius goes on to list a number of offences that were considered so serious that they merited the death penalty (6.37.9–11). These he separates into two categories, one which he refers to as crimes, and the other which he refers to as soldiers disgracing themselves. The crimes are: being absent from one's post while on night watch, failing to ensure the correct orders were given to the guard units or those who reviewed the guard units, stealing something from the camp, giving false evidence, misusing the body, and committing the same minor offence three times. We have already seen how the guard posts were organized and how they were reviewed by members of the cavalry. Polybius says that the watches were scrupulously kept for fear of punishment, implying that this kind of fault was extremely rare. Indeed in Polybius' own account it is not clear how it might happen, as he mentions guard stations being made up of four men, which would make it difficult for a station to be entirely absent and thus unable to hand over its *tessera*. The only reason there would be missing *tesserae* was if the *optio* who organized the guards or the prefect of the cavalry who organized review of the guard stations had incorrectly done his administrative duty. This punishment, exclusive to *optiones* who issued flawed instruction, was the second fault that resulted in the death penalty.

The third offence, that of stealing something from the camp, must have been a capital crime because it was a violation of the camp oath that every member of the camp had taken back at the mustering point. The next crime, 'giving false evidence' is obviously the crime of perjury, which was similarly punishable by death in civil life according to the XII tables (Gell.20.1.53), the Roman law code that dated to the fifth century BCE. This probably pertained to being a witness in the investigations of other soldiers for disciplinary action, as Polybius describes was done for neglect in the night-watches, where the tribunes investigated who was at fault using witnesses (Polyb.6.26.6–9). These witnesses were probably required to swear that they were telling the truth, thus placing perjury in the same category as stealing, crimes that were made more severe by the breaking of an oath.

The significance to an oath was that giving one's word was guaranteed by a divine power. Someone who broke an oath like the *sacramentum* became *sacer*, forfeit to the gods. In taking an oath like this, the soldier was understood to be pledging his person to secure his word, with the gods both as witnesses and guarantors. This idea is made explicit in Livy's account of the oath taken by Scipio Africanus after the Battle of Cannae, as he rallied his companions after the disaster and so prevented them from fleeing from the state:

> 'I solemnly swear,' he said, 'that even as I myself shall not desert the republic of the Roman People, so likewise shall I suffer no other Roman citizen to do so; if I wittingly speak false, may Jupiter Optimus Maximus utterly destroy me, my house, my family, and my estate' (Livy 22.53.10–11).

The next crime punishable by death was 'if one of the young men was discovered to have misused his body.'[7] This is obviously a euphemism for something, but exactly what is unclear. It has been suggested that it means taking the passive role in a homosexual encounter, considered to render a young man unfit to be a soldier.[8] In civil life, violating a freeborn Roman citizen of either sex was the crime of *stuprum*.[9] The historical examples of homosexuality related to the army that we know were punished, however, were of someone in a position of authority using their power to abuse a subordinate. Valerius Maximus includes the tale of Gaius Cornelius, a *primus pilus* from 149 BCE who was convicted of *stuprum* with a young freeborn man. In this case Cornelius claimed that the man had freely prostituted himself, which, it is implied, would have proven that he was not guilty of corrupting an innocent citizen. Similarly, a tribune during the Samnite Wars of the late fourth or early third century was convicted of approaching his adjutant for sexual favours, the attempt apparently constituting the crime.[10] Although these crimes were tried in a civil court after the offender's military service, they point to the older instigator as the criminal rather than the young man, but in Polybius' cited rule he specifies that it was the young person who was punished.

One case might shed some light upon the crime, that of a soldier of the general Marius, who killed a military tribune for attempting to force *stuprum* upon him, and was subsequently acquitted of homicide by Marius himself. This incident was well-known in antiquity and often used as an example in law and rhetoric surrounding justifiable homicide. Although most of the sources report the example in quite basic terms, some others emphasize that the homicide was justified specifically because there was an imperative for young men and women to preserve their chastity.[11] Plutarch adds the significant detail that when called to his own defence, the young man claimed that he had refused the tribune specifically several times and also 'large offers' from others to prostitute himself (Plut. *Mar.* 14.5).

It may be, then, that this crime that merited the death penalty was accepting money for one's body, and this is why Polybius specifies that it applied to 'young men' who were perceived as sexually attractive and were liable to receive such offers. Perhaps, as is implied in the case of the *primus pilus* who offered it in his defence, accepting such an offer released the buyer from crime or at least mitigated the crime, and so military law placed the burden of compliance on the young man. The incident set in Marius' army in 104 BCE was used by some of the later orators to argue that part of the offence was that the soldier had been treated as an adolescent rather than a man, although he ought to have been treated as a man by warrant of being a soldier.[12] The orators' arguments imply that it was more acceptable to proposition someone sufficiently young. The army by the time of Marius no longer had a division of *velites*, required to be young and light, but our Mid-Republican armies did, and it seems that these men may simply have known that they might be approached by older men with offers to prostitute themselves and that, on pain of death, they were to refuse.

The last crime warranting the death penalty was being punished for the same infraction three times, which is discussed more below. There are three further actions that Polybius categorizes, not as crimes, but as shameful and unmanly. They are boasting falsely of bravery to gain distinction, leaving one's station, or throwing away one's arms in battle.[13] Boasting falsely is similar to the crime of bearing false witness, although in this case it appears that aggrandizing oneself for material gain was considered to be shameful rather than unlawful. Polybius specifies that this was falsely boasting 'to the tribunes' and so it must refer to testifying about their acts in the course of a military encounter to gain reward, not merely boasting or exaggerating about their military prowess among fellow soldiers. The next act of shame is leaving one's station, more accurately 'any men who have been placed in a covering force leave the station assigned to them from fear' (Polyb. 6.37.11). This could cover any manner of operation involving a unit or units of the army, like being placed in reserve, as part of an ambush, or guarding a camp.

The last shameful action, throwing away one's arms during battle, is what a soldier would normally do when he fled, dropping sword and shield in order to run away unhindered. Although Polybius specifies that the item was dropped 'through fear', the shame extended to simply losing a piece of equipment, as Polybius goes on to say that soldiers who have lost a weapon of some kind 'often throw themselves into the midst of the enemy, hoping either to recover the lost object or to escape by death from inevitable disgrace and the taunts of their relations' (Polyb.6.37.13). This, of course, implies that the soldier would be alive to face such taunts and would not have been executed just for losing a sword or shield, as long as he had dropped them by accident and not as a preliminary to fleeing. Indeed, for the group of actions that Polybius outlines as being shameful, he does not say that the death penalty applied to them. Elsewhere Polybius says that fleeing one's station incurred the death penalty (1.17.11) and Dionysius of Halicarnassus writes that the commander had the power to put soldiers to death for disobedience or desertion (*Ant. Rom.* 11.43.2).

Dionysius specifically says that desertion and disobedience were capital crimes because they amounted to breaking the soldier's oath, the *sacramentum*. This seems to be the justification behind most, if not all, of the actions that were punished by death. In the case of a minor offence being committed three times, Polybius' Greek makes it clear that this is the same minor fault repeatedly, not three different minor infractions. This perhaps reflects the idea that a soldier could be incompetent or make a mistake twice, but three times proved deliberate disobedience to one's officers, and obedience had been sworn during the *sacramentum*. It is also perfectly plausible that bearing false witness for or against someone else in a military hearing, which could result in dire consequences for the accused, was bound by oath, whereas describing one's own battle conduct for reward was not as serious a matter, and was thus left to be governed by the social weight of shame and dishonour rather than threat of punishment. That leaves only the misuse of the body as a capital crime that seems to have no connection to breaking an oath, and here unfortunately we know so little about this rule that it is impossible to tell why it invoked so serious a penalty.

Fustuarium

Polybius writes that the death penalty in the Roman military of this era was done by a procedure called *fustuarium*, in which 'the tribune takes a cudgel and just touches the condemned man with it, after which all in the camp beat or stone him, in most cases dispatching him in the camp itself' (Polyb. 6.37.2–3). This is a particularly gruesome punishment, with the added dimension that it forced distress and probably guilt upon the soldier's innocent comrades. In fact, Polybius' account of this is problematic, not least because there is not a single recorded instance of a soldier actually being subjected to *fustuarium*. It is mentioned in a few Latin sources, but only as a hypothetical punishment by persons arguing that a soldier who left his standards or abandoned his guard post deserved death by *fustuarium*. This kind of rhetorical usage confirms that the act was known as being a military punishment, but suggests that rather than being the routine punishment for such offences it was legendary or theoretical. A few soldiers over the centuries are recorded as having been beaten to death, but none with the elevated horror of it being done by a collective act of their own fellow soldiers.[14]

There are other reasons to doubt the use of the *fustuarium*. Soldiers convicted of crimes that merited capital punishment do not, in the examples we have, suffer *fustuarium*. Roman citizens who were executed for crimes were most often beheaded, and in the cases of Roman soldiers who had deserted and were executed, we usually hear that they were flogged and then executed in some other fashion, not stoned or clubbed to death by the army. Livy tells the story of 370 Roman deserters from the Second Punic War in 214 BCE taken to Rome, who were scourged and then thrown from the Tarpeian rock, a traditional punishment of criminals. A whole legion of Roman citizens who had taken over the city of Rhegium and were subsequently captured were scourged and beheaded in the forum at Rome.[15] In 201 BCE, after the fall of Carthage, Scipio Africanus had all the Roman deserters found in the city crucified.[16] Sometimes deserters were not executed at all. In 138 BCE deserters from the army were scourged and sold into slavery instead (Frontin. *Str.* 4.1.20).

Theft is another crime that Polybius says would result in *fustuarium*, but apparently there were at least two alternative punishments, depending on the discretion of the commander. From the Elder Cato we hear, as Frontinus records for us, 'Marcus Cato has handed down the story that soldiers caught in theft had their right hands cut off in the presence of their comrades; alternatively, if the authorities wished to impose a lesser sentence, they were bled at the commander's headquarters.'[17] Q. Fabius Maximus is documented as having cut off the hands of Roman soldiers in 141 BCE, men who had deserted and been subsequently captured.[18] Bloodletting as a form of punishment is mentioned also by the antiquarian Aulus Gellius, who writes that it was intended to disgrace the soldier, but he suggests also that it might have been a kind of medical treatment for those who were 'not of sound mind' (Gell. *NA.* 10.8).

The association of the punishment with the *fustis*, a stick or a club, is also problematic. The Mid-Republican soldier did not carry one, nor any type of a cudgel. There is even no evidence for the use of sticks, staffs or clubs by centurions, who by the time of the Empire would famously wield a vine-stick called the *vitis* at disobedient rankers.[19] For a whole camp of soldiers to descend upon one of their number with a *fustis* they would need to be a common item around an army camp, but they are not mentioned in the camp oath in the list of common inexpensive items like spears and spear shafts. Polybius does write that offenders could be beaten or stoned, although the clear link between the Latin *fustuarium* and the word *fustis* does indicate it was very much associated with sticks and clubs rather than stones.

Whether the *fustuarium* was or was not in use during the Middle Republic, and especially whether it was common, would seem to be an important factor in gauging the general tenor of the soldier's experience with the legions. Clearly the point of the *fustuarium* is that it was not done by an executioner but by the soldiers themselves, who were required to beat and eventually kill one of their own colleagues. In reality, however, surely the task would have actually fallen to some of the more violent and unsentimental men among other maniples and divisions, and not to his closest colleagues and friends, who would naturally shrink from participating. This in turn seems to defy the point that the act was not merely to punish the individual soldier but deliberately intended to produce some psychological or emotional effect among the rest of the legionaries as well. Polybius tells us that this effect was terror, with the result that 'the men in covering forces often face certain death, refusing to leave their ranks even when vastly outnumbered, owing to dread of the punishment they would meet with' (6.37.12).

So, we actually find that during this period the most severe and frightening element of Roman punishment never occurs in the sources, in that there is no example in which a group of soldiers was forced to bludgeon one of their number to death. This would mean that in one crucial area of the soldier's experience, service was not as haunting and cruel as we might expect. There were soldiers who acted as executioners, of course, but these would not have been unwilling men spontaneously forced to kill a comrade. Probably they self-selected into this duty, or were chosen by the centurions or tribunes for a particularly calm and stoic temperament in the face of violence and gore. As the unfortunate victim of a Roman soldier at Cerro de la Cruz discovered, it was not always easy to swing the gladius and decapitate someone cleanly. Even in instances where the soldier's comrades were made to watch the executions of guilty men, this would not have had the same nightmarish quality of making the men perform the execution themselves.

Decimation

Polybius explains that in cases where a whole unit of men had fled, instead of having the whole unit subjected to the *fustuarium*, a tenth part of the offending unit was singled out for execution in front of the whole legion, in a practice that Polybius calls 'beneficial and terror-striking' (Polyb. 6.38.1). He goes on to describe how this was done:

> The tribune assembles the legion, and brings up those guilty of leaving the ranks, reproaches them sharply, and finally chooses by lots sometimes five, sometimes eight, sometimes twenty of the offenders, so adjusting the number thus chosen that they form as near as possible the tenth part of those guilty of cowardice. Those on whom the lot falls are cudgelled mercilessly in the manner above described [*fustuarium*]; the rest receive rations of barley instead of wheat and are ordered to encamp outside the camp on an unprotected spot. As therefore the danger and dread of drawing the fatal lot affects all equally, as it is uncertain on whom it will fall; and as the public disgrace of receiving barley rations falls on all alike, this practice is that best calculated both to inspire fear and to correct the wrongdoing.[20]

Although this is perhaps the most famous disciplinary measure of the Roman legions of any time period, just as in the case of the *fustuarium* itself there are very few secure instances of it actually happening, and none at all during the Middle Republic.[21] Like the *fustuarium*, it seems to be something that had been done in an early period or was included in legendary tales about early parts of

Rome's history. Livy writes that in 471 BCE Appius Claudius had a decimation done of his whole army. These men had not merely fled from an enemy, but even before this they had had a terrible relationship with their commander, a man notorious for his supercilious attitude to the plebians under his command. At any rate, the veracity of the story is highly dubious.[22] Even here Livy writes that the decimation was performed by having a portion of the men whipped and beheaded, not beaten to death. There is one more instance from late fourth or early third century of Fabius Rullianus, who punished two legions which had fled from the enemy, '[he] chose men by lot and beheaded them in the sight of their comrades.'[23] There is no *fustuarium* here either, but it is significant that Frontinus makes it clear that the men were beheaded in the sight of the others, a detail that emphasizes the purpose of the decimation in generating fear, just as Polybius had said.

There are no more instances of decimation recorded until Plutarch mentions that Crassus reinstituted it for 500 of his men who had thrown away their arms and fled from an army of Spartacus, 'thus bringing back after a long time an ancestral way of punishing soldiers' (Plut. *Crass.* 10.2). This incident happened in 72 BCE, and Plutarch's remark indicates that decimation had not happened for a long time before that date. It would be consistent with the recorded instances of decimation to think that the ancestral context is the early period of Rome's history and that the hiatus was during the period of the Middle Republic. Probably they were a legendary threat that helped to keep the soldiers careful, which is why Polybius tells us that the threat of *fustuarium* ensured the scrupulous efficiency of the watches. This would explain why these punishments do not seem to have been carried out, because the fear of them was enough to stop soldiers committing the fault.

On other occasions, the Middle Republican officers and members of the Senate simply found another solution for soldiers who had deserted their post or place in the battleline. Those who fled Rome's disastrous defeat at the Battle of Cannae were not decimated, but instead sent away to Sicily while they were still under arms, where they were ordered to remain until the end of the war (Livy 23.25.7). Nor were the mutinous troops of the young Scipio Africanus decimated, when members of the garrison left at the town of Sucro were insubordinate in demanding their long-owed back pay. Instead, Scipio had the core thirty-five ring-leaders killed, while granting the owed pay to the rest of the soldiers.[24]

The assumption that punishments found in the early and late Republics spread also across the Middle period has much to do with later historians associating severe discipline with prestige and exclusivity. It has long been known that the Romans of the later Republic and the Empire romanticized the Middle and Early Republic as a period of moral uprightness, and very much wished to believe that military discipline had been extremely strict and punishments severe.[25] Many people are attracted to the idea of strict codes, extreme discipline and the rigid enforcement of rules. Such attributes add to the perceived prestige of institutions, and many of the exemplary stories of Roman military heroism revolved around an almost shocking enforcement of the very letter of military standards. Two of the stories tell of commanders who had their own sons executed for leaving the ranks to engage in single combat.

While rigid and exacting discipline may make an institution seem exclusive and prestigious to outsiders, being subject to severe punishments for minor transgressions is quite another thing. The exemplary stories of severe discipline were cherished by the ancient world's aristocrats, whose role would have been to enforce them, not to suffer them. For those who lived and worked for years at a time under military rules, any discipline had to be seen as both legitimate and proportional in order to remain unchallenged. In the Middle Republic, the officer class wielded a moral authority as Rome's citizen leaders and in the case of consuls and praetors who served as commanders, in the magisterial positions that bestowed *imperium* and *auspicium*. This could not, however, be stretched into arbitrariness or despotism without the soldiers making their opposition known. Rome's legions were still made up of citizen soldiers, who did not take kindly to being treated unfairly.

In the case of the mutiny at Sucro, the punishments do turn out to be on the severe side for the circumstances. The soldiers had several very legitimate grievances related to the time they had been in service and the fact that they had not been paid for many years. They had, in fact, begun to run short of both food and supplies, and had taken to leaving their posts at night to search for food in the countryside. Their avenue of redress was to bring their complaints to the tribunes, but these officers refused to listen or to address the matter with the commander on the soldiers' behalf. Tempers in the camp began to flare, exacerbated by the class rift between the aristocratic officers and the ordinary soldiers. The mutiny consisted of ejecting the unhelpful tribunes from the camp, while the soldiers remained there. They did not desert, or exert violence on their officers, or ally with any of the local hostile tribes against their colleagues.[26]

When Scipio had the ringleaders of the disturbance executed, this response was less than the standard of ancestral discipline that might have demanded the decimation of the whole garrison, but it was also a heavy-handed response to legitimate grievances that his tribunes had refused to address. An older or more-experienced commander, and certainly more attentive tribunes, might have been able to end the so-called mutiny before it started. The ending of the soldiers' protests in this violent manner makes one wonder what these men ought to have done that would have been in accordance with military disciplinary ideology. The answer is that when the tribunes refused to help them, they were expected to remain hungry and to continue to serve past their time and without pay, which they had not been given for more than five years.

There were very few incidents of real mutiny in the Middle Republic, and the incident at Sucro should hardly be classed as one. It is illustrative nonetheless. The soldiers' situation was extreme, and the fact that they had been compliant for more than five years of extended service without receiving pay indicates that soldiers would generally remain obedient to their officers in less-than-ideal circumstances. Similarly, the fact that they went to the tribunes with their grievances shows that they were allowed to voice legitimate complaints about their service in order that these matters could be dealt with. We find these appeals often, usually written by the historians as if they were made directly to the commander. In 199 BCE, for example, the veterans of the Second Punic War who had been sent out to Macedon with Sulpicius petitioned for their discharge, alleging that they were not, as Livy originally wrote, volunteers, but had been sent to Macedon somewhat against their will and now wished to be discharged. Having an avenue through which to protest unfair treatment was clearly one of the ways that discontent was addressed before the soldiers began to feel that it was necessary to break rules and disobey orders, actions that were, as we have seen, extremely dangerous for them.

Although the soldiers at Sucro had tried to proceed carefully, on that occasion mismanagement among the officer class led to Scipio unleashing aggressive measures on them to scare the rest into obedience. This was the risk of the amount of power that the officers and especially the commanders held, that any dissent, however reasonable, could be squashed by violence. These kinds of tactics, in which soldiers are threatened in order to force compliance, are referred to as coercive. Coercive tactics are often used in the armies of oppressive regimes and the principle behind them is quite simply that the men are induced to fight because the alternative has been made worse. If the soldier perceives that there is a credible threat or certainty of facing death as a punishment if he does not continue to be obedient, then continuing becomes his only true viable option. The same applies to the soldiers that Polybius says 'faced certain death' rather than flee from their post, who did so because the framework of military rules had made fighting the more attractive option.

Threats of capital punishment and social rejection, like the actions that Polybius listed as incurring shame, actually work to promote solidarity within army units. Closing off alternative avenues to safety and advertising credible threats for those who try disobedience or desertion essentially forces soldiers to adhere closer together, as research gathered from the armies of the Soviet Union, the US, North Vietnam, and Israel indicates:

> If soldiers perceive that relatively harmless administrative avenues of escape are open, or if soldiers believe the penalties for desertion are relatively light, cohesion in a unit will be weakened..... a cohesive unit will ensure that the soldier is aware of all legal, moral, and physical barriers that separate him from the civilian world and bind him to his unit.[27]

The threat of death or some other form of severe punishment as a deterrent to desertion and surrender has been instituted many times throughout history. During the Second World War, some 22,750 German soldiers were sentenced to death for desertion, of which sentences approximately 15,000 were carried out.[28] In the late days of the war when the Nazi regime became increasingly desperate, the rules imposed upon the soldiers of the Wehrmacht became more dramatic as the regime had to go to greater and greater lengths to make desertion or surrender a worse option than fighting. The SS divisions deliberately committed atrocities upon enemy civilians and soldiers in front of Wehrmacht troops, telling them that since this was their treatment of the enemy's people, the same would be wrought upon them if they surrendered. German soldiers were told that if they were found to have deserted, their families back home would be hurt or killed.[29]

In 2003, a team of military psychologists from the Strategic Studies Institute of the US Army War College travelled to Iraq in order to study combat motivation among soldiers who had participated in Operation Iraqi Freedom (20 March – 1 May 2003). The Iraqi soldiers, who were all interviewed as EPWs (Enemy Prisoners of War) of mainly low rank, almost universally cited coercion as the reason that they continued to fight. The researchers found that the soldiers lived in fear of punishment at the hands of the Baath party or the *Fedayeen Saddam*, an organized paramilitary force which was entrenched in many of Iraq's cities during the operation. Many of the soldiers had been beaten and jailed for suspected desertion, and deserters from the army consistently retained their weapons to protect themselves from these 'death squads', despite the fact that by remaining armed they exposed themselves to danger from reconnaissance units from the coalition forces who may not have recognized them as deserters.[30]

For the Romans of the Middle Republic, the mere threat of the more severe punishments that a commander could inflict upon them, like *fustuarium* and decimation, might have been enough. Commanders probably did have it in their power to order them, which explains why Polybius listed them as contemporary punishments. There are some examples where we see a Roman commander using fear and coercion to keep their armies in line, in addition to that of Scipio Africanus at Sucro above. In the example of Q. Fabius Maximus, who cut the hands off deserters, Valerius Maximus tells us it was done in such a way as to create fear in the remaining soldiers:

> As they [the deserters] went around with their mutilated arms, they made the others too terrified to desert. By cutting off the hands of rebels from their bodies and throwing them on the ground that was covered with their blood, he proved to the others that they should not dare to do likewise.[31]

Since the fear of mutilation is often stronger than the fear of death, this demonstration was probably a very effective deterrent. We see other examples of soldiers being used as threatening demonstrations of the consequences of desertion, like Scipio Africanus, who had deserters thrown to wild animals during shows, or Aemilius Paullus, who had them trampled by elephants.[32] The soldiers in these cases were specifically said to be foreign and it was unlikely that citizens could be treated the same way, but the fact that these things had been done at all would have reminded every soldier of the consequences of desertion.

Despite these instances of coercive and fear-based punishments used as threats, the evidence shows that the harshest punishments, the famous *fustuarium* and decimation, fell into the periods before and after the Middle Republic, but not during the period of conscripted citizen soldiers. Coercive tactics like those exerted on the Wehrmacht and the Iraqi army were short term measures during periods of extremely high pressure, and we should not expect them to be sustainable as the normal routine of armies over a long period of time. Although the later Romans romanticized the idea of severe discipline, extracting compliance under the threat of death is the product of a very uneven power dynamic that was not usually present when soldiers were citizens and commanders were temporary magistrates. Disciplinary systems need to have legitimacy in order to be effective and to remain unchallenged.[33] In the legions of this era the capital punishments for certain actions were, for the most part, secured by the oaths the soldiers had made pledging their person to their word. The soldiers thus had a high degree of personal awareness of the consequences of violating the oath and the justice dispensed was associated with the divine who had witnessed the oath taking, and not the arbitrary will of the commander.

There are other facets of a citizen army that would have made it less reliant on severe discipline, and in particular the coercive power of the threat of mutilation and death. Although many of the soldiers of this era had stayed in the army by choice because they were suited to the life of a soldier, it still contained many men who were serving only because their time in the legions was compulsory.

There is a sense during this time period that it was better, easier and more effective to sort through men and put them to tasks appropriate to their temperament rather than to attempt to coerce every man to be a proactive and violent soldier. Thus, we can see in the system of rewards and the mechanics of storming a city how the bold and eager were promoted and volunteers were sought out for the most dangerous and daunting tasks. There is an insistent focus in this period on officers watching their men to pick out the bravest and most successful, and on soldiers being recognizable by officers and striving to be noticed for their achievements.

On the other side of the equation, there was also plenty of opportunity to weed out the unwilling by assigning them to various mundane tasks. Individuals and units that were unremarkable, unsuccessful, and untalented in combat situations could be side-lined temporarily during operations through being left to guard the camp or semi-permanently by simply being left behind as a garrison for a town. Even during the Second Punic War, when the need for soldiers was very great, the soldiers who had survived the battle of Cannae were sent to Sicily because they were believed to be unfit for active duty. At the same time the 'weakest' of the soldiers from an active army were picked out of the legions and sent with them (Livy 23.25.8). By contrast, in the late Republican armies led by warlords, and presumably also in the early war bands made up of a clan leader and his followers, the soldiers would have been selected or self-selected professionals who were supposedly willing and able to carry out the most daunting duties of war.

In regard to the two periods before and after the Middle Republic, it should perhaps not be surprising that the harshest punishments fall into those periods where commanders had the most autonomy. When the legitimacy of discipline was not mediated by the state structure and the relationship between the elite classes and the ordinary citizens, it was free to become as harsh or as lenient as particular commanders saw fit. We have seen that when commanders served in a magistrate's position for a year and might be prorogued for several more, they also had advisors from the senatorial class with them, who were almost their equals in rank and were their equals in social status. These men would have served to temper the arbitrariness of punishments. In a structure where both soldiers and officers could swap into and out of units on a yearly basis, temporary commanders did not feel as though they had to assert themselves over their troops to keep control, nor, when they wished to subsequently be elected to further state positions in future, would their officers have particularly favoured having men executed in service if an alternative was possible. Some of the punishments wrought upon soldiers during this period were certainly unpleasant to experience or even to witness, but the men did not regularly serve in fear of their lives for mistakes or hesitations.

Chapter 9

Preparing for Battle

The first time that Ligustinus came to participate in a decisive battle was at Cynoscephalae in 197 BCE, during his fourth year of service. The legions had marched out of their camp in 200 BCE to meet Philip's troops near Acathus, but on that occasion the Roman and allied cavalry had sent the army into retreat before the infantry came to combat (Livy 31.36–7). There had been other kinds of action, including the pillaging of the countryside and the storming of towns, the expedition under the legate Apustius, and the skirmishing during the first year with Sulpicius, when the camp of the Roman army and the camp of Philip had been close together. The whole army forced their way through a guard at the pass to Eordea by moving in a testudo formation (31.39) and captured the town of Pelium (31.40.4–5). After a winter at Corcyra, Villius Tappulus marched the army inland through Epirus as far as the River Apsus, where Philip was holding the pass along the river valley. Since he was unsure of how to proceed, Villius passed command of the army over to T. Quinctius Flamininus without engaging in any larger-scale operations.

The Battle of Cynoscephalae was also the first time that the army in Macedon fought in a battle that turned out to be decisive. It is easy to get the false impression from historical accounts that whenever soldiers were drawn up in battle formation, there would always be combat and it would always be an encounter that was decisive, concluded the war and determined the winner of a campaign. Decisive battles often form an important focal point in historical narratives. On the ground at the time, however, a soldier would have never known how far a particular encounter would escalate, if it even began at all. There were many occasions when the whole army marched out and formed up, only to stand down again at nightfall, only to repeat the same over the course of days or weeks. Sometimes the armies formed up and fought an engagement that was indecisive. On other occasions, they engaged decisively but the battle was not won or lost overwhelmingly enough to end the war.

The few battles that turned out to be decisive to whole campaigns became the ones written to be the centrepieces of historical accounts.[1] But for individual soldiers on the ground, the battles singled out for attention by the historians were not necessarily the highlight of their campaign or career. A significant proportion of the army were left to guard the camp during every battle, rendering perhaps a tenth of the total number of men out of the action completely. No one left behind would have known that morning whether they were going to miss a great historical battle or another day of waiting on the field. Many soldiers would have had their great moment of personal bravery or success during a skirmish or the storming of a town or in a more-minor battle, and the tales that they took home to entertain their family would frequently be from some encounter that was, historically speaking, very minor. In other words, the significance attributed by historians to battles that turned out to be decisive was not at all proportionate to the importance of these battles to individual soldiers.

Whenever a Roman army was close to an enemy army and expecting to offer battle on a particular day, it was necessary to perform a sequence of actions. Firstly, the commander would take the auspices, just as he did before launching any major action. The auspices were followed by a ritual sacrifice, in which an animal was killed and its entrails read by special Etruscan priests called the *haruspices*. Finally, the general gave an exhortation to the troops before sending them out. The two religious rituals ensured that there were no prohibitive signs for that day. If, during the course of the day, it became apparent that the Romans were in a good position to launch an action, then the sequence would be repeated. The auspices checked for any bad omens that might apply to the immediate decision to engage, and the commander made a quick exhortation that had been reduced to a few quick, key points suitable for the moments when battle was imminent.

Auspicium ex tripudiis

If a Roman army was camped with an enemy army nearby and the intention for the day was to send the army out to form up and move into position to offer battle, then the specific time period of that day needed to be queried for its suitability for a potential encounter. In such situations the opposing generals would both be waiting or manoeuvring for an advantage and it was common that the invitation to battle would be declined. The Roman general might not see any satisfactory opportunity on that day himself and retire his troops, or attempt to move them, or, as happened at Cynoscephalae, send only certain units out to skirmish with enemy units.

Before an army could be sent out to draw up in formation for a pitched battle, the Roman general and his attendant had to take the auspices. These were the *auspicium ex tripudiis*, the same type as were taken before crossing rivers, beginning assaults, attempting to take particular strategic spots, and any other engagement or action that was launched. The auspices were always seeking the same information. They brought a particular proposed action before the gods and queried whether any ill omens prevented it.[2] If they were taken in the morning to apply to that day, then the question was if there was any objection on the gods' part to the Romans fighting that day.

The auspices taken prior to a battle had, perhaps, the biggest significance of all the auspices used in a military context, and a kind of mythos had sprung up around them. Generals who did not heed the warnings of their auspices tended to lead their troops into disaster. Perhaps the most famous story of unfavourable auspices is that of P. Claudius Pulcher, who, eager to start a naval battle during the first war with Carthage, could not get his chickens to eat. Becoming frustrated with their reluctance, he cast them into the sea, declaring 'let them drink, if they will not eat!'[3] He was, naturally, defeated. Similarly there was Gaius Flaminius Nepos, who was said to have stumbled into the disastrous Battle of Lake Trasimene against the advice of his chicken-keeper.[4]

The soldiers who were to be sent out to draw up and offer battle would have wanted to make sure that the auspices were good, and would have been cheered by that fact. Although good auspices did not guarantee success, they indicated that any engagement that took place on that day was not doomed from the start. The evidence suggests that the soldiers, or at least some of the soldiers, were witness to the taking of *auspicium ex tripudiis* from captive chickens in the morning while the whole army was still in camp. What this ceremony would have looked like is laid out in an example of one of ancient history's more difficult and intriguing types of evidence, in this case from part of a heavily annotated manuscript of Virgil's Aeneid. The whole manuscript contains a number of fragments of ancient works, but the notes on Virgil are called the *Scholia Virgilii Veronensia* after the manuscript in which the notes were discovered, originating in Verona. These notes were handwritten in the margins by a scholar sometime during the fifth century CE. The scholar has jotted in the margins a quotation that he attributes to an otherwise unknown Sabidius, which describes how a general in the field took the auspices before battle.[5]

The text itself is fractured and difficult, but a number of things can be made out. Sabidius says that the general sat in his tent, orientated in the correct direction. This would have been within the *praetorium*, which during military campaigns acted as an augural space, and the land directly in front of it, designated a religious area called the *templum*, where the auspices were conducted.[6] The chickens were set free, and the soldiers, both infantry and cavalry, Romans, Latins and allies, all dressed and armed for combat, gathered around. The general bid them to be silent. We know from Cicero that the general exchanged a few formulaic sentences with the *pullarius*, although they are not given in Sabidius' text. The last words were a confirmation that the chickens had eaten. At this moment, the general stood up, ordered the legions to say the customary prayers, and reminded them that they owed him obedience and fidelity.

From this account we might surmise that the soldiers were eagerly watching the chickens to see whether they ate or not, but this does not seem to have been the case. The Twelve Tables, the very earliest text of Roman law, stipulated that the oral announcement of the auspice was the law, not the birds' actual behaviour.[7] Thus, for example, we have the story of the consul L. Papirius Cursor, whose army was in such a state of excitement about going to battle that the *pullarius* lied about the results of the ritual, 'the chickens refused to eat, but the *pullarius* ventured to misrepresent matters, and reported to the consul that they had eaten so greedily that the corn dropped from their mouths on to the ground.' The way Livy presents this situation is as if only the *pullarius* was watching the chickens, for Livy continues, writing that 'the consul, delighted at the news, gave out that the omens could not have been more favourable; they were going to engage the enemy under the guidance and blessing of heaven. He then gave the signal for battle' (Livy 10.40.4–6).

In the case of Papirius Cursor, Livy specifically writes that the consul rose in the third watch of the night and sent a *pullarius* to observe the chickens for omens. This would have been before the soldiers were able to gather, with many of them on guard duty and the rest asleep, and heavily implies that only those involved in the auspices were present and only the *pullarii* were paying attention to the chickens. The matter came to light when these attendants argued among themselves about the day's omens and were overheard, at which point it was reported to the consul and the *pullarius* who had lied was placed in front of the battle line, where he was struck and killed by a javelin.

Although Sabidius is definite that the soldiers were present, from Livy's account it seems that they were not, and that all that mattered was the verbal announcement made by the *pullarius* about the result of the auspices. This would parallel the auspices taken before the commander left for the campaign, which were not witnessed by the soldiers personally, as well as the auspices taken in order for the army to cross natural barriers, which cannot have waited for the whole train of the army to catch up to the spot in question. Sabidius might be referring to an earlier period when the army had been smaller, or perhaps at one time it had been normal for the chickens' actual behaviour to be witnessed, even if the sign was solidified by the pronouncement. On the other hand, Livy's wording seems to imply that the consul was not present either, which was certainly not the case in these rituals, and so it is also possible that he has manipulated or rearranged some elements of the story in order to address the obvious difficulty that only the *pullarius* saw the chickens' behaviour.

Sacrifices

The auspices using birds was one of two religious rituals that the Romans used on a day when engaging in battle was proposed. As the auspices solicited the gods for any sign of objection or ill-omen, if the signs were negative then the proposed action would be cancelled. If no ill omen was detected, then the Romans would go on to propose a sacrifice. Livy has the two rituals in this order, auspices followed by sacrifice, with the auspices done first and the sacrifice performed afterward (Livy 38.26.1). During the sacrifice, an appropriate animal, often an ox, was killed and a priest read its entrails for signs. This type of sacrifice, made prior to a battle, was not the same type as the sacrifices that were done at festivals. Those involved an elaborate procession and a feast made from the meat of the animal afterwards, which could not be done while at war.

In the practice of the Classical Greeks, there were two kinds of sacrifices before battle, which were termed *hiera* and *sphagia*. *Hiera* was the type done in the town or camp before the Greeks departed with the intention to offer battle on that day. The *hiera*, like the auspices, had a divinatory capacity, intended to give an indication of the army's prospects that day by searching for omens. For the Greeks the procedure was that an animal, usually a sheep, would have its throat cut. A priest termed a *mantis* would open the body and examine the entrails for signs from the gods. Parts of the animal would then be burnt on the altar as an offering. The second type of sacrifice was done immediately before, and sometimes during, battle. It was termed *sphagia*. This was not a divinatory sacrifice, as it was held too late in the proceedings to be heeded if it threw up a warning, but a sacrifice intended to propitiate the gods and retain their favour.[8]

The Romans also made two sacrifices before engaging in battle and these seem to have been for the same purposes as the sacrifices of the Greeks, one for divination on the day, and the other for favour in the moment. For the Romans, though, the sacrifices were heavily influenced by Etruscan religious practice, and they differed from the Greeks in having their sacrifices interpreted by Etruscan specialists. These diviners were Etruscan priests called the *haruspices*, who would examine the entrails of the sacrificed beast, the *exta*, for any deformity or sign of disease. If there were none, the sacrifice had been accepted and all was well.[9] If there was some fault perceived with the entrails, then the sacrifice had not been accepted and it needed to be repeated until its results were favourable. Thus Aemilius Paullus, before the Battle of Pydna in 168 BCE, was said to have sacrificed twenty oxen to Hercules before the sacrifice was accepted on the twenty-first attempt.[10]

When such sacrifices were made in the Greek world, the soldiers were not present, although the handbook for generals written by Onasander recommends that the officers ought to be there so that they could personally assure the troops that the signs had been positive (Onas. *Strat.* 10.25–7). Perhaps the same was done in the Roman army. Like the auspices, the sacrifice was made at the *praetorium* and the actual sign produced would not have been visible from any sort of distance. In the case of the sacrifice, the reading of the entrails required specialist knowledge and so the declaration of the priest was the only part of the procedure that it would have been useful to witness. In all probability, the soldiers were not present and part of the commander's role was to announce, and hence confirm, that the proper procedures had been performed, the omens had been read, and that they had produced a positive result for action.

If the auspices were good and the sacrifice had been accepted, then the day could be used for offering battle. It would have been normal for the signs to be good and very unusual for them not to be. Cicero tells us that there were methods to get good results from the chickens like feeding them crumbly food or starving them (Cic. *Div.* 2.73). In the case of the sacrifices, they could be repeated until a satisfactory result was obtained. Thus we have scenes like the results being announced to soldiers when they were arming for battle because the assumption was that there would not be a problem (Livy 6.12.7–8).

The Commander's Exhortation

The exhortation of the commander to his troops is often given by historians in elaborate detail. For this reason many of the pre-battle speeches found in Greek and Roman authors have been suspected of being literary conventions, invented in whole or in part by historians who wished to show off their talent and delight their elite audiences.[11] The speeches that appear in the sources purporting to come from the Mid-Republican time period are perhaps the least affected by literary invention, as they are usually not really speeches at all but rather a few pertinent points.[12] As such they are probably closer to reality than many Imperial or Late Republican speeches. Both Livy and Polybius report short exhortations with clear points, but Livy in particular also includes a few elaborate ones that seem to have little basis in a reliable previous source.[13]

The general of the Middle Republic made two exhortations, one in the camp before the army marched out, and then a shorter one to the soldiers when they were drawn up on the battlefield. This is laid out clearly in Livy's account of Cato's addresses in Spain before the battle near Emporiae. Cato made two exhortations, a longer one in camp to the 'tribunes, prefects, cavalry and centurions' and then a short one of only a few sentences to the troops on the battle line. The first speech seems to have been given at the commander's *consilium* on the same occasion as the officers were made aware of the plans for the next day. In Livy's account the whole meeting only consists of the short speech, but in reality the officers must have discussed the precise plans for the next day's attack. On other occasions, we are told that the soldiers were called to an assembly that was held the day before specifically in order to be harangued as, for example, Ligustinus would have been before the Battle of Thermopylae in 191 BCE (Livy 36.17.2).

In the reports of these exhortations, both those done in camp and the shorter speeches on the battleline, a few themes come up repeatedly. This seems to indicate that there was some kind of common body of knowledge among the elite about what topics and points were appropriate to put in exhortations. These repeated and typical themes probably give us the most authentic idea of the sort of thing the soldiers might have heard on any given occasion. The historians are sometimes explicit that they have conveyed the general idea of an exhortation rather than its exact wording. After Cato's speech to the officers Livy qualifies, *in hunc modum maxime adhortatus*. *Maxime* with *modus* in Latin conveys imprecision, and so this translates to 'having made the exhortation in words to that effect' or 'having encouraged them something like that' (Livy. 34.13.10). Livy's source was probably Cato himself, who in turn may only have remembered the points he had made and not the exact wording.

The common themes in the speeches usually come in the form of short, logical points. This is what we would expect, as sometimes the gist of speeches was conveyed to soldiers through their officers, and probably also from soldier to soldier for those who were too far away to hear or attending to other duties at the time. Any message to be relayed would thus need to be short and memorable, with the substance more important than its presentation. When Cato gave his speech to the officers, he made his points knowing that combat was more likely than not, because the next day he planned for the soldiers to go out during the night to take up a position that the enemy would not have expected. This would not normally have been the case, as no-one knew for certain if a day when battle was offered was the day it would actually be fought. Since they had no real certainty about when an encounter might happen, a general could either forgo the exhortation in camp or repeat it on every day when the army was led out to offer combat. If the general chose the latter option, then the points will have been the same in slightly different words every time.

When the general made a speech before the soldiers in the battleline, the points were similarly short and memorable, probably even more so than in camp. Polybius describes Scipio's speech to the soldiers before the Battle of Zama as 'a few words suitable to the occasion' (Polyb. 15.10.1). This was probably about the most that could be conveyed outdoors and over a large area. Scipio was riding along the drawn-up lines as he uttered his speech, which would have been typical practice. What was said in one spot could be repeated again in another, in order to be heard by a greater number of men. Alternatively, a small number of ideas could be passed along the line from one soldier to the next, just as we are told happened in the Spartan battle line.[14]

The most common part of exhortation speeches, both in camp and on the battlefield, was a practical and logical reason why the Romans would defeat the enemy based on their previous experience. The general would point out that they had defeated the same enemy before, like Flamininus did at Ligustinus' first decisive battle at Cynoscephalae, when he evoked the Romans' defeat of the Macedonians at the pass of Eordea a few years before (Polybius 18.23.3–6). If the opposite were true, and the Romans had been defeated by their enemy previously, the general might state why this time would be different, as Scipio did in 210 BCE before leading his troops into unfriendly territory over the Ebro River in Spain. This was an army that Scipio had recently taken over, and he told the soldiers that their previous defeat had been due to the treachery of their Celtiberian allies and that this time, the enemy generals were arguing among each other (Polyb. 10.6.1–5; Livy 26.41.20–21).

Sometimes the speeches mentioned some kind of incentive, like the prospect of booty, wealth, prestige, or some other reward that might result from conquest or victory. Cato did this with his speech near Emporiae when he told the troops that instead of plundering the countryside they could 'drain the wealth of cities' (Livy 34.13.6). During darker moments they were reminded about what they might lose, like the soldiers told before the Battle of Cannae to keep their wives and children in their minds (App. *Hann.* 21). At Zama, facing the prospect of ending the Second Punic War decisively in the Romans' favour, Scipio Africanus tempted his men with 'a rest from their present labours, a speedy return home, and glory forever after.' (App. *Pun.* 42). Fulvius Flaccus in Celtiberia in 180 BCE, when his soldiers were attacked unexpectedly, offered them an enticing vision, that 'they would carry to Rome for the triumph swords bloody with fresh slaughter of the enemy and spoils dripping with gore' (Livy 40.39.9).

On some occasions the speeches mention that the Romans had the blessing or favour of the gods. When the exhortation was made in front of assemblies of the soldiers that were held after the auspices and sacrifices had been performed, this might have been a large part of the point of holding them. This would be because the general, who was the one person on the campaign that had the right to communicate with the gods on behalf of the army as a whole, would wish to personally affirm that the gods had been consulted and that there was no impediment to the army's success. According to Appian, Scipio made a great show of the results of the sacrifice prior to the Battle of Ilipa in Spain in 207 BCE, when he called his troops to an assembly and even bid the priests to bring in the entrails from the sacrificed animal to show them. At the same time he claimed that some birds in the sky were spontaneously giving the best of omens (App. *Hisp.* 26).

Breakfast and March to the Site

Different battles were started in different ways. Sometimes smaller engagements escalated to involve most of the army, and at others the army was led out to form up and offer battle and that offer was accepted by their opposition. In this latter case, the Roman army would be encamped several miles from the camp of the enemy. On a day when the auspices were good they would march out to draw up in a position that was generally favourable to them. The ideal or proper procedure was that the men be allowed to have breakfast first. A fragment of the *Origins* of the elder Cato sums up the list of things that he had done before the soldiers marched out, 'he led out his army, fed, prepared, and encouraged, and drew it up.'[15]

It probably felt reassuring to have breakfast on the day of a battle. It was a good sign that everything was proceeding normally, and that circumstances were under control. A testament to its importance is the fact that it was not omitted from historians' accounts as a trivial detail, but instead often listed as part of the order of things that were done on the morning of a battle. In reference to a battle against the Etruscans near Sutrium in 311 BCE, Livy writes that the consul Quintus Aemilius Barula 'at once commanded the word to be passed round that the men should breakfast, and having recruited their strength with food, should then arm.'[16] This implies that it was known from an early date that the soldiers performed better in a physical fight when they were fed beforehand, and that the advantages of ensuring there was time to eat were respected wherever possible. A character from Plautus' comedy *Amphitryon*, performed around 191 BCE to 189 BCE, claims that a battle was fought from dawn to dusk, and adds indignantly that he remembers this specifically because he didn't get any breakfast![17] The point here is that the character is a glutton and a coward, who ran from the battle he is purporting to describe, and it matters not one bit that he did not eat that morning. But Plautus' audience would have contained many soldiers of Rome, who shared in the joke precisely because they knew the importance of breakfast to an actual fighting man.

We are even shown interrupting or preventing breakfast used as a tactic. Polybius writes that in 218 BCE, just prior to the Battle of the Trebia, Hannibal sent his Numidian cavalry to the Roman camp at dawn to shoot at them and succeeded in tempting their commander to send them out before they had had their breakfasts and become fully prepared (Polyb. 3.71.10–11). A further slog across the frigid River Trebia produced men who were both cold and hungry, a combination that would prove disastrous. The commander Publius Scipio did the same to the army of Hasdrubal before the Battle of Ilipa in Spain in 208 BCE. Polybius tells us that he sent messages around the camp at dawn, ordering his soldiers to do three things: to eat breakfast, arm themselves, and march out. This was done so suddenly that Hasdrubal's troops did not have time to eat their breakfast before going out to defend their camp.[18]

After their food, the soldiers armed and equipped themselves. For the cavalry, this meant having themselves armed, and their horses ready to ride with bits in their mouths and saddles on their back (Livy 28.14.7). Meanwhile infantry soldiers needed to make sure they were properly attired and had all the necessary equipment on their person. Their baggage, including whatever booty they had managed to accumulate thus far, would be left in camp. Not every soldier went to battle. In discussing the distribution of booty after the taking of a town, Polybius says that the proceeds were shared among all, listing those not present as 'the men who are guarding the tents, the sick, and those absent on any special service' (10.16.5). There would also have been men who were designated as messengers and scouts.

There is very little evidence about how many soldiers were left in camp to guard it during a battle, but the examples are diverse enough to show that there was no one standard rule. In the war against Antiochus in 190 BCE, Livy says that a mixed force of 2,000 Macedonians and Thracians was left to guard the camp (37.39.12) out of an army totalling about 29,000. In regard to another encounter, he lists 2 cohorts and the *triarii* of the 2 legions (40.27.7). Two cohorts were made up of 6 maniples of 128 men, totalling 768 soldiers, plus the 1,280 *triarii* of 2 legions, for a total of 2,048 men. On another occasion 1,000 men were left to guard the camp (43.10.4). Aemilius Paullus is reported to have said that a quarter of the forces were guarding the baggage on a day when he declined battle, partly because a quarter of the whole force missing was too many (Livy 44.38.6). Polybius writes that 8,000 men were left to guard the camp during the Battle of Cannae, which is the highest number reported for a camp garrison during this period (6.58.2). Unfortunately, the total number of combatants who fought on the Roman side is vexed and the hence the size of the camp or what percentage of the total number of soldiers this represents is impossible to know.[19]

In general, the scanty evidence points to the number of men left to guard the camp normally being a few thousand, with no real pattern as to the division given this duty or their status as citizens or allies. It is rarely specified who was left in charge of the garrison, although on one occasion Livy writes that a military tribune had been left in charge (37.43.1). The number of those left on guard did not include the sick and wounded, who also stayed in camp. Apparently the standard for being left in the camp as wounded was not excessively strict. We hear of a cavalryman named C. Popilius Sabellus left behind in camp with a wounded foot, although he was evidently capable of fighting under the right circumstances. When the Romans broke into the enemy camp of the Histri in 178 BCE, he and the rest of the ill men left behind took arms to join the slaughter and pillage (Livy 41.4.5–6).

After eating, dressing in armour and checking he had all his equipment, the soldier would have moved into the adjacent road of the camp or the *intervallum* with his unit and waited to march out. As the camp order reflected the battle order, this should have created a neat line that could simply march into place when they reached the battlefield. It must also have involved a great deal of waiting to move, first into the road next to their tents within the camp, then out of the camp, and finally to begin the march towards the chosen site of battle once the whole army was ready. The call to prepare for battle was signalled by the red *vexillum* hoisted above the commander's tent, while the movement of the units was signalled by bugle. The maniple's standard bearer led the unit out.

The Romans did not routinely offer battle immediately outside their own camp unless surprised or pressed. Rather, the army marched for several miles to where they would form a battle line. Armies that intended to confront one another tended to build camps relatively close together, with the idea that the battle would take place at some point between them. On nine occasions in his extant histories, Livy has specified a distance between the Roman camp and the camp of the enemy. These distances range between 1 and 7 miles apart.[20] At Baecula, where Scipio the Younger fought Hasdrubal Barca, the camps of the Romans and the Carthaginians have been located and archaeologically documented. They are more than 5km (over 3 miles) apart in a straight line, and the march taken by the Romans – as evidenced by a trail of lost hobnails from their boots – winds 8km (almost 5 miles) around the hills to where they fought before the Carthaginian camp.[21] This represents a march from camp to battlefield of about two hours. Without baggage and mules, and each man wearing his armour and carrying his weapons only, it would have been a tighter, more efficient journey than when the army was travelling through the countryside.

Drawing Up the Army

The maniples of each legion marched out in their divisions according to numerical order, just as their tents were positioned in the camp, with the first maniple leading and the rest following in order down to the tenth maniple that brought up the rear. It is unclear whether the lines were always led onto the field in the same direction or whether it depended on the terrain whether the maniples ran one to ten from right to left or left to right.[22] As the senior centurion was on the right of the maniple, probably the first maniple drew up on the far right whenever possible. This would result in the first maniple at the end of the line on the right, and the tenth maniple at the end of the line on the left. A Roman citizen soldier might have found himself on the flank of his own legion, but he would never have been on the flank of the whole army, at least at the start of a battle. There would be an interval of unoccupied space and then either another citizen legion or a contingent of the Italian allies, who were stationed on the wings.

Polybius tells us in some detail about how Scipio drew up his troops at the Battle of Zama, a passage that is helpful because the placement of the maniples differed from the usual line. In explaining these differences we are told something about the normal procedure and can deduce the rest. First Scipio lined up the *hastati*, with gaps between the maniples, and then placed the maniples of the *principes* directly behind them. This was in order to create gaps that led in a straight line through the army for the enemy's elephants to charge through. Scipio then stationed the *triarii* directly behind the *principes*, and the *velites* in the spaces between the maniples of the *hastati* in the front line,

> ordering them to open the action, and if they were forced back by the charge of the elephants to retire, those who had time to do so by the straight passages as far as the rear of the whole army, and those who were overtaken to right or left along the intervals between the lines. (Polyb. 15.9.9).

Under normal circumstances there were gaps between the maniples of the *hastati* and the two other divisions were not drawn up directly behind these maniples but, as Polybius says, 'opposite to the intervals separating those of the first line' meaning behind the gap between maniples to create a kind of checkerboard pattern (15.9.7). The *velites* normally opened the battle by skirmishing with enemy light-armed forces but would not usually be able to run straight to the rear of the whole army, but rather would have retreated behind the first line of *hastati*. It is not known whether the *velites* had any relationship to the maniples to which they were attached during a battle situation. They will have needed to retreat periodically to take up fresh javelins, but if these were kept at their own maniple they will have needed to wind their way back through the gaps in the army to reach a unit of *triarii*.

As far as we can tell, the standard formation of a Roman maniple in this period was in a rectangular formation four men deep.[23] This would mean two centuries side by side, with a front line of sixteen men per century, for a total of thirty-two men at the front of the maniple, with three more lines of thirty-two men standing behind them. The division into lines four men deep has obvious advantages and conveniences since it would make it very easy for the eight-man *contubernium* to stand together, and be a natural extension of the way that the army moved out of camp maniple by maniple, century by century, and probably *contubernium* by *contubernium* as well. As they lined up, the standard bearer of each maniple walked out with the standards and planted them where the front line should be. This helped to orientate the soldiers on the battlefield, as they would be able to gauge from the position of the standard where their front line was located and know not to go too far beyond it.[24]

We do not know the exact arrangement of soldiers within the battle line, which, while vital to the battle experience of a Roman soldier, was of no interest to our sources. It could have worked in a variety of ways. An eight-man *contubernium* could have been stretched out in one row, in which case the front of the century would have had the men from two *contubernia* across its front line, and four stretching the length of the whole maniple. Or each *contubernium* could have stood in a square, with four men in the front and four behind, or two in the front and six behind them, making a rectangle across the depth of the formation rather than across its front. In the formations with depth, the arrangements could then be adjusted by the men themselves, who could place their most bloodthirsty and eager members in the front and their steadier men behind. None of the formations would need to be exact, with each man only needing to make sure a member of his *contubernium* was to his right and left, or front and back, rather than this having to be one particular individual. There had to have been a degree of flexibility to all the formations, as the legions themselves varied in size depending on their recruitment, soldiers arriving and leaving year by year, and the casualties they took. The maniple would have needed to adapt to compensate for those who were sick or wounded.

Even when the soldiers had reached the site that had been selected for battle and drawn up in order, there was likely to be more of the waiting and boredom so characteristic of military service in all times and places. A long time could pass between the deployment of the battle line and the beginning of the actual engagement, if it happened at all. At Ilipa in 206 BCE, the two sides repeatedly broke camp and formed up their battle lines day upon day, only to retire again over and over (Polyb. 11.21.7). Livy's version of this contains a line that offers some insight into the often drawn-out and dull process of offering battle. He writes that the Romans and Carthaginians marched out from their camp, faced each other, then retired at sunset:

This went on for some days; the Carthaginians were always the first to get into line and the first to receive the order to retire when they were tired out with standing. No forward movement took place on either side, no missile was discharged, no battle-shout raised (Livy 28.14.2).

So we find the Roman soldier stood waiting, with very little to occupy his time save speaking with his comrades. What conversations might have filled these hours has been lost. Probably such things were never known beyond the rank-and-file soldiers themselves, as the idle discussions of soldiers were unlikely to come to the ears of the elite officers or their companions. Even Polybius, an eyewitness to some of these armies, never stood in their ranks nor is likely to have spent much time with anyone who had.

While a certain amount of vigilance was required for the sudden or unexpected, even if the signal was given to attack, the action would not happen instantly. If the general decided that there was a good opportunity to begin the battle, for example, if the enemy were moving a unit, or had come to the battlefield in a disorganized way, or some other advantage presented itself, then the auspices would be repeated, followed by the second, shorter exhortation. The auspices would not have been performed if the battle was at the instigation of the enemy, as in order to perform the auspices the Romans needed to have a query about a specific action. If it was not their choice to start the battle due to a temporary advantage or opportunity, then the first set of auspices covering action on that particular day would still have applied.

It is uncertain whether it was necessary to repeat the whole sequence of auspices, then sacrifice, then exhortation. A sacrifice was, however, more time consuming and cumbersome than divination using birds. The auspices could be checked swiftly in order to be completed while it was still possible to take advantage of an opportunity, but completing a whole sacrifice and doing divination on the entrails would take longer. There could have been a sacrifice of the type completed by the Greeks immediately before battle, the *sphagia* sacrifice, that was to propitiate the gods. A sacrifice of this sort would not need to be completed before the instigation of action but could be done behind the army while it was already in movement, or even when the battle had begun, as it was among the Greeks.

The second set of auspices cannot have been witnessed by the soldiers, who were arranged in their battle lines by the time it took place. Nevertheless, we are told that it was necessary in order that the soldier could make an oral declaration of his will before three or four of his comrades. This practice was called *testamentum in procinctu*. The Latin word *procinctus* means to be equipped or ready for battle, so the title of the will is simply 'the will [made while] equipped for battle.' After Sabidius has described the auspices taken in camp, he adds that the soldiers were then led out and drawn up in the battle line.[25] Something is missing in the text, which goes on to say that anyone who wished could use this delay to make his will. There are two interpretations of what the missing activity might be that created the delay. One is that it was the sacrifice, and the other is that it was the second set of auspices.[26] It seems more likely that it was the latter, because the making of the will was dependent on the auspices and it could not be done without them. Cicero claims that the *testamentum in procinctu* had fallen into disuse in his time, the 50s BCE, because the generals no longer held auspices and so the soldiers had no opportunity to make them.

The connection between the auspices and the declaration of the soldier's will is quite unclear, as there is no obvious religious connection between this type of divination and the soldier's personal wishes after his death. It might simply be that in the Middle Republic there was a delay while the auspices were taken that did not happen in later eras. Perhaps a declaration as important as the soldier's will needed the solemnity leant by the auspices being conducted simultaneously in order to provide an appropriately weighty moment.[27] The auspices did imply the immediacy of battle, which might have been a necessary legal requirement for the validity of this type of will. Otherwise there seems no reason why the soldier could not have declared his intentions for his will at any point during his military service. The further implication of the *testamentum* would be that when the Roman commander had decided to launch an attack, notification would need to be sent around the soldiers that the auspices were being taken. This seems to point to the origins of the practice being in an early time period when armies were much smaller than in the second century, at a time when the soldiers were not spread out so far and the general's activities were more visible.

The small amount of time set aside for the soldier to make *testamentum in procinctu* would have felt intense. There, with combat all but certain, the soldier was asked to think about his own death and contemplate his last wishes. At the same time he might be asked to bear solemn witness to the wishes of others, which it would be his duty to commit to memory and promise to carry out should his comrade die in the upcoming encounter. Plutarch says that these wills were made as the Romans were girding up their togas and taking up their shields, when they gave the unwritten will to three or four of their comrades (Plut. *Cor.* 9.2). It must have seemed especially poignant when standing gazing across at the men who might kill them, and an intense bonding experience for the handful of men who shared that moment.

The drawn out process of divination, sacrifice, and exhortation, as well as the *testamentum in procinctu*, shows us several elaborate ways in which the Romans laid emphasis on the importance of a pitched battle. Although individual soldiers and units were in danger during skirmishing and the storming of cities, the pitched battle represented a period of elevated risk for the whole army. This collective danger was marked with the careful ceremonies that consulted and solicited the gods, giving the soldiers and their officers reassurance that the cosmic landscape was, if not tipped in their favour, at least free of divine impediment. The experience was also framed by the speeches of the commander, who would exhort the soldiers with an argument for why they were likely to win. Later, in the aftermath, he would lead another ceremony in which he gave out awards and described the deeds of the brave. Not every soldier who served in a Roman army of the Middle Republic would fight in one of these large, deliberately orchestrated, set-piece battles, but for those who did, the experience encompassed much more than combat.

Chapter 10

Fighting a Battle

The *Velites*

When a military unit needs to move while it is on a battlefield or in proximity to hostile forces, its allied units will aid it by deploying missile weapons. In the modern day these missiles are gunfire, and their use for this purpose is referred to as 'suppressive fire' when it is intended to neutralize the enemy's attacking ability, and 'covering fire' when it is specifically to hold the enemy in place so that another unit can move.[1] Although it is not often specifically mentioned, the same was true in the ancient world. In order for the maniples of Roman heavy infantry to move into position on the field, they needed other units that protected them so that they could organize themselves without harassment.[2] The cavalry and the *velites*, as the two units with the greatest speed and range of weaponry, were the natural choice for this task. These would have been sent out to provide cover and to attack the enemy's units mid-deployment if they should see the opportunity. For this reason, Rome's enemies would have needed to protect their own infantry by sending out their cavalry, light-armed infantry or specialist units like archers. Hannibal did this before the Battle of Cannae, sending slingers and javelinmen out in advance of the infantry to form a screen of missile troops while the heavy infantry crossed a stream behind them to reach the battlefield (Polyb. 3.133.6). The Romans did the same thing before the Battle of the Trebia when they needed to cross the river. The cavalry was sent out followed by 6,000 *velites* before the infantry troops left the camp (Polyb. 3.72.1–4).

When the light-armed troops of the enemy and Roman *velites* had been sent out as a screen in this manner, it seems that they often did not begin fighting with the lines of their enemy counterparts, but rather kept apart from each other and maintained a watchful stance in case the other should attack. This would result in both armies being drawn up with a force of light-armed troops stretching across their front line. Presumably this process could also be done in reverse if it became apparent that no fighting would be done that day, with the heavy infantry retiring first, followed by the *velites* and finally, the cavalry covering the *velites* as they too fell back and retired. It ought to be remembered that although their role is often given little attention in the sources, the *velites* were a very large number of men whose presence in front of the army would have represented a substantial force. They made up almost thirty per cent of the total citizen legion and were important to the army's functioning.[3]

As the first units to go out, and the most mobile, it seems that the cavalry often or usually came to fighting with their opposite number. The Battle of Zama in 202 BCE will be used extensively in this chapter, as Polybius provides us a detailed description that is helpful for illustrating several different principles. Polybius mentions that at Zama, by the time both sides were ready for the infantry battle, the Numidian cavalry that were on both sides had 'been skirmishing with each other for some time' (Polyb. 15.12.1). As cavalry could very easily cut through light infantry, both sides would have been trying to protect their own screen of lightly armed men and seeking opportunities to attack that of the other side. On some occasions the first units to come to real blows were mixed, especially if the force had been sent out as reconnaissance to discover the position of the enemy army. This was what happened at Cynoscephalae in 197 BCE, when it was a mixed unit of cavalry and light-armed troops, possibly *velites*, whose conflict escalated into a large and ultimately decisive battle.

In addition to covering the deployment, the *velites* were often given the role of fighting a preliminary stage of the battle, in which they skirmished with light-armed infantry or other units placed in front of the enemy army for this purpose, like the elephants. The tactical purpose of this initial skirmishing in front of the drawn-up armies is not altogether clear. It is a clearly defined part of the battle, spoken of as happening after the whole army was drawn up and ready, and entirely independent of the *velites'* protective duty during the heavy infantry deployment. It might be that, having acted as a screen for deployment on both sides, it was not possible for the light-armed troops to withdraw from the front of the line without leaving the army at a significant disadvantage. The range of the *hasta velitaris* was much longer than the range of the *pilum* thrown by the *hastati*, and the same will have been true of the other side's light-armed missile weapons versus the missile weapons of the heavy infantry, if they had them at all.

One objective of the *velites* would have been to dispose of the enemy's light-armed infantry. If they succeeded in making the lightly-armed soldiers retreat, they could attack the first lines of the heavy infantry while remaining at a distance themselves, aiming to break up or weaken these lines. If their light armed opponents were formidable, their aim would be to at least hold them off until their own heavy infantry units behind them had advanced close enough to force the opposing light infantry to retreat. No light-armed infantry bearing missile weapons wished to have heavily armed and armoured soldiers close to them, as they were dressed for speed, not defence. When the heavy infantry were close enough to engage, the *velites* escaped from the front lines to the rear through the gaps between the maniples.

The Battle of Telamon offers a good illustration of the role of the *velites*, as it was an occasion on which the *velites* were extremely effective with their opening onslaught. The Romans were facing an army made up of different Gaulish tribes. This army did possess its own light-armed infantry, but it had been caught between two Roman armies and, on one side at least, had no protective screen of missile-wielding troops. This meant that the Romans were able to advance upon them with the *velites* close to the *hastati* and unleash a javelin assault without themselves being harassed. The *velites* advanced a little in front of the legions and they threw their javelins thick and fast at the ranks of the Gauls.[4] The number of missiles in the onslaught would have been more important than precise accuracy on the part of the individual. When a large number of missile weapons hurtled down at once, it would have been very difficult to avoid or dodge them. The *velites* in a standard consular army of two legions numbered more than 2,000 and the initial javelin onslaught against a foe ill-equipped to deal with light infantry would have been significant. In other words, one of the primary advantages of the *velites* was the fact that they operated in large numbers. The more of the enemy that could be brought down by the first hail of missile weapons, the greater the chance of sowing disorder. This worked well at Telamon, where the Gauls were unable to reach the *velites* to attack or drive them away. Polybius says the Gaesatae in the vanguard were

> reduced to the utmost distress and perplexity, [and] some of them, in their impotent rage, rushed wildly on the enemy and sacrificed their lives, while others, retreating step by step on the ranks of their comrades, threw them into disorder by their display of faint-heartedness (Polyb. 2.30.4).

The *velites* faired extremely well against heavy infantry, but were vulnerable against certain other units often placed in the front lines like elephants, or if they were left exposed to cavalry. At Zama the *velites* faced Hannibal's elephants that were stationed in front of the Carthaginian army with the light-armed, missile bearing mercenary units behind them (Polyb. 15.11.1). On this occasion, Hannibal started the battle by ordering the elephants to charge, and the *velites*, who had been ordered to open the fighting, had to deal with them. Since orders on both sides were issued by the sound of a trumpets and bugles, the loud noise made some of the elephants panic, with some crashing back into their own side, and others trampling the *velites*. The *velites* had been told to run if they were beaten back by the elephants, ideally to the very rear of the lines, and if they could not make it, to duck between the lines, meaning the spaces between the *hastati* and the *principes* and the *principes* and *triarii*.

The objective of the *velites* at Zama was not to kill the elephants specifically, but to dispose of them in any manner possible, either sending them back upon their own lines or encouraging them to flee the battlefield. For this reason Scipio had ordered the maniples to form up with one long corridor leading straight from the front line to the rear of the Roman army. The task of driving away the elephants was suited to the *velites'* strength in groups or teams rather than as individuals. By creating a shower of missiles, they could scare or hurt the animal into running in the opposite direction. The elephant driver would have been a priority target to unseat or kill, to ensure that if the animal fled through the lines of the Roman maniples and emerged at the army's rear, it could not then be used to turn and attack them.

Polybius here calls the *velites* 'cohorts' which may or may not be an accurate term, given his definition of that word as a unit made up of three maniples. It would make sense for the *velites* to operate like the later cohorts did, which were made of one maniple each from the *hastati*, *principes* and *triarii*. The *velites* attached to the maniples of *triarii* and *principes* could not fight directly in front of their own maniples, which were behind the front lines when the battle started. It would be convenient for the *velites* to organise by number, for example so that the *velites* attached to the third maniples of *triarii* and *principes* would fight with the *velites* of the third maniple of *hastati* in front of that maniple. Their cohorts would thus number 144 men, more or less, in a group, within which individuals could move quite freely, and also push forward singly or in small bands, if they chose and saw an opportunity.[5]

When they skirmished at the opening of a battle, the *velites* could and did make retreats to their maniples, as described by Polybius in his narration of the Battle of Ilipa in Spain in 206 BCE:

> as the day advanced, there was no decisive advantage on either side in the engagement of the light-armed troops, those who were hard pressed always retreating to the shelter of their respective phalanxes and then issuing forth again to resume the combat (11.22.9).

During these intervals the *velites* could pick up more javelins. Since they threw them with the right hand, they had to carry spares in their left hand. The left arm also bore the soldier's small shield and so probably the *veles* could only carry three to five javelins at a time, while a cache of replacements would be left at the soldier's maniple.[6] A trip to replenish these could also provide them time to breathe and receive some words of encouragement from their fellow soldiers.

As lightly armed soldiers, the main exertion of the *velites* would have been the cardiovascular exercise of sprinting and running. Running was a big part of the *velites'* job, both through short dashes towards the enemy and back through their own maniples to retrieve more weapons. On some occasions the *velites* needed to flee from cavalry, elephants, or other light-armed soldiers. Perhaps the most exciting and dynamic role fell to the *velites* with the cavalry, who were borne close to the enemy on horses, and leapt down to dash out of the cavalry's ranks and throw their javelins before swinging back up onto their mounts.[7] Sometimes, as we saw in the chapter on training, the *velites* would come close enough to other light-armed infantry to use their swords and fight side by side with the cavalrymen.

The primary offensive capability of the *velites* was their collective missile power. This type of violence is generally thought to be easier to initiate and carry through than close combat with a sword. It is easier, psychologically speaking, to hurt someone with a missile weapon because the distance makes the harm seem less personal. The *veles* taking aim with the *hasta velitaris* had to concentrate and remember his throwing technique under pressure, to aim and then to throw. Probably he had little time to consider what might happen when it reached its target. Once the throw had been made, the *veles* had relinquished control, and had no power to stop or alter the javelin's flight. When fighting hand to hand, the soldier was in control at every stage of his sword's movement, including vicious cuts and thrusts that sliced flesh in front of his eyes. By contrast, when the *velites'* javelins whipped down thick and fast on an area of enemy soldiers, the *veles* was probably already prepping another, and the sheer number of missiles would have made it very difficult to tell if his own weapon had struck a man, a shield, or the ground.

On the one hand, the young soldiers might have found this disappointing. As we have seen, one of the concerns of the *veles* was to be seen, to stand out for his bravery and to draw the attention of the centurions of their maniples. On the other hand, it may have formed an important psychological stepping stone towards the kind of close and personal violence that was necessary in the front lines of the *hastati* and *principes*. Some of the javelins would have done damage, hitting a leg or an arm or even a face, to cheers of approval from the front lines of the older soldiers. This immediate positive reinforcement for damage inflicted upon an enemy soldier would have helped to ease any initial trepidation on the part of the young soldiers about hurting another person. The anonymity of the javelin strikes would have allowed him to imagine the situation both ways. If he felt nervous or guilty about having harmed someone he could tell himself that he had not, and conversely if he needed to work up his courage to more personal violence he could reassure himself that he had already done it.

The *velites'* battle was not finished when they retreated behind their maniples and the *hastati* advanced to engage in hand-to-hand combat. The maniples of Roman infantry needed to be able to advance, retire, and exchange one line for another. The evidence about how exactly this was done is not described in our extant sources and has puzzled scholars who posed the question of how maniples could exchange places on the battlefield without exposing themselves to attack during the manoeuvre. The answer lies in the previously mentioned military adage, that in order to move an infantry unit anywhere on a battlefield, one needs to lay down covering fire.[8] The *velites* were not the only unit that could do this, as we have seen with the archers and slingers that accompanied some of Ligustinus' armies. They were, however, a unit that was helpfully distributed throughout the maniples, which would make it easy for some of the *velites* to cover the retreat of their own specific maniple while others secured the advance of theirs. This could have involved either reforming a screen in front of their unit or lingering in the gaps between maniples and using their javelins to prevent an enemy advancing.[9] Since under missile fire the Romans closed up their ranks to offer a wall of shields, enemy infantry would be forced to do something similar.

Hastati

The first ranks of the *hastati* were the first static front line, which initially remained in place while the *velites* skirmished in front of it. Each individual soldier was oriented by the standards that marked where the line was supposed to be, and the individuals who stood to their right and left. The ten maniples of the *hastati* made up the front line. When lines were adjusted to make them longer, it was usually accomplished by taking a maniple of *principes* or *triarii* and moving them up into the front line rather than making the *hastati* move into a wider formation by thinning the depth of the line.

By the time the soldier marched on to the field of battle, certain parts of the army might already be fighting. Even if they were not, the *hastati* did not usually start the battle and they would not have had to go into action immediately. Instead they would have settled into a period of waiting while their *velites* and cavalry skirmished with the light-armed infantry of the enemy in the space between the two battle lines. There was initially quite a large space between the two armies, which the heavy infantry would close by advancing when the signal was given. In the very front lines, the soldiers needed to be vigilant for any action that came too close. The enemy light-armed troops would be trying to kill the *velites*, but they would also take any opportunity to break through them and attack the *hastati* with their missile weapons, so the soldiers needed to watch for any signs of impending danger. Depending on the enemy that they faced, they would need to be prepared to defend against slingshots, arrows, javelins, and any other types of missiles that might come flying towards them. They also needed to carefully watch for any sign of the *velites* returning or retreating, either seeking the safety of their lines for rest or to replenish their weapons. If *velites* suddenly came flying towards them because they were being chased by the enemy, they would need to be alert to allow their own men to pass, while being ready to attack their pursuers.

While they waited, the front lines of *hastati* would have been able to gaze straight out across the battlefield to evaluate the appearance of their opponents. Over the course of the second and third centuries BCE the Romans fought a wide range of peoples in the ancient world, from the tribes of Hispania and Gaul to some of the Greek city states and the kingdom of Macedon in the East. During their drawn-out wars with the Carthaginians they would often have looked out to see elephants stationed in front of the enemy lines. When they faced Spaniards, they would have seen them in their national dress, which was a short tunic with a purple trim (Polyb. 3.114.3). Celtiberians wore a black cloak that resembled goat hair, with a round wicker shield, greaves protecting their legs and helmets made of bronze with purple crests (Diod.Sic.5.33.2–3).

Some enemies were more intimidating than others. By the time of the Battle of Cannae in 216 BCE, on the end of a string of Roman defeats, the sizeable contingent of Libyans that were in the Carthaginian army were equipped with their pick of the Roman equipment that they had recovered from the battlefields of their previous victories.[10] It would have occurred to the soldiers facing them that they had stripped those shields and helmets from the corpses of the Romans who had marched out before them. At the Battle of Telamon in 225 BCE, the vanguard of the consortium of Celtic tribes facing the Romans was made up of the Gaesatae, tall, striking-looking warriors who fought naked, thinking that clothing would hinder their path across the brambled battlefield. Their appearance startled the Romans. They were not so intimidating, however, that the Romans did not also notice that they were wearing gold torques and bracelets that would earn them a rich profit as spoils of war (Polyb. 2.29.5–9). On that occasion, there was fear among the lines, but also greed and a sense of opportunity.

This period of waiting while the *velites* skirmished might, at first glance, seem to be an uneventful and relatively easy part of the battle for the soldiers standing in their maniples, but it is likely to have been difficult psychologically. There is no first-hand account of what it was like to wait in these lines watching the youngest members of the army fight, but several considerations should colour our view. Firstly, at least some of the *velites* fighting in front of them were men with whom they had lived and worked for months, if not years. They would not have been familiar with all 1,200 of the *velites*, but those who were fighting directly in front of their units and using them for support and relief were friends and comrades, familiar faces that they saw every day. Secondly, the success or failure of the *velites* had a direct bearing on their own safety and chances of both victory and survival. They had a very limited ability to intervene in the fighting and would only have been able to help if it came close to them.

These conditions exposed the soldier to a number of potentially harrowing experiences that are recognized as profound stressors upon modern military personnel.[11] Firstly, the general condition of being in danger is stressful. The soldier in the front line needed to maintain a state of constant alertness for missiles flying through the air towards him, as well as any threats in the form of light-armed infantry who might come across the field at speed. Someone who perceives themselves to be under threat, as the soldiers certainly were at this time, tends to find it stressful, and this would have provided a general background level of discomfort even while nothing dramatic was happening. This discomfort would be compounded by watching the *velites* fight. Although gladiatorial combats were a form of entertainment in ancient Italy at this time, the soldiers had a personal connection with the *velites* who were in greater danger during this period than the *hastati*. Watching comrades in danger and being unable to help can produce feelings of frustration, helplessness and guilt. If the *velites* started to lose or some of them were struck and killed, or they were run down by enemy cavalry, horror and shock would compound the unpleasantness of the experience.

Of course, the soldiers were not standing silently during this time, lost in their thoughts. They could not physically intervene, but they could raise noise to encourage their own soldiers and to try to intimidate the enemy. At Telamon the soldiers were not only frightened by the appearance of the naked Gauls but also by the noise they made. Polybius says that the soldiers

> were terrified by the fine order of the Celtic host and the dreadful din, for there were innumerable horn-blowers and trumpeters, and, as the whole army were shouting their war-cries at the same time, there was such a tumult of sound that it seemed that not only the trumpets and the soldiers but all the country round had got a voice and caught up the cry (2.29.5–6).

The Romans had their own war cry, although we do not know what it was, or if it was always the same. When they made their final advance they would clash their spears against their shields to raise a noise. During their initial wait, the shouting and clashing of weapons would have risen and fallen as they reacted to the skirmishing.

The opening of a battle was signalled by the sound of the trumpet.[12] The trumpet was a significant sound for a Roman soldier, and we find it in literature, especially epic literature, as a symbol of war. Ennius wrote that its sound, to a Roman ear, said *taratantara* (Enn. *Ann.* 451). There were at least two moments where the battle could be said to begin, once when the skirmishing began with the cavalry and *velites*, and then again when the heavy infantry of *hastati* moved forward to close the space between the opposing lines. At the Battle of Zama, when the *velites* had been held back in the gaps between the maniples, Hannibal opened the battle by ordering the charge of his elephants. As the *velites* fought with them, the *hastati* made their advance. At the Battle of Telamon the Romans seem to have taken the initiative against the front lines of the Gauls because they were undefended by light-armed soldiers. The *velites* were able to unleash their javelins on the unprotected front ranks of the Gauls, and the *hastati* advanced to take advantage of the confusion. Sometimes the battles were started deliberately by neither side, like the Battle of Pydna that started when a runaway horse was pursued by both sides and escalated into a fight between all (Livy 44.40.7–10).

Since there were different stages when the different units began their battle, and it was not always opened at the instigation of the Romans, the commander would only have been able to give a second speech to the soldiers on some occasions rather than all of them. Since the speeches had probably grown out of the ancient practice of the commander announcing the results of the auspices, originally it would not have been given unless the battle was instigated by the Romans. They did not need to take auspices to defend themselves or if the battle began by accident, as auspices were only taken to see if there was any prohibition against launching an attack. Far from there being a clear-cut moment when the battle was started, it seems that often the action of one unit prompted the start of the next. These units were able to move independently by initiative of their own officer, who might be a tribune, a legate or a prefect.[13] The *hastati*, therefore, could have been ordered to advance by the signal of the trumpet, with the commander's words ringing in their ears, or they could hear the signal to attack when the enemy were already advancing upon them.

The *hastati* were probably eager to fight, if only because it meant the end of their uncomfortable, stressful wait. Before they advanced to hand-to-hand fighting, they would throw a volley of *pila* at the enemy. As we have seen, the *pilum* was meant to be thrown at a short distance. Its impact depended on its weight rather than its velocity.[14] The line would have had to advance to a distance suitable for this weapon, which, unlike the lighter and numerous *hasta velitaris*, was supposed to be thrown straight at one particular target, the body of an enemy combatant. Here the strength of the soldier added to the penetrative abilities of the weapon. It could be extremely effective, as was demonstrated by the death of Indibilis, the chieftain of the Ilergetes, in battle against the Romans. Livy writes that his soldiers were fighting around him, while Indibilis 'resisted though half-dead, but was pinned to the ground by a *pilum*' (29.2.15).

If an enemy soldier caught the *pilum* on his shield, it was intended to stick in the shield, rendering it useless because it could no longer be effectively wielded. Most of Rome's enemies had similar missile weapons and the *hastati* would need to be careful to protect themselves against incoming missiles with their shields while at a range close enough to throw their own. Although the use of the *pilum* in Roman combat is frequently attested as a kind of preliminary stage of the battle of the *hastati*, it was not compulsory and it was not used every time.[15] If the enemy were charging in too fast or for some other reason they had no time to throw the *pilum*, the soldier would simply drop it on the ground and draw his sword.

After the volley of *pila* the Roman line would advance to meet the enemy with swords. As they moved forwards, they yelled their war cry and clashed their weapons together. Each soldier had a good amount of space around him, enough to wield his sword and swing his shield around, but otherwise his companions were close. Although he had been trained to fight, ideally the individual soldier did not want to spend too much time fighting hand to hand, as it did not take very long to tire. Fighting vigorously with a sword and shield can only be sustained for fifteen or twenty minutes before men become exhausted.[16] Rather, remembering what he had been taught, the *hastatus* approaching an enemy for the first time was aiming to be quick and vicious. As he and the enemy soldier reached one another he would plant his left leg firmly forward in the ground and crouch a little, from where he could use the power of his leg muscles to thrust up with sword or shield.

The choice of tactics would have varied depending on the foe. The most powerful blow was a cut brought down from overhead, but this involved a certain amount of risk because it took longer to land than a thrust, and would expose the right arm, armpit and side to the enemy's own blade. The same, of course, was true in reverse, presenting the soldier a potential vulnerability in enemies using longswords. Thus for soldiers armed in this way, the Romans preferred to use their swords to thrust.[17] As we saw during the discussion of Roman training, a thrust aimed at the head and eyes was preferred with some enemies, and the signature move of the Roman legionary became the technique of striking the opponent with the shield, ramming the iron rim up into the jaw or smacking him with the boss, before plunging the sword into the side or midriff, aiming at vital organs. Combinations of cut and thrust could also be used, as a thrust that jabbed or cut any part of the body could cause the soldier to flinch and allow the Roman enough time to bring the powerful cutting move down upon his neck or shoulder.

Everything the Roman man had ever learned told him that this moment called for most aggressive acts of violence he could possibly manage. For those soldiers who enjoyed such things, and there were certainly those who did, this would have been an exciting moment, an outlet for gratuitous violence that was welcome, desirable, and positively received. Even now there is a very small percentage of men, referred to as 'aggressive psychopaths' or 'natural killers' for whom combat is enjoyable, and who suffer little to no remorse for killing another human being.[18] Probably these men have always existed, although it is impossible to say whether they existed in greater or lesser numbers than the two per cent found in armies in the Second World War and in the 'less than four per cent' in the modern professional American army.[19] During the Second World War, wide conscription would have diluted the percentage of men who sought out the military as an outlet for violent tendencies, and in the American army, the percentage is probably depressed by a restriction on recruiting men with a criminal record. In the armies of the Roman Republic, we would expect boys who were naturally aggressive and violent to both self-select into the most dangerous parts of service and to elect to stay in the army or volunteer for further campaigns. While others served only the minimum required years of service, men who found their violent tendencies were well suited to the legions would have been able to concentrate in Rome's armies.

Natural killers gravitate to the front of the fighting, where their aggression and fearlessness help to motivate others. These others, we might imagine, were much like the most common type of soldier found in the modern world, quite able to fight given the right training and circumstances, but who did not find it particularly enjoyable. There would also be the more reticent or hesitant men, whose inclination may have been to hang back, either through fear or through an instinctive reluctance to harm another human being at such a close and intimate range. For these last two categories of men, the sporadic method of ancient fighting would have been helpful. The lines clashed, then parted, regrouped, and waited before fighting again, so the actual time spent fighting hand to hand in a battle line was very short.[20] This meant that the soldier only needed to work himself into exercising close, bloodied violence in brief flashes. He did not need to maintain aggression during protracted fighting for many hours while he was tiring both physically and mentally. Rather, he could work himself into short bursts of quick and vicious action. Some circumstances will prompt outbursts of violence even in otherwise mild-mannered men. Notably, the death of a comrade is one of the triggers that can move soldiers to a murderous anger, especially if they witness it personally.[21] A Roman soldier who had seen the death or wounding of one of the maniple's *velites* in the early skirmish was quite likely to harbour anger against the side that had caused it. A soldier whose close comrade was killed or wounded next to him might well react with blinding rage.

Further aiding the Roman soldier in his violent task was the fact that a planned, pitched battle was a very particular endeavour with conditions unlike any other. The ceremonies done before and after battle marked the beginning and end points, separating off a limited period of time within which specific rules and standards applied. The Romans had queried the gods for any impediments to success beforehand, and they only initiated an engagement themselves after querying the gods a second time for the quality of the immediate moment. We have seen that the whole army often deployed and retired many times before actually engaging in combat, which would only have emphasized that the time during which a battle was fought was unique and required specific conditions to enter. Afterwards, if the Romans were victorious, there would be more ceremony to mark what had happened. This included an awards ceremony called the *contio*, in which the commander gave awards and decorations and described the conduct of the soldiers who had performed admirable deeds. This made battle an event marked off by ceremony and ritual that allowed the soldier to prepare himself beforehand and process what had happened afterward.

We should not, therefore, be surprised if the Roman soldier interpreted battle as a short-term discomfort, time limited, during which unique rules and conditions applied. To be successful, a soldier did not have to display continued, sustained violence, or be at the very front of the ranks again and again. The soldier might only need to show conspicuous bravery, or extreme violence, once. Citizen armies are, above all, characterized by being made up of ordinary men who have been drafted, men who would never have chosen to join the military under other circumstances. As we shall see later, sometimes the Romans rewarded acts of courage with discharge, the tacit admission that although these acts were welcome and necessary in the army, one of the lures for completing them was that they would not have to be repeated. The individual progression through the divisions and the relative rarity of pitched battles could mean that in a six to fourteen-year length of service a Roman soldier might only have to be a front line *hastatus* in one of these set-piece battles once or twice, or even not at all.

The Killing Zone

As long as the two armies were actively fighting face to face, there does not seem to have been a large amount of killing. The evidence suggests that most casualties, and thus the most amount of slaughter, was done when one side's line gave way, and the soldiers turned to flee.[22] This almost always turned into a rout as the losing side's soldiers were cut down from behind and killed. As long as the lines on both sides held, frontline troops could be wounded or killed but not in huge numbers. This is reflected in the oath that Livy tells us originated among the soldiers in 216 BCE, 'that they would not leave their comrades for fear or for flight, and that they would not quit the ranks save to fetch or pick up a weapon, to strike an enemy, or to save a comrade' (22.38.4). The core of the oath, not to leave the line for the purposes of fleeing, suggests that it made the battle exponentially more dangerous, as once one soldier ran, another would do so as well, causing a cascading effect.

A further restriction on the number of deaths while both lines held is that it was apparently not easy in a practical sense to kill someone in hand-to-hand combat. When Roman soldiers voluntarily engaged in combat during skirmishing, when obviously there could be no rout, rewards were given for just wounding an enemy (Polyb. 6.39.3). During his description of the Battle of Zama, Polybius says that the mercenaries fighting for Carthage 'at first prevailed by their courage and skill, wounding many of the Romans' (15.13.1). Even while they had the upper hand, the mercenaries only managed to wound, not kill, their opponents. It is only later in the fight, when the mercenaries had begun to turn and flee and were trapped between their own allies and the Romans that Polybius describes a scene of great carnage. The oath is instructive here too, with 'to save a colleague' implying that it was permissible to break the line in a forward direction, and this is perhaps why wounding did not often turn into killing. A soldier could step forward to yank his comrade back out of harm's way or take over the fight for him, and he might have needed to do both. The role of a soldier in the second or third rank of the maniple would thus be to act as both helper and guardian for the colleagues in front of him, with the aim of intervening between a wounding blow or slice and the killing movement that would follow. Anyone who had been wounded could be passed or helped backwards through the maniple from hand to hand.

In his description of a Roman legion versus a Macedonian phalanx, Polybius tells us that there was a space of 3 feet between each soldier and the one next to him, and the same amount of distance between the ranks.[23] This was to allow the soldiers to move around with their shield and sword without getting in each other's way. Facing a Macedonian phalanx, a densely packed square of men who levelled extremely long pikes at their enemies, Polybius remarks that a single Roman was opposite to two men and thus ten pikes. For the Romans, this had the disadvantage of neutralizing the ranks further back than the first, 'as the rear ranks can be of no help to the front rank either in thus forcing the pikes away or in the use of the sword' (18.30.10). This implies that the normal job of these rankers was to turn away weapons with their shields and to attack anyone they could reach. Sometimes, especially under missile fire, the Romans came in close together and formed a *testudo*, a 'tortoise', in which their large shields were lifted above their heads and they moved together. At other times, they banded closely together in order to present a wall of shields to the front.[24] They would then push the formation forward and the rankers behind would help to provide weight and momentum.

Polybius indicates that the proper behaviour of the units stationed behind the front line was to follow and shout encouragement. He describes this dynamic at Zama, in which 'the rear ranks of the Romans followed close on their comrades, cheering them on, but the Carthaginians behaved like cowards, never coming near their mercenaries nor attempting to back them up' (15.13.3). The presence of other soldiers close by was of great psychological importance, and the reassurance that these troops provided had several dimensions. Firstly, they were witnesses to the behaviour of the soldiers in the front lines, and by shouting and cheering they reminded the soldiers who could not see them that they were there and watching. It was important that deeds of valour be witnessed by others so that they would increase the man's reputation and allow him access to tangible rewards like money and military decorations. Secondly, the noise of their reactions would have given immediate reassurance of the positive value of violent and aggressive actions, and the sense of being part of a crowd could even have helped to escalate their efforts.[25] Finally, the noise of the soldiers provided the reassuring knowledge that practical support was at hand, should it be needed.

When enemy soldiers clashed in the area between the two battle lines, they would have parted again when they reached a stalemate, or if one side retreated because it was temporarily getting the worst of the fight. Any retreat could not be a disorderly flight, which would prompt the other side to rush forward in pursuit. Rather, when the Romans needed to make a retreat out of the killing zone, it seems they carefully stepped backwards while continuing to face forward and defend themselves with their shields. Conversely, when they had made progress forward, they stepped over any enemy dead and weapons during their advance. At Zama, the mercenaries stationed in the front gave way and the *hastati* pursued them back upon their rear lines. According to Polybius, the army now had a problem:

> The space which separated the two armies still on the field was now covered with blood, slaughter, and dead bodies, and the Roman general was placed in great difficulty by this obstacle to his completing the rout of the enemy. For he saw that it would be very difficult to pass over the ground without

breaking his ranks owing to the quantity of slippery corpses which were still soaked in blood and had fallen in heaps and the number of arms thrown away at haphazard (15.14.1–2).

The *hastati*, who had taken the principal part in creating the carnage, had advanced past it and needed to be recalled by bugle. They were told to form up in the centre, while the *principes* and the *triarii* were brought up behind them to the left and right and then ordered to advance over the dead to join them. Once again, this manoeuvre seems impossible to complete without the cover of missile fire, and, although Polybius does not mention it, it surely must be the case that either missile detachments aided the process or the *velites* protected the movements of their own units. In particular, the *hastati* that were closest to the enemy while they waited for the other lines to join them would have been especially vulnerable without missile protection.

Finishing

The grim description of the scene left behind the Roman advance at Zama does actually help to elucidate just exactly what the Romans, especially the ranks behind the first, were doing on the battlefield. There is evidence that Roman soldiers did significant amounts of damage to the bodies of their enemies before they continued their advance. This may have included decapitation. While this may have been the result of violent anger, or a product of the group environment of goading and cheering soldiers, it probably also had a very practical purpose of making sure that a seemingly-dead enemy was truly dead. Since the soldiers pressed forward in the battle line by advancing over the bodies of their dead opponents, they would have wanted to leave no chance that someone who had seemingly expired actually still had the strength to slash at their ankles or legs.

The evidence that Roman soldiers routinely or commonly decapitated their enemies comes from various sources. When Livy describes the Macedonians being intimidated by the sorry state of the bodies of dead cavalrymen killed by the Romans in 200 BCE, he lists as the most fearful of the wounds 'arms torn away, shoulders and all, or heads separated from bodies, with the necks completely severed, or vitals laid open' (31.34.4). We have seen that the Roman *gladius* was sharp and powerful enough to cut through bone from the skeleton from Cerro de la Cruz mentioned in Chapter 7. The attacking Roman had apparently attempted to decapitate this man, too, although he was probably a civilian in a town, which may suggest this was a kind of Roman standard or habit. In Silius Italicus' epic *Punica*, the character Laelius kills an opponent by severing his head on the battlefield (15.469–70). It is possible to decapitate a living person quickly with some skill and a sharp enough knife or sword, and civilizations known to have done this during battle include the Nasca of Peru.[26] A painted amphora from Campania and a tomb painting from Paestum, both dating to the third century BCE, show warriors about to deliver a *coup de grace* to a fallen opponent by seizing the head in their left hand and aiming a spear at the base of the neck with their right.[27] Across the Paestum tomb on the opposite side, another warrior has already buried his spear in his opponent's upper body near the collar bone. This iconography is suggestive of a longer tradition within Italy of finishing an opponent by seizing the head and inflicting damage to the neck, where the opening of the carotid artery would cause death quickly.

There is another story, told to us by Livy, that might help both with what exactly the Romans were doing on the battlefield itself and how the third and fourth rankers were participating in combat. It involves the army of criminals and slaves that was recruited after the Battle of Cannae to fight for the Roman state. Their commander, Sempronius Gracchus, promised the men who were enslaved that they could earn their freedom if they could bring him the head of an opponent as proof that they had killed a man in battle. He had to rescind this order, however, when he found that the slave soldiers had paused to take the heads off their dead opponents rather than pressing the attack:

And nothing hampered the Romans more than that enemies' heads were made the price of freedom. For when a man had boldly slain an enemy, in the first place he was wasting time in cutting off the head with difficulty in the confusion and turmoil; and then, as his right hand was occupied in holding the head, the bravest had ceased to be fighters, while the battle was turned over to the spiritless and the fearful. When the tribunes of the soldiers reported this to Gracchus: that they were not wounding a single enemy standing, but butchering the fallen; and that in the soldiers' right hands there were human heads instead of swords, he ordered the command at once given that they should throw away the heads and attack the enemy (24.15.3–5).

There are really two ways to interpret this story. It might be that Sempronius had asked these soldiers to take an extra step in order to provide proof to secure their freedom. It turned out, however, that stopping to remove a head inhibited a man from continuing the attack. The other possible interpretation is that Sempronius had asked for heads in particular because decapitation was a regular method used by Roman soldiers either to finish an opponent or to make certain they were dead, but it turned out that the inexperienced soldiers were unable to do this quickly and efficiently. The final flaw in the plan was the soldiers trying to carry the heads, which would not have been a normal activity in either case.

Whichever of the options is the case, the story does give us a better idea of how the ranks of soldiers operated. If a Roman soldier wounded an opponent while the lines on both sides were still holding, he would have needed to make sure the man was dead before he, and the rest of the line, continued the advance. This probably involved pulling or pushing him to the ground to inflict final blows, and, although this need not have taken a long time, the soldier dealing with a falling or fallen man would have been stooped or hunched over. This would have made him vulnerable to any enemy soldiers coming up behind their comrade, and so a soldier from the ranks behind would have needed to step in to combat the next opponent. When the soldier was finished and absolutely sure that the enemy posed no more threat, he could catch his breath for a moment, protected by the fighters in front of him, before seizing the next opportunity to return to the front. In the case of the enslaved soldiers at Beneventum, instead of plunging back into the fight, they effectively became bystanders. Others, whose natural inclination was to hang back, suddenly found themselves with no choice but to become the front rank.

It is hard to know exactly how accurate Livy's account might be, but the incident with the heads is good for illustrating how eager fighters could repeatedly return to the front rank while others could hang back. There were moments where it was necessary for someone to step into the front rank when a comrade was wounded or had badly wounded his opponent. In times when battle was not going so well for the Romans, they would have had to step in when their own comrades were killed. Livy's description of this battle implies that the eager could simply move past the reluctant to claim these openings, and that the fearful could probably linger for a long time until either the fight was won and the enemy fled, or the soldier became vulnerable and was forced to either fight or flee by an enemy bearing down on him. The dynamic in a battle line that was holding on both sides was much different from a rout. When one line broke, the winning side were no longer obliged to advance slowly and carefully. The pursuit of the fleeing soldiers became the most important thing, and in this circumstance men who were wounded seem to have been simply thrown down and left for dead.

Principes and Triarii

Stationed behind the *hastati*, making up the second line of heavy infantry, were the *principes*. Like the *hastati*, the *principes* would have needed to wait during the skirmishing of the light infantry until the heavy infantry were signalled to advance, although their line of sight to this activity would have been partially obscured by the *hastati* in front of them. The *principes*, as we saw at Zama, followed closely upon the ranks of the *hastati*, cheering them on. Like the other units, they did not need an order directly from the commander in order to react to circumstances on the battlefield, and so at Zama when the *hastati* fell into confusion in the centre, 'the officers of the *principes*, seeing what was happening, brought up their ranks to assist' (Polyb. 15.13.7). The *principes* evidently moved up to press the attack when the Romans gained ground. If the *hastati* lost ground, they would retreat between the intervals left by the *principes* and let them take over as the front line.

The *triarii* were the third of the heavy infantry divisions, and were usually placed furthest to the rear. The soldiers were stationed not standing, but kneeling, with their left leg forward, protected by their shields, and their *pila* embedded in the ground pointing upwards.[28] As this resting stance indicates, under normal circumstances they did not need to anticipate immediate action and were considered to be a reserve unit. Livy tells us that the phrase 'to fall back upon the *triarii*' was used as a saying among the Romans to mean a situation in which someone was in dire straits. The situation that gave rise to this phrase was not an orderly rotation of units, in which the *hastati* and the *principes* were unable to win the battle and the *triarii* were ordered into their place. Rather, he describes a battlefield in which the slow, backward retreat of the *hastati* had brought them to where the *principes* were stationed. The *principes* let the *hastati* retreat through the gaps in their maniples while they took over the front line. They, in turn, were slowly forced back to the line where the *triarii* had been stationed at the beginning of the battle, meaning that the Romans had progressively lost a significant amount of ground.

The regular stationing of the *triarii* as the third and last of the Roman lines reflects the principle that we observed within the units themselves where the aggressive soldiers were at the front and the stalwart at the rear. The *triarii* were men who had seen it all, and thus were the least likely to flee out of fear. They would be called to act in a situation which was among the most precarious and dangerous that the army faced, when a number of their units had already failed. Aggressive and proactive fighting was not the only behaviour that was valued in the legions, as Polybius tells us when he discusses the qualities that were desirable in centurions, who were chosen to be 'men of a steady and sedate spirit... who will hold their ground when worsted and hard-pressed and be ready to die at their posts' (Polyb. 6.24.9). The ability to remain calm and master their fear would have been critical for the *triarii* as well. Since breaking the line and turning to run caused the unit to collapse and usually precipitated a massacre of the fleeing soldiers, the *triarii* had the important job of stepping in to prevent breakdown and panic. Apparently the Carthaginian army under Hannibal used their best troops for a similar purpose, as Polybius tells us:

> the most efficient and steadiest of his troops he had placed behind at a certain distance in order that, anticipating and witnessing from afar what took place, they might with undiminished strength and spirit make use of their qualities at the proper time (15.16.4).

In one sense, the rank-and-file *triarii* were the safest troops in a pitched battle. They were furthest from the killing zone, they were seldom called upon to actually enter the fight, and they were also the most heavily armed. The *triarii*, with many years of war profits in their purses, were the troops most likely to wear the *lorica hamata*, the full panoply of mail.[29] In another sense, the occasional duty of the *triarii* was to enter the most hazardous of situations by taking responsibility for a battle that was already going badly. It might take an extraordinary effort to save the situation. Dionysius of Halicarnassus says of them that the Romans 'fall back of necessity upon these as their last hope when there has been a general slaughter of the younger men and they lack other reinforcements' (*Ant. Rom.* 8.86.4). Like Ligustinus, these men had probably drawn blood for the first time from the distance of the *hasta velitaris*, fought a variety of different nationalities and tribes, and once stood in the places of the soldiers who had faltered and given way.

The fact that the *triarii* were uncommonly used in a pitched battle situation does not necessarily mean that they were rarely in combat. As we have seen, pitched battles that involved one whole army against another did not happen every year or even during every campaign. A large proportion of time on campaign was spent simply moving across enemy lands. The Romans also spent time storming various cities, perhaps not properly categorized as combat because these actions were so often against civilians, and in skirmishing that only involved some army units. Since we start to see authors referring to cohorts when narrating events in the second century and Polybius tells us these were units of mixed division, this would in turn indicate that the *triarii* took an equal role in these operations.

Chapter 11

The Aftermath of Battle

S everal different things could happen in the immediate aftermath of a battle, depending on its outcome. If the battle had been indecisive, it could be ended in an orderly way, with the two sides carefully retreating as darkness fell. The maniples of Roman legionaries and allies fell back from the battlefield in accordance with their usual procedure, followed by the *velites* and the cavalry, and marched the several miles back to their camp. The wounded could be taken with the retreating soldiers, either helped along by their comrades or taken in wagons. The camp would turn to guard duty for the night, while some treated the wounded, and a count would be done of the dead and missing as the soldiers reported the status of their maniples.

If the Roman army had been defeated, there would be a great deal of confusion among the surviving soldiers. In the aftermath of a rout, Roman soldiers often found themselves scattered across the countryside, with no certainty about where they could find safety, where the enemy were, or if those enemy soldiers had also captured their camp, a common occurrence after a defeat. They would have had no idea at all whether their loss had been complete or partial, and whether they were part of only a handful of survivors, or if there were many other lost soldiers wandering the land. In such a situation, the soldiers struck out for the nearest friendly place, whether that was a town or an army camp. After the disaster at the Battle of Trasimene in 217 BCE, the scattered survivors had made their way to Rome, the obvious place to regroup and reconnect with the survivors of their own side and find representatives of the state who could provide them some direction.[1] For those not in the vicinity of Rome nor near friendly territory, as many armies on campaign were not, they could flee to another Roman army, if they knew of one in the area. After their defeat at the Second Battle of Herdonea in 210 BCE, the surviving soldiers fled to the camp of the other consul (Livy 27.1.15).

The aftermath of the Battle of Cannae provides a well-documented example of what might happen to soldiers and officers after a defeat. Here, the dead and soldiers who had been wounded badly enough that they could not walk were left on the battlefield as night fell. Others who had fled from the rout of the army found themselves in groups, alive and out of danger for the moment, but not knowing what had happened to the rest of the army or to the Roman camp. Out in the open fields, they risked being found by detachments of the enemy sent to hunt down survivors. They would not have tried to go back to the camp, knowing that the whole army had been defeated and that the camp was the obvious next target for the enemy to attack. As Cannae was so close to Rome, it was widely feared that Hannibal himself would move to attack it, so they did not try to travel there. The soldiers instead gathered at two nearby allied towns, Canusium and Venusia.

The reason that soldiers looked for a friendly town after a lost battle was in order to regroup, but also to be behind walls and under cover away from enemy detachments. Soldiers who had left a battlefield in defeat would have been uniquely vulnerable. They carried very little, since all their possessions had been left behind in the camp. Most would have turned and fled as it became clear that their maniple's structure had broken and those in front of them were being cut down. When this happened, the soldier's shield, which was heavy, cumbersome, and no longer of use, was dropped immediately. Livy included this detail in describing the actions of the survivors of Herdonea: 'those Romans who escaped from the fatal field fled by various routes, almost wholly weaponless, to Marcellus in Samnium' (Livy 27.1.15). This indicates it was common to drop swords and javelins as well as shields. Thus we find that survivors needed quite a bit of help. When the soldiers who made it to Canusium in 216 BCE were helped by a wealthy woman named Busa, she gave them corn, clothing, and travelling money.[2] Similarly at Venusia, the elite citizens gave the soldiers clothing, money, and arms (Livy 22.54.2).

After a defeat, the regrouping soldiers often had no clear leaders and had to make emergency plans about what to do next. After Cannae, the soldiers who had been left guarding the two Roman camps deliberated about what to do, with the larger camp sending a message to the smaller to come to them by night so that they could all make their way to Canusium. Some of the soldiers attempted the breakout under cover of darkness, making their way to the larger camp and then to Canusium. Some were left in both camps to be captured, and these captives Livy describes as 'the wounded and timorous' (22.52.4).

At Canusium itself there were four military tribunes and several members of the elite classes, who deliberated among themselves what action to take. It seems that there was no hierarchy of command extending down through the ranks that would clearly indicate who was next in line to take charge. This is probably because of the strong religious and legal dimension to the commander's authority, wherein rights of *auspicium* and *imperium* had been bestowed upon a particular individual holding a magistracy that was representative of the whole Roman people, the legitimacy of which was confirmed through consultation with the divine.[3] Such authority was not the sort of thing that could be passed on from one officer to another. Although Livy tells the tale of the nineteen-year-old Scipio, the future Africanus, effectively asserting his leadership by encouraging the wavering nobles to rededicate themselves to the Republic, as soon as it was discovered that one of the consuls was alive at Venusia the remnants of the army were brought back together under his command.[4]

The fact that command did not automatically fall to another officer upon the general's death is illustrated again by events in Spain a few years later, in 212 BCE, when the two Scipios who were commanding as propraetors were both killed. During the disaster one Roman camp was captured and the surviving soldiers made their way to the camp of the other consul, where a legate had been left in charge. We might have expected him to retain this authority beyond its original remit of guarding the camp, given that the commander had died, but apparently this was not the case. Instead, the soldiers decided to hold elections for a new commander, preferring a young member of the equestrian class called Lucius Marcius. An equestrian would not usually be found in such a position, but 'he had a greater spirit and character than the circumstances in which he had been born', says Livy, who clearly anticipated that his audience would regard equestrian status as lowly (25.37.2). It is not entirely clear in what capacity L. Marcius was serving with the army, but it may have been as a member of the *cohors amicorum*, since Livy tells us that he had been personally trained by the commander Gnaeus Scipio.[5] Marcius had collected and rallied the scattered forces from the last Roman defeat, including retrieving some from garrisons in various towns, and he acted exactly as generals did, including signalling attacks and recalls and exhorting his troops.

In summary, after defeat, soldiers often headed for the nearest source of safety and then reorganized in whatever way their circumstances demanded. The soldiers did have other options. Trying to regroup with others from the army was not without its dangers. They might be captured by the enemy on their journey, or they might arrive to find the camp or town under attack or in enemy hands. Some soldiers may have wished to attempt desertion or defection instead. Weighing heavily on their decision would have been how he or his group had become separated from the rest of the army in the first place. If they had become lost in mist or darkness, or won in their part of the field only to discover the rest of the army had lost in theirs, or some similar circumstance, then other soldiers and officers would be glad to see them. If, however, they had fled the battlefield, then their options would seem to be more limited. It was easy for anyone to tell if they had fled by looking to see if the soldier still had his sword and shield. We have seen from the evidence of Polybius that the soldier would be blamed and punished for leaving his station even if there was no real practical point at all in staying until he was killed, and that this caused many men to fight on despite the hopelessness of the situation. At the Battle of Cannae, Livy tells us that 'hardly fifty men shared the consul's flight, nearly the whole army met their death in company with the other consul' (22.50.3). If the soldiers had good reason to believe that they would be punished rather than welcomed, they could seek another way out. They could try to either approach the enemy deliberately in order to become a defector, or to travel out of the area entirely to seek a new life. We will look at what these other options might have looked like in the next chapter.

It was possible to get separated from the bulk of the army even in the case of a victory. Even when the battle was won, there was a degree of disorganization. Most commonly, dispersal of troops happened because the soldiers were chasing down a fleeing enemy. Their aim was to catch and cut down the fleeing men, slashing at their legs as they tried to run with the hope of cutting tendon or muscle. Sometimes the men would have become over eager. The effort to catch the routed soldiers could go on for some time, as there was often an effort to track down fleeing soldiers a great distance past the battlefield. Livy describes a pursuit like this by L. Manlius' army in Galatia in 189 BCE when they had captured the enemy camp and the soldiers were sent to pursue the fleeing Gauls: 'the flight and the carnage extended over all the spurs and ravines of the mountain, and a great many losing their way had fallen into the deep recesses below; many, too, were killed in the woods and thickets' (38.23.6–7). Depending on the needs of the battlefield situation, sometimes the soldiers were not allowed to chase the fleeing soldiers and were recalled to their lines instead. The signal for a recall was conveyed by bugle, as, for example, when the pursuing *hastati* were signalled to return at Zama (Polyb. 15.14.3).

We hear of some soldiers who were missing at the end of winning battles, whose absence was noticed at the time and recorded in our sources because they were elite individuals. Thus we know the story of the seventeen-year-old P. Scipio Aemilianus, the younger of two sons serving with the commander Aemilius Paullus, who failed to return to camp with the rest of the army after the Roman victory at Pydna. Aemilius, of course, noticed his absence, and the soldiers searched for him, looking for his body among the dead by the light of their torches. Plutarch writes that Scipio rode up late in the evening with a couple of his comrades, covered in blood from being caught up in the pursuit and killing of enemy soldiers (Plut. *Aem.* 22.3–7). Scipio was probably part of the cavalry at this point, which would have pursued the furthest. Here Plutarch tells us they had ranged for 15 miles looking for Macedonian soldiers.

Although the infantry would not have pursued nearly as far as the cavalry, it would still happen that foot soldiers went missing when the soldiers were scattered in this way. In the case of the ordinary soldiers, the formulaic nature of the camp would be useful in taking stock of who was present and who was missing. As each *contubernium* returned to its tent they would be able to report to their centurion that they had a full complement, or that some members had definitely been killed, or that a particular individual was missing because they had lost sight of him in a pursuit or retreat. Even if the fighting had been vicious enough that a whole tent of men was missing, this could be reported by their neighbours. As long as they had retained their camp and some semblance of order, the Romans would be able to get a fairly accurate count of what had happened to each of the soldiers, at least for their own citizen legionaries. In the case of a missing, ordinary soldier, it would not be a whole camp of men who searched, but rather it would fall to his comrades to look for his body among the dead.

On the Battlefield

The site where the battle had taken place fell to the control of the victorious side. If the heavy infantry and cavalry that had fought in the battle were restrained from going in pursuit of their defeated opponents, they could be redirected on an expedition to attack the enemy's camp. Any units which had been held in reserve could be directed to the same purposes. At Cynoscephalae we are told that the soldiers only pursued the fleeing Macedonians for a little while, then 'began, some of them, to strip the dead and others to collect prisoners, but most of them ran to plunder the enemy's camp' (Polyb. 18.27.3). In situations like this, soldiers could start to search the battlefield on the same day, for valuables, lost arms and their own wounded. On many other occasions, however, we are told that night had fallen while the two sides were occupied with flight or pursuit. In those cases it would have been extremely difficult to search for anyone who might be lying wounded, and it was probably the responsibility of the soldiers to keep an eye on the whereabouts of members of their own *contubernium* so that, at least in victory, no-one was left behind.

After most battles, the victorious army retired for the night and a contingent was sent out at dawn to pick through the battlefield. They would retrieve dropped weapons, take any valuables, and identify and remove their own dead. Again, the Battle of Cannae is a good example, where soldiers from the victorious army of Hannibal started out the morning after to search through the battlefield. Livy paints a particularly haunting picture of the sight. First they saw the dead, lying where they had fallen, both cavalry and infantry soldiers mixed together as they had happened to be caught by the troops running them down. Livy writes:

Here and there amidst the slain there started up a gory figure whose wounds had begun to throb with the chill of dawn, and was cut down by his enemies; some were discovered lying there alive, with thighs and tendons slashed, baring their necks and throats and bidding their conquerors drain the remnant of their blood (22.51.6–7).

These unsettling apparitions were Romans and Roman allies, who had passed a miserable night alive but unable to escape their fates because their pursuers had cut through the muscles in the back of their legs as they fled. They were finally killed by the Punic soldiers. Some of the dead were found with their heads buried in holes, a bizarre detail that Livy attributes to suicide, and yet hardly seems possible. Some have thought these soldiers who had buried their own heads were the result of irrational, panicked attempts to dig themselves to safety.[6] It is difficult to say for certain what happened to them, as Livy's narrative says only that they had been found in this manner, not whether they had done it during their attempted escape from the battle or at some point during the long hours in which they had lain forgotten on the field. Another possibility is that they had attempted to give themselves a kind of burial, fearing for the fate of their spirit. Some Roman sources demonstrate a belief that an unburied corpse created a wandering or unhappy spirit, and sometimes it was sufficient to put a body to rest symbolically if it was not possible to bury it. In ancient Greece it was sufficient to throw a handful of dirt over a body if complete burial was not possible, and this seems to have been the case in Republican Rome as well.[7]

The overall picture that emerges from each of these battlefield descriptions is one of horror. The dying lay among the dead in darkness for many hours, in great pain but unable to move or help themselves, aware that their ultimate fate would be to die of their injuries or suffer until the enemy returned to kill them. Into this scene of misery, Livy has woven an exemplary tale of how a Roman ought to die. On the field the Carthaginians discovered 'a Numidian who was dragged out alive from under a dead Roman, but with mutilated nose and ears; for the Roman, unable to hold a weapon in his hands, had expired in a frenzy of rage, while rending the other with his teeth' (22.51.9). This is an echo of a martial value that goes back to the famous tale of the 300 Spartans who died in defence of Greece at the Battle of Thermopylae, fighting the Persian invasion. Their determination was illustrated by the will to carry on with whatever weapons they had. After they had been fighting for some time Herodotus tells us 'most of them had had their spears broken and were killing the Persians with swords' (7.224.1). Then a second part of the Persian army attacked them in the rear and they were forced back upon a hill, where 'they defended themselves with swords, if they still had them, and with hands and teeth' (Hdt.7.225.3). This was what a Roman was supposed to do, but many would not have found it enticing.

Capture

We normally hear about soldiers who were captured in large groups, commonly because they had been left to guard the Roman camp and after defeat on the battlefield it had fallen to the enemy. Others, however, must have been captured in small groups or individually in the surrounding country. Probably these men surrendered when they were approached by a larger group of armed enemy combatants, rather than be cut down where they stood. It would have been standard for soldiers from a victorious army approaching groups of the defeated to ask for their surrender as long as the initial rout was over. We have seen that the Romans offered this option to the towns that they stormed. In the case of defeated soldiers, they could be ransomed back to their army or sold as slaves. They could be stripped of their arms and armour just as easily alive as dead, and so on balance, it would have been less dangerous and more profitable to take soldiers prisoner than to kill them, although much may have hinged on the temperament of the soldiers who found them.

For most of the third century BCE, soldiers could and did surrender, and they had a reasonable expectation of being returned to their own side fairly swiftly. Any prisoners kept with an army necessitated extra work in the form of guarding and providing water and food, and so few armies wished to retain their captives for any length of time. Instead they would, as soon as possible, either sell them into slavery or, more commonly, ransom them back to their own people in order to make a profit. The same applied to the *calones* when they were captured from Roman camps, although the ransom demanded was much less than for soldiers.[8] There was no long-standing Roman tradition of refusing the ransom demanded for prisoners of war, and it was normal to pay ransoms until the middle of the Second Punic War. During the First Punic War it was routine for the Romans to swap captives with the Carthaginians after battles, and if there should be more on one side than the other, a price was set as a ransom (Livy 22.23.6). This happened with other enemies too. After the Romans lost to the forces of King Pyrrhus of Epirus at the Battle of Heraclea, envoys were sent from Rome to negotiate the exchange or ransom of the soldiers (Dion. Hal. *Ant. Rom.* 19.13.1). These soldiers were ultimately returned by Pyrrhus without charge, citing principles of justice.[9]

The first signs of a harsher fate imposed upon the captured soldier came during the Second Punic War, when we see the first instances of the Roman Senate being unwilling or unable to pay the ransom for prisoners of war. The soldiers who were captured at the Roman defeat at Lake Trasimene in 217 BCE were returned in a one-for-one exchange between the sides shortly after the battle. The Carthaginians had 240 more prisoners than the Romans, and the amount of money to be paid as a ransom had been agreed between the commanders of the two sides, Fabius Maximus and Hannibal. The Roman Senate, however, were reluctant to pay. The Roman commander ended up paying the ransoms personally, partly, we are told, because he could not bear the thought of 'abandoning his countrymen to their fate' by which he means that they would be sold as slaves (Plut. *Fab.* 7.4).

It is difficult to tell how much of the Senate's reluctance to pay for these prisoners was to do with a new and harsher standard of morality and how much was simply to do with money. It does seem likely that the Senate did not have the money to hand and could not gather it quickly, as we know that during these years it was struggling to continue to finance the war.[10] According to Plutarch, however, the Senate scorned Fabius for trying to recover 'men whose cowardice had made them a prey to the enemy' (Plut. *Fab.* 7.4). On the one hand, this objection, on the grounds that the soldiers' surrender was evidence of their cowardice, could simply be another romanticization of high and exacting standards in the Roman military. As we saw in the case of the Romans' disciplinary system, the idea of such strict rules were popular among the elite classes of the following centuries, who could never be subject to their cruelty and for whom they represented exclusivity and prestige. On the other, although prisoners of war had been ransomed before, it is clear that there already existed the idea that surrender had tainted them, and they suffered punishment and stigma upon their return. The soldiers turned over by Pyrrhus of Epirus were subjected to various slights, with the cavalrymen being sent to serve as heavy infantry and the heavy infantry sent to serve in the light infantry, and all being required to sleep outside the bounds of the camp.[11]

The turning point came after the disastrous defeat of the Romans at the Battle of Cannae. The survivors of this battle fell into two groups. There were those who had escaped the battle and regrouped at Canusium and Venusia, eventually returning to Rome to offer themselves for continued service, and those who were captured, mainly in the Roman camps. Of this latter group, ten were sent back to Rome to negotiate for ransom of all. This time, however, the Senate refused either to pay the ransoms themselves or to allow the soldiers' relations to pay for them. Polybius tells us that this squashed Hannibal's hopes of obtaining funds 'and at the same time established the rule for their own men, that they must either conquer or die on the field, as there was no other hope of safety for them if they were beaten' (Polyb. 6.58.11). Despite the negative sentiment about soldiers surrendering, the outright refusal to allow them to return was not in accord with the prevailing ethos at the time, as all our sources agree. The soldiers, the Roman people in general, and a large proportion of senators were in favour of ransoming the men. Perhaps the majority Senate view that eventually prevailed was a moral decision. Perhaps it was strategic, to deprive Hannibal of the money he desperately needed to continue the war. For the soldiers, the result was the same. The state abandoned them to be sold into slavery.

Thus it seems from this point onwards, in law and in literature, if not in popular opinion, fighting to the death was considered preferable than living to fight another day. The story of the fallen soldier on the battlefield at Cannae, who died still angrily attempting to bite his opponent, illustrates the idealized, stubborn fighter who would not give up. In looking back on the Roman Middle Republic from centuries later, many ancient writers were drawn to this as a Roman virtue, what they considered to be the 'undaunted spirit'.[12] These writers admired the lofty ideal that a Roman soldier should die fighting or face permanent rejection from Roman society, which indeed, after Cannae, seems to have been increasingly made into state policy, as reflected in the laws governing a captured soldier's return to citizenship.

A soldier who was captured in a war, thus forcibly enslaved to an enemy state, was no longer considered to possess citizenship of Rome. The laws of *postliminium* governed how and under what circumstances that citizenship could be regained, and under these laws the soldier's claim was treated differently depending on how he had been captured. If a soldier had surrendered while still armed, or deserted by becoming absent from the army, or had actively gone over to the enemy, he would not legally be able to restore his citizenship.[13] Thus the only means of capture that was valid in the eyes of Roman law was to be captured forcibly, while actively fighting. We are told that this was a deliberate attempt to influence the soldier's behaviour at the moment of capture. The return of citizenship was more heavily regulated in times of peace than when the war was still ongoing, because 'the Romans wished the citizens to place hope for return in martial courage rather than in peace.'[14] In other words, at the moment when the soldier was about to be captured, he would not be reassured that he would automatically be restored to his former status by treaty at the end of the war.[15]

The Wounded

As long as their side was holding its own, those wounded in the course of a battle could be ushered behind the lines to safety. Scipio did this while he was reorganizing troops at the Battle of Zama. With the enemy driven back and the pursuing *hastati* being recalled, the wounded were carried to the army's rear (Polyb. 15.14.3). After the battle, soldiers on the field would make a search for the missing and wounded. The Elder Cato writes of a tribune who was pulled from among the dead suffering from blood loss. He had fortunately received wounds only to the body and not the face, allowing him to be recognized.[16] The implication, of course, is that sometimes those who had received facial wounds were unrecognizable.

When the veterans from the Second Punic war who were in Macedon with Ligustinus protested that after so many years they were 'worn out with wounds', this is almost certainly a rhetorical exaggeration, but it does imply that certain minor wounds, most likely cuts and slashes to the arms and face, were common to all soldiers. Some would have received more serious injuries, and there may not have been medics to help. There were men whose job was to dress wounds on the battlefield by the middle of the first century BCE. Cicero mentions one such person, writing that when the wounded are carried away from the battle line, a new recruit calls out in pain, while an experienced soldier merely looks around for a *medicus*, a physician (Cic. *Tusc.* 2.16.38). This role may not have existed for the times of the Middle Republic, or the person may not have been a properly trained doctor.[17] Pliny cites the earlier historian L. Cassius Hemina as saying that the first doctor came to Rome from Greece in 219 BCE, a man named Archagathus, who was set up with a surgery at the public expense. 'People believe that he was a specialist in wounds,' he writes, 'and that to begin with his arrival was amazingly popular, but that soon the savagery of his amputations and cauterizations made his name change to that of 'executioner', and medicine and all doctors became objects of loathing.'[18] This would suggest that there were no dedicated physicians accompanying the Republican legions, even though it was the practice with armies elsewhere in the ancient world at this time. Classical Greek armies had army surgeons who went along with them to heal the wounded and the sick, although they were not part of any official medical corps, since Greek armies were made up of citizen soldiers just like the Mid-Republican legions.[19]

The wounded seem to have been kept in camp for a short time after battles, especially if the army was under threat. Many of them would have died during the initial days and weeks after the battle. This is because the ancient soldier had a high chance of his wound becoming infected. Tetanus, sepsis and gangrene are all described in medical texts from the ancient world, and there was little that could be done about them.[20] Soldiers who were wounded during the course of storming cities or during minor battles might have had to keep travelling with the army until there was a large enough group of wounded to be left somewhere safe, if indeed there was somewhere safe to leave them. When the Romans were garrisoning the town of Nola under threat from Hannibal's army, for example, the sick and wounded soldiers were kept with the army. Livy tells us that they were grouped together with the *calones* and the *lixae* to stand behind the army in battle array and help raise the shout so that the enemy would overestimate the number of actual combatants (23.16.8).

When it was safe to do so, the wounded seem to have been regularly left behind in allied towns, and apparently exempted from some or all of the rest of the campaign. Livy tells us, for example, that in 211 BCE the commander Marcellus left the wounded at Numistro with a small garrison under the command of a tribune (27.2.10). These details in the historical sources, which specify which towns were garrisoned, where the wounded were left, and sometimes which officer was left in charge, imply that the generals detailed the location of all the army's various groups and detachments when they wrote their dispatches back to the Senate.

In early times, the wounded had been billeted with patrician families in Rome in order to make their recovery (Livy 2.47.12). This was presumably because these wealthy families were the best equipped to feed and look after a convalescent. The soldiers' own families on their small farms would likely have been too poor to feed a man who was not working and too busy to spare another family member as a nurse. Thus, when the wounded soldiers were left in allied towns, they were probably taken into the homes of elite and wealthy families. Just as members of wealthy families had helped the ordinary soldiers at Canusium and Venusia in the aftermath of Cannae, the wealthy of other towns would have taken their wounded. Doing so strengthened the town's ties to Rome and increased the standing of the families involved in respect to their own local politics. Where the wounded were left in a town and a garrison of healthy soldiers was left with them, as at Numistro, it might suggest that there was, or there was suspected to be, a faction of influential families there that were not so friendly or pro-Roman.[21]

There are a few more scattered pieces of evidence about what happened to the wounded when the army was on campaign. In Ligustinus' eleventh known year of service in 181 BCE, he joined another campaign in Spain under the commander Q. Fulvius Flaccus. This army camped near a town called Aebura, about which we know nothing, as it appears in no other source. A garrison was sent to this town while the Romans were camped nearby. This might imply that, just as at Numistro, the commander was uncertain about the loyalty of the locals, or might simply be that it was common to garrison towns that were within a certain proximity of an army camp to make sure they were not infiltrated or used as a stronghold by enemies. The men guarding this town were left out of a subsequent engagement with the Celtiberians but arrived mid-battle to help turn the tide, without any explanation of how they had known to come or if they were acting upon orders. When the army moved on, they first conveyed the wounded to Aebura, where they were apparently left.[22]

Unfortunately, we know nothing about what it was like to be a convalescent soldier in an allied town in Italy or in one of the provinces like Hispania. It seems to have often been the practice to leave a garrison with the wounded. This would have been precautionary, in case the local people turned against the Romans and sought to take advantage of the vulnerable soldiers. There is little evidence for where the wounded soldiers were accommodated within these towns, nor for how a Mid-Republican garrison worked or what it did from day to day, nor for what relationship either convalescents or guards had with the population of the town. This is unfortunate, because it would have been a large part of military service for thousands of soldiers over the centuries.

The fact that the Romans left wounded soldiers in towns must mean that after a battle there was often a fairly large group of soldiers who needed an extended recovery time measured in months rather than days or weeks. The soldiers who made it to these garrisons would have either escaped infection or survived it and were afflicted with conditions that would heal given time. Probably most would have had blood loss like Cato's tribune, which causes weakness and fatigue until the body is able to regenerate its red blood cells, which takes about sixty days. Some would have had broken bones, which can take from only a few months to heal to six months or more, depending on the size of the bone, its location in the body, and the overall health of the individual. The last major category would have been those recovering from stab or slash wounds, which can also take months to heal depending on size and severity. Any soldiers who had several wounds, or combinations of broken bones, wounds and blood loss would naturally have needed to recuperate for much longer.

Soldiers who were wounded probably received very little in the way of medical care during their stay in these towns past the kind of herbal and folk remedies that were common at the time. Pliny tells us that the Elder Cato recommended a poultice of cabbage to apply to wounds to help them heal (*HN* 20.33). Soldiers had the use of bandages, as we hear about them faking injuries by bandaging each other as if wounded (Dion. Hal. *Ant. Rom.* 9.50.5). In friendly towns along campaign routes, soldiers may have had access to local healers.[23] It is also possible that some of the *calones*, so often overlooked in the ancient sources, could have been left with the wounded to attend to them, and any aristocratic soldier would have kept his own private slaves with him. It is unlikely that there was much effective medicine to be had, but the army could offer safety and rest.

We hear nothing about what ultimately happened to wounded soldiers. Perhaps after they were recovered they were sent back to the army, or perhaps they remained in place until the army on its way back to Italy reached their town. Those whose wounds made them unfit for future combat may have been sent directly home, although it is also possible that there were roles for men in the army even if they had serious impairments. We hear one exemplary tale of a man called Marcus Sergius, who served as a disabled soldier. The Elder Pliny says that he lost his right hand in his second campaign but went on to fight with his left hand (*HN* 7.29). 'He had a right hand made of iron and attached to the stump,' writes Pliny, 'after which he fought a battle, and raised the siege of Cremona, defended Placentia, and took twelve of the enemy's camps in Gaul.' This hardly seems credible, especially as Pliny says that he rode a horse in battle, although it is possible, like some of the citizen cavalry we have seen before, that he dismounted in order to fight. At any rate, soldiers with serious injuries like the loss of a hand cannot normally have been expected to resume combat roles. It might have been possible to serve in a non-combat capacity.

The Dead

When Plutarch describes the search for the missing Publius Scipio in the aftermath of the Battle of Pydna in 167 BCE, he writes that the soldiers searched for him among the dead outside the ramparts of the camp. This suggests that in victory, at least, with the enemy chased off the battlefield, the Romans had organized a detail to find the bodies of their own soldiers, retrieve them, and pile them near the camp. They were of course not taken inside, which would have been distressing and unhygienic, but apparently carried off the battlefield and left outside the walls. We are told the soldiers searched through them by torchlight, suggesting that although the bodies had been taken from the battlefield, identification and disposal of them was done later, by daylight.

The unpleasant task of pulling bodies from the battlefield would not have fallen to those who had fought that day. As we have seen, the battlefields were often miles distant from the camps, and those recovering the dead would have needed to take carts or wagons to transport the bodies back. This must have been a task that belonged either to the *calones* or the soldiers who had made up the garrison left behind in the camp. In Plutarch's description of the aftermath of Pydna we hear that the soldiers were met on their way back to camp by slaves carrying torches to light their way, which suggests that they had duties after the battle and may have been responsible for collecting the dead.

It was important to the Romans to recover their own dead, for fear of what might happen to their bodies if left in enemy territory. The fate of the wounded on a battlefield that they did not control was unpleasant to think of, like Livy's staggering, ghost-like figures who had lain wounded in the darkness for so many hours, never to find comfort or see a friendly face again. And it was worse than just the terror of neglect and abandonment, for it was thought that the souls of the unburied dead were restless and would rise to haunt the living.[24] Some of Rome's enemies were even inclined to use the bodies of the dead as trophies.

The Gauls, for example, were known to take the severed heads of their enemies and display them hanging from their horses.

Livy rarely tells us what ultimately happened to the bodies of soldiers killed in battles. Once he says that they were cremated, during a days' pause during the Second Battle of Herdonea, but in other places he uses the Latin verb *sepelio*, which can mean to either bury a body or to cremate and then bury it.[25] Dionysius of Halicarnassus mentions Roman soldiers being cremated once as well, in reference to a very early battle of the Romans against the Sabines c.505–503 BCE (*Ant. Rom.* 5.47.1). The Elder Pliny tells us that the custom of cremation was adopted by Rome's military when they discovered that bodies buried in foreign wars had been disinterred (*HN* 7.54). The evidence is admittedly scant, but it points to the Romans cremating their dead near their camp before they moved on.

The process of cremation in the ancient world required considerable time and effort, much more than simply burying the bodies. Despite the fact that victories resulted in proportionally few deaths compared to the enemy, there could still be tens or hundreds of casualties. The pyre would have needed to have been particularly large and probably on most occasions the Romans would have needed to build several. These were built in a pit, even if it was a shallow one, to allow the flow of air. Each pyre would have needed a significant amount of wood, which was used both as kindling and for the structure of the pyre itself. The pyre was constructed in layers of logs, with the logs of each new layer at a right-angle to the previous layer.[26] Once the pyre had been built and lit, attendants would have been needed to stoke the fire and keep it burning at an adequate heat. This could have been the duty of the *calones*, although a specialist either among the slaves or among the soldiers cannot be ruled out, as it took a certain amount of skill to stoke and rake a pyre to keep an adequate temperature and remove the build-up of ash.[27]

It would have taken many hours for the cremations to be completed. Today a crematorium will burn a body at an average temperature of 900°C, taking one to two hours to complete.[28] The highest temperature achieved by an ancient pyre appears to have been over 800°C, although the entire process took much longer, somewhere in the vicinity of seven to eight hours.[29] We know nothing about any ceremony that might have surrounded the cremation of soldiers outside army camps during this period. In the funerals of famous individuals mentioned in various sources, the moment of lighting the pyre was important, and seems to have been done by someone close to the deceased.[30] In the case of the Romans, the commander seems to have been responsible for all the religious obligations that related to a collective of Roman soldiers, and we would expect this to be the case for any ritual attached to the communal funeral pyre as well.

Similarly, we have no evidence of whether individuals lingered at the pyres, although we are told that in civilian funerals the mourners stayed until the cremation was complete.[31] If the soldiers did stay, it was likely to be a depressing experience. The Romans noted all kinds of unpleasant phenomena witnessed at funerals, including bodies or parts of bodies rolling off the pyres and fat spitting.[32] Even if they did not attend or did not stay by the pyres, the cremations would have been impossible to ignore, sending smoke high into the sky all day and emitting the foul smell of burning flesh. Thus the day after a victorious battle was likely to have been a grim one, as the disposal of the dead took precedence over the rituals and ceremonies that marked the victory.

When the cremations were complete, the remains of the soldiers would be collected from the pyres. The result of the ancient cremation process was not fine ashes, but a collection of small bone fragments, many of which were and are immediately recognizable as parts of particular bones.[33] The Romans used two different types of grave, a type called *ustrinum* where the cremated remains were removed from the pyre and contained in an urn, which was then buried, not necessarily near the site of the pyre. The second type was called *bustum*, when the remains were buried at the site of the pyre.[34] What happened to the communal remains of Roman soldiers of this era is not known. No remains, neither loose nor contained in an urn, have ever been found near the site of a Republican battle. Tradition and religion dictated that the remains needed to be buried, but no source specifies whether this was at or near the camp or battlefield or whether they were transported somewhere else.

Similarly, we do not know how or even if the news of a man's death reached his relatives. There are two possibilities. The first is that a list of the dead was drawn up and sent to Rome in the form of dispatches. The possibility is suggested by part of Livy's account of Cannae, where he writes that the surviving commander, Varro, was able to send to Rome information that allowed families to be informed of their own 'private disasters'.[35] The problem here is that Livy was probably writing about the dead from elite families, not average citizens. While the names of all the dead would be easy enough to source from each maniple, this information reaching Rome would not in itself be sufficient to inform relatives of soldiers from other Italian towns and cities. We would have to speculate that specific messengers were sent out from Rome for this purpose, a speculation which is now several steps removed from the evidence.

The second possibility is that there was not an official means of transmitting the news about casualties and it was instead arranged by the soldier's comrades. If the dead soldier had made his *testamentum* before his immediate colleagues, they would now be responsible for seeing that his wishes were carried out, and this might have included disposing of his possessions as he had requested or informing his family about how he had died. In some cases, this might have obligated the soldiers to transport pay or possessions back to a family. It should have been possible to entrust the news about the man's death to someone from the deceased soldier's village or town, perhaps a man with whom he had travelled to the mustering point or a relation, if there was one serving in the army at the same time. We have seen how, even with the mixing of men from the same tribe, half of those who went to the *dilectus* would be in the same army, and also that any man was locatable by any other as long as he knew the legion, division and maniple. This method seems more likely but also suggests that news would take a long time to get back to the soldier's home, as it would need to wait for either the whole army to return or a soldier who had completed his service to leave the army and come back to that region.

Burning the Arms to Vulcan

After a victorious battle, the soldiers sent to pick through the battlefield retrieved weapons and armour, both their own and those of the enemy, along with any other valuables they might find. This would have entailed searching the bodies of the enemy dead for any concealed jewellery, coins, and anything else that might have some value and could be sold through the *lixae* or to local dealers. Any weapons that the Romans had dropped or lost would be collected and returned to the camp for repair or reuse. There would have been many more weapons and arms to collect from a defeated enemy. The weapons, arms and armour were then separated out into piles, those that were broken or deemed ugly or unimpressive, and those that were considered good enough to display back at Rome, either in a triumphal procession if the commander was awarded one, or as spoils on public buildings.[36] Sorting through these items for the best pieces, perhaps the soldiers thought back to those they had seen mounted on walls in Rome and other Italian towns.

The weapons and armour that were not thought suitable for display were burned. In practical terms this meant that they were no longer available for anyone else to use, since the Romans did not want or need to take them. The burning was also a ritual act, a sacrifice that in its earliest instances was dedicated most commonly to Vulcan. As Vulcan was the god of fire as a destructive force, the choice of dedicatee suggests that the intention was to destroy the weapons and any hostile spirits within them.[37] Once we are told that the dedication was made to Lua Mater, a mysterious and obscure goddess who, like Vulcan, was associated with destruction. Once we hear of them dedicated to Mars, Minerva, and Lua Mater, and once to Mars and Minerva. On two occasions the dedicatees are named simply as the gods of war.[38]

Plutarch describes this ritual as it occurred in 102 BCE, when the commander Marius performed it, and since it was a very old tradition it would have been the same in Ligustinus' day and even earlier. Plutarch writes:

> After the battle, Marius collected such of the arms and spoils of the barbarians as were handsome, entire, and fitted to make a show in his triumphal procession; all the rest he heaped up on a huge pyre and set out a magnificent sacrifice. The soldiers had taken their stand about the pyre in arms, with chaplets on their heads, and Marius himself, having put on his purple-bordered robe and girt it about him, as the custom was, had taken a lighted torch, held it up towards heaven with both hands, and was just about to set fire to the pyre, when some friends were seen riding swiftly towards him.[39]

The soldiers were an important part of this ritual. They had sorted the spoils into piles and they were present to witness the ceremony. Most importantly, it was by their hands that the spoils had been won, and so this marked the beginning of the commemoration of their achievement during the battle. The commander wore the *cinctus Gabinus*, a toga tied up by knotting the corners, which was a special type worn during sacrifices associated with military contexts. The fact that the commander had changed out of his *paludamentum*, the distinctive red cloak that symbolized his military duties, and into the religious *cinctus Gabinus* was a sign that the battle was over.[40] This suggests that dealing with the dead ought to be considered as within the period of time marked off for the battle, which was not over until the dead had been put to rest.

Although the commander appeared in sacrificial garb, the soldiers themselves still bore their arms, as Plutarch goes on to tell us in the case of Marius' army. When the new arrivals turned out to be carrying a message of good news, the soldiers clashed their arms together, which was usually the sword or spear against the shield. The ceremony would have been one in which they turned their attention from what they had lost to what they had gained, and they presented themselves there in the same attire as when they had gained it. There must have been a finality in watching the destruction of these last symbols of the enemy they had defeated turned to ash by the flames as the hostile spirits within were consumed by the power of the god of fire.

The *Contio*

After the burning of arms had taken place, the focus of the army turned from marking an ending of the battle, to reviewing and evaluating what had happened during it. In Chapter 1 we saw that Polybius wrote that the young soldiers were inspired to face danger because they witnessed the honours and rewards bestowed upon those who had distinguished themselves in battle, hung on private houses so that they might attest to the occupant's valour. This was how such deeds became exemplary to the whole of society and were aspirational to those who had not yet entered the army or who had still to complete their service.

These awards were made at a ceremony that took place after the battle at a special assembly of the soldiers called a *contio*. This ceremony was conducted by the commander, who:

> bringing forward those whom he considers to have displayed conspicuous valour, first of all speaks in laudatory terms of the courageous deeds of each and of anything else in their previous conduct which deserves commendation (Polyb. 6.36.2).

As we know from Polybius' previous remarks, it was the centurions and the tribunes who were charged with observing soldiers in battle. Sometime before the *contio*, the centurions, of which there were many, must have passed their recommendations for awards to the tribunes. The tribunes were most likely responsible for drawing up the list of soldiers to be honoured and collecting and supplying the information about their previous deeds to be read aloud in the ceremony.

The *contio* was thus about praise, reward, and story-telling, highlighting individual examples of courage and military excellence taken from all across the battlefield. When it took place, the soldiers had spent days waiting and preparing for battle both in danger and under threat of looming danger. They had spent many hours in the fight itself, and then days afterward dealing with the dead and sorting their arms. Some would have been adjusting to life without certain comrades, or looking after the wounded in critical days when they might die of infection. In the relief of survival, turning for the first time to congratulating each other and enjoying their victory, the *contio* would have been a joyous and perhaps raucous occasion. The fights of individuals and units would have been re-lived by those who were there and described to those who had not been.

A *contio* was held after a victorious pitched, set-piece battle, but also after smaller engagements and operations. It does not seem to have been unusual for a soldier to receive an award. The impression given by the sources is that there were many. In his speech in 171 BCE, Ligustinus claimed to have been awarded for his courage thirty-four times and received six civic crowns. Since he also said he was in service for twenty-two years, or over a period of twenty-two years, this would mean that he received rewards on average once or twice every year that he served. He cannot therefore mean that every reward had been won in a pitched battle or even that he distinguished himself during a very large action, but rather that he must have performed bravely while skirmishing or in storming towns. Regarding his second campaign in Spain, the Elder Cato claimed to have taken 400 towns in 400 days, a statement that barely seems credible, but might reflect a lot of combat done in divisions and detachments operating in different places. Cato also wrote that he gave a pound of silver to every soldier in Spain.[41] The impression is that service in Spain was intense but lucrative, and we saw in Chapter 6 that the Elder Cato was particularly fond of holding *contiones*.

At the *contio*, enthusiasm for battle in particular was celebrated as aspirational and rewarded with tangible gifts of both monetary and symbolic value. Here, each soldier's memories of combat were new and fresh, and the tales of the deeds of his fellow soldiers would have seemed more vivid and poignant than they had ever been. We know that there was a set correspondence between certain deeds and their rewards, mostly commemorating the behaviour of eager risk-takers, those who had pushed forward and gone first over a wall, engaged in single combat, or stood in the face of immense danger to save a comrade.

In the aftermath of a victorious battle, the Romans of this period would have stayed in their camp for several days in order to attend to everything that needed to be done. Sallust says that an army under the commander Metellus lingered in place for four days in order to see to the wounded and hold the *contio* (Sall. *Iug.* 54). This was probably about the usual length of time. Some of this period, as we have seen, was given over to dealing with the dead, some to marking the end of the period of combat. For the soldiers, it would have been a time of processing their experiences and recovering from the stress and danger of the past days. As well as the official *contio*, there were probably late nights of discussing the battle, sharing stories with others, keeping company with the wounded and remembering the dead.

Chapter 12

Getting Out Alive

Broadly speaking, there were only two ways to leave Roman military service, the desirable, appropriate way, and the way that was far less socially acceptable, namely desertion. In the socially and legally desirable route, a soldier completed his required length of service and returned to a normal civilian life somewhere within the boundaries of Roman Italy. The sources show that elite Romans were very invested in the idea of the soldier as a farmer on the land, and some of the laws and conventions designed to keep soldiers in legionary service would only be effective if the soldier desired to return to Roman territory. Polybius' explanation about how decorations motivated young soldiers to emulate or rival their elders in martial courage depended on a constant cycle of soldiers returning to their towns and cities with rewards and honours for display. The threat that the soldier would not be accepted back to his household as a deserter assumes that it was the desire of the soldier to do so, and that closing that avenue would be a distressing loss for him. Similarly, monetary rewards were traditionally given to soldiers on the day of a commander's triumph in Rome, a practice that presupposes that the soldier was present there after a successful campaign. While this would have been true for most soldiers in an early period, by the Middle Republic, Rome was not the hometown of most soldiers, who either needed to wait out the time between the end of a campaign and when a triumph was celebrated in Rome, or make a special trip to attend.

The life of a farmer would not have appealed to everyone, and there were options, although Rome's elites do not often seem to have thought of them. When the Elder Cato wrote that 'the legions set out cheerfully to those places from which they thought they would never return' he meant that soldiers went out to die happily in service to Rome, not that they might choose to live a different life far away.[1] In reality there were, of course, numerous ways for the soldier's story to end that were neither return nor death. The majority of Rome's soldiers were young, unmarried men, who, of all the demographics in the ancient world, had the most freedom and greatest range of opportunity. Since most serving soldiers would not already have had families of their own, the motivation to return to Italy would not have been strong for everyone. Some stayed in the provinces to marry, some to conduct business, and some to take work in areas other than agriculture.

The undesirable way to leave the army was as a deserter, someone who left the army by sneaking away, defecting to the enemy, or leaving a battle or his guard post. These men would have had a restricted range of opportunities in some senses, although there was a good degree of anonymity in the ancient world. Many Roman citizens would be able to live in safety as long as no-one knew their history and was able to denounce them as deserters from the legions. There were less travelled paths to take, both for those who left the legions honourably and for those who deserted. On the margins of society lived all sorts of bandits and pirates, and the whole of the ancient world contained groups of mercenaries who lived by selling their services to various states and kingdoms. For those who sought a life of adventure beyond Italy's borders, there were certainly a number of ways to do it.

The Road Home

The sources for this period usually associate bringing the army back to Italy with a commander holding a triumph at Rome. The prayer of Scipio made at the lustration of the army that we saw in Chapter 5 included the appeal that the gods would allow him to 'bring the victors home with me safe and sound', where 'victors' means the soldiers on campaign with him (Livy 29.27.3). Several parodies of the speech of triumphant generals in plays of Plautus include among the typical boasts that the general returned the victorious army. In these instances it is not specified to where exactly the soldier was obliged to be returned, but when the general made a request to the Senate to be awarded a triumph, one of the criteria was that the army had to have been returned to Rome so that both officers and soldiers could act as witnesses to the account of the war that the general gave as part of his application. This is a point made by C. Aurelius before the Senate in 200 BCE, in regard to the triumph of L. Furius over the Gauls, which was held without the presence of the soldiers:

> 'Our ancestors,' he said, 'laid it down that the lieutenants-general, the military tribunes, the centurions and the soldiers should be present in order that the people of Rome might have visible proof of the victory won by the man for whom such an honour was decreed. Was there a single soldier out of the army which fought with the Gauls, or even a single camp-follower from whom the Senate might have enquired as to the truth or falsehood of the praetor's report?' (Livy 31.49.9–10)

These practices would have been established at an early period, when the armies sent out from Rome were smaller, travelled lesser distances, and routinely returned at the end of every campaigning season. When armies began to be sent out under the control of a representative of the state rather than a private individual, it made sense that they would be witnessed upon their return. Both citizens and officials could see for themselves how many of the soldiers returned and talk with them about the campaign. The general who had been responsible for their safety would not be able to falsify losses or exaggerate his success. By the Middle Republic, of course, most of the soldiers had not left from Rome and could not be thought of as returning there, especially the allies who had mustered in their own towns and had not even been levied at Rome. For most soldiers, going to Rome to participate in a triumph would have been an extra trip at the end of the campaign rather than a homecoming.

The original stipulation for a triumph was intended to be that it was only awarded when a war had been so decisively won and a people so decisively pacified that the whole army could be taken out of the area. As Rome began to fight longer campaigns further afield, this requirement was often complicated by the presence of multiple tribes or areas within one province, where commanders wished to celebrate a triumph over one people but the soldiers were needed to proceed against another. There were sometimes negotiations about when and how commanders were allowed to take soldiers out of the field for the purposes of a triumph. Livy mentions such an assessment happening in Spain in 181 BCE between Q. Fulvius Flaccus and Ti. Sempronius Gracchus. 'In perfect harmony' he writes, 'they arranged which soldiers they should discharge and which they should hold in service' (Livy 40.40.14). Sempronius had taken *supplementa* (reinforcements) along with him, intending to release the veterans and reorganize the legions. On this occasion, release was not merely a matter of the length of the soldier's service. The Senate, in consultation with the new commander and officers from Fulvius Flaccus' army, had set rules about how many soldiers he could take out of the province for his triumph, because the new general Sempronius had objected to being left with an army made up entirely of new and inexperienced soldiers.

Ligustinus tells us that he was one of the soldiers who was chosen to travel back from the war in Spain with Fulvius Flaccus. He says that he was among the soldiers who were released *virtutis causa*, 'on account of valour' (42.34.9). This arrangement was beneficial for both the outgoing commander and the soldiers chosen to return. For the commander, a triumph was more popular and prestigious if there were many soldiers who walked in the procession who could display the declarations they had earned during the campaign.[2] For the soldiers, travelling to Rome would be a safer and easier option than fighting in Spain, and this bonus was capped off at the triumph with double pay and a large donative of 50 *denarii* per legionary and 100 *denarii* for centurions (Livy 40.43.7).

The arrangements for handing over the army from Fulvius Flaccus to Sempronius Gracchus in Spain are instructive of how this was done. The handover of the army was done at Tarraco, modern day Tarragona, which lies in southeastern Spain, down the coast from Barcelona. The army had been marched north and east to the coast on the orders of the incoming consul (Livy 40.39.3) so that its handover and subsequent reorganization could take place at the Roman-controlled port. Once again, the navy were responsible for transport. Livy writes that the retiring troops were relieved of their oath, loaded on the boats and embarked for Rome. These boats would have arrived at Rome's port at Ostia. Although it was possible to sail to the city itself, a triumphing general had to stay outside the city until his triumph, and it is doubtful that a troop transport could be led up the Tiber. The Roman citizen soldiers nevertheless would have been told to continue to Rome. Q. Fulvius Flaccus was standing for the consulship, and so they would have been encouraged to vote for him and to encourage their friends, family and patronage networks to do likewise. At some point during the handover, the incoming commander Sempronius Gracchus apparently extracted a promise from Ligustinus to return to serve with him.[3] We have seen before that self-selection was an important part of the army's functioning, and on the other side, officers were clearly motivated to find and retain good soldiers with experience.

If soldiers were in Italy at the time they were due to leave the army, they were simply dismissed to disperse to their various home towns from that point. Just as the army in Spain had marched to Tarraco, a friendly area near the port, to make the handover, the same happened with armies that travelled on foot to their provinces. Armies that were campaigning in Gaul were mustered at and returned to Ariminum for the purpose of handovers, because it lay at the end of the Via Flaminia and was just 9 miles south of the River Rubicon, the border between Italy and Cisalpine Gaul.[4] Similarly, while the Romans were campaigning in Liguria in the first quarter of the second century, the Etruscan town of Pisae on the border between Etruria and Liguria was where armies mustered and to where they were returned to be handed over and reorganized.[5] Despite the fact that soldiers travelled to and from these border towns on foot, we often find soldiers spending several months in them, either as part of an army ordered to winter there or because whole armies had been held there until or in case they were needed.

It is not clear whether the commander was obliged to return soldiers to Italy when there was no prospect of a triumph. In 167 BCE there was a debate in Rome about whether the commander Aemilius Paullus should be awarded a triumph, with the commander's soldiers opposed to it because they said they had been treated unfairly under his command. Livy narrates that a senator named

M. Servilius addressed the soldiers who had opposed the triumph and asked, rhetorically, why they thought they had been brought back to Italy, if not for a triumph. In doing so he contrasts being 'brought back' (*deportare*) to Italy with being dismissed (*demittere*, literally 'sent away') as soon as the province was settled (45.38.14). This does somewhat imply that Livy, at least, thought that soldiers were only returned to Italy using state resources if they were required for a triumph, and that it was possible to simply dismiss soldiers from the borders of a province to make their own way home.

At various times it seems that orders were given directly by the Senate that a commander should return an army to Italy before it was known whether it would be needed for a triumph or not. Ligustinus' first two armies were both recalled in the same year, although he himself had left the first campaign early. Livy gives the Senate's orders: 'It was decided not to send a fresh army to Macedonia, the one which was there was to be brought back by Quinctius and disbanded, as was also the army with M. Porcius Cato in Spain' (34.43.8). As it turned out, both of these armies took part in triumphal parades, and it may be that the orders were given specifically to allow that possibility to remain open. There is, in fact, more evidence of the soldiers being left in a province despite the commander being awarded a triumph than evidence for soldiers returned to Italy when there was no prospect of such an honour being awarded. In 211 BCE, for example, troops in Sicily were angry that they were not withdrawn from the province when their commander was given an ovation, the lesser form of a triumph (Livy 26.21.17).

It seems most likely that any time a whole army was completely withdrawn from a province, it was provided transport back to Italy, whereas individuals or groups of soldiers who were dismissed from an army were not offered transport. This is not to say that none was available, but it may have depended on whether there was an official deputation travelling back to Italy that the soldier could accompany. When a commander came out from Rome to take over the army of a retiring colleague, for instance, usually new soldiers were sent with him and soldiers who had served their time could be released. These soldiers could then travel back to Italy or to Rome with the outgoing commander. This might have been out of consideration for their convenience, but we might suspect it was favoured by the magistrates themselves, who would have preferred to have a large escort for reasons of both safety and prestige.

Questions remain about the groups of soldiers that were separated from the main campaign before it came to an end, the soldiers who had been left in various towns, either as a garrison, or because they were wounded. We would assume that at the very least, messages were sent to these towns to give the soldiers the opportunity to return to Italy with the army, but we hear little about the process of withdrawing and nothing about the soldiers who had been left to garrison various towns. Those who had recovered from being wounded while away from the main body of the army were presumably also sent for so that they could return, but it was a different story for those who were freshly wounded or remained unfit. Appian tells us that when Scipio left Spain in 206 BCE he 'settled his sick and wounded soldiers in a town which he named Italica after Italy' (App. *Hisp.* 38). On the one hand, since the trip to and from Spain involved a long voyage by ship, it would have been extremely arduous on the wounded. On the other, it seems that any wounded soldier who wished to return to Italy was in the unfortunate position of being trapped in Spain, at least until he was well enough to make the trip home.

Sometimes soldiers would have elected to stay in the province or, in the case where they were required to go to Rome for a triumph, to return there. During their winter camps or when billeted in friendly towns, Roman soldiers interacted with local people and many made connections with them, establishing links for future commercial opportunities or forming personal relationships. In 170 BCE, for example, a deputation of men appeared before the Senate in Rome and identified themselves as the sons of Roman soldiers and local women from Spain (Livy 43.3.1–4). There were some 4,000 of these men. For marriages to be legally recognized in Rome, these non-Roman women would have needed to hold citizenship in a community that enjoyed *conubium*, the right of marriage, with Roman citizens. As they did not, the mothers of these men did not have the sufficient status to contract a legal marriage with a Roman citizen and their sons had not inherited their father's citizenship. These men were granted permission to make a colony at Cartesia, on the modern-day Bay of Gibraltar, which would have Latin status and include the existing inhabitants of that small town if they wished. It was to be called *colonia libertinorum*, 'the colony of freedmen', indicating that the men's Spanish mothers had once been slaves who had been freed along with their sons.[6] Like the town of Italica, the existence of these men indicates a permanent Roman presence in Spain made up of primarily veteran soldiers.

The Release of the Military Oath

When Ligustinus travelled back to Rome from Spain, Livy writes that the soldiers were relieved of their oath before they were loaded onto the naval transports. It was necessary for this to be done every time a soldier retired from a particular campaign. In order to leave the army in the appropriate way, the soldiers needed to be released from the *sacramentum*, the oath they had taken upon recruitment, in which they had promised to become and remain a soldier until appropriately dismissed. A soldier dismissed in this way was termed an *exauctor* or *exauctoratus*, literally an 'ex-actor' in the sense of someone who used to perform deeds or actions, but perhaps more accurately in this context an 'ex-combatant'. In its most important sense, being under oath as a soldier gave the man sanction to kill someone who had been declared an enemy as a legitimate act of war rather than a murder.

It was not appropriate or desirable for a soldier to leave an army unless he had been released from the oath, by his commander specifically. Even if his length of service stretched in excess of the required amount of time, the oath bound him to obedience unless specifically and deliberately released, with the same implications as deserting in the field. Any violation of the oath would have been counted the same as if he had left a guard post or slipped away from the camp without permission during the night. One incident which is enlightening in this regard is from Livy's account of the actions of a tribune in the army of the consul Postumius in 180 BCE. The legions were waiting at Pisae when M. Fulvius Nobilior, either by accident or through incompetence, dismissed the legions without permission.[7] When the consul heard of this, he followed the soldiers but apparently was only able to find some of them. This implies that the soldiers had organized themselves into groups, just as they might when they travelled to a mustering place, and headed for their various home towns. The soldiers were ordered to return to the army and fined half a year's pay, while any who did not return were to be sold as slaves. The punishment here must be because only the commander was able to relieve the soldiers of their oath and the soldiers, not properly dismissed, were therefore not technically *exauctores* either.

That it was necessary to be bound by the terms of the *sacramentum* in order to act in the capacity of a soldier is confirmed by an action of the Elder Cato, as reported by Cicero and Plutarch.[8] According to this story, Cato wrote to his son on campaign when the boy had been dismissed by his commander, but wished to stay on with the army, warning him not to go back into action until he had obtained his commander's permission to do so. In a different version of the same story, he wrote to the son's commander to ask him to give the *sacramentum* again so that the son could return to service.[9] Plutarch's story about the Elder Cato appears in one of his *Roman Questions*, which, just like Polybius' histories, was a book about Romans intended for Greeks. This entry reads, 'Why were men who were not regularly enlisted, but merely tarrying in the camp, not allowed to throw missiles at the enemy or to wound them?'[10] The answer, of course, is that they were no longer under oath. Nowhere is it explained why there were sometimes *exauctores* in army camps. Perhaps individuals were considered to have served their time at the end of the active campaigning season and had been released by the time the soldiers went into winter quarters. In that case they may have stayed with the army waiting for transport back to Italy when a new commander arrived the following spring and the previous one returned.

For most soldiers, when their years of service came to an end, they were released. This, however, was not always done in a timely manner, and sometimes their commanders did not wish to release them at all. We have already seen through the case of the so-called mutinous troops of Scipio's in 206 BCE that the ordinary soldier had very little power to advocate for himself, and that it was very much up to the temperament of the general whether any protest at his treatment would result in resolution of the problem or punishment for insubordination. The status of soldiers in the individual provinces, and whether they could be returned or released, seems to have been discussed by the Senate at the same time as they decided how many soldiers should be raised for the year and where they should go. Soldiers who were kept under arms past their allotted time therefore needed to persuade their commander to intervene with the Senate on their behalf, or to send another officer to do so.

The veterans from the Second Punic War who were taken by Sulpicius to Macedon on Ligustinus' first campaign asked for their release only a year later. When Livy wrote his narrative of the year 200 BCE he listed these men as volunteers, which is likely how they had been put down in records for that year. In the subsequent year, however, they claimed that they had not been volunteers at all and had been sent to Macedon by tribunes who had not listened to their protests. Livy calls this incident a 'severe mutiny' (31.3.2) but does not list any action on the part of the soldiers except advocating for their release. The commander, P. Villius, apparently solved the conflict by promising to petition the Senate on their behalf, but we hear nothing further about these men or Villius' promised appeal. Similarly, in 180 BCE, a legate and two tribunes from the army of Q. Fulvius Flaccus in Spain spoke before the Senate regarding soldiers agitating for their discharge. One legion had been there since 196 and the other since 187 BCE. Although there must have been a great deal of turnover of individual soldiers during that time, enough of them had been held against their will for long enough that they were threatening to desert or mutiny if they were not released.[11]

Deserters

The Roman framework of military rules had, at its heart, the aim of making continuing to fight the better option for the soldier most of the time. These rules aimed to discourage acts like desertion by making it an extremely unappealing road to walk down. The penalty for desertion, either from one's post or battlefield, was death.[12] In addition, rules like that of *postliminium*, which made re-entry to citizenship after surrender very difficult, blocked an easier option of *de facto* desertion by deliberately giving oneself up to the enemy as a prisoner. Similarly, Polybius writes that men who escaped the *fustuarium* were 'not allowed to return to their homes, and none of the family would dare to receive such a man in his house' (Polyb. 6.37.4). The *fustuarium* was supposedly for more minor crimes than desertion. In short, the penalty for not leaving the army in an appropriate way was that the soldier was not supposed to be able to resume any kind of a life within the Roman state.

Of course, it is legitimate to wonder just how far the romanticized idea of severe Roman discipline was actually embraced by the soldiers' families. We know of at least one soldier who was found back at Rome, a certain Caius Matienus, who in 138 BCE was accused of deserting the army in Spain, scourged and sold as a slave (Livy *Ep.* 55). Curiously, he was brought before the tribunes at the levy, although we do not know in what circumstances he was there, or who denounced him. Perhaps, having deserted the army, he had indeed been rejected or even turned in by his family, and taken to the levy by the consuls as an example for the recruits. Perhaps he had attempted to re-join under a different name to try to continue a life as a Roman citizen. One wonders how many soldiers who made it back to Roman territory were never recognized by anyone who knew of their desertion and were never denounced by their families.

There were, no doubt, all kinds of men who left the army and each would have had his own story. Some, perhaps, had fled a crumbling battle line, deciding to live to fight another day despite the dim view taken of men who had done so. Some would have taken badly to the hardships of life in an army camp and left because they found it intolerable. Some would have deserted for profit, selling the location of the army or its camp for a reward. In Ligustinus' first campaign in Macedon, the army of the Romans had not yet encountered the army of King Philip when they were each alerted to the position of the other by deserters (Livy 31.33.11; 34.7). This was after the expedition of Apustius, in which several towns had been sacked. The sole encounter between the forces that came before the desertion of these Roman or allied soldiers had been an attack on the soldiers under Apustius as they returned to the larger part of the army. If they were, in fact, soldiers, these deserters had most likely seen the opportunity to make a quick profit from the enemy rather than being worn down by warfare or plagued by fear. It ought to be remembered, however, that 'deserters' may not in fact refer to former soldiers, but the *calones*, the group of people travelling with the army who had every reason to desert whether they profited thereby or not, since it would mean their freedom.

There were likely also a category of deserters who are hidden from our view, who left the army because they were treated unjustly, or perceived that they had been, and did not think they had any hope of recourse.[13] This is the other side of the framework of legal and social rules that aimed to keep the soldier in service. Even if the path of desertion was fraught and difficult, at a certain point it would have been more appealing than the possible alternatives. We have seen how Roman notions of extreme discipline and the imbalance of power between the elite officers and the ordinary men could lead to soldiers being put in positions where the expectation placed on them was literally to die. Anyone who fled a crumbling battleline, for example, faced the choice of standing his ground and being cut down with no real appreciable benefit to the army, or taking his chances as a deserter. The so-called mutineers at Sucro might have done a great deal better to desert than to be executed for insubordination because they tried to remedy their dire situation. The legions which had escaped from Cannae, also, who were already exiled from Italy with no indication that they might ever be allowed to return, could hardly be blamed if they had sought new lives, but might readily have been considered deserters if they were found in the wrong place.

What a deserter was able to do next would depend on how he had left the army. A man who became separated from his comrades during the chaotic phase of a battle might choose to slip away, shedding shield and helmet as signs of his enrolment in the army and striking out for some new territory. In the situation where the army had been scattered, an individual or even a whole unit could simply choose not to try to seek out the remains of the army and go somewhere else instead. In a defeat, the enemy army controlled the battlefield, and anyone who did not make it back to join the remnants of the army would simply be assumed dead. The disadvantage, of course, would be that just like the soldiers who made their way to Canusium and Venusia after Cannae, deserters from the battlefield would have had only the clothes they were wearing. In such a case, the deserter would have needed to eke out an existence, as the ancient expression was, 'leading the life of a wolf', stealing, or robbing others, or begging, until he could make his way to somewhere he would not be recognized and there were opportunities to live in safety.[14]

There were certainly places in the ancient world where the despised could flourish. In some places we hear mention of congregations of undesirables, who had through crime or flight violated the rules of their societies and become stateless, with no fixed loyalties. One such place was Agathyrna in Sicily, where we are told that in 210 BCE, just as the Carthaginians had been driven from Sicily in the course of the Second Punic War, the Roman consul M. Valerius Laevinus came upon a group of men who had turned to brigandage. Livy was disgusted by such types, calling Agathyrna 'the seat of a motley population' and listing them as refugees, insolvent debtors and those guilty of capital crimes

(26.40.17). These men were a risk to both the locals and to the grain supply, and so Valerius sent them to Regium in Italy as a kind of irregular force, with a specific remit to attack and plunder the nearby town of Bruttium, as it was allied to Hannibal.[15]

None of these men were wanted by their own state. They were certainly, however, useful to another, just as Romans who had deserted their legion would not be welcome at Rome but could sell their services as mercenaries to other entities. This was apparently the plan of some of the tribunes who fled the Roman camp at Cannae and regrouped at Canusium, who, thinking the whole Roman state was lost, were mulling over fleeing overseas and defecting to 'some king'.[16] This passage is somewhat suspect, as we saw in the previous chapter it is a vignette designed to cast a good light upon P. Cornelius Scipio, the future Africanus. Although Scipio buoys and exhorts his colleagues back from their disloyalty, the story eventually comes to nothing, as the party come to realize that the state is intact after all. The mention of the specific proposal to offer their services to a king, however, indicates that it was perfectly possible in the ancient world to do such a thing. There were plenty of kingdoms in the East where a retinue of Roman nobles might be welcomed. The bigger their retinue, the more important and impressive they would seem, and so undoubtedly any ordinary soldiers who wished to join them could have done so.

The life of a mercenary might have been appealing to some whether or not they had left the Roman army honourably. The very violent, those referred to as 'natural killers', gravitate to armies and, in the modern world, they often move on to becoming mercenaries, because routine military life does not provide enough excitement for them.[17] We might suspect that the Roman army remained a suitable and desirable place for such men much more than any modern military. Rome's pattern of warfare meant there was almost always a campaign to join and a great wealth of rewards for the most proactively violent soldiers. Only in the 150s BCE when the campaigns in Spain became desperately unpopular, because they involved too much effort for too little gain, would the most violent of the soldiers have a reason to look for more lucrative prospects by becoming a mercenary. A violently inclined soldier who chafed under strict military rules might have been tempted to do the same.

The key to desertion or defection, of course, was not to get caught. It would have been easy enough in the ancient world to shed an identity and pick up a new one, or to simply invent a different backstory should anyone come asking. Deserters were regularly caught when Rome's enemies were defeated and Rome demanded they be rounded up and handed over as part of the settlement. They were also sometimes caught simply by being in a place where a Roman was not supposed to be, such as when the Romans besieged and forcibly entered enemy towns. There were no trials for such men and, one imagines, few questions asked. In 214 BCE, for example, 2,000 deserters from the Second Punic War were found in Leontini in Sicily, all of whom were scourged and beheaded.[18] This seems a large number for one town and seems likely that some of these men were soldiers who had regrouped after Cannae and had been sent to Sicily with orders not to return within Italian borders. A contingent of these men met the commander of the Roman army sent to Sicily, M. Claudius Marcellus, in order to ask to be allowed to serve with his army. This indicates that the soldiers in Sicily were in fact not soldiers at all, but citizens in exile. Some of them were probably living in Leontini and trapped in the town when it was taken over by an army from the nearby pro-Carthaginian town of Syracuse.

The Rewards of Service

What a soldier could gain from his service in terms of monetary rewards was different depending on the specific era within the Middle Republic in which he lived. A soldier who fought after the Second Punic War was likely to be much better off than one who fought in it, especially in its early years. A large portion of the war was fought within Italy, which impoverished the Roman state instead of enriching it. We have already seen that the state was in great financial difficulty because this was a key point during the discussion of the soldiers who were refused ransom after Cannae. During these years commanders had difficulty even feeding their troops, let alone rewarding them, and Rome was forced to reach out to allied states for help supplying grain and equipment.[19] In addition, there were fewer successes, especially of the particular type of resilience that the Romans wished to encourage and reward at this time. We have here the odd instance of a unit of allies from Praenestae, who had set out late and missed the Battle of Cannae. They ended up in a town called Casilinum, which was besieged by the Carthaginians and eventually forced to surrender. In honour of its long defiance, however, the Roman Senate voted to the surviving soldiers double pay, a five-year exemption from military service, and Roman citizenship, although this last was refused. Why the treatment of these men was so different from the soldiers that surrendered the camp at Cannae is nowhere specified, but it was probably both a political gesture of appreciation for the Italian allies at a time when Hannibal's strategy was to tempt or force them out of their Roman alliance, and the result of a general dearth of acts of spirited resistance to the Carthaginian army.[20]

By the end of the Second Punic War, the Roman victory meant that surviving soldiers were finally able to reap some reward for their many years in service. Around the time that Ligustinus was starting his career, many of these soldiers were ending theirs, and those who ended their service under Scipio in 201 BCE were allocated land in the south of the Italian peninsula. The settlements were in the south largely because the land had been confiscated from cities that had sided with Hannibal during the latter half of the war when most of the fighting was in this region.[21] This land was distributed according to the length of the soldier's service, two *iugera* for every year he had served in Spain or Africa.[22] The plot of land which Ligustinus said was left to him by his father had been only one *iugerum*, however, this had signalled extreme poverty and unless the soldiers had served for a very long time, the plots that resulted from the distribution would still have been considered small. The settlement of veterans on public land would become a feature of the first century BCE, but at the time it was an isolated reward.[23]

The Roman Senate's preferred way of providing a future life for men after their military service was to allocate them a space in a Roman colony. The main principle of these colonies were that they were strategic militarily. In the first quarter of the second century BCE, colonies were started in the Po Valley, north of Ariminum and Pisae, the two towns that had been the mustering points for the wars waged in Cisalpine Gaul and Liguria, as the Romans gradually took over these provinces. The colonies were closely connected to the idea of manpower, as the intention was that the veteran colonists would raise families, including sons who would be eligible to join the Roman army. The soldiers of this era thus were almost exclusively settled to the far north and south of the Italian peninsula. This life was not, apparently, a happy ending for everyone, as there are signs that there was quite a large amount of emigration from these colonies, much of it to the city of Rome itself.[24] Rome had begun to channel its new wealth into extensive public building works, which in turn increased the demand for labour of numerous kinds.

By the time that Ligustinus came to fight in the second century BCE, soldiers who came to the end of a campaign with a victorious army could make a lucrative profit from their service in the form of war booty. Ligustinus, in fact, served in one of the very best periods to be a Roman soldier, at least under the Republic. The period from 200 BCE to 167 BCE was the one in which Rome completed her Mediterranean expansion with the takeover of the lucrative Greek East. After this came a period that was characterized by the notoriously unpopular wars in Spain, unpopular largely because of the lack of profit they provided. Ligustinus, however, participated in some of the most profitable campaigns of the era. Not only was there money to be made from goods stripped from the towns that the Romans took over, there was also a share in the profits of victorious campaigns over kingdoms and states and large donatives from triumphant generals.

Some of these bonuses probably involved a certain amount of luck and being in the right place at the right time. We do not know, for example, how it was decided whether soldiers were eligible to march in triumphs and receive the donative given to soldiers on such occasions. Ligustinus had left the army of Flamininus in Macedon before the campaign came to an end, and while he may have been in Rome in 194 BCE when that triumph took place, we do not know if he was welcome to join if he had not been present at the end of the campaign. He would certainly have been eligible for the triumph of M. Porcius Cato that took place in the same year, where, despite it being the end of a campaign of only a year, the donative was slightly higher than Flamininus', at twenty-seven *denarii* per infantryman and fifty-four per centurion rather than the twenty-five and fifty *denarii* from the Macedonian campaign.[25] Cato was said to have boasted that he gave a pound of silver to every soldier who served in Spain (Plut. *Cat. Mai.* 10.4) which ought at this time have been equivalent to eighty-four *denarii*, although most scholars have assumed that this refers to an exaggeration about the donative on the part of Plutarch or Cato rather than an additional amount.[26] Even omitting the claim of the pound of silver, it seems to have been extremely profitable for a soldier to have fought in Spain with Cato, who is recorded as emphasizing that he allowed the soldiers to take a great deal of booty. He had claimed that 400 towns were taken, and there were also silver mines in that part of Spain.

At other times, such as when he was selected out of Fulvius Flaccus' soldiers in Spain to return for the triumph, other soldiers who had not been as distinguished were left in the province and presumably missed out on the generous donative given on that occasion. Ligustinus himself would have been among the soldiers who complained bitterly to their commander after the Battle of Cynoscephalae, when the triumphant Roman soldiers attempted to strip booty from the Macedonian camp only to find that their Aetolian allies had already claimed it (Polyb. 18.27.3–5). Sometimes, especially when we hear that a commander had sent away the *lixae*, the booty would have been received by the soldiers in kind.[27] The sources are usually not very precise about what sort of items constituted booty, and we should assume it was anything that could be used by the soldiers themselves or anything with a resale value. From camps this might include cattle, horses, mules, and fodder, and from cities and towns, everything from wine to art. Most commonly, everything would be gathered together to be sold and the money then distributed to the soldiers by their officers.[28]

After he returned from Spain in 194 BCE, Ligustinus spent a few years at home before joining several short campaigns. In his speech he claimed to still live on the *iugerum* of land and in the house in which he was born. This is not what we would expect from a man who had been enriched by his service in the legions, but probably Ligustinus' account is intended to appeal to the romanticized views of an aristocratic elite more than it was supposed to be aspirational for a peasant soldier. A strong, sentimental connection to ancestral land was, after all, the root of building and maintaining a culture in which military prowess was prized by the average man. We are left to fill in for ourselves how Ligustinus might have personally improved life for himself and his large family. His original *iugerum* cannot have been a farm that sustained his wife along with eight children. Perhaps he had bought a larger piece of land along with slaves to work it with the proceeds of the profitable wars in Macedon and Spain. Later, he could have bought land or housing for his sons.

Ligustinus never mentions another profession or business besides his repeated service in the army. Despite his declaration that he served for twenty-two years, it is not possible for him to have been on the campaigns that he specified and also have completed twenty-two years of service by 171 BCE.[29] He must instead be referring to the twenty-two-year period between 200 and 179 BCE, the years of the first and last campaign that he specifies. Within this time period we can pin down eleven years of service, with an additional two that are uncertain because Ligustinus is unspecific about when exactly he joined or left a particular campaign.

Ligustinus' service therefore is as follows. After spending five years in Macedon and Greece with Flamininus, he returned to Rome early and joined M. Porcius Cato campaigning in Hispania Citerior. This was one season of campaigning between 195 and 194 BCE. He then returned to Rome and presumably participated in Cato's triumph of 194 BCE. Apparently he then spent two years at home, for he is clear that his third campaign was when he joined the war against Antiochus under M. Acilius Glabrio in 191 BCE. This service may have been one or two years. Livy and Polybius both write that the whole army was handed over from M. Acilius Glabrio to L. Cornelius Scipio after a year, implying that Ligustinus must have been handed over with it, however, reinforcements were also sent out with Scipio, which may have allowed time-expired soldiers to be released if they wished.[30] Between 189 and 183 BCE he served twice, in two legions that served for a year. He then served in the army of Q. Fulvius Flaccus, again in Hispania Citerior. He could have joined this campaign at its outset or been part of the *supplementa* sent to reinforce this army in 181 BCE. As we have seen, he returned with Flaccus to walk in his triumph and must have returned in 179 BCE to serve with Sempronius Gracchus.

After this, Ligustinus mentions no more years of service, and even if he had served thirteen years until 179 BCE and then continuously through the seven campaigning seasons between then and when he came to volunteer again in 171 BCE, he would only have twenty years of service. He therefore must mean that he was a soldier as his primary job for 22 years. During this time he walked in at least three triumphs, with donatives of 54 *denarii*, 100 *denarii* and double pay, and 50 *denarii*. These donatives were some of the best available at the time, and not every soldier would have had the good fortune to serve in one of these campaigns in areas where rich profit could be made. Ligustinus had met many of these less fortunate men during his career, in the form of the Punic War veterans in 199 BCE and the troops of 180 BCE in Spain, who had not been retired for triumphs but rather repeatedly held in service. In 171 BCE the recruiters were not short of young men who had targeted this campaign for their service because of these kinds of donatives and the amount that could be made through booty in the field. They did, however, need experienced hands, which is why Ligustinus had presented himself although he had apparently ceased volunteering eight years before.

In addition to the pay he had drawn over these years, which as a centurion was double that of an ordinary infantryman, and the donatives he had received, Ligustinus mentions being singled out at the *contio* on thirty-four occasions. He is not specific about most of these awards but many of them might have had a monetary value. The account centres more on prestige than financial gain, naming him as the recipient of six civic crowns, which were crowns of oak leaves awarded for saving the life of a Roman citizen in combat. In addition, there is reason to think that Ligustinus had come to the personal attention of some of Rome's most influential aristocrats. As *primus pilus* on more than four occasions, he would have sat in the *consilium* of commanders a minimum of four times. He claims to have been personally picked out by M. Porcius Cato for promotion to first centurion of the *hastati*, by Q. Fulvius Flaccus to walk in his triumph, and then sought out by Ti. Sempronius Gracchus to return to his Spanish campaign. From a very poor man, he had advanced enough in class and social status through his military exploits that he had the ear of the elites.

The campaign which Ligustinus joined in 171 BCE came to a dramatic conclusion in 168 BCE with the Battle of Pydna and the Roman victory over King Perseus of Macedon. If Ligustinus is, as many suspect, either entirely fictional or his career has been massaged into an example of the ideal soldier, it would make sense to imagine his military career ending with the triumph that followed the Battle of Pydna, back in Rome in 167 BCE. This would make him present from beginning to end of this important phase of Rome's expansionist history, the most profitable and glorious phase between the poverty and desperation of the Second Punic War and the relentless grind of the unpopular Spanish wars. It would neatly wrap up a career that would begin and end in Macedon, at the beginning of the First Macedonian War to the conclusion of the Third, when the lucrative East was finally ushered into the Roman fold. For Livy, perhaps, and his audience, Ligustinus was the best of all soldiers, because he was the soldier who won the Empire.

Conclusion

Looking Forward to The Late Republic

T he division of Roman history into periods is a modern one, and it has changed over the years based mainly on our interpretation of the three interconnected themes of land, politics, and the army. The traditional date for the end of the Middle Republic and the beginning of the Late Republic used to be 133 BCE. This was a date largely determined by Roman politics, as it marked the tribunate of Tiberius Gracchus, who was the first to seek to bypass the Senate and send proposed legislation to the assemblies of the people instead. This launched a period of political and military violence, in which the character of the legions would play a pivotal role. As we saw in the introduction, the date of 133 BCE is not universal and the division has sometimes been taken as 146 BCE, the date of the destruction of Carthage and, thus, the removal of Rome's last great enemy in the Mediterranean. The crucial date that marks the most change to the Roman legions and soldiers is also different, set at 107 BCE, the date of the reforms of Marius.

By 107 BCE, Rome had been short of recruits for its legions for decades. The Romans believed that rich landowners in the countryside had expanded their estates by buying up neighbouring plots of land belonging to poorer citizens. As these citizen farmers left their lands, they ceased to meet the property qualification for service in the military. An element of the ruling elite made land reform an important part of their political platform, aiming to take the land back from the rich and redistribute it to the poor so that more men would meet the land requirement to become soldiers. It is now thought, however, that the free population was not in decline at all. Volunteers were easily found to fight in Rome's profitable wars, and so the impression of a manpower shortage was tracked back to men hiding from both recruiters and census takers, lest they be sent to the prolonged, unpopular, and unprofitable wars that Rome was fighting in Spain.[1]

So, not in response to a manpower shortage but rather in the face of the unpopularity of military service, Marius recruited the landless poor as volunteers to serve in his Numidian campaign of 107 BCE. These men were without land because there was little left to distribute.[2] This action has been considered the beginning of momentous change in the nature of Rome's armies, but at the time it probably only inspired doubt and contempt about how well or how loyally men without land could fight for the Republic.[3] Over recent years a scholarly consensus has emerged that the opening of the army to the landless poor had three long term implications:

1) The army gradually became more professionalized
2) There was an increase in *esprit de corps* or cohesion among the legions
3) There was a shift in the loyalty on the part of the Republican soldier from the state to his individual commander.[4]

The main idea behind the professionalization of the Late Republican army is that the soldier from this point onward was no longer a citizen soldier who would return to land he owned in Roman Italy. Instead he served primarily for pay and benefits and so came to resemble a mercenary in his motivations rather than a citizen soldier.[5] The second common characterization of the post-Marian legion is that it experienced increased cohesion and *esprit de corps*, partly caused by the professionalization that caused soldiers to serve for long periods of time with the same comrades, and partly by the deliberate efforts of Marius himself.[6] The legions were provided with a legionary eagle that provided a focal point for the soldiers' loyalty. Although there was still no standing army or permanent institution, there were semi-permanent legions with their own numbers and symbols.

The third significant change for the Late Republic is a shift in loyalty towards the individual commander of legions rather than the Roman state. This is often thought to be the result of a lessened political conscience among the soldiers due to their professionalization and service for pay rather than a higher cause. A large part of the soldiers' loyalty towards their commanders was a refusal on the part of the state to provide for them after their service, even though many of them had been conscripted and sent against Rome's foreign enemies just as their Mid-Republican counterparts had been. Instead, the Roman Senate continually forced these commanders to petition the Senate extensively and make political alliances in order to have land granted to their soldiers.[7]

After following the experiences of the Mid-Republican soldier so closely, we are in a better position to examine whether what these changes say about the soldier before the Late Republic is accurate or not. As a description of the differences between the two eras, these common interpretations are making a statement about the Mid-Republican soldier just as much as about his Late Republican counterpart, to whom he serves as a contrast. If the Late Republican soldier enjoyed increased cohesion, professionalization and loyalty to his commander, then the implication is that the Mid-Republican soldier experienced these to a lesser degree or not at all.

The matter of cohesion is the most obvious place to start, but it is difficult to understand exactly what is meant by increased cohesion or *esprit de corps*. We have seen that cohesion is not best understood as one single element but rather splits into task cohesion and social cohesion, the ability of soldiers to perform the tasks demanded of them as a team and the degree to which they developed bonds of friendship with one another. There is really no reason to think that the Mid-Republican soldier had a less developed sense of social cohesion or *esprit de corps* with his fellows than his Late Republican counterpart. The fact that the Late Republican soldier appears as an obvious example of a soldier with a close and strong bond to his legion, his comrades and his leader does not necessarily mean that there is evidence that the Mid-Republican soldier did not. It may simply be a reflection of the fact that there is better evidence for the later period, both in the number and quality of the sources that we have, including first-hand accounts of soldiers and their behaviour from contemporary sources such as Caesar, and in the fact that we can trace the same soldiers for a longer period of time.

The other consideration is that the elements that served to form group identity, and hence social cohesion, mostly belong to the most overlooked part of Roman military service, the accompanying religious rites and ceremonies. Perhaps also there is a tendency to assume that it would take years to form a strong sense of social cohesion, but modern studies of the topic suggest this should not be the case at all, in fact the contrary, that identification with any group into which people are sorted happens very quickly. Mid-Republican soldiers lived, travelled and fought together for many months, stretching to years in many cases, and we should expect that they, too, had a strong social cohesion that was emphasized and developed through religious rites like the *lustratio* and the burning of enemy arms. It was a common religion that underpinned the soldier's oath to remain under arms, and the basis of the legitimacy of the commander was that he was a magistrate who possessed the authority to interact with the gods on behalf of the army as a representative of the state.

This is not to say that there is not an important point to be made in the idea of the Late Republican legions displaying a particular type of cohesion that is not observed before this time period. In this regard the most important change between the Late Republican and Mid-Republican citizen soldiers did not stem from any difference in their character, but the permanence of the institutions that they joined. Mid-Republican soldiers were part of a unique group of soldiers who made up each legion each year, with veterans moving out and reinforcements moving in. In permanent, numbered legions, elements of army institutions whose absence we have noted in an earlier time, could start to manifest, such as a sense of the unit having a history and its own character, culture or reputation. The numbered legions developed an institutional dynamic wherein, instead of there being only a sense of the soldiers being bonded to each other, there was also a sense that they were bonded to an institution.

Similarly, the claim that soldiers of the Late Republic were particularly mercenary benefits from the perspective of what came before. It is true that the armies that defended Rome in the Second Punic war could hardly be called mercenary and most of them reaped few rewards for what were sometimes extraordinary efforts to defend their state. For most of the second century, however, the soldier's reason to fight was mostly for profit. By the time of Ligustinus, the Republic was not engaged in a fight for survival but in the pursuit of empire and men shirked recruitment when they were sent to places with little prospect of profit. It is hard to see why anyone would expect this to be otherwise. There may have been benefit to the Roman people in the long term from expansionism into poor areas, but in the short term it benefitted only a small number of elites who sought to make their names as generals. It is apparent that the average man in Roman Italy was only willing to risk his life if the undertaking provided a reasonable expectation of reward.

The point that must be emphasized in any discussion of changes between these two eras is that the soldiers themselves were not men of distinctly different character. Despite the fact that Marius recruited the landless poor, there is little to suggest that the Late Republican armies were overwhelmingly made up of these men or that they brought any significant change in culture.[8] Rather, they were the same types of men whose experience of army service happened in different circumstances to the men who came before them. In addition to the three areas mentioned, there were also other distinctive changes to the legions that influenced how the soldier would have perceived serving in this turbulent era.

Technical Changes to the Army

There were technical changes made to the army during the Late Republic that resolved some inefficiencies that were apparent in the Mid-Republican army. In particular, the division of the *velites* fell out of use entirely along with the citizen cavalry. From this period, then, Roman citizens ceased to serve as light infantry or cavalry, with the effect that the Romans of the Late Republic served exclusively in units of heavy infantry. This also meant that the young recruits serving as *velites* no longer had the experience of being attached to a more senior unit of *hastati*, *principes* or *triarii* with which they camped and travelled.

The disappearance of the *velites* is unsurprising, as even by the Middle Republic it had looked like a unit that was somewhat of a relic of the early army. At one time the Romans had provided the complete army themselves from citizens, and this had included light infantry and cavalry, who were necessary to keep the enemy at bay while the heavy infantry deployed. The *velites* also, as we have described, provided a kind of training ground for the youngest troops, who could become acclimatized to warfare and violence from a position where they were more free to retreat and could advance at their own pace. By the second century the Romans were already accompanied by a number of specialist units who were better suited to providing missile cover for heavy infantry, like archers and slingers, who could keep an enemy infantry at a distance while remaining at a safe distance themselves. We have seen that the *velites* carried swords and were sometimes placed in physical danger, which, while it may have seemed to build character and bravery among Rome's recruits, was not tactically optimal.

The other major inefficiency in the existence of the *velites* is that it gave the Mid-Republican army an overly large training burden. The citizen legions of the Middle Republic already had a large training burden due to the large turnover of men caused by the conscription of the majority of male citizens. In addition to this, if a Roman citizen soldier served in first light and then heavy infantry, he would need to learn the different skills for these two positions, which represented double the training of most soldiers in the ancient world. As we saw with divisions of foreign troops like the Cretan archers and the Numidian cavalry, usually national groups specialized in one form of warfare that limited their training and experience to one set of skills. It was unusual in the ancient world for individuals to be expected to progress from one skill set to another. This is obviously because it was better for these divisions to retain soldiers who had become experienced and skilled. In a division like the *velites*, individuals who wished to progress to the heavy infantry would effectively weaken the light infantry by making it a division that was always filled with learners and the inexperienced.

This consideration would lead us to expect that either the division of *velites* was always inefficient and, consequently, an extremely hazardous place to be, or that individuals were detained in that division because they had been particularly young or poor at the time of their first enlistment. So while Polybius says that the 'youngest and poorest' were sent to the *velites*, one would assume that because armies were dissolved and new armies raised so frequently, after a few years a *veles* could join a new army and qualify to be placed into the *hastati*. This is the period, however, where armies were serving for longer periods of time continuously, and it might be that *velites* were not automatically or even routinely moved into other divisions. The *velites* probably had their own leaders, but they had no formal centurion positions to provide an obvious promotional opportunity. Therefore, just as some armies were simply left in provinces year after year, it might be that some soldiers would simply be left serving continuously in the *velites*. Therefore, even beyond their tactical awkwardness, one suspects there are two possibilities of why the *velites* disappeared, which are not mutually exclusive: that they were always an inefficient and dangerous division, or that the division unfairly depressed the prospects of the poor.

The disappearance of the *velites* and the new semi-permanence of army legions in the Middle Republic would have drastically decreased the training obligation of army officers, as there was no longer a high proportion of new entrants and two sets of skills to train simultaneously. This in turn would have mitigated an obvious liability of some Mid-Republican armies that were not battle ready at the beginning of a new campaigning year. This was a significant vulnerability in these legions as they would have needed constant training to bring new entrants up to competence.

The second large technical change to the Late Republican army was that the primary unit of organization came to be the cohort rather than the maniple. The cohort had been in use as a unit as early as the beginning of the second century, as we have seen in its mentions by Polybius and the Elder Cato, and its new primacy as an organizational unit was the logical result of the disappearance of the *velites*. There were now only three divisions of Roman citizen soldiers in the camp rather than four. Where previously one maniple of *hastati*, *principes* or *triarii* had camped with its attached *velites*, now three maniples, one of each division, camped together as a cohort. Consequently, where beforehand it was commonplace for the *velites* to deploy separately from the maniples to which they belonged and even fight in a different part of the field, now soldiers who camped together were stationed together on the field as well.

Further Changes to the Soldier's Experience in Late Republican Armies

There are a few changes, in addition to the three that are most commonly cited, that would likely had a profound effect on how a soldier experienced military service at the end of the second century BCE and after. Firstly, the location of conflicts in the late Republic brought soldiers back to fighting on home ground again, within Roman Italy, one of a number of factors that would greatly change the psychological experience of soldiers. In some decades and for some armies the enemy was broadly the same category as those who had been faced in the Middle Republic, an enemy external to Italy and recognizably foreign, like the Gauls, the Germans, and the Parthians on the Eastern border. By the end of the second century, however, we also start to see the army sent to deal with slave uprisings, first in Sicily and then in Italy itself, culminating in the famous uprising of Spartacus. Then followed the Social War, so named because the Romans fought against the *socii*, their own former allies within Italy. In the aftermath of this war, the Roman citizen body that made up the legions widened and broadened with the integration of the former allies as citizens, giving the original Romans new comrades in their cohorts and the Italian allies new places in the citizen legions. The most significant change of enemy came in the period of the civil wars, which saw a Roman army march on the city of Rome for the first time. One imagines the escalating psychological difficulties as the Roman citizens were faced with fighting their slaves, their allies and eventually each other. This era represents a turbulent age of politics that made enemies of sections and factions of other Romans and conscripted Roman soldiers to fight them.

In addition to new categories of enemy, in the course of the Late Republic there was a general decrease in religious activity surrounding the army. Cicero complains that by his time armies were sent out under commanders who did not have the right of *auspicium* and thus did not take auspices on behalf of their armies (Cic. *Div.* 2.76–7). The significance of the commander had been as the authorized representative of the state who had the power to appeal to the gods on behalf of a group of Roman citizens. This would have served to emphasize that the army was representative of the state rather than a faction or division of it, as many Late Republican armies came to be. The decrease in loyalty to the state that is usually observed in soldiers of this era is therefore perhaps another way of saying that there was a decrease in the reach of centralized authority at Rome. This, of course, was not an exclusively military phenomenon. Loyalty to the state was a much more difficult business when the state, or the Republic, had ceased to be one entity.

Glossary

There were a very limited number of Roman male first names (*praenomen*). Those used in this book are commonly abbreviated as follows:

A. = Aulus, L. = Lucius, C. = Gaius, Cn. = Gnaeus, M. = Marcus, P. = Publius, Q. = Quintus Sp. = Spurius, T. = Titus, Ti. = Tiberius

Auspicium (sg.): The right to take auspices on behalf of a Roman army.

Auspicium ex tripudiis: A means of taking the auspices using the feeding behaviour of chickens. This was done before certain actions and movements to check for objections from the gods.

Calo (sg.) *calones* (pl.): Slaves belonging to the state, who accompanied the army on campaign.

Cohors amicorum: Literally 'cohort of friends', a group of advisors, friends, and sons of friends who were invited by the general to accompany the campaign and provide advice or gain experience.

Consilium (sg.), *consilia* (pl.): The commander's military advisory council.

Consul: The highest magistrate in the state and the usual commander of armies. Two were elected annually.

Contio (sg.), *Contiones* (pl.): An assembly of the soldiers, especially the assembly held after a military engagement in which the commander gave awards to soldiers for their bravery.

Contubernium (sg.) *Contubernia* (pl.): The group of 8 men who shared a tent in the Roman military camp.

Decimation: A form of military punishment in which one out of every ten of the soldiers of a particular unit was executed.

Denarius (sg.), *denarii* (pl.): A denomination of Roman currency.

Dilectus (sg.): The military levy.

Divisions: the four groups into which soldiers were divided based on age and wealth; the *velites*, *hastati*, *principes*, and *triarii*.

Domi Nobiles (pl.): Literally 'the nobles at home', members of the elite class in towns and cities in Italy other than Rome.

Exauctor (sg.), *Exauctores* (pl.): A former soldier or soldiers who had been released from the *sacramentum*, the military oath.

Fustuarium (sg.): A military punishment in which a soldier was beaten to death by other soldiers.

Gladius (sg.) *gladii* (pl.): The Roman military sword.

Hastatus (sg.), *Hastati* (pl.): 'spear men'. The first division of citizen heavy infantry, who were placed in the first line in battle.

Haruspex (sg.) *haruspices* (pl.): Etruscan priests who examined the entrails of sacrificial victims.

Heavy infantry: the soldiers in the divisions of *hastati*, *principes* and *triarii* who were more heavily armed and armoured than the *velites*.

Imperium: The right to command an army on behalf of the Roman state.

Iugerum (sg.), *Iugera* (pl.): The standard measurement of Roman land.

Legate: A lieutenant or ambassador. In the Middle Republic, former commanders or members of the *cohors amicorum* were often given this title when they accompanied an army on campaign as an advisor.

Light infantry: The soldiers in the *velites* and sometimes other contingents from the allies who were lightly armed and armoured.

Lixa (sg.) *lixae* (pl.): camp followers or sutlers, who bought booty and sold goods to the soldiers, and probably also handled the sale of those captured as slaves.

Lustratio: A ritual performed when the army or navy departed for war, asking the gods for protection and success.

Maniple: The base unit of organization in Mid-Republican armies, consisting of two centuries.

Pomerium: The sacred boundary around the city of Rome that separated civil life inside from the military sphere outside.

Postliminium: The law that governed if and how a Roman captured in a war could be restored to Roman citizenship.

Praetor: The second magistrate, besides the consul, who possessed the rights required to command an army.

Princeps (sg.), *principes* (pl.): 'First line men'. The *principes* were the second division of heavy infantry, who were placed in the second line in a battle. Their name suggests that at some point they had been the first line.

Proconsul: Literally 'in place of a consul' or 'acting as a consul'. A former consul whose command had been extended past the year of his consulship by the Roman senate.

Propraetor: Literally 'in place of a praetor' or 'acting as a praetor'. A former praetor whose command had been extended past the year of his praetorship by the Roman senate.

Primus Pilus (sg., also *primipilus*): A centurion of the first maniple of the *triarii*. While the name of the *triarii* 'third line men' changed at some point from *pili*, 'spears' or 'spearmen', the title of the centurions remained the same.

Pilus (sg.), *Pili* (pl.): 'Spearman' or 'spearmen', an older name for the *triarii*.

Pilanus (sg.), *Pilani* (pl.): Archaic. 'Spearman' or 'spearmen'. Another old name for the *triarii* according to Varro, *Ling*. 5.89.

Pullarius (sg.) *pullarii* (pl.) : The chicken-keeper. A man who looked after the chickens on campaign and acted as an assistant during the auspices.

Sacramentum (sg.): The military oath taken by soldiers at the end of the levy, to obey their leaders and to remain a soldier until formally released.

Sodalis (sg.), *sodales* (pl.): 'Swordmates', the name given to soldiers who fought in the war bands of the early Republic.

Stipendium (sg.): The military pay of a soldier. In the second century BCE this was 108 *denarii* per year per infantryman, 216 *denarii* for a centurion, and 324 *denarii* for a cavalryman.

Supplementum (sg.), *Supplementa* (pl.): Troops sent to replace casualties and time-expired soldiers in armies on campaign. They were usually made up of 5,000 citizen soldiers and 7,500 allied soldiers per two legion consular army, but could number more or less.

Testamentum (sg.) *testamenta* (pl.): A will. The *testamentum in procinctu* was a will made orally by a soldier to his immediate comrades while stood on the battle line.

Triarius (sg.) *Triarii* (pl.): 'Third line men', the last division of heavy infantry. Formerly known as *pili*, 'spearmen' or *pilani* meaning the same, a centurion of the *triarii* was still referred to as a *pilus*.

Tribune, or military tribune: Roman military officers who organized the camp and were often placed in charge of units, either in battle or on expeditions. There were six per legion.

Veles (sg.) *Velites* (pl.): The division of light-armed infantry. These men were the youngest and poorest of Rome's citizen soldiers.

Notes

Introduction

1. Astin 1967, 19; 245–6. The conversation is related at Polyb. 31.23.1ff.
2. Polyb.38.19–22.
3. Rawson 1971, Brunt 1971, 625–34.
4. On Polybius' omission of religious elements in the Histories see Vaahtera 2001, 19–30; Vaahtera 2000.
5. For the surviving manuscripts of Livy and their condition, see de Franchis 2014, 3–23.
6. Eckstein 2015, 408.
7. Cf. Clark, 2018, 193: 'it is not that our evidence is "literary" and thus we cannot really know anything. Rather, our evidence is literary and therefore we cannot really know anything *without reading it very carefully*.'
8. Rüpke 2019, 205.
9. Briscoe 1981, 63–66.

Chapter 1

1. See Rosenstein 2004, esp. 26–106.
2. See Rosenstein 2002, especially Appendix 5, and Rosenstein 2004.
3. These types of farming activities are detailed in the agricultural treatises of the authors Cato the Elder, Varro, and Columella, spanning from the second century BCE to the first century CE. See also Rosenstein 2004, 63–106.
4. Cato, in the preface to *De Agricultura* (On Agriculture) wrote that the bravest and sturdiest men come from farming; cf. Cic. *Rep.* 2.4. For modern agreement see Brand 2019, 180.
5. Polyb. 6.19.2 with Walbank 1.698.
6. Rosenstein 2004, 189–90; Brunt 1971, 399–401.
7. The most important scholarly works that address the figure of Spurius Ligustinus are Taylor 2019, Hoyos 2011, Cadiou 2002, Perotti 1974, and Dutoit 1964. On Livy's text of this incident, see Briscoe's commentary (2012).
8. Livy 42.34.3–4, trans Roberts (amended). The manuscript of Livy gives the name of Ligustinus' tribe as 'Crustumina', which is an alternative spelling; Taylor 2019, 271 n.26.
9. Hug 2014, 2–3.
10. Chrissanthos 2004, 348–50.
11. Alföldi 1962, 212.
12. This was the estimation of Syme 1957, 124 and Taylor 2013, 83–4, followed by Taylor 2019, 271. The exact date of the foundation of Forum Novum (or when a prior site acquired that distinctly Roman name) is uncertain. The archaeological work done on the area by the British School at Rome's Tiber Valley Project, e.g. Gaffney *et al.* 2001 and 2004, concentrate on its later time periods and give it simply a 'Republican' origin. Farney 2019, 168, estimates only that it was established 'by the late second century'. Taylor 2013, 84 states that it was probably already an occupied site when the Romans conquered that region in the years leading up to 299 BCE. This uncertainty need not bother us too much, as Ligustinus certainly came from the area that was or would come to be known as Forum Novum, the only town in the Sabine country that had citizens enrolled in the Clustumina (Syme 1957, 124).

13. Farney 2019, 167; Laurence 1999, 29–32 for *fora* as centres of Roman administration, trade, and recruitment.

14. Farney 2019, 163. For the sale of land see Gabba 1988.

15. Horace Odes 3.6 37–9. Dutoit 1964, 187 cites this verse and other similar views of the Sabines.

16. Taylor 2019.

17. Briscoe 2012, 262 thinks he is largely an invention of Livy, Hoyos 2011, 64 that the speech is a Livian elaboration based on a real character and situation, Cadiou 2002 treats Ligustinus as entirely real, Dutoit 1964 fleshes out the ways in which he represents an idyllic Roman exemplum.

18. Soeters *et al.* 2006, 237–8.

19. This is not to say that there were not specific habits and behaviours within an army on campaign, what we might label a 'camp culture' or 'campaign culture' that was particular to that time and place.

20. Polyb. 6.52.7.

21. Polybius describes this process in 6.39.1–11.

22. Milne 2020.

23. The elements of exemplary narratives are the work of Roller 2020, 3–23, also described in his earlier work: Roller 2004.

24. Polyb. 6.55.3–4.

25. Polyb. 6.54.5

26. Val. Max 2.7.6; Liv. 8.7; also referenced by Cic. *Fin.* 2.105; Dion. Hal. *Ant. Rom.* 8.79.2; Sall. *Cat.* 52.30; Hor. *Epist.* 1.5.4–6.

27. Ricks 1997, 239–41.

28. Dion. Hal. *Ant. Rom.* 10.36–7. Siccius Dentatus also appears in Val. Max. 3.2.24, Pliny *HN* 7.101–2, Gell. *NA* 2.11. He may be legendary or semi-legendary. See Forsythe 2005, 208–9 and Oakley 1985, 393; 409–10.

29. Plin. *HN* 35.2.7.

30. For an earlier version of this analysis, see Milne 2020.

31. Polyb. 6.39.3. For the identification of the objects with their Latin names, see Maxfield 1981, 61–2.

32. For a nation who appear more 'naturally' inclined to war in the ancient sources see the Macedonians: Eckstein 2006, 200–16, esp. 202–3.

33. Swank and Marchand 1946, 180.

34. Pierson 1999, 64.

35. *Nulla est ergo tanta humilitas quae dulcedine gloriae non tangatur*, Val. Max. 8.14.5.

36. Hölscher has pointed out that in the ancient world a military victory is 'a momentary factual event, limited in space and time' while political power is, by contrast, 'a long-term structural concept'. On a state level, this has the practical implication that a victory must be capitalized upon (for example, by annexation of territory), something that did not always happen in the ancient world. In another sense, however, it means that the same process must also happen symbolically in order to foster and perpetuate a long-term conceptual sense of superiority and dominance: Hölscher 2006, 29.

37. The two versions of the story come from Livy (2.20.11–12) and Dionysius of Halicarnassus (6.13) respectively.

38. Orlin 1997, 15.

39. Davies 2017, 42, who notes that this building was concentrated in two phases, around the Third Samnite war and the First Punic War.

40. Hölkeskamp 1993, 28.

41. Rüpke 2006, 218–19.

42. Rome full of arms and armour: Plut. *Marc.* 21.2. For a good analysis of the evidence for displayed spoils, from whence it comes and how seriously it ought to be treated, see Rawson 1990.

43. Humm 2009, 117, referencing Livy 22.57.10.
44. Spoils sent to Italy: Cic. *Verr.* 2.1.55, cf. Livy 24.21.9, who writes that Roman spoils were sent to Syracuse.
45. Livy 8.14.12.
46. Despite Cicero's testimony that it was built by Servius Tullius: Humm 2009, 120–21.
47. Hölscher 2006.
48. Humm 2009, 125–6.
49. Welch 2006. Such artwork and statuary in the private homes of Rome's elite was intended to be viewed by friends and clients, to boost the owner's social standing and contribute to their political advancement.
50. On Scipio as legate: Livy 37.1.9; see Wolff 2010, 22 on the motivations of the soldiers who accompanied him.
51. Östenberg 2009, 192–99.
52. Livy 41.28.8.
53. Plin. *HN* 35.7.22–3.
54. Coarelli 1996, 239–57.
55. D'Auria 2017.
56. Fronda 2020 on Flamininus' 'Italian Triumph'. The procession of Scipio is discussed 176–7.
57. Livy 45.35.3.
58. Livy 10.46.2–3, in regard to a triumph over the Samnites that was considered particularly special for the high number of decorated soldiers.
59. For example, Livy 26.21.8 (the triumph over Syracuse) and 39.5.15 (in 187 BCE)
60. For the artfully arranged weaponry of the Macedonians paraded in 167 BCE see Plut. *Aem.* 32.3–4. For descriptions of captives in triumphs see, for example, Flor. 1.37.5 (the Gallic King Bituitus) or App. *Hisp.* 98 (Numantines); Polyb. 2.31.1–6 (Celts).
61. Shay 2002, 152.
62. Mondini 2019, 246–252.
63. The fact that Ligustinus' military life takes place precisely in these years of Rome's growing power (not to mention, as we will see later, that he served with all the famous commanders of his day), ought perhaps to weigh against the idea of him having been a real person.
64. For a straight-forward explanation of the Sibylline books, see Orlin 1997, 76–97.
65. Schultz 2006, 28–33.
66. Livy 28.28; Val. Max. 2.7.15; Polyb. 1.7.6–13.
67. Livy 24.20.6.
68. As Richlin writes of the third century BCE, 'In a century racked by war throughout the Mediterranean, mass enslavements and city sackings filled the landscape with people who had lost everything.' (Richlin 2017, 3)
69. On the soldiers liberated after Cynoscephalae, see Plut. *Flam.* 13.5–9, Livy 34.50.3–7; 34.52.12. On how they might have influenced the views of contemporary Roman society see Richlin 2018, 216–17; Leigh 2004, 86–95.

Chapter 2
1. Harris 1985, 47. For his general estimation of Roman willingness to serve during this era, see 41–53 and more recently, Rosenstein 2004, 58–60.
2. Rosenstein 2004, 81–88.
3. On all of these rules governing recruitment, see Roselaar 2009.
4. For a clear description of the census, and the associated problems that make our understanding of it imperfect, see Northwood 2008.
5. Rosenstein 2004, 57–8. Perotti 1974, 94, explains Ligustinus' enrolment in the legions by referring to the fact that the minimum wealth requirement for qualifying as *assidui* was

lowered during the Second Punic War, but as Rosenstein explains, it was not lowered by very much.

6. James 2011, 22–3; 2002, 38–9.
7. Armstrong 2016, 142–4.
8. Deniaux 2006, 402.
9. Forsythe 2005, 29–31.
10. Armstrong 2020, 92–94; de Ligt 2007, 116 argued that the *dilectus* was in two stages and Polybius is only referring to the second part.
11. Aulus Gellius 16.4.
12. Gargola 2017, 110–18, emphasizes the centrality of the city of Rome to all accounts of the levy. Brunt 1971, 625–34 points out that asking citizens to come to Rome to be sorted into their legions, return to their homes to equip, and then depart to the mustering point seems a waste of time and resources.
13. Livy 43.15.1. Jehne 2006, 253 calculates that the levy must have taken a minimum of 7 and a half days, allowing time for the tribunes to examine the men. The sheer scale of the operation seems to me to make this timeline likely, even perhaps too optimistic. It does seem unlikely that the men were scrutinized, as the tribunes were probably trying to move through the men as quickly as possible and giving them no more than a cursory glance.
14. For this judgment see Hopkins 1991, 489 ff. who emphasizes the ritualistic nature of sorting this amount of men by age, stature, and wealth.
15. Jehne 2006, 253–54 writes that the levy would have had a competitive element, and that the tribunes selected the most suitable-looking men first, causing embarrassment to those left until later. This assessment depends on the assumption that the tribunes were scrutinizing the men as they picked them.
16. Polyb. 6.24.8–9.
17. As far as I know, no scholar has thought to ask the question of what the first soldier might have looked like save Holbrook 2003, 74–5, who suggests that physiognomy mattered, and that perhaps one of the first four soldiers chosen ('of nearly equal age and physique' Polyb. 6.20.2) was suitable; however the idea that the first four soldiers were particular in any way is speculative.
18. Torquatus: Livy 7.10; Claudius Quadrigarius F6 *FRHist.* = Gell. *NA.* 9.13; *De vir. ill.* 28,3. Penula: Livy 25.19.9. Antony: Cic. *Phil.* 2.63: *gladiatoria totius corporis firmitate.*
19. Williams 2010, 139–44.
20. Ov. *Ars.* 1.515; Mart. 2.36.
21. Cic. *De Div.* 1.102, see Brand 1968, 46–7. For *De Div.* 1.102 and propitious names, see the commentary of Pease 1920. It is unclear whether the moment of enrolment was deemed to be when the man was chosen for a legion or when he took his oath, although sheer practicality suggests that there was more time for creating records during the enrolment.
22. These three names are listed by Paul. *Fest.* 250.18–20 L. Valerius is mentioned as a propitious name in Cic. *Scaur.* 30. See Pease 1920 I. 283–5, although some of the names mentioned first appear in the Late Republic, e.g. 'Faustus' and 'Felix'.
23. See Laes 2013, 145–80 and especially 176 on the problem of the identification of this L. Caecilius Metellus, mentioned in Plin. *HN* 11.174, who may have lived in the third or the second century BCE.
24. Livy 30.1.4–5: *Is [Licinius] Romam reverteretur, bello quoque bonus habitus ad cetera, quibus nemo ea tempestate instructior civis habebatur, congestis omnibus humanis ab natura fortunaque bonis. Nobilis idem ac dives erat; forma viribusque corporis excellebat; facundissimus habebatur, seu causa oranda, seu in senatu et apud populum suadendi ac dissuadendi locus esset.*
25. Polybius 6.21.1–4
26. Dion. Hal. *Ant. Rom.* 10.18.2.
27. Polyb. 3.61.10.

28. Frontin. *Str.* 4.1.4.
29. Sabin 2007, 430–1.
30. Paul. Fest. 224
31. See for example, Levinson 1986.
32. Cf. Rüpke 1990, 76–96, whose assessment is far more detailed than the brief statement here.
33. Jehne 2006, 255–56.
34. Simkins 2007: 83.
35. Lord Derby spoke to a local cotton manufacturer in Manchester about a lacklustre recruiter, of whom the manufacturer said, he 'seemed hardly able to grasp the main idea, namely, the better spirit obtained by those acquainted with one another working together.': Arthur Taylor to Derby, 29 August 1914, Derby Papers, LRO 920 DER (17) 14/2. Higher *esprit de corps*: Simkins 2007, 317.
36. King 2006.
37. Reese 1992, 83–5.
38. MacCoun 1993, 291. This distinction is now generally accepted: RAND 2010, 13.
39. Kier 1998.
40. Ben-Shalom, 2005.
41. For a summary of this phenomenon and the studies of it, see Stangor *et al.* 2014, 266–76.

Chapter 3

1. See Jehne 2006, 251–2 and n.33; Brunt 1971, 625–7.
2. Rosenstein 2002, 175–6 argues that citizens were not required to provide their own arms as early as the time of the Punic Wars.
3. Helm 2020, 108–9.
4. There is some doubt about the century as a base unit of the Mid-Republican military, as it may in fact be retroactively applied by later authors. It may also be the case that the centurion gave his name to the number of men that he commanded rather than the other way around. See Armstrong 2020, 86–8.
5. See Rosenstein 2016.
6. Jehne 2006, 261–62. Rathbone 1993, 151–52 has converted the rates from the ones given to us by Polybius (6.39.12) in Greek obols. This is probably the amount established during the monetary reforms in 212/211 and is around the same as was paid before this date as well (Rosenstein 2016, 85).
7. Terrenato 2019, 164–6.
8. Cf. Armstrong 2020, 89–94.
9. Quesada Sanz 2006, 77–8.
10. On both these matters see Armstrong 2020, 83–9, who points out that of the main sources, most discuss the Republican army retroactively and Polybius struggles to translate the Latin technical terms into suitably accurate Greek equivalents. It is his suggestion that *ordo* may be the equivalent of the Greek *tagma* and a quite general term.
11. This passage is always translated to add 'centurion' or 'leader' to the sentence, which does not appear in the original Latin, following the convention that 'tenth *hastatus*' or '*primus hastatus*' was the title of a centurion.
12. Livy 8.8.6, cf. Horsmann 1988, 8, who points out that the *velites* must have been even younger. Livy, of course, had never seen an army of this era and so it is difficult to tell how literally his words ought to be taken.
13. Livy 28.45.16–17. On this occasion the supplies were offered voluntarily, but it does show that Italian towns were capable of producing very large numbers of arms that could be supplied as part of their military service or paid for by the state.
14. Mass production, stamps, and deterioration in quality: Paddock 1993, 45.

15. Sumner 2009, 17–20, with illustrations. Sumner explains that long sleeves were not worn as they were considered effeminate. Illustrations of early Italian peoples and Republican iconography show tunics with varied lengths from the extremely short to midway down the thigh.
16. Sumner 2009, 72.
17. As with the weapons and armour of the Mid-Republican soldier, no source tells us definitively whether clothing of this type was issued by the state or whether it was supplied by the soldier himself. Once again we might suspect that the truth was actually a mixture: that soldiers would take the clothing and equipment with them if they had it, and could obtain it within the legions if they did not. As in the case of the mules below, the advantage of the soldiers carrying necessary items from their homes was that they would have been available when travelling to army service and home from it, making that journey easier, safer and more comfortable.
18. Roth 1999, 158–65.
19. Gilliver 2007, 10.
20. Bellón *et al.* 2017.
21. This was sometimes referred to as a *vas* or a *fascis*: Roth 1999, 72.
22. The spit, pot, and cup were what Scipio Aemilianus allowed his men when he stripped their personal items down to basics: Roth 1999, 73. The waterskin is mentioned in the camp oath (Chapter 5) as a low value item and must have been necessary for the journey to the mustering point. The food and coins are my conjectures.
23. Burns 2003, 73–4.
24. Quesada Sanz and Galán 2017, 27–35
25. Legions dismissed and told to reconvene at a certain place and day: Polyb 6.21.6; Arretium: Livy 34.56.4; Brundisium: Livy 37.4.1; Cales: Livy 23.31.3.
26. Cf. Gargola 2017, 111 with references at n.112.
27. Polybius 3.61.10. The exact circumstances of this army's journey and arrival at 3.68.12–3 are confused in the sources, and Polybius is best read with Walbank's commentary, Vol 1, 396–7 and 402–3.
28. Laurence 1999, 140.
29. This should be a consideration for the debate over whether there was a preliminary stage to the *dilectus* and how much local organization was involved. In the previous chapter we saw the rules for delayed soldiers refer to 'whoever had conducted the levy in that district', the situation with the mules further suggests local organization that was responsible for keeping track of who had departed the district and with what resources.
30. Laurence 1999, 90–93 describes the differences between the two roads. The via Latina, although longer, had more towns along its length that were attractive to the rich making leisurely journeys.
31. The mule road: Strabo 3.6.7; Fronda 2010, 200–1 writes that this route was most likely in place long before Strabo's time (first century BCE) and was probably used by some traders who put 'profit above comfort'.
32. Dobson 2008, 85–90.
33. Cf. Onas. 10.2 'First arming the soldiers, he [the commander] should draw them up in military formation; that they may become familiar with the faces and names of one another; that each soldier may learn by whom he stands and where and after how many. In this way, by one sharp command, the whole army will immediately form ranks.'

Chapter 4
1. McCall 2002, 4–5.
2. Dobson 2008, 51.
3. Pfeilschifter 2007, 3.
4. Harpers 1898, s.v. Umbria

5. Rosenstein 2012, 86.
6. Thus preferring the views of Rosenstein 2012 over that of Pfeilschifter 2007. Rosenstein points to the sheer amount of time that soldiers of all types spent together while on campaigns as suggesting that they necessarily had a lot of interaction, while Pfeilschifter believes that their inability to speak each others' languages would have been a barrier to socializing.
7. For an account of the Numidian cavalry and their actions at the Ticinus, see Sidnell 2006, 172–8.
8. Roth 1999, 89. The five attendants are mentioned in Plut. *Cat. Mai.* 10.5. Apuleius gives him six, having had three of his own and stopping to buy three more at the market before his departure to Spain: Apul. Apol. 17.9–10.
9. Gelzer 1969, 8.
10. For the *calones* see Roth 1999, 101–10.
11. Incidents in which the *calones* play a role in a battle are detailed by Carrandi 2020, 110–17.
12. Veg. *Epit.* 3.6, trans. Milner, 1996, 108.
13. See Feig Vishnia 2015, Roth 1999, 93–101.
14. Feig Vishnia 2015, 267–8.
15. Festus, *de Verb. Signif.* s.v. *calones*.
16. Ripat 2006.
17. Joseph and Wallace 1992. The most well-known of these pronunciation differences is *o* for *au*, where the *o* came to be considered as a mark of low class.
18. Suolahti 1955, 55.
19. Helm 2020, 111–114.
20. Livy 28.9.19, see further Milne 2020, 148–9 on triumphal songs as reviews of military officers.
21. On the development of the praetorship and the argument that the consulship grew out of the praetorship, see Drogula 2015, 183–93.
22. Brennan 2000, 166–7.
23. Livy 41.15.10; 42.31.2–3.
24. A. Atilius Serranus; C. Licinius Crassus, the consul's brother; and M. Valerius Laevinus. (MRR 171 BC, *Legates, Lieutenants*). The consul and praetors of that year were allowed to select military tribunes for the army headed to Macedonia, instead of the usual practice of having them elected. Livy 42.31.5.
25. See, for example, Scipio Aemilianus who went on campaign to Macedon in 168 BCE at the age of sixteen or seventeen (the exact year of his birth is not known): Astin 1967, 245–7. The Elder Cato started to serve at seventeen: Plut. *Cat. Mai.* 1.6.
26. Ward 2016, 310–313.
27. For examples and for the legates in general, see Johnston 2008, 13–16.
28. Rawson 1971, 13–23.
29. Suolahti 1955, 57–145.
30. See Johnson 2008, 12. The identification of the first man elected as the *primus pilus* at Polybius 6.24.2 is that of Walbank, op. cit. but there is no other real evidence for the Mid-Republican period.
31. On Scipio as legate: Livy 37.1.9; see Wolff 2010, 22 on the motivations of the soldiers who accompanied him.
32. Wolff 2010 has collected these incidents.
33. Jehne 2006, 257; Brunt 1971, 393.
34. Age of 46: Southern 2006, 94; for the profitable campaigns in Macedonia and Rome recruiting for *evocati* see Livy book 42.31.4; 42.33.4.
35. Jehne 2006, 264.
36. Golden 2013, 44–5, within a detailed account of the *tumultus* 44–86.
37. Ser. on *Aen.* 8.1 and 7.
38. Livy 33.3.10; 42.35.6.

39. Livy 24.49.7; Diod. Sic. 29.6.1
40. Livy 37.39.12; 42.35.6. On all the instances of mercenaries in the Roman armies see Griffith (1935) 234–5. On *auxilia* that might be mercenaries, see Lendon 2007, 508 and n.49.
41. See Düll 1964, i.134–41
42. Gell. *NA.* 16.4. Trans. Rolfe, amended.
43. Davies 1971, 132, writes that the soldiers were allowed to carry off *poma pabulum*, but he does not explain why he has apparently taken the two words together or what he understands the sum of them to mean. Roth 1999, 42 has *pomum pabulum* as referring to a fruit, apparently following Davies, and Düll 1964, 135–6 has *napum* (turnip) followed by *pabulum* (fodder) apparently following a variant manuscript. According to the early edition of Lion (1824), the surviving codices had mixed these words into a nonsense (popabulum, pompabulum, pombabulum) for which he gave the simplest and most convincing amendment *poma, pabulum*.
44. Roth 1999, 122; Volken 2008, 270.
45. Rüpke 2019, 78.
46. Brand 1968, 97.

Chapter 5

1. Livy 31.12.5–10, with Briscoe 1973, 88–9, who points out that these lists probably stem from Livy's consultation of the Annales Maximi, a record of events from each year that included prodigies. It is unclear whether prodigies were left to be expiated all at one time or were done as they occurred during the year. On this occasion it seems that at least some were being expiated so close to the planned departure that it was making the consuls anxious to get going (Livy 31.13.1), in particular a matter of sacrilege at Locri.
2. The implication being that the lictors, who attended upon the consul, were required to witness the commander performing the correct rituals before they would put on his *paludamentum* at the *pomerium*. On C. Claudius and other examples of commanders who neglected the correct procedures, see Drogula 2015, 105–11.
3. For an explanation of the names of warships and their various levels: De Souza 2007, 357–8.
4. Casson 1995, 85. Casson is describing a Greek *trireme* but the design of the Roman *quinquereme* was the same in this regard. The ancient ship is difficult to describe and I have adhered closely to Casson's language here: 'Half-way up the stem post, the point where the waling pieces on port and starboard came together was capped by a subsidiary spur (*proembolion*).'
5. Adams *et al.* 2013, 63.
6. For photographs and depictions of the various *proembolia* see D'Amato 2015.
7. A picture of this monument can be found in D'Amato 2015, 15.
8. De Souza 2007, 364.
9. De Souza 2007, 364–5.
10. Kromayer and Veith 1928, 620–1 and n.3; the authors note that the Roman fives were large enough to transport a limited number of troops. The evidence for Kromayer and Veith's number of troops carried by each transport ship all dates to the late Republic, and the evidence of Livy 43.9.5f is misunderstood (Erdkamp 1998, 59 n.48).
11. Thiel 1946, 212–3.
12. Erdkamp 1998, 58–9.
13. For example, Livy 29.25–7, who records that the soldiers boarded the transports and spent the night there before a favourable sign was obtained to sail the next morning and a lustration was done at that point.
14. This is the interpretation of Scheid 2016, 203–9 and Rüpke 2019 [1990], 147–9.
15. Rüpke 2019 [1990], 146.
16. Knapp 1980, 27–8 and n.26.
17. Livy 31.14.2; Briscoe 1973 s.v. and 31.3.2.

18. On the 'Roman Protectorate' and its strategic importance, see Hammond 1989, 23–5.
19. Livy 34.9.11, but see Knapp 1980, 28 and n.29 who suspects this is exaggerated to increase the sense of Cato's speed.
20. Dobson 2013, 225.
21. On these equivalent measurements see Dobson 2008, 71.
22. Dobson 2008, 71ff.
23. Dobson 2008, 79–80.
24. Dobson 2008, 109.
25. This description is taken from Polybius' digression on Greek and Roman methods of building camp walls at 18.18.1–18.
26. Polyb.6.42.5
27. Luttwak 1976, 56; Phang 2001, 69; Veg. *Mil.* 1.21.4–5; 3.8.1–3.
28. Dobson 2013, 225–6.
29. Milne 2012.
30. Habinek discusses the various etymological theories in connection with the phrase's suspected connection to dancing (Habinek 2005, 23–4 and n.78).
31. Cic. *Div.* 2.76–7. 'Military enterprise' is *bellicam rem*.
32. Cic. *Div.* 2.35; It is not certain that this would also apply to the time of the Middle Republic, as Cicero is criticizing the lapsed standards of his own time, but it seems a very obvious consideration not to feed the birds before they were due to be consulted.
33. For a discussion of the total number of mules with the legions and various estimates, see Laurence 1999, 128–9.
34. Marine Corps Small Wars Manual, 1940, 19.
35. Ogburn 1956, 143.

Chapter 6

1. Livy 24.48.11. *Ordines* as a unit of the army is a problematic term, as neither Livy nor Polybius had great concern about using the correct technical military terms, if indeed there was any such rigid terminology. Armstrong notes that *vexillum* and *manipulus* seem to refer to the group of men following that type of standard and may not be a uniform number of men. Instead a *manipulus* or a *vexillum* would refer to any group formed and sent to do a task under that standard. Similarly *ordines*, translated here as ranks, might simply mean 'a group in formation': Armstrong 2020, 83–9.
2. App. *Pun.* 43; Vegetius 2.22 says that the trumpeter *ad bellam vocat milites* 'calls the soldiers to war', as imprecise in Latin as it is in English. The trumpeter also *rursum receptui canit*, 'sounds the retreat' although *receptus* can also mean 'to retire', a rather more mundane action than pulling back troops engaged in combat, and which could simply mean an army that had been offering battle standing down and returning to camp. In fact it seems the trumpet issued all orders applicable to the whole army: Appian *Hisp.* 89 has Scipio recall his soldiers from a village by trumpet, *Pun.* 21 the trumpet signals the army to move out of camp.
3. Serv. on *Aen.* 11, 870; [Aur. Vict.] *Origo gentis Romanae* 22; Ov. *Fast.* 3.115–118; see Quesada Sanz 2007, 95. Varro *Ling.* 6.85 suggests that *manipulus* comes from *manus*, a hand, and means literally a handful, but in another place he suggests it is a handful of men under a particular standard, *Ling.* 5.88.
4. Quesada Sanz 2007, 87.
5. Polyb. 3.106.3–5.
6. For some examples of such training and their effects, see Taylor *et al.* 2014; Thompson and McCreary 2006; Booth-Kewley and McWhorter 2014.
7. The timeline for Cato's campaign in Spain is quite unclear, as at this point the Roman calendar was out of sync with our own by a considerable margin. See Knapp 1980.

8. Livy 34.9.11. This was probably in June or July 195 BCE, see Knapp 1980, 28–30. For Livy's reliance on a speech of Cato, either directly or through an intermediary, see Briscoe 1981, 63–6.
9. Cadiou 2017, 581–2.
10. ORF3 , Cato fr. 35, trans. Astin 1978, 37.
11. Polyb. 11.23.1, where he has transliterated the Latin term *cohors* into Greek, leaving us in no doubt that this was the exact word under discussion.
12. A good discussion of the cohort and its origins can be found in Dobson 2008, 57–64.
13. This brings up again the question of the age of the *velites* and whether Ligustinus was too old by the age of twenty to serve in that division. Livy writes that the 'youth coming to maturity' were in the front lines of maniples of the *hastati*, and so it has been suspected that the *velites* were typically younger (Horsmann 1991, 7.) The association with the cavalry and the fact that the *velites* rode on the cavalry's horses certainly seems to imply younger men.
14. Walbank 1. 701–2
15. Klejnowski 2015.
16. Livy 24.34.5.
17. Klejnowski 2015; Murray *et al.* 2010; Connolly 2000; Harris 1963.
18. Klejnowski 2015.
19. Kanz and Grossschmidt 2006, 210–11.
20. Klejnowski 2015.
21. Quesada Sanz 2003, 175; Sabin 2000, 8; Goldsworthy 1996, 218.
22. The shield is recorded by Kimmig 1940 as originating from a site called 'Kasr El-Harit', but no such place appears to exist. An examination of the original excavation report (Grenfell *et al.* 1900) suggests that Kimmig has mistakenly amalgamated the two sites of Kasr El-Banat and Harit into one fictious site and that this has been reproduced into subsequent scholarship where the item is sometimes referred to as the 'Kasr El-Harit shield' (Bishop 2020, 8–11). The shield has a rather dubious provenance, with the original finders recording no more than it 'originated' from a building that was apparently a house in the cemetery of Harit (Grenfell *et al.* 54–62).
23. Polybius 6.23.2 gives the dimensions in Roman feet. A foot then, as it is today, measured about 30cm, making his measurements 120cm by 75cm.
24. Bishop and Coulston 2006, 62.
25. Livy 26.51.4. For readers with some Latin training, it is important here to carefully distinguish between some similar words in Latin military vocabulary: *pilum, i* (nt) the neuter noun is the Roman heavy javelin, plural *pila*, connected to *pilus, i* (m) the older word for a *triarius* ('one who carries the *pilum*') or in the plural *pili*, as it sometimes appears in the names of centurion positions. *Pila, ae* (f) the feminine noun means a ball, hence *pila praepilata* are 'balled-in-front *pila*' not, as it might seem at first glance, '*pila* before *pila*' or '*pila*-fronted *pila*'.
26. Following Carter 2006, who argues that Polybius' Greek here means only that the buttons were leather, not that the whole practice sword was covered with leather.
27. Bishop 2017, 11. Ancient authors using the world *pilum* are referring to any weapon of this construction. Bishop 2017 and Connolly 2000 both consider the *hasta velitaris* to be a type of *pilum*.
28. Connolly 2000.
29. Bishop 2017, 45–53, with pictures. There is no ancient evidence for exactly how the *pilum* was thrown, but from experimentation and descriptions that show it was done from standing, this is a convincing reconstruction.
30. Bishop 2016, 12–25.
31. Bishop 2016, 31.
32. Miks 2015.
33. See Quesada Sanz 2017, 251–4 on these sources; Miks 2015.

34. Quesada Sanz 2017, for the evidence showing that the original sword of the Romans was a *xiphos* type for thrusting, and the adoption of the Spanish sword added the ability to cut. Bishop 2020, 8–11 and table of blade lengths at 31 for the longer *gladius* in the Mid-Republican period.
35. Liston 2020, 84–5.
36. Liston 2020.

Chapter 7
1. See Levithan 2013, 49.
2. Levithan 2013, 56–7.
3. On tactics of intimidation see Levithan 2013, 57–60; on the general principle of sparing places and peoples who surrendered, see Baker 2021, 79–86.
4. Levithan 2013, 43–4.
5. Sall. *Iug.* 57.4–6, trans. Hanford and adapted by Levithan, 2013, 43–4.
6. Levithan 2013, 44.
7. Baker 2021, 59.
8. Ziolkowski 1993.
9. Ziolkowski 1993, 83.
10. On these skeletons see Quesada Sanz *et al.* 2014, pages 243–54.
11. On beheading as the usual practice of the Romans and the organization of prisoners, see Baker 2021, 46–50.
12. The methods and extent of the destruction of the physical parts of a city: Baker 2021, 51–8.
13. Livy 31.35.1–2 with commentary of Briscoe 1973, 141 for the Tralles and the Cretans.
14. Anders 2015, 279–81.
15. Polybius 6.35.12; 6.36.5, Walbank 1, 719. Livy records the night watches being signalled by the *bucina* at 7.35.1.
16. Dobson 2008, 85–90.
17. The perimeter of the camp is calculated from the scale diagram in Dobson 2008, 103. This has six gates but certain other evidence suggests four, e.g. Livy 40.27.2.
18. Varro *Ling.* 5.91; Paulus ex. Fest. s.v. optio.

Chapter 8
1. *FRHist.* Cato F82.
2. Livy 34.15.4 translation from *FRHist.* Cato F82.
3. The praetor in 319: Livy 9.16.17–19; Petillius: Val. Max. 2.7.15; The dismissed soldiers: Livy 40.41.7–11.
4. Walbank, I, 720.
5. Livy. *Per.* 57, translation modified from McDevitte.
6. Kiesling 2006, 235–6.
7. This very literal rendering is the translation of Leitao 2013, 235.
8. Phang 2001, 282–3; Leitao 2013, 235–7; Walters 1997, 29–45.
9. Williams 2010, 103. For the concept of *stuprum* in Roman life and law, 103–36.; Walbank, *Commentary* I, 720 thought this was the offence of *stuprum cum masculo*, punishable under Early Republican law.
10. Val. Max. 6.1.10 and 6.1.11. In the latter Valerius uses the word *cornicularius*, an anachronistic imperial term meaning an adjutant for a tribune or centurion. Since the story takes place during the Republic this man, a freeborn Roman citizen as opposed to an officer's slave, must have been an *optio*.
11. Langlands 2006, 265–75. The complete set of sources are: Calp. *Flacc.* 3; Val. Max. 6.1.12; Cic. *Mil.* 9, *Inv.* 2.124; Quint. *Inst.* 3.11.14; [Quint.] *Decl. Maior.* 3; Plut. *Marius* 14.

12. This theme is in Calpurnius Flaccus and Pseudo Quintilian, see Langlands 2006, 270–2.
13. Polybius lists these last three offences as ἀδικήματα, 'crimes', but elsewhere he says that death is the penalty for deserting either post or battlefield (1.17.11–2), as is confirmed by Dionysius (Dion. Hal.11.43.2).
14. Tac. *Ann*.3.21.1; Val. Max. 6.3.9; Vell. Pat. 3.78.3. This is referred to not as a *fustuarium* but as being beaten or killed *fusti* 'by means of a stick' or simply 'by stick'. It is not impossible that the whole legion was involved in these punishments, but it would be strange if they were and not one of the three authors thought it worthy of record.
15. The Tarpeian rock: Livy 24.20.6; The legion: Livy 28.28.2, Polybius says there were only 300 of these men (1.7.11).
16. Livy 30.43.13; Val. Max. 2.7.12.
17. *FRHist.* Cato F134.
18. Front. *Strat.* 4.1.42; Val. Max. 2.7.11; Oros.5.4.12.
19. This point is made by Kiesling 2006, 242–3.
20. Polybius 6.38.2–4, trans. Paton, modified by Phang 2008, 124.
21. Goldberg 2016, 160 lists as a 'possible' instance of decimation the actions of Cn. Cornelius Scipio in 218 (Polyb.3.76), where Polybius states that he 'inflicted the customary penalty on those responsible for what had happened'. It is, however, not at all clear what had happened nor who was responsible, as the sailors had been wandering too far from their ships with insufficient care for their surroundings, and many were killed before the others made it back to their ships. Only if they were accused of deserting their posts would this have been a capital crime, and one suspects that it was rather the officers in charge, who had allowed the sailors too much licence to wander the countryside, who were at fault. A further instance of an 'Aquilius' who ordered a decimation (Front. *Strat.* 4.1.36) cannot be dated.
22. Livy 2.58–9; Dion. Hal. *Ant. Rom.* 9.50; Front. *Strat.* 4.1.34. For the dubious historicity of this account, see Goldberg 2016, 143.
23. Front. *Strat.* 4.1.35. Rullianus in this account is given the alternative name Rullus.
24. App. *Hisp.* 34–7; Livy 28.24–32; Polyb. 11.25–30; Zon. 9.9–10.
25. Phang 2008, 113–15.
26. On the mutiny at Sucro from the perspective of the soldiers, see Chrissanthos 1997.
27. Henderson 1985, 16.
28. Kitterman 1991, 450–462, 456.
29. Shils and Janowitz 1948, 292.
30. Wong, *et al.* 2003, 455.
31. Val. Max. 2.7.11, trans. Walker.
32. Val Max. 7.2.13–14.
33. Phang 2008, 111.

Chapter 9

1. Cf. Quesada Sanz 2015, 601.
2. Linderski 1986, 2196, from the evidence of Serv. on. *Aen.* 3.89.
3. Suet. *Tib.* 2.2; Cic. *Div.* 2.71.; Liv. *Per.* 19, 22.42.9; Flor. 1.18.29; Eutrop. 2.26.1; Val. Max. 1.4.3, 8.1. abs 4. See Engels 2007: 405–7.
4. Cic. *Nat. D.* 2.8. For all the signs Flaminius allegedly ignored see Engels 2007: RVW 92, 100, 102.
5. Schol. Ver. Aen. 10.243–244, ed. Baschera 1999, 123–124.
6. Rüpke 1986, 2174.
7. Scheid 2012, 115–19, referencing the law of the Twelve Tables, on which see also Crawford 1996, 580, 652.
8. For the Greek sacrifices before battle see Pritchett 1974, 109–115.
9. Scheid 2003, 84.

10. Plut. *Aem.* 17.11; a delay of some sort in the sacrifices is mentioned by Livy when Aemilius' critics complain that he was 'wasting time on the pretext of offering sacrifice' Livy 44.37.12.
11. See, for example, Hansen 1993.
12. Note that even Hansen, who argued convincingly that elaborate speeches in Thucydides, Xenophon, Caesar and others were mostly fiction, allowed for 'a brief exhortation of the troops, unit by unit, while the commander walked along the front' (Hansen 1993, 171).
13. For example, 36.17.2–16; 21.40–41.
14. Anson 2010, 305, quoting Xen. *Lac.* 13.9.
15. *FRHist.* Cato F97.
16. Livy 9.32.5;
17. Plaut. *Am.* 253–5.
18. Polybius 11.22.4–8, cf. Livy 28.14.6.
19. For the number of Roman troops serving at Cannae see Daly 2002, 25–29.
20. Sabin 1996, 64 and n.27. The nine instances are: Livy 22.15, 22.24, 23.29, 24.14, 25.39, 27.41, 30.5, 30.8 and 30.29.
21. Bellón *et al.* 2017.
22. Speidel 2005, 286 states that they were lined up right to left, but neither explains why he thinks this nor addresses whether it would always have been the case.
23. The figure of four is given twice for the Mid-Republican period by Cato in *De re militari* and by Livy in connection with the Battle of Pydna (44.9.6), numbers given by other sources for the Late Republic and Imperial Period list numbers from three to ten: Taylor 2014, 309–10.
24. Anders 2015, 266 and n.19.
25. The most recent version of the Scholia Verona on the Aeneid can be found in Baschera 1999.
26. Very little attention has been paid to the details of the Romans' divination and sacrifice before battle, which are regularly omitted from accounts of Roman warfare. The different editions of the Scholia Verona emend the text differently to account for the missing verb that gives us the action causing the delay. Baschera 1999, 123–24 and Funaioli 1907, 110–11 amended the text as <*ibi auspicaba*>*tur*, following Hagen 1887, 446, indicating that the delay was the second auspices being taken. A second emendation reads [*morabantur, ut immolare*]*tur*, by Marquardt and Mommsen 1876, 81 n.5 and followed by Bruns 1909, 77–78, indicating that the delay was the sacrifice of an animal. Zablocki 2009 follows this second option (although he seems to mistakenly attribute the second emendation to Hagen, who favoured the first).
27. This is the view of Karlowa 1885, 851–53.

Chapter 10

1. Bowyer 2007, s.v. suppress; suppression; cover; covering fire.
2. Cf. Daly 2002, 172.
3. Quesada Sanz 2006, 77–78.
4. Polybius 2. 30.1, 'thick and fast' is the translation of Walbank 1.206, contrary to Paton, 'well-aimed'.
5. Anders 2015, 263–300.
6. Klejnowski 2015.
7. Following Livy's description of these tactics at 26.4.7.
8. Cf. Slavik 2017, with examples of the *velites* 'pinning down' enemy infantry.
9. Taylor 2014, 319–20, who suggests that enterprising members of the *velites* could stay in the gaps to pick off any intruders, but does not place the whole unit there, and Slavik 2017, who argues convincingly that it was the job of the *velites* to cover the maniples while they exchanged places.
10. Polyb. 3.87.3; 3. 114.1; Livy 22.46.4; see Daly 2002, 89.
11. For each of the following see Bouchard *et al.* 2010.
12. See Plaut. *Amph.* 227; Virg. *Aen.* 9.503. Veg. *Mil.* 2.22.

13. McCall 2020, 228–9.
14. Bishop and Coulston 2006, 51–2.
15. Slavik 2017.
16. Goldsworthy 1996, 224.
17. James 2011, 34–7, who discusses the various sword strokes used by the Roman soldier.
18. Pierson 1999.
19. Swank and Marchand 1946, Pierson 1999.
20. The sporadic manner of heavy infantry fighting, done in loose groups or 'clouds', has emerged as the scholarly consensus over the last few decades. See Taylor 2014, Quesada Sanz 2006, and the seminal work of Sabin 2000.
21. Grossman 2009, 179; Pierson 1999.
22. Sabin 2000, who points out that casualty numbers given to us by the ancient sources were very large for defeated armies but very small for victorious armies, suggesting that most killing was done during the rout.
23. There is a great deal of discussion around the amount of space occupied by each soldier and hence the length of a battle line, which I have not attempted to review and discuss here. I have accepted that Polybius is correct in allowing the soldier sufficient space to wield a weapon and turn a shield, whether or not this is precisely three feet. Taylor 2014 has shown that formations could be drawn close together when necessary.
24. Taylor 2014, 307–9.
25. Ward 2016, 304–5.
26. Proulx 2021. Roman monuments often feature soldiers carrying severed heads from battles, although it is harder to know whether they are the result of the actual method of killing or reflected trophy taking from the battlefield afterward. Trajan's column does depict a scene in which a still-fighting soldier carries a severed head with him. See Fields, 2005.
27. Ville 1981, 22–35, especially 34 n.78. Ville's citations are now outdated, for the amphora (A. 3550, held in the Musées royaux d'Art et d'Histoire in Brussels) see Trendall 1967, 322, no.704, pl. 126. For the tomb at Paestum with illustrations, see Graells 2013.
28. Livy 8.8.10. Varro, quoting Plautus, agrees that they crouched or kneeled, *Ling.* 5.89. The Latin word used here is *subsido* and does not mean 'sit' in this context as rendered in the Loeb translation; Livy at 28.2.8 has *subsidunt Hispani adversus emissa tela ab hoste*, 'the Spaniards crouched down to avoid the missiles thrown at them by the enemy' which shows a similar usage and cannot mean to sit.
29. Quesada Sanz 2006, 247.

Chapter 11
1. The soldiers made their way to Rome: *FRHist*. Fabius Pictor F23.
2. Livy 22.52.7, cf. Val. Max. 4.8.2.
3. Clark 2018, 196 n.19.
4. Livy 22.53.1–54.6. We should not make too much of these tales of individual valour, especially those which lead nowhere. As Clark (2018, 195–6; 2014, 45, 54–55, 64–67) describes, in narrating defeat the historians often use the motif of 'small victories' among larger defeats, in which they move the focus from the greater loss to individual tales of bravery or soldiers displaying the resilience of their spirit.
5. Livy 25.37.3. Cicero says that this man was a *primus pilus* (Cic. *Balb*.34). One of the two sources must be mistaken, as an equestrian with a personal connection to the commander would surely have a more authoritative role than centurion, even the most senior centurion, a position which could be held by rising up through the rank and file.
6. Heidenreich and Roth 2020, 136.
7. Graham 2011, 93–4, citing Horace Odes 1.28. With respect to Greece, the accomplishment of burial via a scattering of earth is a key point in the story of the mythological figure Antigone,

daughter of Oedipus. In this story, Antigone buries her brother Polynices despite a decree forbidding it, with the burial consisting only of piling earth upon the body.

8. Livy 22.58.4; See also the fragment of Aelius Gallus at Festus p. 244 L, which shows that the laws of *postliminium* also applied to the recovery of slaves as well as mules, horses, and ships.

9. Enn. Fr. 6. 183–90, discussed by Skutsch 1985, 347–53 and Elliott 2013, 167–69.

10. Ñaco del Hoyo 2011, 376–392.

11. Val. Max. 2. 7. 15b; Frontin. *Strat.* 4. 1. 18; Eutr. 2. 13. 2. For this incident in the context of the history of thought about Roman soldiers and surrender, see Leigh 2004, 57–97.

12. Barton 2001, 54.

13. Digest 49.15. See Leigh 2004, 64–5 for the applicability of this late evidence to the Republican period.

14. Tryphoninus *Disputationes* 4 = *Digest* 49.15.2. Trans. Leigh 2004, 63.

15. Leigh 2004, 63–4.

16. *FRHist.* Cato F76 = Gell. *NA.* 3.7.19.

17. Scarborough 1968, 256, suggests that Cicero's *medicus* is simply a fellow legionary considered to be skilled with bandages, although there is no evidence that this is the case.

18. *FRHist.* Cassius Hemina F27 = Pliny *Nat.* 29.12–13, with translation from *FRHist.* Vol 2. 263.

19. Gabriel 2012, 148.

20. Salazar 2000, 30–34.

21. On this point see Fronda 2010, 205–6 and n.6. On the factions of aristocratic families in the towns of Italy during the Second Punic War, see also 65–7.

22. Livy mentions this sequence of events in 40.30.1 – 33.1.

23. This is the speculation of Salazar 2000, 75–6. Pages 74–79 contain a complete account of all that is known about medical treatment of wounds in the armies of the Republican period.

24. Graham 2011, 93–4; Hope 2002, 105–6.

25. Herdonea: Livy 27.2.9., *sepelio* e.g. 23.46.5.

26. The details of how to build a pyre: Noy 2000b.

27. Noy 2000a, 187.

28. Noy 2000a, 187.

29. Over 800°C was the finding of Dutour *et al.* 1989, seven to eight hours is the estimate of McKinley 1989.

30. Noy 2000b, 41.

31. Serv. on *Aen.* 6.216, quoting Varro.

32. Noy 2000a, 187–90.

33. McKinley 1994.

34. Noy 2000b, 31–5.

35. Livy 22.56.1–4. The connection between this incident and the transmission of information about the dead is made by Pearson 2021, 53.

36. App. *Pun.* 8.48; Plut. *Mar.* 22.1

37. Rüpke 2019, 205–7.

38. Lua Mater: Livy 8.1.6; Mars, Minerva and Lua Mater: Livy 45.33.1; Mars and Minerva: App. *Lib.* 133; 'the gods of war': App. *Hisp.* 57, *Mith.* 45. See Rüpke 2019, 205–6.

39. Trans Perrin 1920, modified.

40. Rüpke 2019, 205 and 155 n.11.

41. *FRHist.* Cato F135.

Chapter 12

1. *FRHist.* Cato F114.

2. Milne 2020, 145–6.

3. Ligustinus specifies that he joined Sempronius Gracchus at his request (43.34.10). Cadiou 2009, 85–6 points out that the general must have made this request during the handover in

Spain, extracting a promise from Ligustinus and others that they would return. Cadiou also notes that the timing of Flaccus' triumph means that Ligustinus cannot have participated in that continued campaign until 179 BCE.

4. Armies either mustered or stationed at Ariminum: Polyb. 3.61.; 3.86; Livy 31.10.5; 31.11.1; 41.5.7; armies handed over at Ariminum: Livy 21.63.1; 27.7.10.

5. Mustered at Pisae: Livy 40.41.7; 41.5.6; 41.17.7; Wintered at Pisae: Livy 40.17.7; 42.9.2; 43.9.1–3 (Italian allies only, citizen legions were dismissed). In 193 BCE Pisae itself was overrun by the Ligurians and the army was mustered at Arretium to the South and East instead: Livy 34.56.2; 35.6.1.

6. Wilson 1966, 24–5.

7. The story is told at Livy 40.41.7–10. There are certain problems with the text and the identity of the tribune involved is uncertain: see Briscoe 2008, 513–16.

8. Cic. *Off.* 1.36, Plut. *Quest. Rom.* 39.

9. Cicero has both versions of the story, but one appears to be either a textual interpolation or an earlier version of the other, although they involve different sons on different campaigns. See Linderski 1984, 75–6. Plutarch does not specify either which son or which campaign his story involves.

10. Plut. *Quest. Rom.* 39.

11. Livy 40.35.3–6, with Briscoe 2008, 498 on the original dates that the legions had begun their service.

12. Polyb. 1.17.11–2, cf. Dion. Hal. *Ant. Rom.* 11.43.2.

13. This is an important point made by Wolff 2009, 69–70.

14. 'Leading the life of a wolf' is reported to us as a common expression of the second century BCE by Polybius (16.24.4) in reference to Philip V's starving army.

15. Rawlings 2016, 208–11, who points out the strategic significance of these men and their contribution to the Roman side.

16. *Rex aliquis*, Livy 22.53.4.

17. Dyer 1985, 117–18.

18. Livy 24.30.6; Plut. *Marc.*14.2.

19. Kay 2014, 15–17.

20. Clark 2014, 76–8; Fronda 2010, 123–4.

21. Kay 2014, 167.

22. Livy 31.4.1–3; 31.49.5.

23. Broadhead 2007, 155. There was another allocation in 199 BCE, but also to Scipio's veterans: Livy 32.1.6.

24. Kay 2014, 168; Broadhead 2007, 156.

25. Donatives are given at Livy 34.46.2 and 34.52.4; donatives for the period 200–167 BCE and references are tabulated by Brunt 1971, 394.

26. On the conversion between silver and denarii, see Taylor 2020, 111–12. Briscoe 1981, 122 writes that Livy's figure was probably based on an official record and should be preferred to Plutarch's pound of silver, and Astin 1978, 53, assumes that Livy is simply being more precise than Plutarch.

27. Coudry 2009, 25–6.

28. Polybius describes this procedure: 10.16–17.

29. This was also the conclusion of Cadiou 2009, who thinks that Ligustinus served for eleven years in a twenty-two-year period.

30. The army handed over: Polyb. 21.5; Livy. 37.7.7; reinforcements sent with Scipio: Livy 37.2.2. Cadiou 2009, 83–5 discusses the possibility that Ligustinus spent only one year on this campaign.

Conclusion

1. Rosenstein 2004, 156; Cagniart 2007, 81; Rich 1983, 317–18; Shochat 1980, 56–60.
2. Cagniart 2007, 82.
3. Lintott describes Marius' critics as 'more likely to have seized on the breach of a principle at the root of Roman society, one which it shared with classical Greek cities, whereby the defence of a community was entrusted normally to those with a considerable stake in it through property… Thus Marius would have been charged with buying worthless men, who were more likely to damage Rome by desertion than subversion.' (Lintott, CAH² IX. (1994) 92).
4. For an account that summarizes all three of these elements, see Le Glay, Voisin, and Le Bohec 2001, 114.
5. Cagniart 2007, 82; 'Consequently, from 107 onward, soldiers joined the army expecting their generals to provide financial rewards at the end of the campaign. In addition to the booty soldiers could gain from a war, the anticipation of tangible benefits at the time of discharge became the motivation to serve, and this transformed the Roman soldier into a mercenary.' cf. Gabba 1976, 25: 'the impulses and sentiments of the masses must have been influenced only by considerations of an economic kind: *stipendium*, the booty which followed a war, and finally a plot of land as a reward for service.'
6. De Blois 2007, 167, Potter 2004, 71.
7. Cf. Campbell 2004, 9–10; Cagniart 2007, 82.
8. On this point see Cadiou 2018.

Bibliography

Ancient Sources

Appian. *Roman History, Volume I: Books 1-8.1.* Translated by Horace White. Loeb Classical Library 2. Cambridge, MA: Harvard University Press, 1911.

Appian. *Roman History, Volume IV: The Civil Wars, Books 3.27-5.* Translated by Horace White. Loeb Classical Library 5. Cambridge, MA: Harvard University Press, 1913.

Cicero. *On Old Age. On Friendship. On Divination.* Translated by W. A. Falconer. Loeb Classical Library 154. Cambridge, MA: Harvard University Press, 1923.

Dionysius of Halicarnassus. *Roman Antiquities, Volume VI: Books 9.25-10.* Translated by Earnest Cary. Loeb Classical Library 378. Cambridge, MA: Harvard University Press, 1947.

Dionysius of Halicarnassus. *Roman Antiquities, Volume VII: Books 11-20.* Translated by Earnest Cary. Loeb Classical Library 388. Cambridge, MA: Harvard University Press, 1950.

Gellius. *Attic Nights, Volume III: Books 14-20.* Translated by J. C. Rolfe. Loeb Classical Library 212. Cambridge, MA: Harvard University Press, 1927.

Livy. *History of Rome by Titus Livius: The Epitomes of the Lost Books.* Translated by William A. McDevitte. London: Henry G. Bohn, 1850.

Livy. *History of Rome.* Translated by Rev. Canon Roberts. New York: E. P. Dutton and Co, 1912.

Livy. *Livy with an English Translation.* Foster, B. O. *et al.* (eds). 14 volumes (Vols. 6–8 translated by Frank Gardner Moore; Vols. 9–12 by Evan T. Sage; Vols. 13–14 by A. C. Schlesinger). Loeb Classical Library. Cambridge, MA: Harvard University Press, 1922-59.

Onasander. *Aeneas Tacticus, Asclepiodotus, Onasander.* Translated by Members of the Illinois Greek Club (Loeb Classical Library). London: Heinemann; New York: G. P. Putnam's Sons, 1923.

Pliny the Elder. *The Natural History.* Translated by John Bostock. London: Taylor and Francis, 1855.

Plutarch. *Lives, Volume IX: Demetrius and Antony. Pyrrhus and Gaius Marius.* Translated by Bernadotte Perrin. Loeb Classical Library 101. Cambridge, MA: Harvard University Press, 1920.

Plutarch. *Lives, Volume VI: Dion and Brutus. Timoleon and Aemilius Paulus.* Translated by Bernadotte Perrin. Loeb Classical Library 98. Cambridge, MA: Harvard University Press, 1918.

Plutarch. *Lives, Volume X: Agis and Cleomenes. Tiberius and Gaius Gracchus. Philopoemen and Flamininus.* Translated by Bernadotte Perrin. Loeb Classical Library 102. Cambridge, MA: Harvard University Press, 1921.

Plutarch. *Moralia, Volume IV: Roman Questions. Greek Questions. Greek and Roman Parallel Stories. On the Fortune of the Romans. On the Fortune or the Virtue of Alexander. Were the Athenians More Famous in War or in Wisdom?.* Translated by Frank Cole Babbitt. Loeb Classical Library 305. Cambridge, MA: Harvard University Press, 1936.

Polybius. *The Histories.* 6 Vols. Translated by W. R. Paton. Loeb Classical Library 128. Cambridge, MA: Harvard University Press, 1922-27.

Sallust. *The Jugurthine War [and] The Conspiracy of Catiline: Translated with an Introduction by S.A. Hanford.* Baltimore: Penguin Books, 1963.

Vegetius. Milner, N. P. *Vegetius: Epitome of Military Science. Translated with notes and introduction.* 2nd ed. Liverpool: Liverpool University Press, 1996.

Modern Sources

Adams, J.R. *et al.* (2013) 'The Belgammel Ram, a Hellenistic-Roman Bronze Proembolion Found off the Coast of Libya: test analysis of function, date and metallurgy, with a digital reference archive', *International Journal of Nautical Archaeology*, 42(1), pp. 60–75.

Alföldi, A. (1962) 'Ager romanus antiquus', *Hermes*, 90(2), pp. 187–213.

Anders, A.O. (2015) 'The "Face of Roman Skirmishing"', *Historia: Zeitschrift für Alte Geschichte*, 64(3), pp. 263–300.

Anson, E. (2010) 'The General's Pre-Battle Exhortation in Graeco-Roman Warfare', *Greece & Rome*, 57(2), pp. 304–318.

Armstrong, J. (2016) *Early Roman Warfare: From the Regal Period to the First Punic War*. Barnsley: Pen and Sword.

Armstrong, J. (2020) 'Organized Chaos: Manipuli, Socii and the Roman Army c. 300', in M.P. Fronda and J. Armstrong (eds) *Romans at War: Soldiers, Citizens, and Society in the Roman Republic*. Oxon and New York: Routledge, pp. 76–98.

Astin, A.E. (1967) *Scipio Aemilianus*. Oxford: Clarendon Press.

Astin, A.E. (1978) *Cato the Censor*. Oxford: Clarendon Press.

d'Auria, D. (2017) 'Immagini allusive a vittorie militari in ambito domestico nel II sec. a.C.', in S. Mols and E. Moormann (eds) *Context and meaning. Proceedings of the twelfth International Conference of the Association Internationale pour la Peinture Murale Antique (Athens, September 16–20, 2013)*. Leuven: PEETERS, pp. 259–264.

Baker, G. (2021) *Spare No One: Mass Violence in Roman Warfare*. London: Rowman & Littlefield.

Barton, C.A. (2001) *Roman Honor: The Fire in the Bones*. Berkeley, Los Angeles and London: University of California Press.

Baschera, C. (1999) *Gli Scolii veronesi a Virgilio*. 1. ed. Verona: Mazziana.

Bellón Ruiz, J.P. *et al.* (2017) 'Archaeological methodology applied to the analysis of battlefields and military camps of the Second Punic War: Baecula', *Quaternary International*, 435, pp. 81–97.

Ben-Shalom, U., Lehrer, Z. and Ben-Arı, E. (2005) 'Cohesion during Military Operations: A Field Study on Combat Units in the Al-Aqsa Intifada', *Armed Forces & Society*, 32(1), pp. 63–79.

Bishop, M.C. (2016) *The Gladius: The Roman Short Sword*. Oxford and New York: Bloomsbury Publishing.

Bishop, M.C. (2017) *The Pilum*. Oxford: Osprey Publishing.

Bishop, M.C. (2020) *Roman Shields*. New York: Bloomsbury Publishing.

Bishop, M.C. and Coulston, J.C. (2006) *Roman Military Equipment: From the Punic Wars to the Fall of Rome*. Oxford: Oxbow Books.

de Blois, L. (2007) 'Army and General in the Late Roman Republic', in P. Erdkamp (ed.) *A Companion to the Roman Army*. Oxford, UK: Blackwell Publishing Ltd, pp. 164–180.

Booth-Kewley, S. and McWhorter, S.K. (2014) 'Highly Realistic, Immersive Training for Navy Corpsmen: Preliminary Results', *Military Medicine*, 179(12), pp. 1439–1443.

Bouchard, S. *et al.* (2010) 'Selection of Key Stressors to Develop Virtual Environments for Practicing Stress Management Skills with Military Personnel Prior to Deployment', *Cyberpsychology, Behavior, and Social Networking*, 13(1), pp. 83–94.

Bowyer, R. (2007) *Dictionary of Military Terms: Over 6,000 words clearly defined*. 3rd edn. London: A&C Black.

Brand, C.E. (1968) *Roman Military Law*. Austin: University of Texas Press.

Brand, S. (2019) *Killing for the Republic: Citizen-soldiers and the Roman Way of War*. Baltimore: Johns Hopkins University Press.

Brennan, T.C. (2000) *The Praetorship in the Roman Republic* (2 vol). Oxford: Oxford University Press.

Briscoe, J. (1973) *A Commentary on Livy Books XXXI - XXXIII*. Oxford: Oxford University Press.

Briscoe, J. (1981) *A Commentary on Livy, XXXIV-XXXVII*. Oxford: Clarendon Press.

Briscoe, J. (2008) *A Commentary on Livy, Books 38–40*. Oxford: Oxford University Press.

Briscoe, J. (2012) *A Commentary on Livy: Books 41–45*. Oxford: Oxford University Press.

Broadhead, W. (2007) 'Colonization, Land Distribution, and Veteran Settlement', in P. Erdkamp (ed.) *A Companion to the Roman Army*. Oxford, UK: Blackwell Publishing Ltd, pp. 148–163.

Bruns, C.G., Mommsen, T. and Gradenwitz, O. (1909) *Fontes iuris Romani antiqui*. Tubingae: In Libraria I.C.B. Mohrii (P. Siebeck).

Brunt, P.A. (1971) *Italian Manpower: 225 BC–AD 14*. Oxford: Oxford University Press, USA.

Burns, M.T. (2003) 'The Homogenisation of Military Equipment Under the Roman Republic', *Digressus Supplement 1*, pp. 60–85.

Cadiou, F. (2002) 'À propos du service militaire dans l'armée romaine au IIe siècle avant J.-C.: le cas de Spurius Ligustinus (Tite-Live 42, 34)', in P. Defosse (ed.) *Hommages à Carl Deroux. II, Prose et linguistique. Médecine*. Bruxelles: Latomus, pp. 76–90.

Cadiou, F. (2017) *Hibera in terra miles : Les armées romaines et la conquête de l'Hispanie sous la république (218–45 av. J.-C.)*, Hibera in terra miles : Les armées romaines et la conquête de l'Hispanie sous la république (218–45 av. J.-C.). Madrid: Casa de Velázquez (Bibliothèque de la Casa de Velázquez).

Cadiou, F. (2018) *L'armée imaginaire. Les soldats prolétaires dans les légions romaines au dernier siècle de la République*. Paris: Les Belle Lettres.

Cagniart, P. (2007) 'The Late Republican Army (146–30 BC)', in P. Erdkamp (ed.) *A Companion to the Roman Army*. Oxford: Blackwell Publishing, pp. 80–95.

Campbell, J.B. (2004) *Greek and Roman Military Writers: Selected Readings*. London and New York: Routledge (Routledge classical translations).

Carrandi, J.P. (2020) 'Calones: esclavos del ejército romano', *Revista Universitaria de Historia Militar*, 9(19), pp. 98–120.

Carter, M.J. (2006) 'Buttons and Wooden Swords: Polybius 10.20. 3, Livy 26.51, and the Rudis', *Classical Philology*, 101(2), pp. 153–160.

Casson, L. (1995) *Ships and Seamanship in the Ancient World*. Baltimore: The John Hopkins University Press.

Chrissanthos, S.G. (1997) 'Scipio and the Mutiny at Sucro, 206 B.C', *Historia: Zeitschrift für Alte Geschichte*, 46, pp. 172–184.

Chrissanthos, S.G. (2004) 'Freedom of speech and the Roman Republican army', in I. Sluiter and R.M. Rosen (eds) *Free Speech in Classical Antiquity*. Leiden and Boston: Brill, pp. 341–367.

Clark, J.H. (2014) *Triumph in Defeat: Military Loss and the Roman Republic*. Oxford: Oxford University Press.

Clark, J.H. (2018) 'Defeat and the Roman Republic: Stories from Spain', in J.H. Clark and B. Turner (eds) *Brill's Companion to Military Defeat in Ancient Mediterranean Society*. Leiden and Boston: Brill, pp. 189–212.

Coarelli, F. (1996) *Revixit ars: arte e ideologia a Roma : dai modelli ellenistici alla tradizione repubblicana*. Roma: Quasar.

Connolly, P. (2000) 'The reconstruction and use of Roman weaponry in the second century BC', *Journal of Roman Military Equipment Studies*, (11), pp. 43–46.

Corps, U.M. (1940) *Small Wars Manual*. Washington: University Press of the Pacific.

Coudry, M. (2009) 'Partage et gestion du butin dans la Rome républicaine: procédures et enjeux', in M. Coudry and M. Humm (eds) *Praeda, Butin de guerre et société dans la Rome républicaine / Kriegsbeute und Gesellschaft im republikanischen Rom*. Stuttgart: Franz Steiner Verlag.

Crawford, M.H. (ed.) (1996) *Roman Statutes, 2 vols* (2 vol). London: Institute of Classical Studies (BICS Supplement, 64).

Daly, G. (2002) *Cannae: The Experience of Battle in the Second Punic War*. London: Routledge.

D'Amato, R. (2015) *Republican Roman Warships 509–27 BC*. Oxford and New York: Osprey Publishing.

Davies, P.J.E. (2017) *Architecture and Politics in Republican Rome*. New York: Cambridge University Press.

Davies, R.W. (1971) 'The Roman Military Diet', *Britannia*, 2, pp. 122–142.

De Ligt, L. (2007) 'Roman Manpower and Recruitment During the Middle Republic', in P. Erdkamp (ed.) *A Companion to the Roman Army*. Malden, MA; Oxford: Blackwell, pp. 114–131.

Deniaux, E. (2006) 'Patronage', in N. Rosenstein and R. Morstein-Marx (eds), R. Morstein-Marx and R. Martz (trans.) *A companion to the Roman Republic*. John Wiley & Sons, pp. 401–420.

Dobson, M. (2008) *The Army of the Roman Republic: The Second Century BC, Polybius and the Camps at Numantia, Spain*. Oxford: Oxbow Books.

Dobson, M.P. (2013) 'No Holiday Camp: The Roman Republican Army Camp as a Fine-Tuned Instrument of War', in J. DeRose Evans (ed.) *A Companion to the Archaeology of the Roman Republic*. Chichester, West Sussex, UK: Wiley-Blackwell, pp. 214–34.

Drogula, F.K. (2015) *Commanders and Command in the Roman Republic and Early Empire*. Chapel Hill: University of North Carolina Press.

Düll, R. (1964) 'Zum Lagerfund im Römischen Recht', in Arangio-Ruiz, V., Guarino, A., and Labruna, L., *Synteleia: Vincenzo Arangio-Ruiz*. Napoli: Jovene, pp. 134–141.

Dutoit, E. (1964) 'Tite-Live 42, 34: l' "exemplum" d'un soldat romain', in M. Renard and R. Schilling (eds) *Hommages a Jean Bayet*. Bruxelles: Latomus, pp. 180–189.

Dutour, O. *et al.* (1989) 'Analyse de la température de crémation d'incinérations antiques par diffractométrie R.X. (Nécropole du Haut Empire de Saint Lambert de Fréjus, Var)', *ArchéoSciences, revue d'Archéométrie*, 13(1), pp. 23–28.

Dyer, G. (1985) *War*. New York: Crown Publishers.

Eckstein, A.M. (2006) *Mediterranean Anarchy, Interstate War, and the Rise of Rome*. Berkeley: Univ of California Press.

Eckstein, A.M. (2015) 'Livy, Polybius, and the Greek East (Books 31–45)', in B. Mineo (ed.) *A Companion to Livy*. New Jersey: Wiley-Blackwell, pp. 407–422.

Elliott, J. (2013) *Ennius and the Architecture of the Annales*. Cambridge: Cambridge University Press.

Engels, D. (2007) *Das römische Vorzeichenwesen (753–27 v. Chr.). Quellen, Terminologie, Kommentar, historische Entwicklung*. Stuttgart: Franz Steiner.

Erdkamp, P. (1998) *Hunger and the Sword: Warfare and Food Supply in Roman Republican Wars (264–30 BC)*. Amsterdam: J.C. Gieben.

Farney, G.D. (2019) 'Forum Novum and the Limits of Roman Colonization', in A.U. De Georgi (ed.) *Cosa and the Colonial Landscape of Republican Italy (Third and Second Centuries BCE)*. Ann Arbor: University of Michigan Press, pp. 159–81.

Fields, N. (2005) 'Headhunters of the Roman Army', in A. Hopkins and M. Wyke (eds) *Roman Bodies: Antiquity to the Eighteenth Century*. Rome: British School at Rome, pp. 55–66.

Forsythe, G. (2005) *A Critical History of Early Rome: From Prehistory to the First Punic War*. Berkeley, Los Angeles and London: University of California Press.

de Franchis, M. (2015) 'Livian Manuscript Tradition', in B. Mineo (ed.) *A Companion to Livy*. New Jersey: Wiley-Blackwell, pp. 3–23.

Fronda, M.P. (2010) *Between Rome and Carthage: Southern Italy during the Second Punic War*. Cambridge: Cambridge University Press.

Fronda, M.P. (2020) 'Titus Quinctius Flamininus "Italian triumph"', in M.P. Fronda and J. Armstrong (eds) *Romans at War*. London and New York: Routledge, pp. 171–190.

Funaioli, G. (1907) *Grammaticae Romanae fragmenta. Collegit recensuit Hyginus Funaioli (Gino Funaioli)*. Stuttgart: Teubner (Bibliotheca scriptorum Graecorum et Romanorum Teubneriana).

Gabba, E. (1976) *Republican Rome, the Army and the Allies*. Berkeley: University of California Press.

Gabba, E. (1988) 'Aspetti militari e agrari', *Dialoghi di archeologia*, 6(2), pp. 19–22.

Gabriel, R.A. (2012) *Man and Wound in the Ancient World: A History of Military Medicine from Sumer to the Fall of Constantinople*. Dulles, VA: Potomac Books, Inc.

Gaffney, V. *et al.* (2001) 'Forum Novum–Vescovio: Studying urbanism in the Tiber valley', *Journal of Roman Archaeology*, 14, pp. 58–79.

Gaffney, V. *et al.* (2004) 'Multimethodological approach to study and characterize Forum Novum (Vescovio, central Italy)', *Archaeological Prospection*, 11(4), pp. 201–212.

Gargola, D.J. (2017) *The Shape of the Roman Order: The Republic and Its Spaces*. Chapel Hill: University of North Carolina Press.

Gelzer, M. (1969) *The Roman Nobility*. Translated by R. Seager. Blackwell.

Gilliver, K. (2007) 'Display in Roman warfare: The Appearance of Armies and Individuals on the Battlefield', *War in History*, 14(1), pp. 1–21.

Goldberg, C. (2016) 'Decimation in the Roman Republic', *The Classical Journal*, 111(2), pp. 141–164.

Golden, G.K. (2013) *Crisis Management During the Roman Republic: The Role of Political Institutions in Emergencies*. Cambridge: Cambridge University Press.

Goldsworthy, A.K. (1996) *The Roman Army at War: 100 BC–AD 200*. Oxford: Oxford University Press.

Graells, R. (2013) 'Panoplias pintadas: estudio anticuario de las armas pintadas en una tumba de Paestum recuperada en 1854', *Lucentum*, (32), pp. 53–92.

Graham, E.-J. (2011) 'From fragments to ancestors: Re-defining the role of os resectum in rituals of purification and commemoration in Republican Rome', in *Living Through the Dead: Burial and Commemoration in the Classical World*. Oxford: Oxbow Books, pp. 91–109.

Grenfell, B.P. *et al.* (1900) *Fayûm towns and their papyri*. London: Offices of the Egypt exploration fund.

Griffith, G.T. (1935) *The mercenaries of the Hellenistic world*. Cambridge: Cambridge University Press.

Grossman, D. (2009) *On Killing: The Psychological Cost of Learning to Kill in War and Society*. Rev. ed. New York: Back Bay.

Habinek, T. (2005) *The World of Roman Song: From Ritualized Speech to Social Order*. Baltimore: Johns Hopkins University Press.

Hagen, H. and Thilo, G. (1887) *Servii Grammatici qui feruntur in Vergilii carmina commentarii: Appendix Serviana ceteros praeter Servium et scholia Bernensia Vergilii commentatores continens*. Lipsiae: Teubner.

Hammond, N.G.L. (1989) 'The Illyrian Atintani, the Epirotic Atintanes and the Roman Protectorate', *The Journal of Roman Studies*, 79, pp. 11–25.

Hansen, M.H. (1993) 'The Battle Exhortation in Ancient Historiography. Fact or Fiction?', *Historia: Zeitschrift für Alte Geschichte*, 42(2), pp. 161–180.

Harris, H.A. (1963) 'Greek Javelin Throwing', *Greece & Rome*, 10(1), pp. 26–36.

Harris, W.V. (1985) *War and Imperialism in Republican Rome, 327–70 B.C.* Oxford: Clarendon Press.

Heidenreich, S.M. and Roth, J.P. (2020) 'The Neurophysiology of Panic on the Ancient Battlefield', in L.L. Brice (ed.) *New Approaches to Greek and Roman Warfare*. Hoboken, NJ: John Wiley & Sons, pp. 127–138.

Helm, M. (2020) 'Poor Man's War - Rich Man's Fight: Military Integration in Republican Rome', in M.P. Fronda and J. Armstrong (eds) *Romans at War: Soldiers, Citizens, and Society in the Roman Republic*. Oxon and New York: Routledge, pp. 99–115.

Henderson, W.D. (1985) *Cohesion: the human element in combat: leadership and societal influence in the armies of the Soviet Union, the United States, North Vietnam, and Israel [by]Wm. Darryl Henderson*. Washington, DC: National University Press.

Holbrook, A. (2003) *Loyalty and the Sacramentum in the Roman Republican Army*. Thesis. McMaster University.

Hölkeskamp, K.-J. (1993) 'Conquest, Competition and Consensus: Roman Expansion in Italy and the Rise of the "Nobilitas"', *Historia*, pp. 12–39.

Hölscher, T. (2006) 'The Transformation of Victory into Power: From Event to Structure', in K.E. Welch and S. Dillon (eds) *Representations of War in Ancient Rome*. New York: Cambridge University Press, pp. 27–48.

Hope, V.M. (2002) 'Contempt and Respect', in E. Marshall and V.M. Hope (eds) *Death and Disease in the Ancient City*. London and New York: Routledge, pp. 116–139.

Hopkins, K. (1991) 'From violence to blessing: symbols and rituals in ancient Rome', in K. Raaflaub, A. Mohlo, and J. Emlen (eds) *City States in Classical Antiquity and Medieval Italy: Athens and Rome, Florence and Venice*. Stuttgart: Franz Steiner Verlag, pp. 479–498.

Horsmann, G. (1991) *Untersuchungen zur militärischen Ausbildung im republikanischen und kaiserzeitlichen Rom.* Boppard am Rhein: Harald Boldt Verlag.

Hoyos, D. (2011) 'The Age of Overseas Expansion (264 - 146 BC)', in P. Erdkamp (ed.) *A Companion to the Roman Army.* Malden, MA; Oxford; Chichester: Wiley-Blackwell, pp. 63–79.

Hug, A. (2014) *Fecunditas, Sterilitas, and the Politics of Reproduction at Rome.* University of Toronto.

Humm, M. (2009) 'Exhibition et "monumentalisation" du butin dans la Rome médio-républicaine', in M. Humm and M. Coudry (eds) *Praeda: Butin de guerre et société dans la République romaine.* Stuttgart: F. Steiner, pp. 117–152.

James, S. (2011) *Rome & the Sword: How Warriors & Weapons Shaped Roman History.* London: Thames & Hudson.

Jehne, M. (2006) 'Römer, Latiner und Bundesgenossen im krieg. Zu Formen und Ausmass der Integration in der republikanischen Armee', in M. Jehne and R. Pfeilschifter (eds) *Herrschaft ohne Integration? : Rom und Italien in Republikanischer Zeit.* Frankfurt: Verlag Antike, pp. 243–267.

Johnston, P.D. (2008) *The Military Consilium in Republican Rome.* Piscataway, NJ: Gorgias Press.

Joseph, B.D. and Wallace, R.E. (1992) 'Socially determined variation in ancient Rome', *Language Variation and Change,* 4(1), pp. 105–119.

Kanz, F. and Grossschmidt, K. (2006) 'Head injuries of Roman gladiators', *Forensic Science International,* 160(2–3), pp. 207–216.

Karlowa, O. (1885) *Römische Rechtsgeschichte.* Leipzig: Verlag von Veit & Comp.

Kay, P. (2014) *Rome's Economic Revolution.* Oxford: Oxford University Press.

Kier, E. (1998) 'Homosexuals in the U.S. Military: Open Integration and Combat Effectiveness', *International Security,* 23(2), pp. 5–39.

Kiesling, E.C. (2006) 'Corporal Punishment in the Greek Phalanx and the Roman Legion: Modern Images and Ancient Realities', *Historical Reflections / Réflexions Historiques,* 32(2), pp. 225–246.

Kimmig, W. (1940) 'Ein Keltenschild aus Ägypten', *Germania: Anzeiger der Römisch-Germanischen Kommission des Deutschen Archäologischen Instituts,* 24(2), pp. 106–111.

King, A. (2006) 'The Word of Command: Communication and Cohesion in the Military', *Armed Forces & Society,* 32(4), pp. 493–512.

Kitterman, D.H. (1991) 'The Justice of the Wehrmacht Legal System: Servant or Opponent of National Socialism?', *Central European History,* 24, pp. 450–462.

Klejnowski, G. (2015) 'Hasta Velitaris - The first edge of the Roman army', in K. Andula (ed.) *Res Militaris. Studia nad wojskowością antyczną tom II.* Warsaw: Tetragon, pp. 69–91.

Knapp, R.C. (1980) 'Cato in Spain, 195–194 BC: Chronology and Geography', in C. Deroux (ed.) *Studies in Latin Literature and Roman History II.* Brussels: Latomus, pp. 21–54.

Kromayer, J. and Veith, G. (1928) *Heerwesen und Kriegführung der Griechen und Römer.* Munich: C.H. Beck.

Laes, C. (2013) 'Silent History? Speech Impairment in Roman Antiquity', in C.F. Goodey, M.L. Rose, and C. Laes (eds) *Disabilities in Roman Antiquity.* Leiden: Brill (Memosyne Supplements), pp. 145–180.

Langlands, R. (2006) *Sexual Morality in Ancient Rome.* Cambridge: Cambridge University Press.

Laurence, R. (1999) *The Roads of Roman Italy: Mobility and Cultural Change.* London: Routledge.

Le Glay, M. *et al.* (2001) *A History of Rome.* 2nd ed. Malden, MA: Blackwell Publishers.

Leigh, M. (2004) *Comedy and the Rise of Rome.* Oxford: Oxford University Press.

Leitao, D.D. (2013) 'Sexuality in Greek and Roman Military Contexts', in T.K. Hubbard (ed.) *A Companion to Greek and Roman Sexualities.* Chichester, West Sussex, UK: John Wiley & Sons, Ltd, pp. 230–243.

Lendon, J. (2007) 'War and society', in H. van Wees, M. Whitby, and P. Sabin (eds) *The Cambridge History of Greek and Roman Warfare: Volume 1: Greece, The Hellenistic World and the Rise of Rome.* Cambridge: Cambridge University Press, pp. 498–516.

Levinson, S. (1985) 'Constituting Communities through Words That Bind: Reflections on Loyalty Oaths', *Michigan Law Review,* 84, pp. 1440–1470.

Levithan, J. (2013) *Roman Siege Warfare*. Ann Arbor: University of Michigan Press.

Linderski, J. (1984) 'Rome, Aphrodisias and the Res Gestae: The Genera Militiae and the Status of Octavian', *The Journal of Roman Studies*, 74, pp. 74–80.

Linderski, J. (1986) 'The Augural Law', *Aufstieg und Niedergang der römischen Welt*, 2.16.3, pp. 2146–2312.

Lion, A. (ed.) (1824) *Auli Gellii Noctes Atticae*. Göttingen: Vanderchoeck und Ruprecht.

Liston, M.A. (2020) 'Skeletal Evidence for the Impact of Battle on Soldiers and Non-Combatants', in L.L. Brice (ed.) *New Approaches to Greek and Roman Warfare*. John Wiley & Sons, Ltd, pp. 81–94.

Luttwak, E. (1976) *The grand strategy of the Roman Empire from the first century A.D. to the third*. Baltimore: Johns Hopkins University Press.

MacCoun, R.J. (1993) 'What is known about Unit Cohesion and Military Performance', in B.D. Rostker and S.A. Harris (eds) *Sexual Orientation and US Military Personnel Policy: Options and Assessment*. Santa Monica, CA: RAND, pp. 283–331.

Marquardt, J. and Mommsen, T. (1876) *Handbuch der Römischen Alterthümer: Erster Band*. Hirzel.

Maxfield, V.A. (1981) *The Military Decorations of the Roman Army*. London: Batsford.

McCall, J.B. (2002) *The Cavalry of the Roman Republic*. London: Routledge.

McCall, J.B. (2020) 'The Manipular Army System and Command Decisions in the Second Century', in J. Armstrong and M.P. Fronda (eds) *Romans at War: Soldiers, Citizens, and Society in the Roman Republic*. Oxon and New York: Routledge, pp. 210–231.

McKinley, J.I. (1994) 'Bone Fragment Size in British Cremation Burials and its Implications for Pyre Technology and Ritual', *Journal of Archaeological Science*, 21(3), pp. 339–342.

Miks, C. (2015) 'Sword, gladius', in Y. Le Bohec (ed.) *The Encyclopedia of the Roman Army*. Chichester: Wiley, pp. 948–970.

Milne, K. (2012) 'Family Paradigms in the Roman Republican Military', *Intertexts*, 16(1), pp. 25–41.

Milne, K.H. (2020) 'The Middle Republican Soldier and Systems of Social Distinction', in J. Armstrong and M.P. Fronda (eds) *Romans at War: Soldiers, Citizens, and Society in the Roman Republic*. Oxford and New York: Routledge, pp. 134–153.

Mondini, M. (2019) 'Brothers and Heroes. Literary Sources on Death in the First World War (the Italian Case).', in M. Giangiulio, E. Franchi, and G. Proietti (eds) *Commemorating War and War Dead: Ancient and Modern*. Stuttgart: Franz Steiner Verlag, pp. 239–253.

Murray, S.R. *et al.* (2010) 'Efficacy of the ankyle in increasing the distance of the ancient Greek javelin throw', *Nikephoros*, 23, pp. 329–333.

Ñaco del Hoyo, T. (2011) 'Roman Economy, Finance, and Politics in the Second Punic War', in D. Hoyos (ed.) *A Companion to the Punic Wars*. Oxford, UK: Wiley-Blackwell, pp. 376–392.

Northwood, S. (2008) 'Census and Tributum', in S. Northwood and L. De Ligt (eds) *People, land, and politics: demographic developments and the transformation of Roman Italy, 300 BC–AD 14*. Leiden and Boston: Brill.

Noy, D. (2000a) "Half-burnt on an Emergency Pyre': Roman Cremations which Went Wrong', *Greece & Rome*, 47(2), pp. 186–196.

Noy, D. (2000b) 'Building a Roman Funeral Pyre', *Antichthon*, 34, pp. 30–45.

Oakley, S.P. (1985) 'Single Combat in the Roman Republic', *The Classical Quarterly*, 35(2), pp. 392–410.

Ogburn, C. (1959) *The Marauders*. New York: Harper & Brothers.

Orlin, E.M. (1997) *Temples, Religion, and Politics in the Roman Republic*. Boston and Leiden: Brill.

Östenberg, I. (2009) *Staging the World: Spoils, Captives, and Representations in the Roman Triumphal Procession*. New York: Oxford University Press.

Paddock, J.M. (1993) *The Bronze Italian Helmet: The development of the Cassis from the last quarter of the sixth century BC to the third quarter of the first century AD*. University College London.

Pearson, E.H. (2021) *Exploring the Mid-Republican Origins of Roman Military Administration: With Stylus and Spear*. Abingdon, Oxon: Routledge (Routledge monographs in classical studies).

Pease, A.S. (1920) *M. Tulli Ciceronis de Divinatione Liber Primus.* Urbana: University of Illinois.

Peck, H.T. (ed.) (1898) *Harper's dictionary of classical literature and antiquities.* New York: Harper.

Perotti, G. (1974) 'Sp. Ligustino "agente provocatore" del senato', in M. Sordi (ed.) *Propaganda e persuasione occulta nell'antichità.* Milan: Vita et Pensiero, pp. 83–96.

Pfeilschifter, R. (2007) 'The allies in the Republican army and the Romanization of Italy', in J. Keller, E. Flaig, and R.E. Roth (eds) *Roman by Integration: Dimensions of Group Identity in Material Culture and Text.* Portsmouth, RI: Journal of Roman Archaeology, pp. 27–42.

Phang, S.E. (2001) *The Marriage of Roman Soldiers (13 B.C.-A.D. 235): Law and Family in the Imperial Army.* Leiden: Brill (Columbia studies in the classical tradition).

Phang, S.E. (2008) *Roman Military Service: Ideologies of Discipline in the Late Republic and Early Principate.* Cambridge: Cambridge University Press.

Pierson, D.S. (1999) 'Natural Killers-Turning the Tide of Battle', *Military Review*, 79(3), p. 60.

Potter, D. (2014) 'The Roman Army and Navy', in H.I. Flower (ed.) *The Cambridge Companion to the Roman Republic.* 2nd edn. Cambridge: Cambridge University Press (Cambridge Companions to the Ancient World), pp. 54–77.

Pritchett, W.K. (1974) *The Greek State at War. Part I.* Berkeley: University of California Press.

Proulx, D.A. (2021) 'Ritual Uses of Trophy Heads in Ancient Nasca Society', in E.P. Benson and A.G. Cook (eds) *Ritual Sacrifice in Ancient Peru.* Austin: University of Texas Press, pp. 119–136.

Quesada Sanz, F. (1997) 'Gladius Hispaniensis: An Archaeological View from Iberia', *Journal of Military Equipment Studies*, 8, pp. 251–70.

Quesada Sanz, F. (2003) 'El legionario romano en la época de las Guerras Púnicas: formas de combate individual, táctica de pequeñas unidades e influencias hispanas', *Espacio Tiempo y Forma. Serie II, Historia Antigua*, (16), pp. 163–196.

Quesada Sanz, F. (2006) 'Armamento indígena y romano republicano en Iberia (siglos III-I a. C.): compatibilidad y abastecimiento de las legiones republicanas en campaña', in A. Morillo (ed.) *Producción y abastecimiento en el ámbito militar: arqueología militar romana en Hispania II.* León: Universidad de León, pp. 75–96.

Quesada Sanz, F. (2007) 'En torno al origen de las enseñas militares en la Antigüedad', *Marq, arqueología y museos*, (2), pp. 83–98.

Quesada Sanz, F. (2015) 'La Batalla de "Baecula" en el contexto de los ejércitos, la táctica y la estrategia de mediados de la Segunda Guerra Púnica: una acción de retaguardia reñida', in J.P. Bellón *et al.* (eds) *La Segunda Guerra Púnica en la península ibérica: Baecula : arqueología de una batalla.* Jaén: Universidad de Jaén, pp. 601–620.

Quesada Sanz, F., Muñiz Jaén, I. and López Flores, I. (2014) 'La guerre et ses traces: destruction et massacre dans le village ibérique du Cerro de la Cruz (Cordoue) et leur contexte historique au IIe s. a.C.', in F. Cadiou and M. Navarro Caballero (eds) *La guerre et ses traces: conflits et sociétés en Hispanie à l'époque de la conquête romaine (IIIe-Ier s. a. C.).* Bordeaux: Ausonius Éditions (Mémoires (Ausonius (Institut))), pp. 231–272.

Quesada Sanz, F. and Galán, C.R. (2017) 'Las armas y el contexto del guerrero de "Las Atalayuelas"(Jaén): una escultura de época ibérica tardía/romano republicana', *Gladius*, 37, pp. 7–51.

RAND: Rand National Defense Research Institute (2010). Sexual orientation and U.S. military personnel policy: an update of RAND's 1993 study (Report No. MG-1056-OSD).

Rathbone, D.W. (1993) 'The census qualifications of the assidui and the prima classis', in H. Sancisi-Weerdenburg (ed.) *De Agricultura: In Memoriam Pieter Willem de Neeve (1945–1990).* Amsterdam: J.C. Gieben, pp. 121–52.

Rawlings, L. (2016) 'The significance of insignificant engagements: Irregular warfare during the Punic Wars', in J. Armstrong (ed.) *Circum Mare: Themes in Ancient Warfare.* Boston: Brill (Mnemosyne Supplements), pp. 204–234.

Rawson, E. (1971) 'The Literary Sources for the Pre-Marian Army', *Papers of the British School at Rome*, 39, pp. 13–31.

Rawson, E. (1990) 'The Antiquarian Tradition: Spoils and Representations of Foreign Armour', in W. Eder (ed.) *Staat und Staatlichkeit in der frühen römischen Republik: Akten eines Symposiums 12.-15. Juli 1988, Freie Universität Berlin*. Stuttgart: Franz Steiner Verlag, pp. 158–173.

Reese, P. (1992) *Homecoming Heroes: An account of the re-assimilation of British Military personnel into civilian life*. London, Leo Cooper.

Rich, J.W. (1983) 'The Supposed Roman Manpower Shortage of the Later Second Century B.C.', *Historia: Zeitschrift für Alte Geschichte*, 32(3), pp. 287–331.

Richlin, A. (2017) *Slave Theater in the Roman Republic: Plautus and Popular Comedy*. New York: Cambridge University Press.

Richlin, A. (2018) 'The Ones Who Paid the Butcher's Bill: Soldiers and War Captives in Roman Comedy', in J.H. Clark and B. Turner (eds) *Brill's Companion to Military Defeat in Ancient Mediterranean Society*. Leiden and Boston: Brill, pp. 213–39.

Ricks, T.E. (1997) *Making the Corps*. New York: Scribner.

Ripat, P. (2006) 'Roman Omens, Roman Audiences, and Roman History', *Greece & Rome*, 53(2), pp. 155–174.

Roller, M.B. (2004) 'Exemplarity in Roman culture: the cases of Horatius Cocles and Cloelia', *Classical Philology*, 99(1), pp. 1–56.

Roller, M.B. (2018) *Models from the Past in Roman Culture: A World of Exempla*. Cambridge: Cambridge University Press.

Roselaar, S. (2009) 'Assidui or proletarii? Property in Roman Citizen Colonies and the vacatio militiae', *Mnemosyne*, 62(4), pp. 609–623.

Rosenstein, N.S. (2002) 'Marriage and Manpower in the Hannibalic War: "Assidui", "Proletarii" and Livy 24.18. 7–8', *Historia*, 52(2), pp. 163–191.

Rosenstein, N.S. (2004) *Rome at War: Farms, Families, and Death in the Middle Republic*. Chapel Hill and London: University of North Carolina Press.

Rosenstein, N.S. (2012) 'Integration and armies in the Middle Republic', in S. Roselaar (ed.) *Processes of Integration and Identity Formation in the Roman Republic*. Leiden: Brill (Mnemosyne Supplements), pp. 85–103.

Rosenstein, N.S. (2016) 'Bellum se ipsum alet? Financing Mid-Republican Imperialism', in H. Beck, M. Jehne, and J. Serrati (eds) *Money and Power in the Roman Republic*. Brussels: Éditions Latomus, pp. 114–30.

Roth, J.P. (1999) *The Logistics of the Roman Army at War: 264 BC–AD 235*. Brill.

Rüpke, J. (2006) 'Triumphator and ancestor rituals between symbolic anthropology and magic', *Numen*, 53(3), pp. 251–289.

Rüpke, J. (2019) *Peace and War in Rome: A Religious Construction of Warfare*. Translated by D.M.B. Richardson. Stuttgart: Franz Steiner Verlag.

Sabin, P. (1996) 'The Mechanics of Battle in the Second Punic War1', *Bulletin of the Institute of Classical Studies*, 41(S67), pp. 59–79.

Sabin, P. (2000) 'The Face of Roman Battle', *The Journal of Roman Studies*, 90, pp. 1–17.

Sabin, P. (2007) 'Land Battles', in P. Sabin, H. van Wees, and M. Whitby (eds) *The Cambridge History of Greek and Roman Warfare, Vol. 1, Greece, the Hellenistic World and the Rise of Rome*. Cambridge: Cambridge University Press.

Salazar, C. (2000) *The Treatment of War Wounds in Graeco-Roman Antiquity*. Leiden: Brill.

Scarborough, J. (1968) 'Roman Medicine and the Legions: A Reconsideration', *Medical History*, 12(3), pp. 254–261.

Scheid, J. (2003) *An Introduction to Roman Religion*. Translated by J. Lloyd. Bloomington: Indiana University Press.

Scheid, J. (2012) 'Le Rite Des Auspices à Rome : Quelle Évolution ? Réflexions sur la Transformation de la divination publique des Romains entre le IIIe et le Ier Siècle avant Notre Ère', in S. Georgoudi, R.K. Piettre, and F. Schmidt (eds) *La Raison des signes.: Présages, Rites, Destin dans les Sociétés de la Méditerranée Ancienne*. Leiden and Boston: Brill, pp. 109–128.

Scheid, J. (2016) 'Le lustrum et la lustratio: En finir avec la "purification".', in V. Gasparini (ed.) *Vestigia. Miscellanea di studi storico-religiosi in onore di Filippo Coarelli nel suo 80° anniversario.* Stuttgart: Franz Steiner Verlag, pp. 203–209.

Schultz, C.E. (2006) *Women's religious activity in the Roman Republic.* Chapel Hill: University of North Carolina Press.

Shay, J. (2002) *Odysseus in America: Combat Trauma and the Trials of Homecoming.* New York: Scribner.

Shils, E.A. and Janowitz, M. (1948) 'Cohesion and Disintegration in the Wehrmacht in World War II', *Public Opinion Quarterly*, 12(2), pp. 280–315.

Shochat, Y. (1980) *Recruitment and the programme of Tiberius Gracchus.* Bruxelles: Revue d'Études Latines (Collection Latomus).

Sidnell, P. (2006) *Warhorse: Cavalry in Ancient Warfare.* London: Hamledon Continuum.

Simkins, P. (2007) *Kitchener's Army: The Raising of the New Armies 1914–1916.* Barnsley, Pen and Sword.

Skutsch, O. (1985) *The annals of Q. Ennius.* Oxford: Oxford University Press.

Slavik, J.F. (2017) 'Pilum and Telum: The Roman Infantryman's Style of Combat in the Middle Republic', *Classical Journal*, 113(2), pp. 151–171.

Soeters, J.L., Winslow, D.J. and Weibull, A. (2006) 'Military culture', in G. Caforio and M. Nuciari (eds) *Handbook of the Sociology of the Military.* Boston: Springer, pp. 237–254.

Southern, P. (2006) *The Roman army: a social and institutional history.* Santa Barbara: ABC Clio.

de Souza, P. (2007) 'Naval Forces', in P. Sabin, H. van Wees, and M. Whitby (eds) *The Cambridge History of Greek and Roman Warfare.* Cambridge: Cambridge University Press, pp. 357–367.

Speidel, M.P. (2005) 'Centurial Signs and the Battle Order of the Legions', *Zeitschrift für Papyrologie und Epigraphik*, 154, pp. 286–292.

Stangor, C., Jhangiani, R. and Tarry, H. (2014) *Principles of Social Psychology.* BCcampus Open Textbook Project.

Sumner, G. (2009) *Roman Military Dress.* Stroud: History Press Ltd.

Suolahti, J. (1955) *The Junior Officers of the Roman Republican Army. A Study on Social Structure.* Helsinki: Suomalainen Tiedeakatemia.

Swank, R.L. and Marchand, W.E. (1946) 'COMBAT NEUROSES: Development of Combat Exhaustion', *Archives of Neurology & Psychiatry*, 55(3), pp. 236–247.

Syme, R. (1957) 'The Origin of the Veranii', *The Classical Quarterly*, 7(3–4), pp. 123–125.

Taylor, L.R. and Linderski, J. (2013) *The Voting Districts of the Roman Republic: The Thirty-five Urban and Rural Tribes.* Ann Arbor: University of Michigan Press.

Taylor, M.J. (2014) 'Roman Infantry Tactics In The Mid-Republic: A Reassessment', *Historia: Zeitschrift für Alte Geschichte*, 63(3), pp. 301–322.

Taylor, M.J. (2019) 'A Census Record as a Source in Livy?: The Life and Career of Spurius Ligustinus', *Mnemosyne*, 73(2), pp. 261–278.

Taylor, M.J. (2020) *Soldiers and Silver: Mobilizing Resources in the Age of Roman Conquest.* Austin: University of Texas Press.

Taylor, M.K. *et al.* (2014) 'Sex differences in cardiovascular and subjective stress reactions: prospective evidence in a realistic military setting', *Stress*, 17(1), pp. 70–78.

Terrenato, N. (2019) *The Early Roman Expansion into Italy: Elite Negotiation and Family Agendas.* Cambridge, UK and New York, NY: Cambridge University Press.

Thiel, J.H. (1946) *Studies on the History of Roman Sea-power in Republican Times.* Amsterdam: Amsterdam, North-Holland publishing company (N. v. Noord-hollandsche uitgevers mij.).

Thompson, M.M. and McCreary, D.R. (2006) *Enhancing mental readiness in military personnel.* Toronto: Defence Research And Development Toronto (Canada).

Trendall, A.D. (1967) *The red-figured vases of Lucania, Campania and Sicily* (2 vol). London: Clarendon (Oxford monographs on classical archaeology).

Vaahtera, J.E. (2000) 'Roman Religion and the Polybian politeia', in C. Bruun (ed.) *The Roman Middle Republic: Politics, Religion, and Historiography c.400 - 133 B. C.* Rome: Institutum Romanum Finlandiae, pp. 251–264.

Vaahtera, J.E. (2001) *Roman augural lore in Greek historiography: a study of the theory and terminology.* Stuttgart: Franz Steiner Verlag.

Ville, G. (2014) *La gladiature en Occident des origines à la mort de Domitien.* 2nd edn. Rome: Ecoles françaises de Rome.

Vishnia, R.F. (2002) 'The Shadow Army: The Lixae and the Roman Legions', *Zeitschrift für Papyrologie und Epigraphik*, 139, pp. 265–272.

Volken, M. (2008) 'The water bag of Roman soldiers', *Journal of Roman Archaeology*, 21, pp. 264–274.

Walbank, F.W. (1957) *A Historical Commentary on Polybius* (3 vol). Oxford: Oxford University Press.

Walker, H.J. (2004) *Valerius Maximus: Memorable Deeds and Sayings: One Thousand Tales from Ancient Rome.* Indianapolis: Hackett Publishing Company.

Walters, J. (1997) 'Invading the Roman Body: Manliness and Impenetrability in Roman Thought', in J.P. Hallett and M.B. Skinner (eds) *Roman Sexualities.* Princeton: Princeton University Press, pp. 29–45.

Ward, G.A. (2016) 'Individual Exploits in Warfare of the Republic', in *The Topography of Violence in the Greco-Roman world.* Ann Arbor: University of Michigan Press, pp. 299–324.

Welch, K.E. (2006) '"Domi militiaeque": Roman Domestic Aesthetics and War Booty in the Republic', in K.E. Welch and S. Dillon (eds) *Representations of War in Ancient Rome.* New York: Cambridge University Press, pp. 91–161.

Williams, C.A. (2010) *Roman Homosexuality.* 2nd edn. New York: Oxford University Press, USA.

Wilson, A.J.N. (1966) *Emigration from Italy in the Republican age of Rome.* Manchester: Manchester University Press.

Wolff, C. (2009) *Déserteurs et transfuges dans l'armée romaine à l'époque républicaine.* Napoli: Jovene.

Wolff, C. (2010) 'Les volontaires dans l'armée romaine jusqu'à Marius', *Latomus*, 69(1), pp. 18–28.

Wong, L. *et al.* (2003) *Why they fight: combat motivation in the Iraq war by Leonard Wong et al.* Carlisle, PA: Strategic Studies Institute (Strategic Studies Institute).

Zabłocki, J. (2009) 'Le più antiche forme del testamento romano', in P. Mach, M. Nemec, and M. Pekarik (eds) *Ius romanum schola sapientiae: Pocta Petrovi Blahovi k 70. narodeninám.* Trnava: Právnická Fakulta Trnavskej Univerzity, pp. 549–560.

Ziolkowski, A. (1993) 'Urbs direpta, or how the Romans sacked cities', in J. Rich and G. Shipley (eds) *War and Society in the Roman world.* London and New York: Routledge, pp. 69–91.

Index

Acathus, 106, 138
M. Acilius Glabrio, 64, 206
Adjutant, *see Optiones*
Aebura, 183
Q. Aemilius Barula, 146
L. Aemilius Paullus, 13, 46, 93–4, 101,
    103–105, 136, 142, 147, 176, 195
Aetolians, 56, 205
Agathyrna, 201
Alexander The Great, 29
Allies, 54–6
Altar Of Domitius Ahenobarbus, 46,
    101
Animals, 59
Antiochus, 147, 206
Antipatrea, 108, 111–14, 118
M. Antonius, 29
Apollonia, 81, 107
Apsus River, 106–107, 138
Archagathus, 182
Ariminum, 31, 47, 195, 204
Armour, 45–6, 84–5, 188
Arretium, 43, 46
Assassination, 20, 119, 122
Assidui, 21
Athacus, 59
Augury, *see* Auspices
Augustus, 78
C. Aurelius Pecuniola, 125
Auspices, 87–8, 139–43, 145–6, 151–2, 162
Auspicium, 63, 74, 133, 174, 214
Auspicium Ex Tripudiis, 88, 139–40
Auxilia Externa, see Foreign Allies

Baecula, Battle of, 45, 148
Baggage, 57–8, 77, 83, 85, 90, 147–8
Bandages, 184
Bandits, 47, 193
Battle;
    preparation for, 138–53
    fighting in, 154–72
    aftermath of, 173–91

Battlefield;
    distance from camp, 148
    deployment onto, 148–51
    after a battle, 177–8
Beheading, 16, 112–13, 129, 132, 203
Beneventum, 48, 170
Booty, 13, 28, 110, 125, 145, 147, 203–206
Breakfast, Before Battle, 146–7
Brundisium, 13, 43, 46–50, 52, 75–7, 79–81
Bruttium, 202
Buccinator, 118
Bugle, 92, 118, 148, 156, 168, 176
Burial, 187
Busa, 174

L. Caecilius Metellus, 30
Caligae, 45, 60
Calones, 57–8, 70, 77, 80, 112, 121, 179, 182,
    184–6, 200, 215
Camillus, 104
Camp;
    built at the mustering point, 49–51
    camp oath, 70–2
    built at the point of disembarkation,
        81–5
    navigation, 85–7
    guarding of, 118–22
Campanians, 16
Cannae, Battle of, 11, 68, 91, 93–4, 126,
    132, 137, 145, 147, 154, 160, 169, 173–4,
    176–7, 180–1, 183, 187, 201–203
Canusium, 174, 180, 183, 201–202
Captives, 16, 58, 112–13
Capture, 179–81
Capua, 97
Carthage, 12, 79, 101, 109, 111–13, 116, 129,
    140, 166, 208
C. Cartilius Poplicola, 76
Casilinum, 203
Castramentation, *see* Camp
Casualties, 34, 74, 150, 165, 186–7, 217
Cato, *see* M. Porcius Cato

Cavalry;
 citizen cavalry, 53–4
 allied cavalry, 55–6
 areas in camp, 84
 working with *velites*, 97–9
 skirmishing, 114–15
 in battle, 154–5
Celtiberians, 70, 145, 160, 183
Censor, 20
Census Class, 20–1, 27, 37, 46, 53
Centurions, 39–40, 41–2, 67, 85, 92–3
Cerro de la Cruz, 112–13, 131, 168
Chalcis, 118
Chicken-keeper, *see Pullarius*
Chickens, 53, 59, 80, 87–8, 140–1, 143
Cincinnatus, 30
Cinctus Gabinus, 189
M. Claudius Marcellus, 174, 183, 203
C. Claudius Nero, 68
C. Claudius Pulcher, 64, 140
P. Claudius Pulcher, 140
Ap. Claudius Sabinus Regillensis, 132
Clustumina, 4, 15
Cnidus, 118
Coercion, 134–6
Cohesion, 18, 33–6, 135, 209–10
Cohors Amicorum, 65, 86, 120, 175, 215–16
Cohort, 54–6, 95–6, 147, 157, 213
Colonies, 54, 76, 197, 204
Combat, *see* Battle, Skirmishing, Sacking
 of Cities
Comitia Centuriata, 23–4
Comitia Tributa, 66
Comitium, 11
Commander, 62–3
 advisors to, 63–5
 departure from Rome, 73–5
 making exhortations, 143–6
 duties after a battle, 188–91
 releases soldiers from their oath, 197–9
Coniuratio, 69
Consilium, 64, 67, 143, 207, 215
Contio, 95–6, 189–91
Contubernium, 50, 86, 89, 122, 150, 177, 215
Convalescents, 183–4
Conversantibus, 84, 86
Corcyra, 81, 138
L. Cornelius Scipio, 70, 206
P. Cornelius Scipio Africanus, 12–13, 68,
 77–80, 116, 126, 129, 132–4, 136, 144–5,
 149, 157, 175, 181, 193, 202, 204

P. Cornelius Scipio Africanus Aemilianus, xi,
 42, 58, 65, 89–90, 125
Cremation, 186–7
Cremona, 185
Crimes, 125–30, 200–201
Criminals, 16, 19, 68, 113, 129, 169
Cumae, 88
Cynoscephalae, Battle of, 16, 107, 138–9,
 145, 155, 177, 205

Dead, 185–8
Decapitation, 131, 168–9
Decimation, 131–3, 135–6, 215
Decorations, 8–13
Defeat, 14–16, 145, 173–81
Defection, 175–6, 193, 202
Delecti Extraordinarii, 54, 85
Deployment, 154–5
Desertion, 128–36, 175, 192–3, 199–203
Deterrent, 72, 112, 135–6
Dilectus, 18, 21–8, 47–9, 66–7
Discipline, 123–37
Disobedience, 33, 124, 128, 134
Divination, xi–xii, 53, 59, 88, 142, 151–2
Divisions, Sorting of, 37–42
Domi Nobiles, 53, 98, 216
Donatives, 194, 204–207
Donkeys, 47
Dyrrachium, 81, 103

Elephants, 53, 59, 102, 136, 149, 155–8,
 160, 162
Eligibility for Service, 19–21
Engineers, 24
Enrolment, *see Dilectus*
Eordea, 138, 145
Equestrian Class, 21, 23–4, 46, 53, 66, 175
Esprit de corps, 34, 209–10
Evocati, 68, 85
Evocatio, 10
Exauctores, 198, 216
Executions, 8, 17, 113, 130–1, 182
Exemplarity, 6–14, 178
Exhortations, 61, 86, 139, 143–5, 151–3
Extraordinarii, 49, 54–5, 85

Q. Fabius Maximus Aemilianus, 130, 136
Q. Fabius Maximus Cunctator, 88, 180
Q. Fabius Maximus Rullianus, 132
Face, as a target, 103–105
Facula, 70–1

Festivals, 1, 10, 60, 142
Fighting, *see* Battle, Training
Fines, 124–5, 198
Firewood, 58, 71
Flamininus, *see* T. Quinctius Flamininus
C. Flaminius Nepos, 140
Foreign Allies, 56
Forum, 4, 11, 16, 43, 47–8, 83, 86, 129
Forum Novum, 4, 43, 47–8
Fregellae, 12
M. Fulvius Nobilior, 198
Fustis, 130
Fustuarium, xvi, 129–32, 135–6, 200

G. Cornelius, Primus Pilus 149 BCE, 127
Gaesatae, 156, 160
Galba, 62, 64
Galearii, 57
Gangrene, 182
Garrisons, 118, 123, 137, 147, 182–5,
    196–7
General, *see* Commander
Gerronius, 107
Gladius;
    training in use of, 102–105
    evidence of use at Cerro de la
        Cruz, 112–13
Goats, 2
Greaves, 24, 45, 160
Guard Duty, 118–22, 125–6

Hannibal, 15, 68, 94, 146, 154, 156, 162, 172,
    174, 180–1, 203
Haruspices, 59, 139, 142, 216
Hasdrubal, 147–8
Hasta, 45, 70–1
Hastati;
    training of, 100–105
    in battle, 159–70
Hasta Velitaris, 99–100, 155, 158, 162, 172
Helmets, 44–6
Heraclea, Battle of, 179
Herdonea, 173–4, 186
Hispania, 62–3, 94–5, 107, 160, 183, 206
Homosexuality, 127
Horatius Cocles, 7
Horn, 19, 92
Horn-blowers, 24, 161

Horses, 24, 43, 48, 53–4, 59, 77, 89–90, 97–9,
    120–1, 147, 158, 205
L. Hostilius Mancinus, 12

Ilipa, Battle of, 96, 145, 150, 157
Illyria, 81, 115
Illyrians, 56, 115
Injuries, *see* Wounded
Instruments, 92
Insubordination, 132, 199, 201
Iusiurandum, 31

Juno, 10, 11, 73
Jupiter, 74, 126

Killing, in Battle, 163–70
Kindling, 113, 186
Kitchener, Field Marshal H.H., 34

L. Apustius, legate, 107–109, 111–18,
    138, 200
L. Marcius, elected commander of the army
    in Spain in 212 BCE, 175
Land, 3–6, 20–1, 204–206, 208–209
Landless Poor, 208–209, 211
Latins, 53, 140
Lectisternium, 15
Legates, 66
Levy, *see* Dilectus
P. Licinius Crassus, 3, 30, 64
Lictors, 74
Light-armed, *see* velites
Ligna, 70–1
Liguria, 195, 204
Sp. Ligustinus, 3–5
    at the mustering point, 49–52
    career, 204–207
    census class placement, 21, 42–3
    departure from Italy, 75–81
    enrolment and preparation, 42–6
    in Macedon 200–199 BCE, 106–22
    travel to the mustering point, 46–9
Lilybaeum, 77, 79
M. Livius Salinator, 62
Livy, xii–xiii
Lixae, 58, 70, 112, 121, 182, 188, 205
lorica hamata, 46, 172
Lua Mater, 188
Lucania, 73
Lusitania, 112
Lustratio, 22, 78–80, 193, 210, 216

Macedon, 16, 52, 64, 70, 81, 106–22, 134, 138, 160, 182, 199–200, 205–207
Geminus Maecius, 8
C. Maenius, 11
Mainz-type Gladius, 102–103
T. Manlius Torquatus, 8, 29
Marcellus, *see* M. Claudius Marcellus
Marching, 88–90
    to the site of battle, 146–8
G. Marius, 71, 127, 189, 208–209, 211
Mars, 78–80, 188
C. Matienus, Deserter, 200
Medicine, 130, 182, 184
Medicus, 182
Mercenaries, 69–70
Messengers, 86, 147, 187
Miles Gregarius, 42, 48
Minerva, 188
Q. Mucius Scaevola, 64
C. Mucius Scaevola, 20
Mules, 45, 47–8, 53, 57–9, 77, 80, 83–4, 88–90, 148, 205
Mutilation, 136, 178
Mutiny, 40, 133–4, 199, 201
Mylae, 12

Navy, 75–8, 195
Nazis, 135
Non-combatants, 56–8
Numidian Cavalry, 56, 146, 155, 178, 208, 212

Oaths;
    breaking of, 125–9
    camp oath, 70–2
    coniuratio, 69
    iusiurandum, 31
    military oath, *see sacramentum*
Oculus, 76
Officers, 59–62
Omens, 78, 87, 139–43, 146
Oneraria, Transports, 76
Optiones, 39, 121, 126
Ostia, 76, 195
Oxen, 2, 59, 83, 142

Pabulum, 70–1
Paeligni, Cohors Paeligna, 55
Paestum, 169
Pals Battalions, 34–6

Paludamentum, 74, 189
L. Papirius Cursor, 141
Patricians, 23–4, 59–60, 62, 183
Patronage, 22–3, 37, 41–2, 61, 195
Pectoral, 45, 52, 114
Pelium, 138
Perjury, 126
Q. Petillius Spurinus, 124
Philip V, King of Macedon, 106–107, 114–15, 138, 200, 207
Pilum;
    training with, 101–103
    use in battle, 162–3
Piracy, 11, 81
Pirates, 193
Pisae, 195, 198, 204
Placentia, 185
Plebians, 23–4, 59–60, 62, 132
Polybius, x–xii
Poma, 70–1
Pomerium, 74, 87, 216
Pompeii Type Gladius, 102–103
C. Popilius Sabellus, 148
M. Porcius Cato, xiii, 52, 57, 60, 63–5, 81, 95–6, 107, 116, 124, 130, 143–6, 184, 191–2, 196, 198, 205–207
M. Porcius Cato Licinianus, 65
Portents, 88
Postliminium, 181, 199
A. Postumius, 198
Praenestae, 11, 47, 203
Praepilatus, 'ball-topped' (*pilum*), 101
Praetorium, 53–4, 59, 61, 83–6, 120–1, 140, 143
Praetors, 62–4, 77, 133
Prefects of the Allies, 49, 67, 83, 124–5, 143, 162
Priesthoods, 22–3, 59
Priests, 19, 53, 59, 73, 78, 139, 142–3, 145
Primus Pilus, 3, 40–1, 51, 64, 67, 93, 118, 207
Principes;
    training of, 100–105
    role in battle, 170–1
Proconsul, 63, 88
Proembolion, 75–6
Professionalization of the Army, 209
Propraetor, 63, 88
Psychopaths, 9, 164
Pullarius, 59, 87–8, 140–1

Pydna, Battle of, 15, 58, 65, 142, 162, 176, 185, 207
Pyres, for Cremation, 186–7, 189
Pyrrhus of Epirus, 59, 179–80

Quadriremes, 75
Quaestor, 67, 85, 112, 119, 120
Quaestorium, 54, 84–6, 119, 121
T. Quinctius Flamininus, 13, 16, 62–4, 89, 106–107, 138, 196, 205
Quinqueremes, 75–7

Rank, 39–40
Ransoms, 68, 179–80, 203
Retreat, 155, 159, 167–8, 171–2
Rewards, 8–10, 96, 107, 110, 123, 137, 167, 190–2, 203–207
Rudes, 101

Sabidius, author, 140–1, 152
Sabines, 3–4, 186
Sacramentum, 28–33, 36, 66, 69, 126, 128–9, 197–8
Sacrifices, 73–5, 78–80, 83, 86, 139, 142–3, 145–6, 151–2, 188–9
Sailors, 76–8, 80
Sarcina, 45
Sardinia, 12, 44, 62
Scipio Aemilianus, *see* P. Cornelius Scipio Africanus Aemilianus
Scipio Africanus, *see* P. Cornelius Scipio Africanus
Self-sacrifice, 7–8, 17
M. Sergius, 20, 185
Sertorius, 103
Shield, training with, 100–101
Ships, *see* Navy
L. Siccius Dentatus, 8
Sicily, 13, 26, 44, 62, 76–7, 132, 137, 196, 201, 203, 214
Skirmishing;
    as training, 93–6
    on campaign, 114–17
    in battle, 154–9
    observed by heavy infantry, 159–61
Slashing, 103–105, 176
Slavery, Threat of, 16–17, 125, 130, 179–81, 198
Slaves, Private, 56–8, 64, 67, 70, 169, 184
Slaves, State-owned, *see Calones*

Slaves in service to Rome in 216 BCE, 68, 91, 169
Socii Navales, 76
Spartacus, 132, 214
Spartans, 178
Spatha, 103
Sphagia, 142, 151
Standard-bearer, 92, 121
Standards, 91–4, 124, 129, 150, 159
Stipendium, 30, 40, 125, 217
Storming of cities, 107–14
Stuprum, 127
Sucro, Mutiny at, 132–4, 136, 201
P. Sulpicius Galba, 62, 64, 73–4, 77, 79, 106–8, 134, 138, 199
Supplementa, 194, 206
Surrender, 135, 179–81, 200
Sword, *see Gladius*
Syracuse, 203

Tarpeian Rock, 16, 129
Tarracina, 76
Tarraco, 195
Telamon, Battle of, 156, 160–2
Testamentum in Procinctu, 151–2
Theft, 70, 72, 122–3, 130
Thracians, 70, 147
Ti. Sempronius Gracchus, Consul of 177 BCE, 12, 63, 194–5, 206–207
Ti. Sempronius Gracchus, Consul of 215 BCE, 88, 91, 169
Ticinus River, Battle of, 15, 56
Training, 91–105
    through skirmishing, 93–6
    of the *velites*, 97–100
    of the *hastati* and *principes*, 100–105
Tralles, 115
Transports, Naval, 75–8, 197
Trasimene, Battle of, 15, 140, 173, 179
Trebia, Battle of, 15, 146–7, 154
Triarii, 39–40, 120–1, 147, 149, 157, 159, 168, 170–2
Tribunes, 66
    at the *dilectus*, 26–8
    at the *sacramentum*, 28–33
    sorting divisions and maniples, 38–9, 41–2
    tents of, 83–4
    maniples on duty to, 120
    authority to punish soldiers, 124–5
Tributum, 40

Triremes, 75
Triumph, 13, 16, 62, 79, 145, 192–7, 205–207
Trumpet, 80, 92, 156, 161–2
Trumpeter, 79, 92
Tumultus, 69
Turma, Cavalry Unit, 84, 95, 121
Tusculum, 11

Uter, 70–1

M. Valerius Laevinus, 77, 201–202
Veii, 10
Velites;
    composition, 38–9
    training of, 97–100
    Ligustinus as, 21, 42–3
    role in early part of campaigns, 113–18
    in battle, 154–9
    disappearance of, 211–13

Vexillum, 92, 148
Via Appia, 48
Via Principalis, 54, 56, 83–4, 86
Via Quintana, 83–6
P. Villius Tappulus, 62, 64, 106, 138, 199
Viriathus, 112
Volunteers, 3, 12, 67–8, 109, 117, 134, 137, 199, 208
Vulcan, xii, 188

Warships, 75–7
Weapons, *see*: *Gladius, Hasta Velitaris, Pilum*
Wehrmacht, 135–6
Wounded 147–8, 166, 173, 181–5
Wounding, of an enemy, 9, 166

Zama, Battle of, 50, 100, 144–5, 149, 155–7, 162, 166–8, 171, 176, 181